Calvin Miller   Empowered Lea...

SWINDOLL'S

NEW TESTAMENT

INSIGHTS

INSIGHTS ON
1 & 2 TIMOTHY, TITUS

CHARLES R. SWINDOLL

SWINDOLL'S
NEW TESTAMENT
INSIGHTS

INSIGHTS ON
1 & 2 TIMOTHY, TITUS

ZONDERVAN

ZONDERVAN.com/
AUTHORTRACKER
follow your favorite authors

We want to hear from you. Please send your comments about this book to us in care of zreview@zondervan.com. Thank you.

ZONDERVAN

Insights on 1 and 2 Timothy, Titus
Copyright © 2010 by Charles R. Swindoll

This title is also available as a Zondervan ebook. Visit www.zondervan.com/ebooks.

Requests for information should be addressed to:

Zondervan, *Grand Rapids, Michigan 49530*

Library of Congress Cataloging-in-Publication Data

Swindoll, Charles R.
    Insights on 1 and 2 Timothy, Titus / Charles R. Swindoll
        p. cm. (Swindoll's New Testament insights)
    ISBN 978-0-310-28433-8 (hardcover printed)
    1. 1. Bible. N.T. Pastoral Epistles—Commentaries. I. Title
    BS2735.53.S85 2010
    227'.83077—dc22   2010009043

Scripture quotations are taken from the *New American Standard Bible.* Copyright © 1960, 1962, 1963, 1968, 1971, 1972, 1973, 1975, 1977, 1995 by The Lockman Foundation. Used by permission.

Maps by International Mapping. Copyright © 2010 by Zondervan. All rights reserved.

Published in association with Yates & Yates, www.yates2.com.

Cover design: Rob Monacelli
Cover photography: PixelWorks Photography
Interior design: Sherri Hoffman

Printed in the United States of America

10 11 12 13 14 15 16 17 18 19 20 21 /DCI/ 23 22 21 20 19 18 17 16 15 14 13 12 11 10 9 8 7 6 5 4 3 2 1

CONTENTS

AUTHOR'S PREFACE

For almost sixty years I have loved the Bible. It was that love for the Scriptures, mixed with a clear call into the gospel ministry during my tour of duty in the Marine Corps, that resulted in my going to Dallas Theological Seminary to prepare for a lifetime of ministry. During those four great years I had the privilege of studying under outstanding men of God, who also loved God's Word. They not only held the inerrant Word of God in high esteem, they taught it carefully, preached it passionately, and modeled it consistently. A week never passes without my giving thanks to God for the grand heritage that has been mine to claim! I am forever indebted to those fine theologians and mentors, who cultivated in me a strong commitment to the understanding, exposition, and application of God's truth.

For more than forty-five years I have been engaged in doing just that — *and how I love it!* I confess without hesitation that I am addicted to the examination and the proclamation of the Scriptures. Because of this, books have played a major role in my life for as long as I have been in ministry — especially those volumes that explain the truths and enhance my understanding of what God has written. Through these many years I have collected a large personal library, which has proven invaluable as I have sought to remain a faithful student of the Bible. To the end of my days, my major goal in life is to communicate the Word with accuracy, insight, clarity, and practicality. Without resourceful and reliable books to turn to, I would have "run dry" decades ago.

Among my favorite and most well-worn volumes are those that have enabled me to get a better grasp of the biblical text. Like most expositors, I am forever searching for literary tools that I can use to hone my gifts and sharpen my skills. For me, that means finding resources that make the complicated simple and easy to understand, that offer insightful comments and word pictures that enable me to see the relevance of sacred truth in light of my twenty-first-century world, and that drive those truths home to my heart in ways I do not easily forget. When I come across such books, they wind up in my hands as I devour them and then place them in my library for further reference ... and, believe me, I often return to them. What a relief it is to have these resourceful works to turn to when I lack fresh insight, or when I need just the right story or illustration, or when I get stuck in the tangled text and cannot find my way out. For the serious expositor, a library is essential. As a mentor of mine once said, *"Where else can you have 10,000 professors at your fingertips?"*

In recent years I have discovered there are not nearly enough resources like those I just described. It was such a discovery that prompted me to consider becoming a part of the answer instead of lamenting the problem. But the solution would result in a huge undertaking. A writing project that covers all of the books and letters of the New Testament seemed overwhelming and intimidating. A rush of relief came when I realized that during the past forty-five-plus years I've taught and preached through most of the New Testament. In my files were folders filled with notes from those messages that were just lying there, waiting to be brought out of hiding, given a fresh and relevant touch in light of today's needs, and applied to fit into the lives of men and women who long for a fresh word from the Lord. *That did it!* I began to pursue the best publisher to turn my dream into reality.

Thanks to the hard work of my literary agents, Sealy and Matt Yates, I located a publisher interested in taking on a project this extensive. I thank the fine people at Zondervan Publishing House for their enthusiastic support of this multivolume venture that will require over ten years to complete. Having met most of them over the years through other written works I've authored, I knew they were qualified to handle such an undertaking and would be good stewards of my material, staying with the task of getting all of it into print. I am grateful for the confidence and encouragement of both Stan Gundry and Paul Engle, who have remained loyal and helpful from the beginning. It is also a pleasure to work alongside Verlyn Verbrugge; I sincerely appreciate his seasoned wisdom and keen-eyed assistance.

It has also been especially delightful to work, again, with my longtime friend and former editor, John Sloan. He has provided invaluable counsel as my general editor. Best of all has been John's enthusiastic support. I must also express my gratitude to both Mark Gaither and Mike Svigel for their tireless and devoted efforts, serving as my hands-on, day-to-day editors. They have done superb work as we have walked our way through the verses and chapters of all twenty-seven New Testament books. It has been a pleasure to see how they have taken my original material and helped me shape it into a style that remains true to the text of the Scriptures, at the same time interestingly and creatively developed, and all the while allowing my voice to come through in a natural and easy-to-read manner.

I need to add sincere words of appreciation to the congregations I have served in various parts of these United States for almost five decades. It has been my good fortune to be the recipient of their love, support, encouragement, patience, and frequent words of affirmation as I have fulfilled my calling to stand and deliver God's message year after year. The sheep from all those flocks have endeared themselves to this shepherd in more ways than I can put into words ... and none more than those I currently serve with delight at Stonebriar Community Church in Frisco, Texas.

Finally, I must thank my wife, Cynthia, for her understanding of my addiction to studying, to preaching, and to writing. Never has she discouraged me from staying at it. Never has she failed to urge me in the pursuit of doing my very best. On the contrary, her affectionate support personally, and her own commitment to excellence in leading *Insight for Living* for more than three decades, have combined to keep me faithful to my calling "in season and out of season." Without her devotion to me and apart from our mutual partnership throughout our lifetime of ministry together, *Swindoll's New Testament Insights* would never have been undertaken.

I am grateful that it has now found its way into your hands and, ultimately, onto the shelves of your library. My continued hope and prayer is that you will find these volumes helpful in your own study and personal application of the Bible. May they help you come to realize, as I have over these many years, that God's Word is as timeless as it is true.

The grass withers, the flower fades,
But the word of our God stands forever. (Isaiah 40:8)

Chuck Swindoll
Frisco, Texas

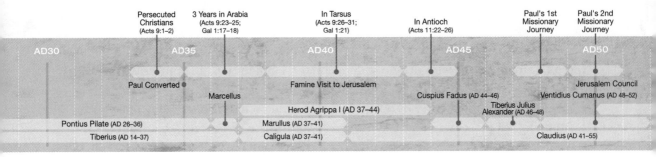

| AD30 | | AD35 | | AD40 | | AD45 | | AD50 |

Persecuted Christians (Acts 9:1–2)

3 Years in Arabia (Acts 9:23–25; Gal 1:17–18)

In Tarsus (Acts 9:26–31; Gal 1:21)

In Antioch (Acts 11:22–26)

Paul's 1st Missionary Journey

Paul's 2nd Missionary Journey

Paul Converted

Marcellus

Famine Visit to Jerusalem

Cuspius Fadus (AD 44–46)

Jerusalem Council

Ventidius Cumanus (AD 48–52)

Herod Agrippa I (AD 37–44)

Tiberius Julius Alexander (AD 46–48)

Pontius Pilate (AD 26–36)

Marullus (AD 37–41)

Tiberius (AD 14–37)

Caligula (AD 37–41)

Claudius (AD 41–55)

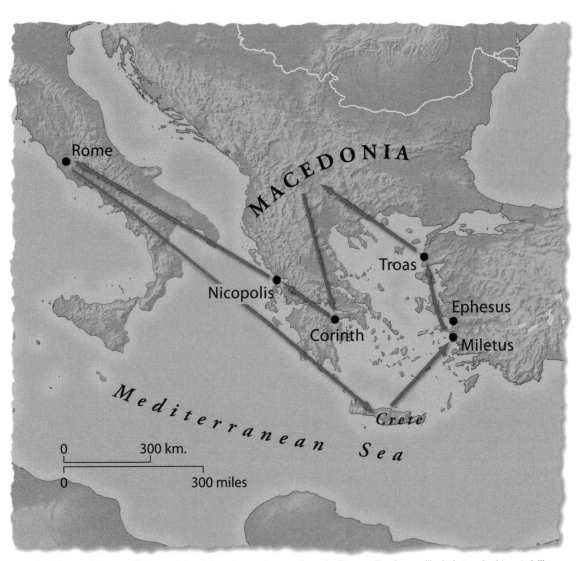

Paul's Planned Farewell Tour—After his release from prison in Rome, Paul very likely intended to stabilize the churches around the Aegean Sea before beginning his mission to evangelize Spain via Rome.

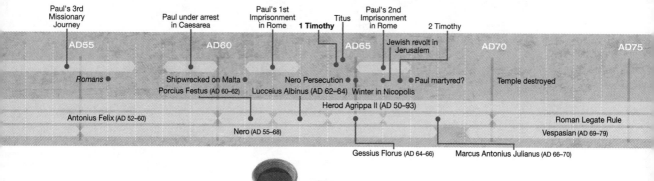

Paul's 3rd Missionary Journey

Paul under arrest in Caesarea

Paul's 1st Imprisonment in Rome

1 Timothy

Titus

Paul's 2nd Imprisonment in Rome

2 Timothy

Jewish revolt in Jerusalem

AD55   AD60   AD65   AD70   AD75

Romans ●

Shipwrecked on Malta ●

Nero Persecution ●

● Paul martyred?

Temple destroyed

Porcius Festus (AD 60–62)

Lucceius Albinus (AD 62–64)

Winter in Nicopolis

Herod Agrippa II (AD 50–93)

Antonius Felix (AD 52–60)

Roman Legate Rule

Nero (AD 55–68)

Vespasian (AD 69–79)

Gessius Florus (AD 64–66)   Marcus Antonius Julianus (AD 66–70)

1 TIMOTHY

Introduction

It had been a long five years. Half a decade on the sidelines, forbidden to travel, unable to conduct ministry among the churches. Five years of lawyers, courts, politics . . . and the hardest of all, waiting. For a man of action like Paul, the waiting must have felt unbearable, but the Lord knew His tireless apostle needed rest after three missionary journeys. Robbers, exposure, stoning, flogging, prison, riots, murderous plots, renegade disciples, and fickle fellowships (2 Cor. 11:26–28) had taken their toll. After more than ten years and twenty thousand miles logged—some by sea, mostly on foot—any traveler would be weary and need time to recharge. For two years, Paul waited in Caesarea as Governor Felix teased Jewish officials with the prospect of execution (Acts 24:27). Further trials under Governor Festus forced an appeal to Caesar in Rome (25:1–12), leading to a treacherous journey and two more years of house arrest in the seat of Roman power (Acts 27–28).

As God would have it, and given Paul's relentless drive, the time didn't go to waste. Paul's captivity in the governor's palace in Caesarea gave him plenty of time to receive visitors and to reflect on his experiences, which he described freely with Israel's rulers (Acts 24–26). Then a relatively comfortable sojourn in Rome allowed him unprecedented access to the political elite in Nero's court (Phil. 1:13). And, of course, he wrote. He celebrated the supremacy of Christ to the Colossians. He praised the Philippians for their constant prayers and generosity. He reasoned with Philemon to receive his runaway slave, Onesimus, as a new brother in Christ. And

The Ministry as God Intended It

Greeting and Salutation	Personal Encouragement and Exhortation	The Ministry
"Grace, mercy, and peace..." (1:2)	• Timothy's task • Paul's testimony • Gospel's trust	**Chap.2:** Men and Women (Prayer and Submission) **Chap.3:** Elders and Deacons (Qualifications and Leadership)
1:1-2	1:3 1:20	Chapters 2 and 3

Emphasis	The Work of Ministry	
Command	Be True!	Be Wise!
"Musical" Interludes	Hymn 1:17 *"Now to the King Eternal"*	Hymn 3:16 *"He who was Revealed"*

The Minister

Chap.4: Seeing and the imporance of:

- Faithful teaching
- Sound doctrine
- True godliness
- Perseverance

Chap.5: Paying attention to:

- Various age groups
- Widows
- Elders
- Wisdom

Chap.6: Maintaining balance with:

- Masters and Slaves
- Rich and poor
- Internals and Externals

Chapters 4 through 6

The One Who Ministers

Be strong and faithful!

Hymn 6:16
"Blessed, Only Sovereign"

"Grace be
with you"
(6:21)

he urged the Ephesians to affirm their unity in the love of Christ as well as to stand firm against the Adversary's attacks.

After five years on the sidelines, however, Paul was released from his house arrest, his freedom and energy returned, and he was ready to resume his plans. Before the Jewish officials in Jerusalem had forced him into protective custody, Paul planned to visit Rome and then spearhead an evangelistic tour of the Western Empire, as far as Spain (Acts 19:21; Rom. 15:28). During his absence, however, false teachers had filled the vacuum he left in Macedonia and Asia, polluting the gospel with gnostic-like philosophies (Rom. 16:17; 2 Cor. 11:4; Gal. 1:6; 1 Tim. 1:3–4; 6:3; Rev. 2:6, 15). Moreover, his brief visit to Crete on the way to Rome revealed a great need for structure (Titus 1:5), as leaderless congregations had fallen prey to the Judaizers' legalism and Greek dissipation (Titus 1:10–14). Before launching anything westward, Paul would have to stabilize these troubled churches.

Clues to Paul's Whereabouts between First and Second Roman Imprisonments

After Release from First Roman Imprisonment

"As I urged you [Timothy] upon my departure for Macedonia, remain on at Ephesus ..." (1 Tim. 1:3).

"I am writing these things to you, hoping to come to you before long" (1 Tim. 3:14).

"Until I come ..." (1 Tim. 4:13).

"For this reason I left you [Titus] in Crete ..." (Titus 1:5).

"When I send Artemas or Tychicus to you [Titus], make every effort to come to me at Nicopolis" (Titus 4:12).

"Erastus remained at Corinth, but Trophimus I left sick at Miletus" (2 Tim. 4:20).

During Second Roman Imprisonment

"Titus [has gone] to Dalmatia" (2 Tim. 4:10).

"Tychicus I have sent to Ephesus" (2 Tim. 4:12).

"When you come bring the cloak which I left at Troas with Carpus, and the books, especially the parchments" (2 Tim. 4:13).

The time between Paul's first and second imprisonments in Rome remains a mystery. We can arrange only tidbits from his letters to Timothy and Titus to form a hypothetical timeline. He most likely departed Rome for a kind of farewell tour (refer to the map, "Paul's Farewell Tour"), during which he deployed his assistants for long-term assignments. After several weeks on Crete, he left Titus there (Titus 1:5), taking the rest of his entourage with him to Miletus, where he left a sick Trophimus in the care of friends (2 Tim. 4:20).

Before departing, Paul probably sent for Timothy, whom he had sent from Rome to serve in Ephesus. He most likely avoided visiting the city to reduce the possibility of becoming entangled in local affairs (cf. Acts 20:16). Regardless, he "urged" Timothy to remain on in Ephesus, originally intending him to serve there for the rest of his life. Paul sailed from Miletus to Troas, where he probably spent the winter of AD 64, taking time to write Titus. As soon as weather permitted, he departed for Macedonia (Philippi, Thessalonica, Berea), leaving his cloak and books behind (2 Tim. 4:13), perhaps with instructions for Carpus to send his belongings to Rome via ship after the apostle himself arrived there.

After a brief visit with the churches that he had established during his third missionary journey, Paul *intended* to turn south for Corinth and then over to Nicopolis, where he planned to spend the winter with Titus (Titus 3:12) before setting sail for Rome again. But something interrupted his plans. Troubling news arrived from Ephesus. During his brief visit with Timothy in Miletus, he implored the younger minister to remain at his post, but the difficulties Timothy faced required a letter of support and then a personal visit by the apostle (1 Tim. 3:14–15; 4:13). He probably cut short his visit to Macedonia and then retraced his steps through Troas and over to Ephesus.

After stabilizing the church in Ephesus, Paul left Timothy in charge and then resumed his original plan to winter in Nicopolis with Titus. The following spring (AD 65), he departed for Rome, intending to launch his mission westward, but tensions between Nero and Christians escalated out of control. Paul eventually landed in prison again, where an executioner took his life, the same fate experienced by many believers during that awful time at the whim of a crazed emperor.

"A TRUE CHILD IN THE FAITH"

Paul first encountered Timothy in the early months of his second missionary journey. He arrived in Lystra to hear the elders speak with such glowing praise of a young man that the apostle felt compelled to meet him. Born of a believing Jewish mother and a Greek father (presumably an unbeliever), Timothy was an ideal pupil for Paul, an individual much like himself: an evangelist with one foot in the Jewish world and the other in the Gentile.

As the years passed, Paul also found in Timothy a kindred spirit—studious (2 Tim. 3:14–15), emotional (2 Tim. 1:4), dedicated (Phil. 2:22), and resolute (1 Tim. 1:18). From his youth, Timothy had been steeped in the Scriptures of the Old Testament, thanks to his mother, Lois, and grandmother, Eunice (2 Tim. 1:5; 3:15). In return, Timothy found Paul to be a worthy model, a man gifted in many ways, but called to fulfill a mission ill-suited for his natural inclinations. Paul had not been trained to speak publicly, his appearance and demeanor apparently lacked polish, and his poor health made traveling a burden (1 Cor. 1:17; 2:3; 2 Cor. 10:10; 11:6; 12:7; Gal 4:13–14). Both men would have to carry out their ministries through a shared dependence on God to equip and direct them.

> ### TIMOTHY IN THE NEW TESTAMENT
>
> | | |
> |---|---|
> | Acts 16:1–3 | Philippians 1:1 |
> | Acts 17:14–15 | Philippians 2:19–24 |
> | Acts 18:1–5 | Colossians 1:1–2 |
> | Acts 19:21–22 | 1 Thessalonians 1:1–2 |
> | Acts 20:1–5 | 1 Thessalonians 3:1–6 |
> | Romans 16:21 | 2 Thessalonians 1:1 |
> | 1 Corinthians 4:16–17 | Philemon 1 |
> | 1 Corinthians 16:10–11 | Hebrews 13:22–24 |
> | 2 Corinthians 1:19 | |

For Timothy to become a part of Paul's ministry, he had to be circumcised (Acts 16:3)—not for spiritual reasons, but for practical ones. While Paul considered himself an apostle to the Gentiles (Eph. 3:1), he always first took the gospel to the synagogue when entering a new region (Acts 13:46; 17:2–3), and only then to the marketplace. Paul preached to Jews first because it was right, not because it was easy or even effective. Timothy had heard the stories of Paul's first visit to the lower Galatian region. The Jews in Derbe, Lystra, and Iconium had persecuted Paul and Barnabas, eventually stoning Paul and leaving him for dead (Acts 14:19). Nevertheless, Paul returned, employing the same methods that had earned him such hardship before. Timothy, by now a dutifully circumcised Jew, stood alongside his mentor in the synagogues.

In time, Paul came to see Timothy as an extension of himself, sending his "true child in the faith" to solve problems he normally would have undertaken. On his second missionary journey, when Paul worried that the churches in Macedonia—Thessalonica in particular—might have succumbed to Jewish persecution, he sent Timothy into the unknown to "strengthen and encourage" the members of the church (1 Thess. 3:1–2). During his third missionary journey, he sent ahead Timothy (and Erastus) from Ephesus to prepare the churches in Macedonia and Greece for his visit (Acts 19:21–22). Then, in final preparation for his long-anticipated journey to Spain—he never expected to see most of his pupils again—Paul placed Timothy in charge of the church in Ephesus, the most strategically important congregation in Asia and the church most susceptible to corruption.

"REMAIN ON AT EPHESUS"

Of all the cities in the Roman Empire, Ephesus would have been one of the most difficult places in which to lead a "tranquil and quiet life" (2:2), let alone to lead a tranquil and quiet church. This port city sat alongside the Aegean Sea at the mouth of the Cayster River near the intersection of two important mountain passes. Ephesus, therefore, commanded a strategic position, offering access in all directions from the sea, making the city an unusually busy and affluent economic hub for the Roman province of Asia. Materials and knowledge flowed into the city from all over the world, feeding its voracious appetite for more wealth and new philosophies.

"Epigraphic, numismatic and literary evidence reveals that the people of Ephesus worshiped up to fifty different gods and goddesses."[1] None, however, challenged the economic and mystical power of the towering temple of Artemis, one of the seven wonders of the ancient world. Worship of the Earth Mother had become a huge attraction, combining tourism and sensual idolatry with such success that it fueled the city's core economy (Acts 19), despite its already burgeoning import-export trade.

The people of Ephesus worshiped Artemis (a.k.a. Diana) the mother goddess, depicted here with multiple breasts. Her value to the city was more than religious. Much of the city's economy depended upon the influx of worshipers' money.

© William D. Mounce

City officials set aside one month of every year to honor the goddess with a grand celebration, during which all work ceased. The stadium hosted athletic games, the theater produced plays, the Odeon held concerts, and people flocked from every corner of Asia and beyond to make offerings in the sacred grove, the mythical birthplace of Artemis. Worship of the goddess brought such enormous sums of money into the temple that it became an important banking institution, perhaps the first of its kind in Asia. Moreover, the city of Ephesus became a sanctuary for debtors,[2] a place of refuge for anyone seeking to avoid his creditor's demands.

If the lure of money and magic didn't add enough chaos, the city of Ephesus also attracted schools of philosophy. Around 500 BC, Heraclitus, a Greek noble of Ephesus, taught that the universe operates according to a unified ordering principle that he called *logos*, "word, reason." Later philosophers built on this theory, claiming that all the laws of physics, mathematics, reason, and even morality can be traced back to an impersonal divine mind. By the time of Paul, Ephesus had become a veritable cauldron of competing philosophies and a celebrated repository of texts on Greek philosophy.

For all its temptations and challenges, "roads from Ephesus radiated in every direction along the coast and through the interior of the province,"[3] making the city a perfect location for Paul's base of operations in Asia. To ensure the church would remain morally uncorrupted, doctrinally pure, and spiritually vibrant, he spent more time in Ephesus than in any other Gentile city. Moreover, he nurtured the congregation from afar, sending envoys to check on its members' well-being, writing at least one letter, and—perhaps most significant of all—placing them in the hands of his star disciple, Timothy.

"IT IS FOR THIS WE LABOR AND STRIVE"

Ephesus was a city built of marble. Marble paved the streets, lined the foundations, supported the monuments, and channeled rainwater to the sea. Even the public toilets were constructed from polished marble. The city gleamed with white iridescence, as if to say to the world, "This city will shine forever." (Even today, tour guides encourage visitors to the magnificent remains of the ancient city to wear sunglasses at midday to avoid eye damage.) So, the church in Ephesus had to be built of equally sturdy stuff. To withstand the crashing chaos battering its foundations, the congregation needed order above all; and with so many strong personalities, their pastor would have to lead with a firm, yet loving hand.

Paul expressed the central purpose of his letter in 1 Timothy 3:15: "I write so that you will know how one ought to conduct himself in the household of God, which is the church of the living God, the pillar and support of the truth." While the apostle did discuss important theological truths, he wrote primarily in order to equip Timothy for the task of leading and stabilizing the church. He began by offering personal encouragement, exhorting Timothy to fight hard for the gospel (1:3 – 20). The opponents of the truth would fight ruthlessly to tear it down. He described the essential qualities Timothy should cultivate within the congregation (2:1 – 3:16), which he hoped would influence the city at large. Then Paul instructed his student on the role of a shepherd: the faithful teaching and preaching of the Word, his conduct among the flock, and the inevitable resistance he would face from within as well as from without (4:1 – 6:21).

Throughout this letter, Paul kept Timothy's eye focused on the ultimate prize of a shepherd: a godly congregation. "Bodily discipline is only of little profit," he wrote, "but godliness is profitable for all things, since it holds promise for the present life and also for the life to come" (4:8). Paul "labored and strived" for this in every church he established and strengthened. In this letter, the apostle laid his shepherd's mantle across the shoulders of his pupil, Timothy. If you serve today as a pastor or spiritual leader, it has passed to you as well.

NOTES:

1. C. E. Arnold, "Centers of Christianity," *Dictionary of the Later New Testament and Its Developments*, ed. Ralph P. Martin and Peter H. Davids (Downers Grove, IL: InterVarsity Press, 1997), 147.
2. *Plutarch's Morals*, ed. William W. Goodwin (Boston: Little, Brown, & Company, 1878), 5:414.
3. Arnold, "Centers of Christianity," 147.

APOSTLE PAUL TO PASTOR TIMOTHY (1 TIMOTHY 1:1–20)

What's a Pastor to Do? (1 Timothy 1:1–11)

¹Paul, an apostle of Christ Jesus according to the commandment of God our Savior, and of Christ Jesus, *who is* our hope,

²To Timothy, *my* true child in *the* faith: Grace, mercy *and* peace from God the Father and Christ Jesus our Lord.

³As I urged you upon my departure for Macedonia, remain on at Ephesus so that you may instruct certain men not to teach strange doctrines, ⁴nor to pay attention to myths and endless genealogies, which give rise to mere speculation rather than *furthering* the administration of God which is by faith. ⁵But the goal of our instruction is love from a pure heart and a good conscience and a sincere faith. ⁶For some men, straying from these things, have turned aside to fruitless discussion, ⁷wanting to be teachers of the Law, even though they do not understand either what they are saying or the matters about which they make confident assertions.

⁸But we know that the Law is good, if one uses it lawfully, ⁹realizing the fact that law is not made for a righteous person, but for those who are lawless and rebellious, for the ungodly and sinners, for the unholy and profane, for those who kill their fathers or mothers, for murderers ¹⁰and immoral men and homosexuals and kidnappers and liars and perjurers, and whatever else is contrary to sound teaching, ¹¹according to the glorious gospel of the blessed God, with which I have been entrusted.

Of all of the vocations one might enter, Christian ministry would have to be the most confusing. For a person who finishes his or her medical school training, hanging out a shingle and practicing medicine is the logical next step. The details of running a practice can be overwhelming, but the mission remains clear. Everyone knows the job description of a physician: treat patients and help them stay healthy.

The same can be said of an attorney. Once law school is complete and the exacting bar exam passed, a lawyer uses his or her know-how to advise and represent clients in legal matters. A CPA earns a degree, passes a difficult exam, and then applies his or her expertise in the field of finance.

The job profile of a minister, however, isn't nearly so clear-cut. To enter ministry is to step into a milieu of high and lofty, yet utterly ambiguous expectations. A young minister might unwittingly step into the shoes of a legendary predecessor, which he can never hope to fill. Or, someone reared and trained in one part of the country follows God's leading to another region, with just enough cultural differences to frustrate everyone. Or, as occurs often, a church diligently seeks an expert in theology with years of pulpit experience, only to resist his spiritual leadership, criticize his temperament, and complain about his preaching once he arrives.

Then, there's the whole realm of theology. So many books and articles written, so many voices, so many alleged authorities with all sorts of perspectives on innumerable topics related to the church. The pastor is expected to be a walking encyclopedia of Bible knowledge, an expert on all the latest theological trends, a flawless public speaker, an inspiring executive leader, a servant-hearted shepherd, a gifted counselor, an authority on children and youth, a caretaker of the aged, sick, dying, and grieving—as well as a dedicated husband and faithful family man!

With so many hats to wear, so many shoes to fill, so many expectations to meet and roles to play, a young pastor can forget why he entered the ministry in the first place. So, what's a pastor to do? Fortunately, the Holy Spirit inspired a remarkable servant of God to write a gifted pastor so that shepherds today might know for certain what the Lord expects of them, how other ministers can serve under his leadership, and how congregations may encourage and support all full-time vocational ministers.

— 1:1–2 —

The letter opens with a warm greeting from one close friend to another. A seasoned and scarred apostle, bearded and no doubt balding, writes as a man who understood the rigors of ministry. Nevertheless, Paul includes the title "apostle," which might seem strange in a personal greeting to his closest associate. That would be like my signing a letter to one my sons:

Dad,

Senior Pastor

Paul inserts the title "apostle" for two reasons.

First, for the benefit of the church in Ephesus. Paul writes to Timothy, intending every word to be heard by the churches in public readings. "Apostle" describes someone sent to accomplish a task on behalf of a sender. And all first-century cultures recognized the same basic rule: treat an envoy as you would the sender, for that will determine how you are treated in return. God sent Paul, and Paul sent Timothy.

Second, for the benefit of Timothy's confidence. Only here and in his greeting to Titus does Paul use the phrase "according to the command of God" (cf. Titus 1:3). Paul's authority to preach, teach, write, and lead came from God's command, which he passed to Timothy upon sending him to Ephesus. This is not to suggest any sort of "apostolic succession." Once the last of the apostles died, the title and authority of apostleship ended. Before the New Testament Scriptures had been collected and vetted by the churches, however, one depended on the recommendation of a trusted source before receiving anyone's teaching as authentic.

Just as God had authorized Paul's ministry, so Timothy stood among the Ephesians with the same authority to teach and to lead.

Paul may have intended another benefit. It may have helped Timothy, a soldier in God's army, feel less alone by reading the words of a comrade-in-arms. Unfortunately, ministry brings its share of loneliness, for a pastor especially. He dare not share too much of his life with any but the most trusted associates, and ideally they should be peers outside the church.

Paul's affection for Timothy as a pupil comes through in calling him "my true child in the faith," similar to the apostle's greeting to Titus (Titus 1:4). The phrase "true child" depends on the technical word *gnēsios*, which, when used with "child," distinguished a natural-born heir from an adoptee. Paul's benediction also suggests an added affection. He frequently imparted "grace" and "peace" in his greetings, but to Timothy alone the apostle wishes for "mercy" (cf. 2 Tim. 1:2), a highly emotive word in Greek and the most common translation of the Hebrew term *chesed*, "gracious, faithful love." Perhaps Paul recognized that Timothy's tender disposition would cause him to need the Lord's empathy while serving in the tumult of Ephesus.

— **1:3–4** —

After a relatively short greeting, Paul gets down to business. He offers his younger friend four specific directives, presumably in response to something specific Paul either has heard from Ephesus or knows about the city from his own experience.

First, *stay at the task* (1:3).

Paul urges Timothy to remain. The simple Greek verb *menō* means "stay" or "remain," often used in the sense of "take up residence." But Paul chooses *prosmenō*, meaning "wait" or "continue remaining." Furthermore, the Greek term for "urged" implies a strong exhortation. Paul probably urged Timothy while they were together in Miletus, just before the apostle resumed his itinerary north to Troas and then over to Macedonia. He apparently received word that Timothy was struggling more than either of them had anticipated and so changes his travel plans to double back to Ephesus, promising Timothy he will arrive soon (3:14–15; 4:13).

From My Journal

"You Pray ..."

Sometimes a minister needs to recognize when the time has come to move on.

In 1965, I accepted a call to be the senior pastor of a church in Waltham, Massachusetts. As if the cultural mismatch of two native Texans in the land of Yankees didn't present challenge enough, my wife, Cynthia, could not adjust to the weather. To this day, she'll tell you she didn't feel warm for two years.

Now, I'm not one to run from a challenge, but the difficulties we had adapting to ministry in New England made it clear that we were not serving in the right place. So, I put the word out that I was open to a change. In the meantime, we committed ourselves to the care of God's people in Waltham and left our future in the Lord's hands. We stayed faithful "in season and out of season."

Before long, I received an invitation to lead the congregation of Irving Bible Church in the suburbs of sunny, much-warmer, Dallas, Texas. Naturally, I wanted some certainty about the rightness of this move, so I said to Cynthia, "I'll need to pray about this." Without missing a beat, she replied, "You pray while I'll pack!"

Most church members would feel shocked to know how many times the thought of resigning crosses a pastor's mind, especially when serving congregations in which encouragement is virtually nonexistent. Legitimate reasons exist for a shepherd to leave his post to go somewhere else, but a pastor usually brushes up his resume in response to challenges that leave him feeling hopeless, unappreciated, and alone. Monday mornings can be especially difficult. Emotionally spent and lacking any tangible results in return for his best effort on Sunday, a pastor wonders if he really has anything worthwhile to offer.

Timothy had seen his share of hardship, having often traveled with Paul, and he had taken on tough assignments before; so the trouble in Ephesus must have been extraordinary. Nevertheless, Paul urges the embattled pastor to stay at his task.

Second, *communicate the truth* (1:3–4).

Paul did not expect Timothy to remain idle in Ephesus. He urged him to carry out his mission of teaching, with even greater determination.

The NASB rendering "instruct" is perhaps too understated. "Command" or "order" better captures the authoritative nuance of the Greek verb. Paul expected the pastor to use his authority to forbid two specific distractions from the gospel: theological innovation and appealing to myths and genealogies for authority.

"Teach strange doctrines" translates the compound word, *hetero* + *didaskaleō*, or "to other-teach" (cf. 6:3). Ephesus had long been the place where teachers established schools and attracted students to their newly invented philosophical systems. No teaching in the church, however, can contradict prior revelation—which is, for us today, Scripture. For the Ephesians, no teaching could contradict the verbal instruction they received from men instructed by Jesus and commissioned to be His envoys (apostles.)

Ancient cultures gave the greatest credence to that which was old. Myths are stories that recount supposedly ancient events for the purpose of explaining how or why people believe a certain thing. People use genealogies to link themselves to something everyone respects in order to establish credibility or legitimacy. The term translated "pay attention to" means "to devote thought or effort toward" something (cf. 4:13; Acts 16:14). It appears the Ephesians sought to link Christian teaching to myths and genealogies to give them an air of authority rather than to stand confidently on God's Word alone.

Ultimately, Paul's command applies to everyone in ministry. The truth for you may have a relatively narrow application. Your discipline may be music, special needs, women's ministries, men's ministries, pulpit ministry, feeding and clothing the poor, or evangelism. Whatever your calling, wherever your ministry occurs, communicate the truth boldly, confidently standing on the authority of Scripture.

From My Journal

Watch Your Target!

After several weeks of rugged physical training, close-order drill (marching), and "snapping in," our Marine Corps drill instructor finally led us to the rifle range. He had us lie down in the dirt with our rifles and look down-range at markers set at 200 yards, 300 yards, and ultimately 500 yards out. Then the captain of the rifle range yelled three words over the P.A. system, "Watch your targets!" And up they'd come, followed by the random cracks of rifle fire all around.

All the while, the captain kept repeating, "Watch your targets! Watch your targets!" which might seem an obvious command. We came for target practice, after all. But if you've never experienced a firing range, the distractions can overwhelm you at first. I had to repeat the captain's three-word command in orvder to keep my mind focused on the target.

Every once in a while those words come back to me. I still hear them in my head. And they're right out of 1 Timothy 1:5. *Watch your target! Love from a pure heart. Love from a good conscience. Love from an unhypocritical faith. Watch your target!*

— 1:5 —

Third, *concentrate on the goal* (1:5).

God gives us His Word and then clarifies the reason we are to stay at the task and communicate the truth: love. The goal is love. The motivation and the message from minister to congregation is love. When your people depart for home after your instruction, when they step out of the counseling room where you have discussed the realities of life, when they think back on that chance encounter or that lunch you scheduled, or whatever situation gave you an opportunity to impart truth, they will remember seeing love in action. Moreover, they will have seen it modeled and understand how to do the same for another.

The minister must not teach truth for the sake of being right or appearing intelligent. The Lord does not want doctrinal purity because He wants the church to be a repository of knowledge. Doctrinal purity cultivates a clean heart, a good conscience (1:5, 19; 3:9; 4:2), and "unhypocritical" faith, which in turn produces love for God and love for others.

— 1:6–7 —

The verb *astocheō* means "to miss the target," as in archery. Figuratively, of course, it describes one's failure to accomplish what he or she intended. Certain men were engaging in theological discussions that failed to produce either love or good works. Paul calls such discussions "fruitless discussion" or "empty prattle."

There's a time and place for splitting theological hairs. Men and women preparing for ministry, for example, should be encouraged to stretch their theological muscles in the academic gymnasium of seminary. Nothing like a good seminary debate to work out the kinks in one's doctrine! A minister, however, always rests his or her teaching on sound doctrine. And a pastor always preaches from solid exegesis toward practical application based on his intimate knowledge of the congregation's needs.

Practical application forbids "fruitless" or "empty" teaching.

— 1:8–11 —

Fourth, *remember the standard* (1:8–9, 11).

All instruction must ultimately support the gospel, even when one is teaching on the law of Moses. The syntactical construction of these verses and how it employs the phrase "according to the glorious gospel" suggests the good news is the baseline against which all teaching must be measured. In other words, the "sound teaching" at the end of verse 10 has the "glorious gospel" as its basis. Sound teaching builds on the basic foundation — the norm or the standard — of the gospel.

Paul defends the law as good and as an expression of God's holy character, given to humanity for the purpose of redemption. God gave us the law so we might measure ourselves against His righteous standard, find ourselves wanting, and then turn to Him for grace. No one can earn salvation by obeying the law because all of us have failed. Therefore, the law is intended for the lawless.

Those who have recognized their helplessness and have received God's free gift of eternal life through faith in His Son now have a different relationship with the law. Believers are no longer "under" the law — that is, subject to its condemnation — but now embrace the law as a means of knowing God and seeking to please Him.

Ministry can be a terribly disillusioning, even confusing vocation. I have counseled many individuals who were contemplating vocational Christian service to test their calling with a simple question: "Will *any* other vocation potentially offer you reasonable fulfillment?" If so, I encourage them to pursue that before making any significant life changes in the direction of ministry.

At the same time, I don't want to paint a bleak picture of ministry, especially that of a shepherd. If God has called you to serve as a pastor, then no other role will suffice. Any other position — regardless of pay, perks, power, or pomp — will prove only frustrating, and very quickly. To borrow from the old Peace Corps slogan, "It's the toughest job you'll ever love."

I have discovered that the best way for a pastor to avoid disillusionment and to cut through innumerable and endless distractions is to choose what he will lean on and to whom he will listen. Those men who depend on popularity for successful ministry and who listen to popular opinion doom themselves to disappointment and insecurity. Those who lean on the Lord and listen to His Word may struggle and even suffer, but they remain focused on the target, persevere through difficulties, slice through distractions, and thrive on the challenge of ministry. They grow in their enthusiasm and they shred their resumes before Tuesday morning.

Application

A Church for the Ages

The church is headed for a split. Not my church, and I hope not yours. I'm referring to *the* church. I see on one side a deeper commitment to tradition than to Scripture, and on the other a wholesale rejection of tradition — and with it, divine truth. And postmodernism is the blade that would make the final cut.

Postmodernism is an insidious philosophy that—among many other failings—leads to an ethic of pragmatism, determining right from wrong based on the immediate needs of the majority. Consequently, churches have redefined success, becoming less concerned with such intangible factors as spiritual maturity or congregational unity, obsessing over programs that "work," and finding ways to "meet needs." I am grieved to see church growth gurus elevating their own status by offering innovative programs, stimulating plans, and motivational talks, all of which dupe insecure pastors into thinking they're missing out on some secret, megachurch formula. Inevitably, these church-growth strategies convince leaders they must change the church to become less offensive to a suspicious world.

Traditionalists, however, don't have much to offer in response. They rely on tried-and-true methods and labor to keep them in place because they appear to have served the church's needs. They resist every attempt to keep up with the times by repeating a seven-word, church-numbing mantra: "We've never done it that way before." In truth, for all its sanctimonious talk, traditionalism is just pragmatism of another kind, no better and no worse than church growth strategies.

The church is about neither traditionalism nor pragmatism. Should we respond to the needs of people? Absolutely! Should we honor our God-honoring biblical traditions? We would be foolish not to. But we must not look to either tradition or pragmatism as the guiding principle of ministry. I don't mean to oversimplify the issue, but when I enrolled in seminary in 1959, I dedicated myself to learning how to teach the Bible. After I completed my four years of training, I devoted the rest of my years to teaching its truths. And in my considerable experience, God's Word is more than enough to meet the needs of people, fill a sanctuary to overflowing, inspire new ministries, energize community change, and even keep worthwhile traditions alive.

No gimmicks needed. No flashy PR campaigns required. Just preach the Word faithfully and consistently, and let God take care of the numbers. The Holy Spirit will guide the message of grace to meet the needs of every individual within hearing.

Battle Cry for a Weary Soldier
(1 Timothy 1:12–20)

---

[12]I thank Christ Jesus our Lord, who has strengthened me, because He considered me faithful, putting me into service, [13]even though I was formerly a blasphemer and a persecutor and a violent aggressor. Yet I was shown mercy because I acted ignorantly in unbelief; [14]and the grace of our Lord was more than abundant, with the faith and love which are *found* in

Christ Jesus. ¹⁵It is a trustworthy statement, deserving full acceptance, that Christ Jesus came into the world to save sinners, among whom I am foremost *of all.* ¹⁶Yet for this reason I found mercy, so that in me as the foremost, Jesus Christ might demonstrate His perfect patience as an example for those who would believe in Him for eternal life. ¹⁷Now to the King eternal, immortal, invisible, the only God, *be* honor and glory forever and ever. Amen.

¹⁸This command I entrust to you, Timothy, *my* son, in accordance with the prophecies previously made concerning you, that by them you fight the good fight, ¹⁹keeping faith and a good conscience, which some have rejected and suffered shipwreck in regard to their faith. ²⁰Among these are Hymenaeus and Alexander, whom I have handed over to Satan, so that they will be taught not to blaspheme.

Seasoned commanders know the dangers of discouragement. It can shut down an otherwise good soldier and quickly spread like a disease, affecting everyone around him. A military commander may have superior numbers, better weapons, extensive intelligence, and a flawless plan, but if his troops lose heart, he may as well start digging graves. The enemy has already won.

Timothy had been ministering in Ephesus for an unknown time by the time Paul wrote to him. During a brief visit — probably in Miletus on his way to Macedonia (1:3) — Paul undoubtedly noticed the early signs of battle fatigue on Timothy's face and urged the younger minister to remain at his post, despite the church's failure to respect Timothy's role as their spiritual leader. In my experience, a pastor can endure almost any hardship with the support of his church, but nothing will destroy his will to "fight the good fight" faster than lack of respect from the congregation. Then, something — perhaps news of Paul's release from prison — convinced the apostle to pay a personal visit to Ephesus (3:14–15; 4:13). He needed to rally the beleaguered soldier's spirits and reaffirm his authority to lead and teach the church in Ephesus.

— 1:12–14 —

Great movements usually begin with a strong leader who has a new message. That's the way of the world, and it's not always bad. We need powerful political leaders with godly character to defeat evil and to restore order. Thank God for the good-hearted men and women who led their countries in the fight against Nazi Germany. I am thankful for the founding fathers of the United States, charismatic characters who inspired their fellow citizens to found a new nation on principles of government radically different from the norm.

Paul, however, carefully removes himself from this role. He states plainly that the gospel did not originate with him; the good news of grace comes from God. He also removes himself as the chief scholarly authority on the subject. His knowledge of grace surpasses that of others only because he once stood in the greatest need of it. He feels uniquely qualified to proclaim the wonders of God's mercy, not because he has studied harder, spoken more eloquently, or stood taller than others, but because he has benefited more than any other servant of God—at least in his own mind.

Beginning in verse 11, Paul's emphasis shifts to reflect on himself. The pronouns "you," "yours," "they," and "them" give way to "I," "me," "my," and "mine." Paul does not treat the gospel with professional detachment, like an exciting new theory or a grand scientific discovery. Nothing could be more personally significant to him. Having benefited so powerfully and so deeply from the wonders of God's grace, he could hardly remain idle. Paul explains the amazing reason he—of all people—has been entrusted (v. 11) with the proclamation of the good news.

Christ Jesus our Lord:

"strengthened me"
"considered me faithful"
"put me into service."

At first, Paul's declaration that Christ "considered me faithful" might seem boastful, as if to say, "The Lord looked down on all humanity and saw that I was faithful, so He put me into service." A subtle detail in his use of Greek, however, makes all the difference.

The term rendered "considered" is *hēgeomai*, which means "to lead, think, regard." The Lord decided within Himself, apart from outside influence, that Paul would be faithful and regarded him as such. As a result, he called Paul into his service. Note the order in which Paul presents the verbs. Christ strengthened him first, *then* decided to believe in him (in a manner of speaking), and then placed the apostle into service.

Naturally, this has impacted Paul's perspective on ministry. It isn't a drag. It isn't a hassle. It isn't a burden. It isn't an interruption. It isn't an inconvenience. He doesn't even call ministry a sacrifice. He describes his work as *diakonia*, "deacon's work." Servanthood lies at the root of this Greek term for "waiting tables," the duty of a kitchen servant.

Right about now, a novice might think, This man Paul must have been something else. He really must have had it all together. For God, the Originator of the gospel, to give His truth to this man and for this man to have it to share in the service of his life—Paul must have been one phenomenal individual!

Wrong.

—1:13–14—

If, in fact, Paul had been such a great man before receiving the gospel, verse 13 would have extolled his virtues. Instead, he reveals his incredible lack of moral qualifications, attaching to himself three negative descriptions.

- a *blasphemer*, who injures others with his words and insults or speaks lightly of sacred things
- a *persecutor*, who puts someone to flight, taking every opportunity to assault and, if necessary, annihilate
- a *violent aggressor*, who mistreats others with hubris or an insolent attitude

Paul assures Timothy and the church in Ephesus that his authority to preach the gospel did not come from his own greatness, but from God despite the greatness of his need. Because Timothy already knew this, Paul probably writes this for the benefit of those hearing the letter read in public. This leads me to speculate that the trouble Timothy encountered in Ephesus stemmed from their stubborn attachment to Paul.

I have seen this problem far too often in my own lifetime. A highly esteemed, faithful minister of the gospel leaves a massive void when he departs, especially if he has occupied the same position for many years. Imagine the pressure placed on the successor to Charles Haddon Spurgeon after his untimely death left the pulpit empty at the Metropolitan Tabernacle in London.

I found a newspaper clipping from the *New York Times* from that period.

Mr. Spurgeon's Possible Successor

The Rev. Dr. Arthur T. Pierson, who may fill the pulpit of the London Tabernacle, preached in the Reformed Church of Brooklyn Heights last evening. Dr. Pierson has been much discussed recently as the probable successor of Dr. Spurgeon. Shortly after Dr. Spurgeon's death, Dr. Pierson, who hails from Philadelphia, was invited to preach in the London Tabernacle, and he remained there for a year under a temporary call. He became a great favorite with the congregation, and would in all probability have been made the permanent pastor before this except for a strong feeling among some of the members of the church that Dr. Spurgeon's son should succeed to the place made famous by his father.

In order to test the younger Spurgeon's strength, he was recently installed on a year's trial. At the expiration of this time the Londoners will decide whether they want to keep him or have Dr. Pierson.

Dr. Pierson has a fine delivery and is a most eloquent preacher.[1]

Apparently, the congregation found "the younger Spurgeon's strength" substantial enough to leave him in place. He served the congregation faithfully for the next fifteen years. Most churches, however, don't fare so well.

Paul reinforces his undeserved place of honor in the ministry of the gospel by calling attention to the mercy he has received. He has been entrusted with the good news, strengthened by God, and given success despite his ignorance. God's mercy has afforded him the opportunity.

Perhaps this is Paul's subtle call for Timothy's critics to extend some divine mercy to the "undeserving" younger leader.

—1:15–17—

What caused God to interrupt Saul of Tarsus and take command of his life to demonstrate His grace? According to Paul, the Son of God entered the world to save sinners, and the apostle just happened to be the best example of a sinner needing salvation. He said, in effect, "If the Lord came to earth looking for sinners, I was too big a sinner to ignore."

Paul also suggests that no other sinner would have been a better subject to demonstrate the Lord's magnificent transforming power. He calls himself a *hypotypōsis*, a prototype, a model, a pattern after which one might reproduce many more.

Now, when the Lord transforms a life so dramatically—essentially turning a maniacal religious murderer into a prototype follower of Jesus Christ—one can only respond with praise. Having reviewed his own testimony of divine mercy and transforming grace, Paul breaks out in song, which draws heavily on the Hebrew Scriptures:

Eternal King (Ex. 15:18; Ps. 145:13)
Immortal (Ps. 90:2; 102:26–27)
Invisible (Job 23:8–9)
"Only" (Dt. 4:35; Isa. 44:6)

Paul, because of God's matchless grace, is a blasphemer no more!

—1:18–20—

To summarize 1:3–17, Paul has said to Timothy, in effect: "Stay at your appointed task in Ephesus, teaching others to remain faithful to the gospel of God's grace and to avoid teaching anything else. As an expert in the law of Moses, I can personally attest to the power of the gospel and the powerlessness of the law to save. Nevertheless, the authority of this truth does not rest on me or any other man; it is divine truth from God's Word." He then resumes the solemn charge he began in v. 3—again for the benefit of the Ephesians hearing the letter read in public, as well as for Timothy's withered confidence.

While the gospel is divine in origin and therefore rests on divine authority, Paul nevertheless affirms Timothy's teaching credentials in two ways. First, Timothy had been commissioned by an acknowledged apostle, Paul himself; second, the young man had received a call of God by means of prophecy. Based on these two affirmations, the apostle charges Timothy with the responsibility to "fight the good fight" (cf. 2 Cor. 6:7; 10:4; Eph. 6:12; 1 Tim 6:12; 2 Tim 2:3–4; 4:7). A more nuanced translation of the Greek phrase would be, "commit yourself fully as a soldier in this present campaign for good."

Verse 19 explains just how Paul expects his lieutenant to carry out the general order to "fight the good fight": hold onto "faith" and maintain "a good conscience." In other words, "continue to do as you have been commanded despite the *apparent* futility of your efforts. And then rest in the confidence that you have done all the Commander has required of you."

Unfortunately, some in Ephesus have abandoned the authentic teaching they received. And because "nature abhors a vacuum," false teaching quickly filled their empty heads and hearts. Paul names two such men, Hymenaeus and Alexander, presumably because they have become Timothy's most distressing opponents in Ephesus. According to Paul's second letter to Timothy, written close to the end of his life, Hymenaeus and Philetus "upset the faith of some" by teaching "the resurrection had already taken place" (2 Tim. 2:16–18). The church in Ephesus apparently respected the oratory skills of Alexander the coppersmith, a Jewish believer (Acts 19:33), but he turned from the gospel as well. Although we don't know what he taught, he did "much harm" and "vigorously opposed" the teaching of Paul and Timothy (2 Tim. 4:14–15).

Paul considers the teaching of Hymenaeus and Alexander to be "blasphemy," the sin of defaming God's character, a sin he knows well, having been guilty of it himself (1:13). Therefore, he has "handed [them] over to Satan," strongly suggesting he has put Hymenaeus and Alexander out of the church, just as he had the young man in Corinth who refused to repent of his sexual affair with his stepmother (1 Cor. 5:1–13). As a strong spiritual leader, Paul deals with unrepentant sin and open rebellion forcefully, not only to protect the integrity of the church, but to allow the consequences of sin to discipline wayward believers (1 Cor. 11:32; Heb. 12:7–10). He undoubtedly expects Timothy to follow suit.

Young men and women often enter ministry only to become disillusioned when evil undermines their idealism. At some point, a minister must come to terms with the reality of ministry without sacrificing his or her idealism. The earth is a war zone in an invisible, all-out struggle of evil to destroy good. Satan *hates* God and everyone serving Him. The minister who fails to see, or refuses to acknowledge, the unseen warfare taking place all around him or her will inevitably quit the fight, disillusioned, distraught, disappointed, and disaffected. Pastors—especially those serving alone in small congregations—struggle with this more than most.

Paul encourages Timothy to stay in the battle despite the apparent gains won by the enemy. Jesus already has assured us of ultimate victory over evil; therefore, the only way for a minister to suffer personal loss is to quit the fight. Satan cannot destroy the souls of God's redeemed, but if he can get them to lay down their arms and surrender to discouragement, he can continue to ravage the rest of the world unimpeded.

In the now-famous words of Winston Churchill, who rallied his country to fight Nazi Germany, "This is the lesson: never give in, never give in, never, never, never, never—in nothing, great or small, large or petty—never give in except to convictions of honour and good sense. Never yield to force; never yield to the apparently overwhelming might of the enemy."[2]

NOTES:

1. *The New York Times*, "Mr. Spurgeon's Possible Successor," September 18, 1893, p. 1.
2. Winston Churchill, in his speech to Harrow School, October 29, 1941.

THE WORK OF MINISTRY
(1 TIMOTHY 2:1–3:16)

Sometimes a pastor needs reassurance—not merely to boost his morale or stroke his wounded ego, but to remind him that the gospel really does change lives and that the work he does will not go to waste. He needs that from time to time because—I'll be honest here—the work of ministry can feel futile, like trying to empty the ocean with a teaspoon. The needs of the world are so great and the impact we have seems so insignificant by comparison. Nevertheless, we have been called to a well-defined set of duties, tasks that must be completed by the church—day by day, week by week. Either the pastor must carry them out personally, or he must build a godly, well-trained staff of men and women, and then lead them effectively.

Paul's lengthy introduction offered more than the usual amount of personal encouragement and professional exhortation. He reaffirmed Timothy's task, reflected on his own experience in ministry, praised the trustworthiness of the gospel, and encouraged the beleaguered pastor to remain steadfast in his work. Then he turned his attention to describing the work of pastoral ministry in a fair amount of detail, giving special attention to the establishment and maintenance of church order. According to Paul, who wrote under the inspiration of the Holy Spirit, every person has a role to fill in God's household, and every role has responsibilities.

What's First in a Meaningful Ministry?
(1 Timothy 2:1–8)

¹First of all, then, I urge that entreaties *and* prayers, petitions *and* thanksgivings, be made on behalf of all men, ²for kings and all who are in authority, so that we may lead a tranquil and quiet life in all godliness and dignity. ³This is good and acceptable in the sight of God our Savior, ⁴who desires all men to be saved and to come to the knowledge of the truth. ⁵For there is one God, *and* one mediator also between God and men, *the* man Christ Jesus, ⁶who gave Himself as a ransom for all, the testimony *given* at the proper time. ⁷For this I was appointed a preacher and an apostle (I am telling the truth, I am not lying) as a teacher of the Gentiles in faith and truth.

⁸Therefore I want the men in every place to pray, lifting up holy hands, without wrath and dissension.

KEY TERMS

ἀνήρ [anēr] (435) "man, husband, male, humanity"

The term for "man," and its plural form, ἄνδρες [andres], generally refers to a male, but can mean specifically a husband or an adult male as opposed to a mere boy. Greek literature also uses this word to include the entire human race. For example, "The anger of man does not achieve the righteousness of God" (Jas. 1:20).

γυνή [gynē] (1135) "woman, wife, female"

Paul uses this term eight times in this section. It can refer to a woman in general or to a wife; context tells the reader how to interpret the author's intent. In some circumstances, the word is used a form of address, as when Jesus called his mother, "woman" (John 2:4).

διάκονος [diakonos] (1249) "deacon, servant, table waiter"

In its most basic, literal sense, the term means "one who serves at-table." By extension, it carries the idea of serving obediently and willingly, offering service with a submissive attitude. When the first church needed men to oversee the distribution of food to widows, the leaders created this office (Acts 6). Although the duties of a deacon expanded, the people serving in this capacity were never to forget their table-waiting roots.

ἐπίσκοπος [episkopos] (1985) "overseer, elder, protector, patron"

The most general sense this word describes one who watches over an institution or a territory. Athens called its state officials episkopoi, the plural form of the word. In the Septuagint (the Greek translation of the Old Testament), an episkopos was one who served as judge, treasurer, or as supervisor of the priests and the Levites serving the temple. In the New Testament, Peter calls Jesus the "Guardian" or overseer (episkopos) of our souls (1 Pet. 2:25). In this sense, the church official designated by this term serves as an undershepherd to the Lord, leading His flock on His behalf and under His authority.

σώφρων [sōphrōn] (4998) "self-control, moderation"

The root term, which is loosely based on a combination of sōzō ("to save, be safe") and phrēn ("mind"), rarely appears in the Bible but ranked high among secular Greeks as a civic virtue. The word in its various forms has "sensibility" or "clear thinking" at its core.

Approximately once a year, I travel with ministry interns to visit six to ten churches in order to discuss the work of leading a congregation. Some churches are small, others are large. Many are growing, a few struggle to survive. We always make a point of visiting at least a couple of large churches. Almost without exception, we encounter the same challenge: maintaining priorities. A pastor fights this battle right out of seminary, and he will fight it until he retires or dies. Men and women serving in other ministerial roles—part-time or full-time, vocational or volunteer—will find themselves asking the same questions as the senior pastor. There's so much need! Where do I begin? What should I do first?

Richard De Haan offered the following description of a particular minister's day in his book *Men Sent from God*, published in 1966. Despite its age, his description is remarkably up-to-date.

> Arriving in the church office at 8 o'clock in the morning, [the pastor] had intended to spend at least two hours in preparation for his Sunday sermons, a noonday talk to a local service club, and five radio talks during the coming week. However, he was reminded by his secretary that he had agreed to write an article for the church bulletin, scheduled to go to press at noon. He was also obligated to make three telephone calls, one of them to the Chairman of the Church Finance Committee. After finishing with these duties, only 30 minutes were left for the preparation of his messages, since at 10 o'clock he was to meet with the Program Committee of the Ministerial Association. Just as he began to study again he received word that the mother of the President of one of the Women's Societies in the church had passed away, and his presence was wanted in their home at once. This, of course, caused him to miss his meeting with the Ministerial Association; but he was able to attend the 12:30 luncheon of the Women's Auxiliary. Following this he spoke to a study class. At 2 p.m. he officiated at a wedding ceremony. At 3 o'clock he began his regular visit in the city hospitals, and finished just in time to make the Men's Supper, where he gave the invocation. The supper lasted until 7:30 allowing the pastor to get away just in time to attend a meeting of the Every Member Canvas Committee. He was on hand simply to make suggestions and to boost the Committee morale. Having done that, his day of service was finally ended and he arrived home about 9:30 that evening.[1]

If you aren't in full-time vocational ministry, you might think that's an extreme exception. Trust me, it's no exception. This could easily describe the day of any pastor in any developed country, even one serving a smaller congregation with minimal staff, and especially one who is intimidated by a congregation and has somehow mistaken servanthood for people-pleasing.

Paul undoubtedly knew the temptation to please people would be especially difficult to resist for a man suffering the stings of criticism and struggling to maintain a congregation's confidence. Having addressed the minister personally, the apostle turned his discussion toward the minister's work. He begins by reminding Timothy of his first duty: *prayer.*

— 2:1-2 —

"First of all." Those aren't throwaway words. Prayer must be the first priority of any vocational minister for the sake of any ministry he or she may serve. Prayer reminds the minister that God is in charge, not people—not even the congregation, the senior pastor, the staff, or the elders. The minister serves God first and people second. Furthermore, prayer releases the minister from the tyranny of the urgent and the demands of the immediate to focus on one's calling.

Paul "urges" (same word as in 1:3) that prayers "be made." The verb is present tense, which gives the action an ongoing, continual quality. Furthermore, his use of the passive form begs the question, "By whom?" The answer: by everyone, with Timothy as the leader. He does not lay the responsibility for prayer on the pastor alone. The burden of ministry, beginning with prayer, falls on the entire fellowship.

Paul uses four distinct, yet closely related, terms to delineate four kinds of communication with God:

- "entreaty" (*deēsis*)—a need presented to God for the sake of having it met
- "prayer" (*proseuchē*)—the most common term for this spiritual discipline, denoting the act of calling on God in a general way, including the presentation of needs (*deēsis*)
- "petition" (*enteuxis*)—informal, intimate, free-flowing conversation with God
- "thanksgiving" (*eucharistia*)—the expression of gratitude or appreciation

Paul calls on Timothy and the church in Ephesus to employ every dimension of prayer—formal and informal, petitioning and thanking—on behalf of *all* people, saved and unsaved. Some have taught that we should pray only for people within the family of God; and when we do pray for the unsaved, we should pray only for conviction of sin and salvation. But Paul clearly commands Timothy to lead the church in praying for the needs of government officials, thus employing every dimension of conversation with God, just as one would pray for a close friend or a family member.

This could not have been an easy request in Ephesus, where city officials considered the church a threat to the local economy (Acts 19:23–27). To make things worse, the Roman Empire rested in the blood-soaked hands of an insane leader named Nero. Nevertheless, the apostle expects the church to pray for these leaders, just as they would for a loved one.

Why? Why pray for the welfare of those who would do you harm? Paul explains two benefits that result from our prayers: freedom from persecution (v. 2) and the redemption of the world (vv. 3–4).

The apostle explains that praying for the well-being of our government leaders sets the stage for a live-and-let-live existence under their authority. He uses two Greek adjectives that describe the "life" of peace: *ēremos*, which denotes "tranquility arising from without,"[2] while *hēsychios* denotes "tranquility arising from within."[3] Generally speaking, all governments want little more than for their citizens to remain peacefully productive and to pay their taxes. While exceptions exist, when most governments feel no threat coming from the church, they generally leave believers to worship as they please.

"Godliness" and "dignity" share the same root term in Greek, which is *sebomai*, "to reverence." The first describes an attitude of worshipfulness toward God, while the second denotes a general deportment of dignity arising from within. In other words, freedom from persecution allows us to be respectful of the Lord and the earthly authorities He allows to rule (Rom. 13:1–2). But to enjoy this benefit, we must pray for the good and well-being of our leaders—even when we disapprove of their character and oppose their policies.

—**2:3-4**—

Verses 3–4 reveal the Lord's ultimate motivation for our prayer. In addition to praying for the overall well-being of our government officials, we must pray for their salvation. The Lord, very simply, wants *all* people—including those in authority—to recognize the truth of the gospel and then submit to the authority of divine truth (cf. 1 Tim. 2:6; 4:10; Titus 2:11; 2 Peter 3:9).

Please observe Paul's careful use of verb tenses and moods in this declaration of God's desire. He does not write, "God ... who desires to save all men," but "God ... who desires all men to be saved." It does not invalidate the Scriptural doctrine of election to say that God desires *all* people to embrace the truth of the gospel and receive eternal life.[4] Paul does not attempt to unravel the mystery of how God's sovereignty and the limited autonomy of humanity impact a person's salvation. He merely affirms the fact that the Lord does not delight to see people perish for their sin (Ezek. 18:23; 33:11).

While the ultimate issue of salvation rests in God's hands, He nevertheless calls us to pray for the salvation of every person, including those who rule over us, and especially our enemies. As with all matters of prayer, He will act in perfect accord with His loving, righteous nature for the highest, greatest good of all people. Regardless of their eternal fate, the act of praying impacts the person offering the prayers. Personally, I find it impossible to criticize or despise someone I am asking the Lord to bless. In fact, I find my perspective gradually change to reflect God's as I pray.

— 2:5-6 —

Having mentioned divine truth, Paul cannot resist the opportunity to restate the gospel. Only now, he presents the gospel in the context of his urging prayer. Jesus assured His disciples on the eve of His atoning sacrifice for all of humankind (cf. 1 John 2:1–2), "I am the way, and the truth, and the life; no one comes to the Father but through Me" (John 14:6). Paul brings that idea forward by describing Jesus as the one and only "mediator" between God and humanity.

The Greek term translated "mediator" has the principal meaning of "trustworthy neutral." The English word invokes a poor image, unfortunately. Paul does not intend to portray God and humanity as disputants in a court case. He has a "priestly intercessor" more in mind. Humans need someone prepared by God to help them overcome their insufficiency.

PRAYER AS A CIVIC DUTY

Amazingly, the church has been faithful to pray for its pagan leaders, even during times of terrible persecution. Take note of these quotes from church fathers living in difficult times.

> To our rulers and governors on the earth — to them Thou, Lord, gavest the power of the kingdom by Thy glorious and ineffable might, to the end that we may know the glory and honour given to them by Thee and be subject to them, in nought resisting Thy will; to them, Lord, give health, peace, concord, stability, that they may exercise the authority given to them without offence.[5]
>
> Clement of Rome, ca. AD 96, during the brutal reign of Domitian

> Whence to God alone we render worship, but in other things we gladly serve you, acknowledging you as kings and rulers of men, and praying that with your kingly power you be found to possess also sound judgment.[6]
>
> Justin Martyr, AD 110–165, written to Emperor Antonius Pius,
> and also addressed to "Verissimus the Philosopher,"
> a.k.a. Marcus Aurelius, under whom Justin suffered martyrdom

> Does the sovereign order the payment of tribute, I am ready to render it. Does my master command me to act as a bondsman and to serve, I acknowledge the serfdom. Man is to be honoured as a fellow-man; God alone is to be feared.[7]
>
> Tatian (AD 110–172), around the time of Marcus Aurelius, the philosopher emperor

> Wherefore I will rather honour the king [than your gods], not, indeed, worshipping him, but praying for him. But God, the living and true God, I worship, knowing that the king is made by Him. You will say, then, to me, "Why do you not worship the king?" Because he is not made to be worshipped, but to be

Sin has separated humanity from God. Sin carries the penalty of eternal death (Rom. 6:23; Rev. 20:14–15) that must be paid in order to satisfy God's justice, yet He wants all people to live with Him forever. Humanity, however, cannot pay this penalty and live. In this sense, a mediator helps each party find mutual satisfaction for their interests. Jesus, the God-man, is uniquely qualified to represent both parties. Moreover, He has resolved the issue by suffering humanity's death on our behalf, which the Father has accepted as the just penalty of sin. Now, through Him alone (Acts 4:12), we have unfettered access to the throne of heaven, which gives us the ability to bring the needs of others before God—including those who do not know Him.

The phrase "the testimony given at the proper time" is difficult to interpret and not everyone agrees what it means. But if we avoid the temptation to overthink its

reverenced with lawful honour, for he is not a god, but a man appointed by God, not to be worshipped, but to judge justly. For in a kind of way his government is committed to him by God.... Accordingly, honour the king, be subject to him, and pray for him with loyal mind; for if you do this, you do the will of God.[8]

Theophilus, ca. AD 181, shortly after the death of Marcus Aurelius, during the reign of his notoriously capricious and corrupt son, Commodus

Without ceasing, for all our emperors we offer prayer. We pray for life prolonged; for security to the empire; for protection to the imperial house; for brave armies, a faithful senate, a virtuous people, the world at rest, whatever, as man or Caesar, an emperor would wish.[9]

Tertullian, AD 160–225, written during the reign of Septimius Severus, a brutal persecutor of Christians

[Christians] always exult in the Lord, and rejoice and are glad in their God; and the evils and adversities of the world they bravely suffer, because they are looking forward to gifts and prosperities to come.... And yet we always ask for the repulse of enemies, and for obtaining showers, and either for the removal or the moderating of adversity; and we pour forth our prayers, and, propitiating and appeasing God, we entreat constantly and urgently, day and night, for your peace and salvation.[10]

Cyprian, ca. AD 252, in reply to Demetrianus, the proconsul of Africa, who contended that Christians should be blamed for wars, and famine, and pestilence because they do not worship the gods

Isn't that a remarkable attitude to have toward those in leadership? How do you regard those in political leadership today? Do you spend as much time praying for them as you do criticizing them? Paul expects Timothy to lead his flock in prayer for *all* who are in authority, even if they rule as enemies of the church.

From My Journal

Applying "Knee Grease"

What's first in a meaningful ministry? According to Paul, for a seasoned spiritual leader, it's prayer. And he's not alone in his opinion.

The Twelve urged the congregation in Jerusalem, "Brethren, select from among you seven men of good reputation, full of the Spirit and of wisdom, whom we may put in charge of this task. But we will devote ourselves to prayer and to the ministry of the word" (Acts 6:3–4).

The author of Hebrews exhorted believers to take full advantage of their access to the Father through prayer. "Let us draw near with confidence to the throne of grace, so that we may receive mercy and find grace to help in time of need" (Heb. 4:16).

James rebuked Christians who had been satisfying their needs by taking advantage of one another. He traced their difficulties to a simple source: "You lust and do not have; so you commit murder. You are envious and cannot obtain; so you fight and quarrel. You do not have because you do not ask" (James 4:2).

John assured the churches suffering persecution in Asia, "This is the confidence which we have before Him, that, if we ask anything according to His will, He hears us" (1 John 5:14).

Peter saw prayer as a chief ministry of the church. "The end of all things is near; therefore, be of sound judgment and sober spirit for the purpose of prayer" (1 Peter 4:7).

My grandfather used to say that getting something going might require "elbow grease," his euphemism for hard manual labor. I guess we might say that ministry needs to start with "knee grease." Prayer isn't the most glamorous ministry of the church. Make no mistake, it is difficult work, requiring a selfless attitude and a willingness to put in hours of solitary labor. But it's well worth the investment. As the martyred missionary Jim Elliot once wrote, "The saint who advances on his knees never retreats."

meaning, one possibility appears clear. The arrival of Jesus to suffer the penalty of sin on our behalf is undeniable proof of God's desire that "all men ... be saved."

— 2:7 —

Because God desires that all people be saved by submitting to the truth of the gospel, and because Paul shared the Lord's desire so intimately, the Lord appointed him to be a messenger of this wonderful news. Paul called himself a herald ("preacher") and an envoy ("apostle") and a "teacher of the Gentiles."

In keeping with his common practice, Paul includes an assurance of truthfulness (cf. Rom. 9:1; 2 Cor. 11:31; Gal. 1:20), not because the Ephesians might accuse him of lying, but to stress the importance of his words.

— 2:8 —

Having urged Timothy to make prayer his top priority in ministry, Paul explains how it should be implemented church-wide. He wants people "in every place" to pray. He doesn't want them to construct a special building. He doesn't want them to consecrate a sacred spot. He doesn't want them to reserve a special time. He doesn't want them to gather in only one place. There's nothing wrong with those things, but Paul doesn't want anything to become a distraction to the top priority: ongoing, coordinated, congregation-wide prayer for the salvation and well-being of every person living in Ephesus. D. L. Moody is quoted as saying, "Satan will do anything to keep you from praying, even if it means adjusting a window shade." How true!

Paul calls for prayer by "lifting up holy hands." His emphasis is on "holy," not "hands." While the posture of prayer can either help or hinder concentration, Paul doesn't care as much about the position of the body as the purity of the person offering the prayer. In that day and culture, people prayed with their hands and faces lifted toward heaven. It was as common as people in Western churches bowing their heads. In our culture, Paul might have said, "bowing holy heads and closing holy eyes."

The term "holy" doesn't mean "perfect." It means consecrated, kept from contamination, set apart for God's special purposes. The Lord wants the people of His church to keep themselves from sin so that they may intercede for "all men," much like a Hebrew priest entering the temple on behalf of Israel.

And Paul instructs Timothy and the Ephesians to pray without "wrath," the passionate "upsurging" of anger toward someone, or "dissension," the contentious kind of disputing that undermines unity. Disharmony appears to inhibit prayer (1 Peter 3:7), although Scripture doesn't explain how or why. Regardless, Paul calls for the congregation to set aside anything that keeps them from banding together as a unit so that the ministry might accomplish its divine purpose: to bring all people to a knowledge of the truth and be saved.

I have spent two-thirds of my lifetime serving in pastoral ministry, and I can assure you the urgency of the immediate screams just as loudly for attention as the day I started. Details and meetings impatiently tug at my sleeve, vying for first priority, all the while trying to convince me that prayer is an admirable waste of time, a spiritual duty rather than an energizing joy. Moreover, I have been charged by Paul, who wrote under the direction of the Holy Spirit, to lead God's people to unite in prayer. Fortunately, I have failed in ministry enough times to remember that the Lord signs my paycheck, not my calendar, not the congregation, not even those serving as elders. Therefore, it only makes sense that I check in with the Final Authority of my life before heading off to work.

First things first. And for a meaningful, God-honoring ministry, that's prayer.

Application

Prayer Made Practical

As Paul began his discourse on the work of ministry, he highlighted the priority of prayer. "First of all . . ." He commanded Timothy to pray for the well-being of non-believers in Ephesus, to ask God for blessing, and to offer thanks on their behalf. He then expected Timothy to lead the church leaders in doing the same, who were, in turn, to lead the congregation.

If you are a leader in ministry, your first responsibility is to lead others in prayer. That certainly includes opening meetings with prayer and praying on behalf of those you lead, but there's more. Spiritual leadership requires leaders to cultivate a life of natural, habitual conversation with God, and then to help others do the same. Here are a few simple guidelines that I have found helpful in my own ministry.

Form a habit. Setting aside a regular time each day is an obvious suggestion, and while I highly recommend it, I'm also realistic enough to know that most people won't. Like New Year's resolutions and the best of intentions, the practice will fade before habit takes over. Instead, let a regular activity initiate your conversation with God. If you exercise regularly, pray as you walk, run, bike, lift weights, or swim. Instead of listening to music in the car, let your regular commute become your quiet time with the Lord. Transform any solitary time performing a mundane task into your habitual time of prayer.

Set no limit. The enemy will spin one of two lies to keep you from praying. First, he'll try to convince you that you can handle challenges without any help from God. You've heard it before: *Don't bother Him with this little matter; you know what to do.* Second, he'll tell you the challenge is not something the Lord wants to address. *Don't bother Him with your troubles; He's too busy to trifle with your everyday concerns.*

Both of these lies place limits on prayer. God says we should pray without losing heart (Luke 18:1), pray at all times (Eph. 6:18; 1 Thess. 5:17), pray confidently (Heb. 4:16), pray in faith (Matt. 21:22; James 1:6), in all places (Titus 2:8), and for all matters (Phil. 4:6).

Reject all substitutes. Before you reach for a book, before you dial the phone, before you take any action, stop. Take the matter to God. Pray first. I'm not suggesting you substitute prayer for responsible action, but please don't become guilty of the reverse. Don't substitute anything for prayer. Make talking with Him your first priority.

What about Women in the Church? (1 Timothy 2:9–15)

---

⁹Likewise, *I want* women to adorn themselves with proper clothing, modestly and discreetly, not with braided hair and gold or pearls or costly garments, ¹⁰but rather by means of good works, as is proper for women making a claim to godliness. ¹¹A woman must quietly receive instruction with entire submissiveness. ¹²But I do not allow a woman to teach or exercise authority over a man, but to remain quiet. ¹³For it was Adam who was first created, *and* then Eve. ¹⁴And *it was* not Adam *who* was deceived, but the woman being deceived, fell into transgression. ¹⁵But *women* will be preserved through the bearing of children if they continue in faith and love and sanctity with self-restraint.

Imagine yourself a modern-day Rip Van Winkle, waking after a slumber that began in 1970. After a long stretch and a wide yawn, you return to a culture that has changed significantly. Technology, transportation, economics, government, and even family life have changed radically while you were asleep. Now imagine returning to church the first time after awakening. The hymnals are gone, there's a coffee shop right next to a bookstore in the oversized vestibule, a rock band has replaced the pipe organ, and the guy next to you is reading his Bible from a handheld computer. You might also notice a significant change in the women around you.

Today's woman barely resembles the woman of 1970. In fact, I see at least three realms that have seen dramatic changes for women.

The first is *the domestic realm*. Before 1970, most women tended the home and nurtured their children while their husbands earned the income for the entire family. Now, the majority of women hold jobs outside the home, either to supplement the household income or because they head a single-parent family.[11] The dwindling numbers of stay-at-home moms frequently feel scorned rather than supported for their dedication. Furthermore, they are often misunderstood as lazy or weak.

The second is *the business realm*. Some things a lady just didn't do before the 1970s. Women didn't report the news, or cover a sporting event, or go to combat, or fly airplanes, or run corporations, or take up any role traditionally filled by men. Today, not only do most adult women earn a wage outside the home, they make up nearly 50 percent of the workforce. Now she is respected far more than exploited. Laws do a better job protecting her from harassment or abuse from coworkers, and she's encouraged to be not only assertive, but aggressive in pursuit of her career. Consequently, men have gradually accepted female coworkers as peers in the business world, which undoubtedly has impacted their view of women as mates and mothers as well.

The third is *the church realm*, without a doubt the most complicated and confusing of all. Today's woman inhabits a much broader secular world than the narrow path our culture expected her to walk before the 1970s. Many would naturally expect her role within the church to change just as dramatically. It should be no surprise, then, to see that many mainline denominations and several independent associations have adjusted their interpretation of Scripture—or simply ignore it altogether—and started ordaining women as priests and senior pastors. After all, if a woman can steer a corporation, or pilot a commercial airliner, why can't she shepherd a flock?

Some conservative churches responded by adjusting their interpretation of Scripture, adopting an overly literal hermeneutic. This took the role of women backward, forcing them to wear hats and forbidding them to say anything while on church property. Unfortunately, they did just as much violence to the words of the apostles Peter and Paul as their liberal counterparts. They claimed to hold Scripture as their primary authority. While I don't doubt their sincerity, it appears the "ideal" they tried to uphold didn't come from the Bible as much as from popular culture icons of the 1950s. Televisions shows such as *Leave It to Beaver* and *Father Knows Best* cemented a particular image of women in the minds of most Americans, which easily can become the grid through which we read God's Word in the twenty-first century. And I admit, because that era defined my own childhood, I must be careful to set aside my preconceptions.

The fact is, the family of two thousand years ago did not fit the modern, "nuclear family" model we have come to regard as ideal. Moreover, the woman of Proverbs 31:10–31 describes a remarkably powerful, business savvy, entrepreneurial, partner coleading a large, extended family enterprise with her husband. The sage described a woman that many ultraconservatives would find presumptuous or even threatening.

While believers must be careful not to separate their lives into sacred and secular realms—we are, after all, "consecrated" men and women wherever we go—we must, nevertheless, recognize that the church is not the world. "You've come a long way, baby" has no place in the Lord's domain. Neither does the heartwarming, postwar prototype of June Cleaver. The Lord doesn't expect us to shed our society completely upon entering the church; He patiently endures the ebb and flow of cultural trends. In His house, however, our attitudes and fashions must fit within certain guidelines. Those guidelines are set forth in the timeless words of Holy Scripture.

The male-dominated culture of Ephesus worshiped the power of Artemis, the earth mother, yet regarded women as chattel, just like the rest of the Roman Empire. This must have been terribly confusing for women living in those conditions—prized, yet dominated; possessed, yet worshiped. Then an apostle bearing good news from God teaches, "There is neither Jew nor Greek, there is neither slave nor free man, there is neither male nor female; for you are all one in Christ Jesus. And if you belong to Christ, then you are Abraham's descendants, heirs according to promise" (Gal. 3:28–29). And suddenly, the value of womanhood takes a giant leap upward to share equality with men. In fact, *everywhere* Christianity takes root, the status of women improves dramatically.

Just as unity does not mean uniformity, however, so equal does not mean identical. The Son of God shares complete equality with the Father, yet submits to His headship. Meanwhile, the Father loves the Son and glorifies Him, giving Him all authority over creation. In that same manner, the Lord describes the distinct roles given to man and woman despite their equal value. No study of the issue would be complete without a detailed study of these passages:

- 1 Corinthians 11:1–16
- 1 Corinthians 14:34–35
- Titus 2:3–5
- 1 Peter 3:1–6

Let me be clear; our purpose here is not to study the issue of men and women in the church, but to examine this passage within Paul's message to Timothy and the Ephesian believers. The context is the public worship service of a church and the subject has been the priority of prayer *for the purpose of influencing the nonbelievers of Ephesus.*

— **2:9–10** —

Paul frequently uses "man" to refer to all of humanity, both male and female (cf. 2:1–7). In 2:8, however, "men" refers to the male members of the body in Ephesus. We know this because Greek uses two terms for "man," *anthrōpos* for humanity in general and *anēr* for "husband" or "male person."

He's not suggesting that only men should pray and that women refrain from praying. Instead, he calls on men to lead the congregation and insists that the responsibility for praying falls on the men. Paul writes, in effect, "I command that men set the pace, that men lead by example, that men become the means by which prayer occurs in the church." Then, having established the responsibility of men to pray and lead the church in prayer *for the sake of influencing the nonbelievers in Ephesus,* the apostle turns to the women with the word, "likewise." Women have their responsibility too.

Paul used three descriptive Greek phrases concerning women's appearance in public: "proper clothing," "modestly," and "discreetly."

The two-word phrase in Greek translated "proper clothing" allows for either "orderly demeanor" or "orderly apparel." The rendering "proper" carries the unfortunate nuance of "matronly," which is not what Paul intended. Instead, we might use the slang expression "put together." In other words, Christian women need not be dowdy or completely unaware of fashion in order to be godly. She's free to dress according to her times, according to the style of the day, according to the custom of the place where she lives. Some expositors imply that women should take note of the current clothing trends and then do the opposite, or deliberately dress in such manner as to be completely unnoticeable. Paul encourages Christian women to avoid that extreme, encouraging them to take delight in their appearance, as many women naturally do.

To avoid the other extreme, Paul also encourages the women to dress modestly (lit., "with modesty"). The Greek term has ancient roots in the concept of "shamefulness," but by the time of Paul, the definition had evolved to mean "with reverence," "with respect," or "with reserve." It encompasses more than merely covering up. The idea is to avoid any manner of dress that suggests sensual appeal or sexual availability.

"Discreet" renders the two-word Greek phrase meaning (lit.) "sensible order." "Sensible" is a favorite term in the Pastoral Epistles, which means "moderate, prudent, modest, restrained, and disciplined."[12] This is the only term Paul applies to both genders and all ages.

To clarify his command concerning women's appearance, the apostle notes three specific trends that are not immoral in and of themselves. Like Peter, Paul uses the combination of braided hair, costly jewelry (cf. "gold" in 1 Peter 3:3), and expensive clothes to illustrate a kind of self-centered vanity that detracts from the kind of beauty the Lord wants to cultivate in all believers, both male and female: godly character expressed through good works (Eph. 2:10; Titus 2:12). Paul neither rails against outward beauty nor discourages women from enjoying their outward beauty. He merely expects the Ephesian women to avoid the silly, ostentatious extremes we often see among those in the film industry or the fashion runways of New York and Paris. He says, in effect, "Instead of devoting untold hours and exorbitant sums to improve your outward beauty, direct your energy to cultivating inner beauty. Outer beauty fades; inner beauty becomes more radiant with age" (cf. 1 Tim. 4:8).

— 2:11–12 —

Paul then shifts his discussion from beauty to behavior. As we examine his words, I urge you to allow the text to speak for itself, and at the same time I urge you to set aside the perspective of God's critics. They have come and gone throughout history, along with their fleeting fads, yet Scripture continues to stand. The Word of God gives three instructions in verse 11, amplifies them in verse 12, and explains the Lord's reasoning in verses 13–15. The three instructions in verse 11 are:

- She is to remain quiet rather than become vocal.
- She is to receive instruction rather than do the instructing.
- She is to refrain from the act of exercising authority rather than taking charge.

To "quietly receive instruction" carries the idea of remaining mentally calm. It is not a stern gag rule for women while on church property. Extremists like to apply this teaching in a strictly literal fashion because it suits their worldly agenda: to dominate and control women. God, however, does not consider women inferior. He never treats women like second-class citizens. Jesus equipped and trained a small group of men to lead the church upon His ascension, but He also instructed many women disciples (e.g., Matt. 27:55; Mark 15:40; Luke 8:1–3; 23:55–56; 24:10).

Furthermore, Paul recalled the significant contributions of women in his letters (Rom. 16:1, 6; 1 Cor. 16:19; Phil. 4:1–2; Philem. 2). This instruction came in the context of teaching and leading the church, for which men must take responsibility.

Bear in mind, churches in the first century didn't offer children's Sunday school, women's classes, adult teaching outside the worship service, or the host of other programs that churches provide today. Paul directed this to women attending the public gathering for worship and instruction. The responsibility for preaching fell to the male leaders, not to women. Furthermore, they were to receive this instruction alongside their male counterparts, who also received it with a submissive, willing spirit (cf. 1 Cor. 16:15; Heb. 13:17). While Scripture calls for the submission of a wife to her husband (Eph. 5:22–24; 1 Peter 3:1–2), submission here refers to the attitude of all believers to the instruction of church leaders. This does not teach that women in general should submit to men in general.

Today, we might look at this instruction through a negative lens, focusing on what women could *not* do. But we must also take into account the practice of the Jerusalem temple and the local synagogues, where women were not allowed to stand alongside men during worship and instruction. Women in Ephesus heard the reading of Paul's letter as a part of the main congregation, not standing on the periphery in the gallery. First-century women would have regarded this portion of Paul's instruction a major victory for women's equality!

Under the direction of the Holy Spirit, Paul affirms the status of women as equal to that of men in the body of Christ. Nevertheless, I repeat, he held men responsible for leading the church. He amplified the instruction of verse 11 by forbidding women to lead the church as an ordained authority, such as apostle, pastor, or elder. (The office of "deacon" during New Testament times carried no ruling authority.)

— 2:13–14 —

Some expositors point out that Paul wrote this instruction to a church living in a culture very different from our own. They claim the apostle forbade female leadership in that time and place so the church would not compromise its honorable standing in the community. In other words, female leadership might have been seen as too radical, or even subversive, potentially distracting nonbelievers from the real issue at hand: their need for the gospel. To avoid too much change too quickly, Paul advises slowing down.

The apostle's rationale in verses 13–15, however, anchors his teaching in something far more timeless and permanent than the needs of the community. He reaches all the way back to the first days of life on earth to reestablish a forsaken principle of creation. Paul offers two proofs from Genesis.

First, in the beginning, the Lord created humanity in His image to become His vice-regents over creation (Gen. 1:26). He first created Adam and placed him in Eden to carry out the ordained purpose of humanity (Gen. 2:15). The man could not fulfill his created purpose, however, without a "corresponding opposite" to supply what was missing. So the Lord created Eve, the first woman, to be his essential "help" (cf. Ps. 30:10; 37:40; 54:4; 118:7).

God created and tasked humanity to fulfill a purpose, and by the order of creation, laid the responsibility of leadership on the man. And with responsibility comes accountability, which is the point of Paul's second proof.

Eve sinned because Satan deceived her. Adam sinned, not as a result of deception, but by freewill choice. Arguably, Eve had an excuse. Adam, without question, had none. When the Lord confronted the first humans concerning their sin, He addressed Adam as the leader. He held Adam accountable because Adam was the responsible head. Unfortunately, the man tried to pass the buck to his wife (Gen. 3:12), who bore the negative consequences of her sin through the pain of childbirth (Gen. 3:16), but He returned to the man last. The buck stopped with Adam.

Some expositors foolishly suggest that the issue of deception in the beginning goes to the mental weakness of women compared to men. This is nothing short of hogwash. Frankly, I've seen too many marriages that suggest the opposite is true! The issue here is not ability, but responsibility. God tasked the man with leadership and He will hold men accountable for the performance of their duty. Adam let Eve down in the beginning by failing to lead and protect. Therefore, both men and women continue to suffer the judicial sentence of the man's disobedience. For men, work became toil (Gen. 3:17); for women, the joy of childbirth comes through distressing pain (Gen 3:16).

— **2:15** —

Paul concludes this segment with a statement many regard as notoriously difficult to interpret. Read in isolation, I can appreciate the confusion; but it doesn't stand alone. Paul places this comment at the end of his instruction to settle the matter and to reassure women that the Lord's arrangement is for their good.

Jesus Christ came to earth to redeem all of humanity from the curse of sin. That's the heart of the gospel. And one day yet future, He will return to replace this broken, twisted creation with a new heaven and a new earth (Rev. 21:1), saving all believers from the curses — the judicial sentence — of the Fall. The man will no longer toil for provision and the woman will no longer endure suffering in childbirth. In the meantime, however, the whole earth groans for redemption like a woman in labor (Rom. 8:22).

Until the Lord returns to consummate His redemption of creation at the end of days, He has commissioned the church—His faithful followers, led by redeemed and transformed men—to become a token of the new creation. People will be saved by the grace of God and preserved to the end (Rom. 8:26–39), and the Lord will use the church as a means of this salvation and preservation.

Male leadership failed to provide and protect in the beginning, and women have been suffering ever since; *redeemed* male leadership should be their means of provision and protection until the return of Christ. Upon His return, He will remove the curse of sin.

Therefore, based on this background, I would paraphrase verse 15 this way (per the literal Greek): "Women will be saved as they continue to suffer the judicial sentence of labor pains if they continue to live out the gospel and persevere to the end of days."

If Paul had written this letter today, these seven verses might have become seven chapters. We have come a long way in the last two millennia, but I wouldn't necessarily call it progress. I don't think Paul ever thought his words would be used as a club to pummel women into submission or to suggest they are second-class citizens of the kingdom. Yet, somehow, men have exaggerated, expanded, and exploited them to satisfy their fleshy compulsion to dominate.

Paul wrote these words to an obsessively male-dominated culture. We're correct to understand that he wrote them not to limit women, but to reassure them. Paul explained the role of women in the church not to empower men, but to challenge them. He looked out on the congregation, as it were, and encouraged women to rest in the leadership of the men. Any man hearing those words would have understood Paul's indirect message to them: *It's time to man up and lead! These women are counting on you not to blow it this time.*

While Paul wrote to an ancient culture, the Holy Spirit inspired these words to guide all cultures throughout all time. The Lord is not surprised to find us reading them two thousand years later. While first-century Ephesus would have ridiculed the remarkable equality of men and women in the church, twenty-first-century Western culture chastens the church for resisting progress. Nevertheless, the message has not changed despite the shifting attitudes of its audience.

Men, hear this! We are to man up and lead. Provide and protect. Just as we find greater freedom in the leadership of Jesus Christ, so Christian women should enjoy greater liberty in the male leadership of the church.

Application

Liberty or Limits for Women?

I love optical illusions. I especially enjoy watching people as they move from confusion, to realization, to laughter, and finally to fascination. One of the most popular optical puzzles dates back to an 1888 German postcard depicting a beautiful young woman or a scraggily old hag, depending upon how your mind interprets the image. Interestingly, most people see the beautiful woman first and, only after coaching, see the hag's features take shape. And equally interesting, whichever woman you see first will forever be the primary image for you. These visual dilemmas prove that vision may be concrete, but perception can be quite subjective.

Viewing Paul's portrait of women in church can appear vexing or promising, all depending on your point of view. From today's post-women's-revolution vantage, we're more inclined to see Paul relegating women to the periphery of church life, giving the most honored places only to men. That is, in fact, what many denominations have done. Both men and women today stare at the picture painted by 1 Timothy 2:9–15 and see the word "limits" boldly stamped across the page.

If you want to see real restrictions, rewind the clock and travel to Herod's temple in Jerusalem. Unlike Solomon's temple or the tabernacle that came before it, Herod's complex featured two exclusive zones. A first wall restricted Gentiles, allowing only Jews and Jewish converts to pass. A second wall restricted women from entering the place of worship, where only men could bring sacrifices and participate in the rites of worship. Synagogues in the first century featured a *mechitza*, a partition separating the genders, and restricted women from participation in worship services except to observe. These restrictions, however, did not come from Scripture. You won't find them in the Old Testament. The Pharisees introduced them, along with a host of other legalistic traditions after the exile.

From this perspective, Christians in the first century gazed at Paul's portrait of women and saw the word "liberty" in bold relief. No longer separated by a partition, women stood or sat with men in the congregation and received instruction along with them. We also find women participating in Christian work with unprecedented freedom throughout the New Testament. While Paul did affirm male leadership in the church and, therefore, reserved the position of "overseer" for men, he also encouraged women to participate in every aspect of ministry, so long as men did not abdicate their responsibility to lead.

So, how do we apply a passage like this in today's post–1970s era? Let us begin with a shift in perspective. Where we might be inclined to see "limits," let us see "liberty." Rather than using this and other passages of Scripture to prevent women from serving in the church, let us exercise strong, confident, Christlike male leadership and seek every opportunity to grant liberty for all to engage in ministry.

I'm not suggesting we set aside the relatively few restrictions set down by the Holy Spirit in the New Testament. I merely mean for us to begin viewing the role of women in the church through a lens of opportunity instead of constraint.

Checklist for Choosing Church Leaders (1 Timothy 3:1–7)

---

¹It is a trustworthy statement: if any man aspires to the office of overseer, it is a fine work he desires *to do.* ²An overseer, then, must be above reproach, the husband of one wife, temperate, prudent, respectable, hospitable, able to teach, ³not addicted to wine or pugnacious, but gentle, peaceable, free from the love of money. ⁴*He must be* one who manages his own household well, keeping his children under control with all dignity ⁵(but if a man does not know how to manage his own household, how will he take care of the church of God?), ⁶*and* not a new convert, so that he will not become conceited and fall into the condemnation incurred by the devil. ⁷And he must have a good reputation with those outside *the church,* so that he will not fall into reproach and the snare of the devil.

The church is not made of timber, tile, bricks, and mortar. God's people are the church. Therefore, it stands to reason that the leadership of the church must be the finest. As one author has noted, "As go the leaders, so goes the church."[13] If the leadership falters, the people lose their way. If the leaders lack the necessary qualifications, the church withers and dies. Unfortunately, it's been my observation throughout my fifty years in ministry that most local churches choose their leaders based on one of four erroneous qualifications.

Popularity. Some people exude enthusiasm and charisma, often in greater supply than wisdom. Yet, because they know how to win friends and influence people, popular opinion buoys them to the top of any organization they join. They easily obtain office and rarely lose their positions, even after the kind of stunning embarrassments that would ruin any other person.

Posterity. Tradition often dictates that a person who has held a position should always hold it. And when that person retires or dies, a son or daughter should naturally take up the mantle. In my experience, these types of leaders rarely possess the right qualifications and usually keep the church rooted in the past.

Politics. These leaders rise to the top because they have the right name, or pull the right strings, or shake the right hands, or leverage the right asset. Politicians know how to land the office they want and retain power for as long as they want it, but they don't always make good leaders. In fact, their political skill might be a strong indication of their failings as a leader.

Prosperity. Wealthy church members often find their way into positions of leadership. There's nothing wrong with wealth, of course, but people often associate material blessings with God's favor and assume that wisdom accompanies wealth. Sometimes, great business sense comes at the expense of humility, cooperation, teachability, and restraint. However, let us remember that a wealthy person with a good perspective on material blessings can become an effective leader. Either way, a large and impressive portfolio means nothing in terms of qualifications to lead the church.

Paul recognizes the importance of church leadership, especially in the turbulent city of Ephesus. Timothy needs a team of qualified elders, not only to help guide the congregation but also to support and encourage him. But rather than turn to the four Ps — Popularity, Posterity, Politics, or Prosperity — the apostle produces an excellent checklist of essential character traits that each elder must possess.

— **3:1** —

The word translated "overseer" is *episkopos*, which means "watcher, patron, protector." Athenians, for example, used the term for state officials. Paul considers the work of an *episkopos* to be noble, a role worthy of pursuit. Today, many would call this man a "pastor" if he is a vocational minister serving the church, or an "elder" if he leads in addition to his regular occupation. Presbyterians often distinguish them as "teaching elders" and "ruling elders," vocational pastors and lay leaders respectively. Baptists typically think of the pastor as the spiritual director of the church and then combine the offices of elder and deacon to form a ruling board for the operation of the church. For the purposes of this discussion, I will use the term "elder" to describe those men vested with the responsibility to lead the church in both spiritual and operational matters.

When I first read this verse, I had to shift my perspective. I had to appreciate the critical difference between ambition and aspiration. Ambition seeks to gain and wield power for the sake of self. Aspiration, by contrast, cares less about the position as becoming worthy of it. As Paul will explain, to qualify for the position of "overseer," one must ideally become a model Christian. That's why he quickly follows this affirmation with a daunting list of qualifications drawn from every quarter of the prospective leader's life. Verses 2 and 3 reveals the man's inner life, verses 4 and 5 examines his home life, verse 6 describes his manner in the church, and verse 7 outlines his conduct in the world at large.

—3:2–3 (The Overseer Within)—

"Above reproach" (lit., "blameless, without accusation") does not denote a requirement for sinless perfection or a pristine past; it's a general assessment of a man's maturity and reputation. John Calvin paraphrased this idea as "not marred by disgrace." This general quality of character frames all the rest, which can be divided into three broad categories: home life, public life, and church life.

"The husband of one wife" (lit., "a one-woman man") describes a man who is married to one woman and continues to live in fidelity and harmony with this same woman. (See the excursus "A One-Woman Man" in my comments on Titus 1:6 in this volume for an extended discussion of this qualification.)

"Temperate" translates a Greek word describing a sober, or nonintoxicated, state of mind. A "sober" or "temperate" man remains in complete control of his faculties, giving no quarter to any kind of influence that would have him behave poorly. He allows nothing to cloud his thinking, keeps everything in balance and within limits, and avoids excess, even in good things, such as work, medications, food, or sex. He also remains free from addiction to destructive things, such as illegal drugs, alcohol, or pornography.

"Prudent" suggests being reasonable, sensible, having sound judgment. This favorite term of Paul's appears throughout his letter to Titus as "sensible" or "self-controlled," a quality he wants to see in "older men" (2:2), "younger women" as taught by the older women (2:5), "younger men" (2:6), and the church at-large (2:12). In other words, sensibility should be the defining quality of the congregation, starting with its spiritual leaders.

"Respectable" renders an adjectival form of the Greek word *kosmos* that means "orderly." Ancient philosophers widely understood the universe to be complex, yet logical and systematic, operating according to mathematical principles. Greek and Roman society, therefore, venerated men whose actions were not capricious or random, but were guided by respectable ideals or "virtues."

"Hospitable" (lit., "loving of strangers") in the ancient mind refers to attitudes toward someone foreign or different. A hospitable man welcomes those who are different and easily overcomes the natural tension that exists between them because of their differences.

"Able to teach" comes from the Greek word for "teach," describing the aptitude for communicating knowledge. This does not require the elder to teach; he must simply have the ability to explain the Scriptures and help others to understand and apply them.

"Addicted to wine" comes from a Greek word meaning "staying near wine." It describes someone who habitually has alcohol nearby or cannot be far from it. The

From My Journal

Men of Dignity and Their Lasting Impact

Whenever I recall my growing-up years in Houston, Texas, I always thank God for a small group of men who took a personal interest in me. I didn't understand how the Scriptures could be so relevant to life until a couple of deacons pulled me aside after a Sunday school class and said, "You know, Charles, we notice that you have a real interest in the Bible. And we think this little Scripture memory program will help get you underway." And they introduced me to a program developed by The Navigators.

They were right. Their discernment helped me recognize an affinity for studying and explaining Scripture. Their wise guidance set me on a path that would lead me to where I am today. They helped me recognize something within a late-blooming, older teenager that I never could have seen in myself.

Trust fund

young back

devoted potential

idea is not restricted to alcoholism. This idea includes those who frequently fail to recognize their limits regarding alcohol. Overseers must avoid overdependence on any substance.

"Not pugnacious" describes a man who is neither contentious nor quarrelsome. Whereas the Greek term for "pugnacious" means (lit.) "a striker," a godly overseer is not someone apt to clench his fists; he doesn't allow emotions to fuel his interactions with others, even in the midst of disagreement.

"Gentle [and] peaceable" is the opposite of a "pugnacious" man, who is apt to punch someone. "Gentle" means "moderate, reasonable, what is right or fitting." His response is always appropriate for the occasion, even when he feels harshly criticized or verbally attacked (Prov. 15:1). Moreover, he is a "not-fighter" (the literal rendering of the word translated "peaceable"). Such a person walks away from physical altercations. While he may have the strength and skill to fight, he is known as a peacemaker, a man willing to keep a loose grip on his rights.

"Free from the love of money" describes a disposition that is not overly motivated to pursue material wealth. Godly men can become successful businessmen who earn large sums of money without necessarily "loving money." People who have their wealth in perspective usually give generously.

These inner qualities describe a man who can be a team player, yet has the strength and wisdom to think for himself. He can lead, but he doesn't seek to be in control. He speaks his mind, but he doesn't need to be heard and he doesn't crave attention. He stands his ground and doesn't compromise his standards, but he freely embraces those who differ from him.

—3:4–5 (The Overseer at Home)—

Whenever we seek to add a new elder or a new pastor, we always like to meet the man's wife and children. The church, after all, is not a corporation but a family. If there's any true reflection of an overseer's spiritual qualifications, it's the home he leads.

We're wise to allow plenty of leeway in this realm. I don't know any good parent whose children are well-behaved 100 percent of the time. In fact, I don't think highly of a household in which the children never misbehave or appear overly mature. More often than not, it's a family ruled with an iron fist rather than "with all dignity."

Instead, we should apply this in a broad sense. Generally speaking, recognizing that healthy children act their age and teenagers sometimes spin out of control, we should ask, does the man create a calm, structured home environment? Does he hold his children to reasonable expectations that instill a sense of personal dignity? Do they esteem him and show him honor? Are his children on the right track to becoming fine young men and women, or without intervention, do you see them headed for trouble?

Children are a remarkably accurate barometer of a man's character and ability to lead. That's why Paul adds a sobering parenthetical aside in verse 5. I see two practical implications from the apostle's statement. First, a man who rears children who lack either control or dignity — running wild or quietly self-destructing — most likely cannot lead adults with any greater success. Second, an otherwise qualified man cannot possibly give adequate attention to leading the church when his home is in chaos or his children are in crisis. If a leader's home life suffers an extended period of difficulty, which can happen to the best of men, he should be asked to take a sabbatical long enough to rescue his family.

Garden paths, Blockades —

— 3:6 (The Overseer within Church) —

I love being around new Christians, especially those who have come to believe in Christ later in life. They help me remember why I devoted my life to pastoral ministry. Still excited. Still rough around the edges. Still enthralled with the freedom of the gospel and just beginning to discover the wonders of God's grace. They soak up Scripture like a sponge and cannot fathom why established believers don't live out God's Word with more consistency. But for all their authenticity and enthusiasm, they cannot offer stable leadership. The overseer's role calls for stability — roots planted deep in the soil of the new covenant, fed by Scripture, nurtured by the Holy Spirit, tested by wind and drought. This proven ability to live the gospel and lead others in that life cannot develop overnight.

Paul echoes the old saying, "A little knowledge is a dangerous thing." The Greek term translated "conceited" literally means "wrapped in smoke." We would say "he has his head in the clouds." That's because new believers allow their enthusiasm and idealism to carry them headlong into trouble. Big talk, purist thinking, headstrong opinions, rash decisions made "in faith," and then ... a thundering crash. The "condemnation incurred by the devil" was a tragic fall precipitated by overreaching pride. His leadership, untempered by humility, led to rebellion.

Respect is modeled / taught)

— 3:7 (The Overseer in the World) —

Conventional wisdom among believers states that the believer can expect only strife from the world, but Paul rejects that notion. While the world system does oppose

God's way, and we will feel less at home in the world as the Holy Spirit transforms us, there's little reason we can't maintain a good rapport with nonbelievers. People outside the church appreciate honesty, fair play, integrity, kindness, hospitality, sensibility, and all the best qualities we hope to find in an overseer. Cultivating a good reputation with those outside the church, generally speaking, says a lot about a man. We are, after all, hoping to influence our communities for the sake of the gospel (2:1–6; Col. 4:5; 1 Thess. 4:12); therefore, our good reputation should begin with our church leaders.

"The snare of the devil" has two different meanings, depending on whether the person is a believer or an outsider. Paul uses the phrase in 2 Timothy 2:26 to describe the fate of "those who are in opposition." Nonbelievers are "held captive by him to do his will" and ultimately suffer eternal torment, having died in their sin. Believers cannot suffer this fate, but the devil's snare can nullify their testimony and bring them to an early physical demise (1 Tim. 6:9).

This is Paul's second reference to the devil's designs on church leaders. We should not be surprised to discover that Satan has his sights trained on overseers for the same reason military snipers target opposing high-ranking military officers. If the devil can take out the leaders, the congregation will fall into confusion. Then the church's influence in the community will bring disgrace to the gospel instead of converts.

Throughout the Pastoral Epistles, Paul expresses concern for the character of the church, which can be boiled down to two terms: *order* and *sensibility*. *Order* means resting on a solid foundation (Eph. 2:19–22) and rising like rows of stones, course by course, held together by the mortar of the gospel, withstanding the chaos of the world, and raising a permanent edifice of honor for the Architect. *Sensibility* denotes giving purpose to every stone in God's great monument to grace.

But, as any stonemason can tell you, each course of stones must be plumb, level, and square with the one below it, or successive layers will wander farther out of alignment with the Cornerstone. Then, shoddy construction will become plainly obvious to everyone, even to the untrained eye.

Let us choose our leaders well.

Application

Choosing Leaders We Can Follow

It may surprise some to know that their church elders may have been elected simply because their names appeared closer to the top of the ballot. All too often, those top names receive the most votes because most people don't really know the candidates and simply check off the requisite number. If a church arranges the ballots in alphabetical order, chances are good in a sizable congregation that the elders are populated with last names between 'A' and 'G.' Poor Mr. Zucker may be the most qualified man in the church … but no one will ever know.

That might be an exaggeration, but I can assure you, it's only slight. The other reasons people vote for elders aren't much better. Let me suggest at least three questions to ask and answer before placing a man in a position of spiritual leadership in the church.

First, does his inner life match his public image? A man can speak well in public and carry himself with an impressive demeanor, but what about behind the scenes? Does he have a spiritual life that he cultivates away from public view? Getting the answers to those questions will require one-on-one conversations, as well as adequate time for observation.

Second, would his wife and children verify that he is qualified? Would the suggestion draw a sarcastic chuckle from them, or would they affirm him as a capable, authentic spiritual leader? It might be a question worth asking them in private.

Third, would the general public—his colleagues and business competitors—affirm him or express concern about his qualifications? This is not a popularity contest, but elders should maintain a good rapport with those outside the church. It's not a good sign if a nonbeliever expresses concern about his honesty, or purity, or some other matter of character.

When evaluating the suitability of a man for leadership in the church, we need to be careful, but we also must be reasonable. While the job description doesn't call for moral perfection or superhuman spirituality, he should embody the qualities you would hope to see in the rest of the congregation someday.

Also, before the next elder is chosen, the congregation should be prepared, starting a few weeks in advance. Sermons or Bible lessons from 1 Timothy 3:1–7 and Titus 1:5–9, highlighting the vital role of pastor or elder and explaining the qualifications in detail, will give the congregation a good set of criteria to consider. Then, take time to introduce the men—in a church service, at a special event, or during the teaching hour in classrooms. A brochure with a photograph and short biography of each man would also help the members know their potential leaders ahead of time.

When selecting their spiritual leaders, most churches do little more than announce a business meeting from the pulpit and then, at the evening service, pass out ballots. But since when are elders to be chosen by congregational vote? Go back to the New Testament. Pay attention to the way elders were selected. They were appointed, not elected. Of all the decisions a church might make each year, the selection of elders ranks among the most crucial. Therefore, let me challenge you with one last suggestion. Examine the amount of time and effort given to other decisions made by the church each year. How does the appointment of elders compare? Take plenty of time choosing anyone appointed to a position of leadership. You'll never regret it.

The Dignity of Servanthood (1 Timothy 3:8–13)

[8]Deacons likewise *must be* men of dignity, not double-tongued, or addicted to much wine or fond of sordid gain, [9]*but* holding to the mystery of the faith with a clear conscience. [10]These men must also first be tested; then let them serve as deacons if they are beyond reproach. [11]Women *must* likewise *be* dignified, not malicious gossips, but temperate, faithful in all things. [12]Deacons must be husbands of *only* one wife, *and* good managers of *their* children and their own households. [13]For those who have served well as deacons obtain for themselves a high standing and great confidence in the faith that is in Christ Jesus.

It's doubtful that anyone who decides to live for Christ while rubbing shoulders with the world can do so without earning a nickname. Military men and football players, especially, love to call the believer in their midst "Deacon," "Rev," or "Preacher." During my tour in Okinawa with the Third Marine Division, one cynical sergeant delighted to call me "Friar Chuck." I think he would have shaved my head and exchanged my uniform for a brown robe with a hood and a pair of sandals if not for Marine protocol. Regardless, the name stuck.

I wouldn't have minded the nickname "Deacon," although the Lord never intended the term to be used that way. I would have enjoyed the irony. What the sergeant would have intended as an insult is actually a great compliment in the Christian realm. "Deacon" is transliterated from the Greek word *diakonos*, which means "servant" or "one who waits on tables." The Christians living in Jerusalem during the earliest days of the church selected this lowly term to designate a highly esteemed role within the congregation.

According to Acts 6, the ranks of believing Jews began to swell immediately. Tens of thousands flocked to the risen Messiah, including Jews who had adopted the Greek language and culture (Hellenists). The rapid influx of people naturally created turbulence. Great success always upsets peace and creates challenges to overcome. In this case, Hellenistic Jews complained that Hebrew Christians were overlooking Hellenized widows in the distribution of food at communal meals.

Details, Details, Details...

I cannot stress enough the wisdom of the church leaders in appointing deacons to carry out the details of ministry (Acts 6:1–7). The overseers—which consisted of the Twelve in the early days—chose to keep their priorities in place despite the overwhelming urge to get involved in the nuts and bolts of ministry operations. Every pastor and every elder struggle with this temptation, especially in smaller congregations where help is difficult to find. The budget can't sustain paid staff and volunteers don't exactly line up at the pastor's door begging for things to do. Nevertheless, pastors and elders must accept their limits, maintain clear boundaries, and devote themselves to their primary responsibilities: prayer, Spirit-filled leadership, and high-quality biblical teaching.

This will not be easy. In fact, it may prove to be the greatest challenge a pastor or elder has to face. Few congregations allow a pastor or pastoral staff or body of elders to maintain their priorities. Most congregations will drive a pastor crazy with complaints and ugly email messages and disparaging comments and critical tirades because he wasn't there when such-and-such happened, or he wasn't on hand when someone endured this difficult circumstance. Regardless, pastors and elders must accept that misunderstanding is the occupational hazard of leadership and stay the course. But congregations that help their leadership maintain proper priorities are rare and precious in the ministry world.

The apostles could not be everywhere at once. Furthermore, it wouldn't have been a wise use of their time to oversee each growing ministry of the church in person. They needed trustworthy people of godly character to carry out the details of ministry on their behalf and — this is vitally important — with the same level of integrity.

Thus, they commissioned the office of "deacon" — initially, to serve food to the hungry. They charged the congregation to find "seven men of good reputation, full of the Spirit and wisdom" (Acts 6:3). They then officially ordained them through a solemn ceremony of consecration and put them to work as headwaiters, supervising ministry helpers and serving tables themselves. This freed the apostles to concentrate on their primary roles in the church — prayer and preaching (Acts 6:4).

By the time Paul wrote to the believers in Philippi, the office of deacon had become a standard element of church life (Phil. 1:1). The practice had spread from Jerusalem to Antioch, across Asia and the Aegean, all the way to Macedonia, the eastern edge of Europe. While the scope of deacon responsibilities widened as the church grew in numbers and complexity, the spirit of the role remains closely tied to that of a waiter. The next time you sit down for a meal at a restaurant and encounter a particularly good table server, take note of his or her qualities. Observe the skills required to serve hungry diners. The whole idea of being a deacon carries with it this same basic servant mentality. A deacon serves the needs of the congregation with sensitivity, efficiency, compassion, and skill.

— 3:8–9 —

Paul turned from the qualifications of an *episkopos*, "overseer," to those of a deacon, introducing this section with the word *hōsautōs*, meaning "likewise, in like manner, in the same way." While the apostle lists several other qualities, I take the phrase "men of dignity" here to envelop the basic characteristics of a deacon — perhaps with less exacting measurement, but present nonetheless. The Greek term translated "dignity" literally means "majestic, splendid, worthy of respect." It carries the idea of determination, commitment, and stability. In other words, the candidates for deacon should be the kind of men who might become overseers, given time for seasoning.

Three negatives — three "not" statements — add clarity to the meaning of dignity.

"Not double-tongued" refers to discretion as well as being without duplicity. Qualified deacons know how to keep matters in confidence (Prov. 11:13). Furthermore, they have integrated lives, so deacons behave the same during the week as they do in church. The truth doesn't change depending on their audience. Words, deeds, and reality remain in sync.

"Not addicted to wine" (see comments on 3:3). Obviously, "much wine" (cf. Titus 2:3) would make little sense if it were nothing more than unfermented grape juice. However, we shouldn't overemphasize Paul's including the word "much." Addiction to a little wine versus a lot of wine makes no sense. His point is the same. Put practically, he's saying, "Don't commission a deacon who drinks too much."

"Not fond of sordid gain" refers to a disposition that is not "sordidly greedy of gain" or "insatiable of wealth and ready to procure it by disgraceful means," as translated from the classical Greek writers Herodotus and Aristophanes. Again, there's nothing innately wrong with money or being wealthy. May we all enjoy great abundance! Deacons should, however, pursue honest gain and then cultivate

Qualifications of Overseer and Deacon in 1 Timothy

Overseer	Deacon
above reproach	beyond reproach
the husband of one wife	the husband of one wife
temperate	
prudent	
respectable	man of dignity
hospitable	
able to teach	
not addicted to wine	[not] addicted to [much] wine
[not] pugnacious	
gentle	
peaceable	
free from the love of money	not fond of sordid gain
one who manages his own household well	one who manages his own household well
not a new convert	tested
a good reputation with those outside the church	holding to the mystery of the faith with a clear conscience
	not double-tongued

a spirit of generosity. In modern churches, this quality carries particularly high importance. Deacons typically receive the offering and later prepare the cash for deposit.

Take note of yet another reference to a "clear conscience" (cf. 1:5, 19). A deacon must "hold to the mystery of the faith with a clear conscience." This is a call to deep spiritual commitment to the mission of the church. The "mystery of the faith" is the gospel, revealed through Jesus Christ, witnessed and taught by the apostles, and entrusted with the church to proclaim throughout the world. The deacon must cling to the gospel in faith and consistently live out its truth by serving. Deacons are the hands and feet of the church, more directly than the other offices. Therefore, the apostle called for deacons to embody sincerity, moral purity, and submission to biblical truth.

—3:10—

The key Greek term in the phrase "these men must also first be tested" is a passive imperative form of the verb *dokimazō*. Based on the root word *dokeō*, "to watch," this was a term commonly used in the trade and crafting of metals. The most reliable means of determining the worth of a coin or ingot is to heat it to the point of melting and to observe its behavior. Both secular and religious writers used the term figuratively of warriors in battle and leaders in adversity.

Deacons must be people who have been observed—not spied on, but watched over a period of time to see how they respond to difficulties.

—3:11—

Suddenly, Paul shifts his discussion on church leadership to the subject of women. Again, he introduces it with the word *hōsautōs* (see comments on 3:8), meaning "likewise, in like manner, in the same way." Three possibilities present themselves.

(1) *The verse describes the wives of deacons, or perhaps wives of all church officials (overseers and deacons).* Some reliable expositors make a good case for the translation "wives." The Greek noun *gynē* can be rendered either "wife" or "woman," depending on the context. Paul could have intended to address wives of men in leadership because they serve alongside their husbands in a supportive role.

I'm not convinced of this interpretation, however, for two reasons. First, I find the absence of any possessive pronoun too difficult to ignore. The verse begins, "Women …," not "*Their* women (wives) …" The apostle takes such great care to identify his subject in other places that omitting it here makes little sense.

Second, the phrasing of verse 11 parallels verse 8 almost exactly, which tends to link Paul's instruction to "women" with that of "deacons" specifically, not to leaders (overseers and deacons) generally. This would mean that Paul addressed the wives of deacons and ignored the wives of overseers completely.

Verse 8	*Diakonous*	*hōsautōs*	*semnous*
	Deacons	likewise	dignified (masculine form)
Verse 11	*Gynaikas*	*hōsautōs*	*semnas*
	Women	likewise	dignified (feminine form)

(2) *The verse refers to women in general.* I'm even less convinced by this option. Paul has already addressed women in general in 2:9–15, so sandwiching an additional comment between two instructions to deacons is dizzying. Paul has been known to interrupt himself, but never like this.

(3) *The verse addresses women who serve as deacons.* Some have called this office "deaconess." This makes the best sense of the parallel between verses 8 and 11, both of which establish qualifications to serve the church. Furthermore, it appears in the context of official church roles.

Some present-day denominations combine the offices of overseer and deacon into one and then object to the third possibility on the grounds that women were not permitted to "teach or exercise authority over a man" (2:12). But the early church didn't combine these offices, and the deacon did not exercise authority over anyone; he or she simply served the congregation.

Like their male counterparts, women deacons are to exercise control over their tongues, remain "temperate" (see comments on 3:2–3), and faithfully carry out their duties. Again, the parallel to verse 8 is noteworthy.

— 3:12 —

Paul returns to his description of male deacons to round out their qualifications, stressing the importance of a strong family life. A deacon must serve the people under his own roof before seeking to serve anyone outside the home. Like overseers, they must be a one-woman kind of man and able to function as an overseer of their children and homes (cf. 3:2, 4; Titus 1:6).

— **3:13** —

The world system doesn't resent people who give of themselves and seek nothing in return, but neither does it reward selfless servanthood. The way to climb the corporate ladder is to get noticed, to take high-profile risks, and to downplay one's failures. Unsung heroes rarely reap the rewards of success in today's culture.

God's kingdom, however, works differently. Jesus turned the corporate ladder upside down to declare, in effect, "The way up in My kingdom is to descend to the lowest rung and become the servant of all" (Matt. 20:26–28). Paul echoed the Lord's words, promising that the table-waiter earns two rewards for service to others. First, the faithful deacon earns the esteem of his or her fellow believers today and high standing in the kingdom tomorrow. Second, the faithful deacon will cultivate an unshakable confidence in the truth of the gospel. Doing good deeds always enhances our assurance of salvation because it resonates with the godly person the Holy Spirit is creating within us.

The idea of servanthood did not sit well with Greek and Roman culture. People holding high political office were said to be servants of the people, but no one "served" without the benefits of land, title, adulation, and perquisites. Let's face it; who wouldn't want to "serve" as emperor of Rome? Aside from the constant threat of assassination, of course, this kind of servanthood isn't a bad job if you can get it! The real job of service went to slaves, whom Greeks and Romans considered inferior—on the same level as oxen or horses.

Jesus turned the idea of servanthood upside down by becoming the servant of all (Matt. 20:28; Luke 22:26–28). In His kingdom, the servant is the greatest of all. In the Christian world, no title bears greater honor or more dignity than that of "servant." What a marvelous compliment to be called "deacon," a faithful, caring, and diligent table-server. Of the official roles within the church, it is the most Christlike of all; therefore, the qualifications must remain stringent. Not everyone has what it takes to bear so noble a title.

Application

Creating a Culture of Service

This old world groans under the burden of human pride. How men and women cherish their positions of power, how they love authority, how they derive such significance from hierarchy! Rare is the man or woman who feels no urge to name-drop or advertise or boast. Sadly, though, the pride of position or power doesn't limit itself to the world; we see it in the church as well. Most churches have a large pool of would-be overseers from which to draw—but servants? Well, that's another story.

Paul concluded his short discourse on the dignity of the church's table-waiters, declaring, "Deacons obtain for themselves a high standing and great confidence in the faith that is in Christ Jesus" (3:13). I don't doubt the great confidence part. The Lord will be faithful to use the good work of the church's servants to bolster their belief in the gospel and to strengthen their personal assurance of salvation. But what about the "high standing" part? Seems that responsibility rests in the hands of the church they serve, at least this side of heaven.

Does your church honor servants? Some churches require would-be elders to serve a couple terms as deacons in order to be eligible for consideration as elder. But aside from that, does your church value and honor those who selflessly and quietly give of themselves? Here are some ideas you might consider, either officially through the church or informally on your own.

Thank them privately. Preferably in writing and make it personal . . . a hand-written note is best. No form letters. Acknowledge some specific areas of service for which you are grateful and resist the urge to include a gift or a tangible token of thanks. Trust me; they will treasure your sincere expression of admiration and gratitude.

If you are a pastor, elder, or other church official, don't try to send these in bulk at the same time each year. People are smart enough to know when they're on the receiving end of a pastoral obligation. Instead, add an agenda item to every meeting with elders or staff, asking them to praise a few people who serve well or have given of themselves above and beyond. Jot these down, and no less than once a month, send a note of thank to three or four.

Honor them publicly. Take note of unsung heroes among your congregation and express your admiration to others. No need to make a big show or become overly dramatic. Simply point out selfless deeds of service in casual conversation. If you are a pastor, use a selfless act of service as an illustration when preaching or teaching—after asking permission, of course.

Reward them collectively. The church would do well to hold a special banquet each year honoring those who faithfully serve the congregation. Make this a time of great celebration. If possible, invite the whole church, reserving tables of honor for those special servants. Pull out all the stops to make it as classy and memorable as possible. As an added touch, invite the congregation to help prepare the room, cook the meal, clean the venue, and—best of all—wait tables.

If we genuinely want to give "high standing" to servants of the church, we must create a culture of service and give priority to expressing appreciation for selfless devotion. Think of ways you can get started today.

A Hope, A House, A Hymn (1 Timothy 3:14–16)

14I am writing these things to you, hoping to come to you before long; 15but in case I am delayed, *I write* so that you will know how one ought to conduct himself in the household of God, which is the church of the living God, the pillar and support of the truth. 16By common confession, great is the mystery of godliness:

> He who was revealed in the flesh,
> Was vindicated in the Spirit,
> Seen by angels,
> Proclaimed among the nations,
> Believed on in the world,
> Taken up in glory.

The first section of Paul's message to his discouraged protégé in Ephesus focused on the work of ministry (1:3–3:13). Paul reminded Timothy of his duty as a pastor (1:3–20), named prayer as the first priority of ministry (2:1–8), clarified the position and role of women in the church (2:9–15), set out the qualifications of church elders (3:1–7), and celebrated the noble title of deacon and deaconess (3:8–13). The second section (4:1–6:21) will probe the inner life and conduct of the minister, with particular emphasis on the shepherd. Between these two sections of teaching we find a seam (3:14–16), a short, personal, and intriguing interlude linking them together.

Our temptation might be to overlook these little seams between great sections of practical teaching, but like the soft, flexible joints in a suit of armor, this is where we find the flesh-and-blood man exposed. First Timothy 1:3–3:13 and 4:1–6:21 show us Paul, the battle-hardened apostle; 3:14–16 reveals Paul, the intimate friend of Timothy. Passages like this are some of my favorite portions of Scripture. They are Spirit-inspired reminders that God's Word is for real people who live real lives, given through men who struggled to overcome the same feebleness of flesh we endure today.

— 3:14 —

I believe Paul intended to complete a two-year farewell circuit around the Aegean, spending the first winter in Troas and the second in Nicopolis before returning to Rome. In constructing his itinerary after the first Roman imprisonment, we know he "left" Titus on Crete (Titus 1:5) and encouraged Timothy to "remain" at his post in Ephesus while on his way to Macedonia (1:3). Most likely, Timothy had been ministering in Ephesus for some time during Paul's imprisonment and met the apostle for a brief visit in Miletus. Paul had used that port once before to avoid becoming entangled in the affairs of Ephesus (Acts 20:15–17). Furthermore, there is every reason to believe he spent some time in Troas, where he left his cloak and books (2 Tim. 4:13). At the time he wrote Titus, Paul intended to spend the next winter in Nicopolis, on the far side of mainland Greece, a long distance from Ephesus. Then, something changed his plans.

—3:15—

We don't know if Paul ever made it to Macedonia. I tend to think he did, but Timothy's crisis in Ephesus persuaded him to reverse course. Whatever the circumstances, he clearly sent this letter ahead to buoy Timothy's confidence, to establish an enduring charter for the church in Ephesus, and to reinforce Timothy's authority as their spiritual leader. Unfortunately, he couldn't race to his friend's side. The Greek form of the verb "delay" suggests an element of uncertainty, but Paul chooses the active rather than passive mood. It is better translated "if I delay," rather than "if I am delayed." He obviously wants to support his friend—preferably in person and sooner rather than later—but the apostle also has to maintain his own priorities in ministry.

Paul's purpose for writing, "so that you [singular] will know how one ought to conduct himself," could not have offered new information for Timothy. The older minister had diligently trained his student for the day when he would shepherd a church on his own. Sometimes, however, a mentor has to recenter his student's thinking and bring him back to basics. He draws on three images to describe the local body of believers: a household, a civic assembly, and a pillar of truth.

"The household of God" draws on the patriarchal, multigenerational family structure found in most Ancient Near Eastern cultures. When a young man married in those days, his father expanded the family home to prepare separate quarters for the new couple. Everyone contributed to meet the needs of the extended family household, taking orders from the patriarch. Often, the father of the clan placed the reigns of leadership in the hands of another, usually his eldest son (see comments on 1:2), an adopted heir, or even a trustworthy servant (Gen. 15:2).

"The church of the living God" uses the Greek term *ekklēsia*. Secular Greek most commonly used the word to describe a gathering of citizens convened for a specific cause (cf. Acts 19:32, 39–40). Paul probably had the Greek translation of the Old Testament in mind, which used the term in reference to God's covenant people, Israel (e.g., Deut. 23:2), the "assembly" of the Lord.

"The pillar and support of the truth" draws on very familiar imagery in Ephesus. The imposing Temple of Artemis featured 127 pillars soaring sixty feet (18.3 m.)

overhead to support a roof 60 percent larger than a regulation football field (425 ft by 225 ft. [130 m. by 69 m.]). According to Paul, the Lord established the local church to become the support structure of divine truth.

— **3:16** —

The very mention of truth prompts Paul to recall a song. New Testament scholars see strong enough elements of rhythm and meter to set verse 16 into six strophes, forming a hymn to the deity and triumph

Top: This crude stack of pillar sections, surrounded by marsh, is all that remains of the great Temple of Artemis, one of the ancient world's seven wonders. Bottom: In the late sixth century A.D., Justinian used the mighty pillars to support the great dome of Hagia Sophia basilica in present-day Istanbul, Turkey.

of Christ. It is the unanimous affirmation of this divine truth that unites all believers.

He who was revealed in the flesh. "He" refers to God the Son, of course, which means the pronoun will not have an antecedent. This is typical of Greek poetry and is not uncommon for Paul (cf. Phil 2:6; Col 1:15). While the apostle John would not pen the prologue of his gospel (John 1:14) for some time yet, early Christians sang of God coming to earth in human flesh. Ephesus, the birthplace of the *logos* concept in philosophy, would not have welcomed the idea with open arms.

Paul's use of the word "revealed" echoes the New Testament idea of Christ's manifesting God when He entered the world (1 Peter 1:20; 1 John 3:5, 8).

Was vindicated in the Spirit. "Vindicated" is an unusual form of the Greek word for "righteousness." It means "shown to be righteous." In the Gospels, Jesus frequently referred to the hour in which He would be "glorified," usually in response to accusations of blasphemy from the religious authorities in the temple. The Lord's crucifixion, resurrection, and ascension and the subsequent coming of the Holy Spirit vindicated the truth of His teaching and confirmed His identity as the Son of God.

Seen by angels. This is a poetic way of saying Christ took up residence in the heavenly realm after completing His earthly ministry. He commissioned His disciples to evangelize the world and then ascended to Heaven, where He remains until His promised return.

EPHESUS: THE BIRTHPLACE OF "THE WORD"

Around 500 BC, a Greek noble of Ephesus named Heraclitus taught that the universe operates according to a rational structure, a unified ordering principle, which we can discern if we carefully observe its patterns and solve its many riddles. According to this theory, all the laws of physics, mathematics, reason, and even morality can be traced back to this one ordering principle, which he called *logos*, "the Word."

Other philosophers, such as the Stoics, adopted this seminal idea and added their own doctrines, even going so far as to describe "the Word" as a divine, animating (life-giving, life-moving) principle permeating the universe. Philo (20 BC–AD 50), a Jewish philosopher heavily influenced by Plato, taught that the *logos* was God's creative principle, which was necessary because God, in the realm of pure thought, cannot have any direct association with anything in the tangible realm of matter.

Ephesus, in addition to popularizing the *logos* idea, became a celebrated repository of Greek texts and attracted many schools of philosophy. Some scholars have suggested that John fell prey to the Greek *logos* idea, accusing him of leaning toward Gnosticism. Greek philosophers, however, would have strongly objected to the *logos* becoming flesh. John merely affirmed the parts of Greek philosophy that were valid in order to preach the truth of Christ on common ground, yet without compromising the distinctly Hebrew concept of the *logos* that he understood from the Old Testament. In Genesis, all things came into existence by God's Word.

Eventually, the church in Ephesus became a fortress of Christian theology.

Proclaimed among the nations. Though past tense, this refers to the work of evangelization conducted in the first century and continuing via the church today.

Believed on in the world. This doesn't mean to imply that everyone in the world will believe the gospel, but that some from every part of the world will place their trust in Christ.

Taken up in glory. The past tense views the event of Christ's ascension (Acts 1:2, 11, 22) as a true past event while simultaneously looking to the future with such certainty it's considered an accomplished fact. This future event is nothing less than Christ's accession, His receiving all authority to rule the earth and to judge every soul at the end of days. His ascension and his accession bookend the present church age.

Like many expositors, I see a chronological progression in the six strophes of this ancient hymn. The life of Jesus is recounted from His coming to earth in the form of human flesh, through His resurrection, ascension, and ultimate victory over all evil. For Paul's purposes in this letter, the fourth and fifth lines stand out in bold relief. Jesus involves His church in the proclamation of the gospel "among the nations" and He has vested the success of "believed on in the world" with us, the work of the Holy Spirit notwithstanding. We have a responsibility to confirm

Strophe of song	Stage of Jesus' life	Scriptural references
He who was revealed in the flesh	Incarnation	John 1:14; Rom. 1:3; Gal. 4:4; Phil. 2:5–7; Heb. 2:14; 1 John 1:1; 4:2; 2 John 7
Was vindicated in the Spirit	Resurrection	Rom. 1:4; 1 Peter 3:18; John 13:31–32
Seen by angels	Ascension	Mark. 16:19; Luke 24:51; Acts 1:9–11
Proclaimed among the nations	Evangelization	Matt. 28:16–20; Acts 1:8
Believed on in the world	Affirmation	Rom. 10:17–18; 14:11; Phil. 2:10–11; Rev. 5:9; 7:9–11
Taken up in glory	Accession	Dan. 7:13–14; 1 Cor. 15:27; Eph. 1:20–22; Phil. 2:9–11; Rev. 1:6

From My Journal

The Seeds of Truth

Do you remember the first place you heard the truth of the gospel? My mind returns to a little church in El Campo, Texas, where I, as a little boy, used to stretch out between my mom and dad on a wooden pew and count the tile squares on the ceiling during the sermon. I don't remember any particular sermon; I just remember the consistent message coming from the pulpit. My young ears heard of the reality of hell and the certain hope of heaven for all who believe in Jesus Christ. I also remember the pastor loving his family and faithfully caring for the family of God. I remember his personal sorrow through the loss of a child. My childish mind couldn't fully comprehend the magnitude of his suffering, but I recall the respect he earned with my mother and father as he remained faithful to the message, Sunday after Sunday, even as he grieved. I remember all of that as clearly as if it happened last week.

It was there the seeds of truth were first planted deep in my soul. The message was faithfully proclaimed that God came in the flesh, that the Spirit validated His work, that the host of heaven affirmed His mission, that the gospel must be proclaimed, that lost sinners will believe, and that Jesus will one day reign supreme over a transformed creation. Many in that church probably wondered if a restless little blonde-headed tyke named Charles would ever do more than count ceiling tiles in church. But thanks, in part, to the consistent life and message of a faithful minister, I not only heard the good news, I believed it with all my heart.

divine truth by conforming to it rather than inventing our own message. Moreover, our "common confession" centers on the person and work of the Lord Jesus Christ.

Paul closes this section of his teaching on the work of ministry with a hymnic confession of divine truth. While the Lord calls ministers to feed the hungry, clothe the naked, shelter the homeless, advocate for justice, call for mercy, and return good for evil, everything in the work of Christian ministry must point to the message, the "common confession," the good news of Jesus Christ.

NOTES:

1. Richard W. De Haan, *Men Sent from God* (Grand Rapids: Radio Bible Class, 1966), 26.
2. W. E. Vine, Merrill F. Unger, and William White, *Vine's Complete Expository Dictionary of Old and New Testament Words* (Nashville, TN: Nelson, 1996), 2:503.
3. Ibid.
4. I offer a more complete examination of this issue in "Straight Talk about Predestination (Romans 9:1 – 33)," found in my *Insights on Romans* (Grand Rapids: Zondervan, 2010), 186 – 202.
5. *1 Clement* 61, in *The Ante-Nicene Fathers Translations of the Writings of the Fathers Down to A.D. 325*, ed. and trans. Alexander Roberts, James Donaldson, and A. Cleveland Coxe (Grand Rapids: Eerdmans, 1968), 10:247.
6. *First Apology*, 17, in ibid., 1:168.
7. *Address to the Greeks* 4, in ibid., 2:66.
8. *Apology to Acrolytus* 1.11, in ibid., 1:92.
9. *The Apology* 33, in ibid., 3:42.
10. *Treatise 5: Address to Demetrianus* 20, in ibid., 5:463.
11. According to Department of Labor Statistics, 2009.
12. Gerhard Kittel and Gerhard Friedrich, ed., *Theological Dictionary of the New Testament: Abridged in One Volume*, trans. Geoffrey W. Bromiley (Grand Rapids: Eerdmans, 1985), 1150.
13. Peter Scazzero, *The Emotionally Healthy Church* (Grand Rapids: Zondervan, 2003), 36.

THE ONE WHO MINISTERS (1 TIMOTHY 4:1–6:21)

It should come as no surprise that the vast majority of Paul's teaching on Christian ministry focuses on ministers themselves. Personal integrity and strength of character have a bearing on all occupations, but none more than the unique and holy calling of teaching and leading God's people. An honest surgeon does better work in the operating room than one with a guilty conscience, but dishonest surgeons can—and do—cure the ills of patients. An immoral police officer can uphold the law, an underhanded businessman can turn a profitable deal, a shifty salesman can sell a quality product at a fair price, and a shady politician can establish good public policy. Hypocrisy in most vocations can detract from professional accomplishments, but it doesn't necessarily prevent them.

Christian ministry, however, cannot tolerate hypocrisy without serious repercussions, sooner or later. The moral purity of a minister directly impacts the effectiveness of his or her work. A minister leads, first and foremost, by example, becoming a living, breathing, authentic, transparent model of the gospel from the moment of salvation, through the process of transformation, and in the ultimate journey from this life to the next. He or she teaches Scripture, first and foremost, by becoming its most ardent student and then by allowing sound doctrine to permeate his or her life, resulting in godliness that is observable. The minister also propagates gospel truth through relationships—in the context of programs and services, yes—but primarily through personal interaction with people inside the church and among the surrounding community.

Having outlined the work of ministry in terms of its leadership and general order, Paul devotes the greater part of his letter to reminding Timothy of his identity as a man of God. He describes the role of pastor in terms of how he should relate to various age groups and levels of society. He writes, in effect, "This is how a pastor confronts false teachers. This is how he should behave with elderly men. This is how he deals with young widows versus older widows. Now let me explain how to encourage slaves." By the end, Timothy receives practical, real-life advice on how to conduct himself as the leader of a church with many differing perspectives and competing interests.

The Inevitable Attack of Apostasy (1 Timothy 4:1–6)

¹But the Spirit explicitly says that in later times some will fall away from
the faith, paying attention to deceitful spirits and doctrines of demons, ²by

KEY TERMS

διδασκαλία [*didaskalia*] (1319) "teaching, doctrine"

Paul uses this term no less than eleven times in his instruction to Timothy and four times in his letter to Titus. It appears alongside several synonymous terms, such as "faithful word" (Titus 1:9), "sound speech" (2:8), and "truths" (3:8). This teaching, which is so essential to Christian maturity and especially needed on the island of Crete, is based on "the knowledge of the truth that is in keeping with godliness" (1:1 NET).

εὐσέβεια [*eusebeia*] (2150) "godliness, piety"

The word typically translated "godliness" stems from the root term *sebomai*, which means (lit.) "to fall back before" or "to shrink from," as one would do in the presence of a deity. The fully developed meaning of *sebomai* is "to reverence." Therefore, *eusebeia*, the noun form, describes an attitude of worshipfulness toward God that can be seen a person's demeanor and interpreted through his or her actions.

καλός [*kalos*] (2570) "good, healthy, serviceable, virtuous, orderly"

The meaning of this term in secular Greek thought is "that which is orderly or sound." Morality is included in the idea, but the word has a more functional nuance, in the sense that gold is a "good" metal because of its usefulness, beauty, and value in the market. Paul takes this idea to a higher level throughout his Pastoral Letters, so that it bears the "philosophical sense of 'right,' 'orderly,' or 'excellent,' manifested in such things as right conduct, correct teaching, and a proper attitude to the world."[1]

πίστις [*pistis*] (4102) "faith, confidence, reliance, trust"

Timothy and the believers in Ephesus would have known the word as it was used in the Septuagint (the Greek translation of the Old Testament). For the Jew — and therefore the Christian — *pistis* is the means by which he or she relates to God. The term also refers to the content of one's belief in which he or she has placed "trust" or "confidence" (i.e., "the faith"). For Paul, "the faith" referred to a correct understanding of the Old Testament, the original teaching of Jesus Christ, and the teachings of the men trained by Jesus. "The faith" is correct Christian belief and practice.

χήρα [*chēra*] (5503) "widow, forsaken, deprived"

The core idea of this word is "forsaken," as it is derived from the Greek term for deficiency. Unfortunately, for much of history, a woman left without a man could not expect to survive long, as many died from hunger, exposure, or assault. Uncivilized cultures valued people to the extent they served the community. Women past the age of childbearing couldn't build the population and were too old for labor. Therefore, women feared the prospect of widowhood without children.

means of the hypocrisy of liars seared in their own conscience as with a branding iron, ³*men* who forbid marriage *and advocate* abstaining from foods which God has created to be gratefully shared in by those who believe and know the truth. ⁴For everything created by God is good, and nothing is to be rejected if it is received with gratitude; ⁵for it is sanctified by means of the word of God and prayer.

⁶In pointing out these things to the brethren, you will be a good servant of Christ Jesus, *constantly* nourished on the words of the faith and of the sound doctrine which you have been following.

A man confronted me one Sunday morning, desperate to hear my answer to a question burning in his breast. "I waited till the end to talk to you, because I've got a question that may take a long time to answer." His wild-eyed intensity took me aback at first.

"Ask," I invited.

"I want to know from you, what is the truth? I've heard you talk, and I've listened to other preachers, and I hear other people refer to it. What do you mean when you refer to the truth? Remember, Pilate asked the question when interviewing Jesus, 'What is truth?' "

I saw a Bible cradled in his folded arms. I reached for it and thumped it playfully a couple of times. "Everything between the covers of that Book."

He blinked a few times, apparently turning the answer over in his mind, perhaps expecting me to continue with a more complicated reply. "What you have in the Scriptures," I continued, "is the truth you need to know. All truth is God's truth, but the Bible is 100 percent authentic, reliable information from Him to you."

That seemed to satisfy him, and he left apparently satisfied, I hope, to read his Bible with renewed confidence and deeper interest. If so, he will have joined the ranks of a widely misunderstood minority. Not only do most people doubt the truthfulness of Scripture; increasing numbers doubt the very existence of any truth at all! But we need not worry. God is not surprised. The enemies of truth are not new, and neither are their methods.

Paul closed the previous section with an ancient hymn, singing the good news of Jesus Christ. He now opens this next section with a sober warning. God came to earth in the form of a human — Truth incarnate — but the world system, advanced by Satan, rejected Him. Moreover, the world system continues to reject truth. Paul's warning can be outlined this way:

The Fact of Apostasy (v. 1a)
Its Nature (vv. 1b–5)

Its Characteristics (1b–3a)
Its Error (3b–5)
Its Defeat (v. 6)

— 4:1 —

Paul sets this instruction apart from the hymn (3:16) with the small contrasting conjunction "but." He had written earlier that the church is to be "the pillar and support of the truth," but we should not be surprised to see some fall away, pursue rival systems of thought, and become enemies of the truth. The Greek verb is *aphistēmi*, which literally means "fall away from." It is always used in the sense of betraying something or someone. It's a choice. One cannot accidentally become an "apostate" (*apostasia* is the noun form.)

The Lord had already warned us that in the "latter days," that is, the time between His ascension and His return, many would exchange the truth of the gospel for apostasy (Matt. 24:10–11; Mark 13:22; 2 Peter 3:3–4; Jude 17–18). In fact, Paul had warned the church in Ephesus of this danger before his arrest in Jerusalem (Acts 20:29–30). Now, apparently, the predicted danger had hit the congregation under Timothy's leadership, and hit them with force. Paul described the apostasy as "paying attention" (same verb as 1:4) to lying spirits and accepting as truth the doctrines of demons (cf. Eph. 6:12). Strong words shape his warning.

Rest assured that apostasy will not bear the obvious imprint of demons. False teaching will never enter your church with the name "Church of Satan" printed all over it. Deceitful spirits cleverly drape their doctrines in the respectable, even pious robes of religion. The teaching appeals to the flesh and is presented with charm and charisma. False teachers speak convincingly to the issues of their day and often use the Scriptures (almost always out of context) to give the appearance of good-faith teaching (cf. Matt. 4:6). It is true that some will be fooled — but not without their consent. They will be drawn in by the power of an error they desperately want to believe … again, because it appeals to the flesh.

— 4:2 —

Paul describes how apostasy can take root in an otherwise sound church. The false teaching will enter by means of hypocrisy. *Hypokrisis* means "pretense" or "pretext." This word illustrates better than any other the difference between the world system and the gospel. The verb *hypokrinomai* means simply "to answer back," usually in the context of debate or acting. Secular Greek writers used the term both positively and negatively, depending on the situation. For example, the White House Press Secretary can present and defend the American president's policy on a given matter, even if he or she disagrees with it personally. According to the Greek mind-set, this individual is dutifully placing his or her private opinion in the background in order to fulfill a public role.

Hebrew writers, however, almost always used the term with a negative connotation. For the New Testament writers, behaving one way while thinking another made one an actor in the worst sense of the term. "The stage is a sham world and actors are deceivers."[2] Paul follows the pattern of Jesus, who used *hypokritēs* to describe people who had fallen away from truth as received from God, but who pretended otherwise.

Paul vividly depicts the false teachers' damaged conscience as "seared." The whole phrase "seared as with a branding iron" derives from a single Greek word that means (lit.) "to burn with a glowing iron." The English medical term "cauterize" comes to us from Latin, which borrowed the word from Greek. The Greek term combines two important images that tend to get lost in translation. First is the idea of marking. False teachers bear the mark of their owner, Satan. Second is the idea of deadened nerves. The moral nerve endings of false teachers have been destroyed by the process of branding. Therefore, we can easily identify apostates if we carefully observe their response to sin.

False teachers minimize their own sin or fail to take their own guiltiness seriously. They might put on a good show if caught, but they quickly rebound to resume their positions of power and influence after public outrage has subsided. Furthermore, their response to the sin of others depends entirely on convenience. They brutally punish the sin of those they do not favor, while they minimize or rationalize their own sin and the sin of their cronies.

— **4:3–5** —

While Gnosticism did not take definite shape as a philosophy until the second century AD, early forms of the heresy began to trouble churches as early as AD 50. This incipient teaching relied heavily on the influence of Plato, whose basic understanding of the universe has informed virtually all of Western thought, including religion and philosophy.

Plato saw the universe as existing in two realms: the realm of *idea*, where concepts exist perfectly and incorruptibly; and the realm of *substance*, in which tangible examples of ideas exist, but suffer imperfection and corruption. In the realm of idea, the concept of an apple exists eternally perfect; in the realm of substance, apples exist as tangible representations of the perfect idea, except here they possess flaws and eventually rot. For Plato, God exists in the perfect realm of idea, while we exist in the flawed realm of substance.

Gnostics reasoned that anything associated with the realm of substance must therefore be inherently bad or sinful, while all things in the realm of idea remain pure or sinless. They reasoned further that a person possesses some elements of both realms: a soul, which is associated with the purity of the idea realm, and a body, which is part of the corrupted substance realm. Some early gnostic corruptions of Christianity taught that the soul or spirit can be nurtured only by denying or abusing the body. This is called asceticism, which condemns any activity that satisfies the body's craving beyond what is absolutely necessary to live. If you're hungry, suppress it. If you're thirsty, ignore it. If you're tired, work harder.

Paul denounces specifically those who condemned marriage and restricted the diet to include only the barest essentials (cf. Col. 2:20–23). He denounces the false teaching of asceticism to show that *anything* given by God must be good, for a holy God cannot provide anything that is evil. The Lord ordained marriage and gave it to humanity as a blessing before sin entered the world (Gen. 2:18, 21–25). He also filled the earth with food, forbidding the first people to eat from only one tree.

Paul declares that people who know these truths also believe in Christ for their righteousness and do not submit to the bondage of asceticism. Believers may freely partake of any blessing received from God with thanksgiving and without guilt (Gen. 1:29–30; 9:1–3; Acts 10:9–15).

— **4:6** —

Having described the particular form of apostasy attacking the church in Ephesus, its characteristics, and its error, Paul explains how to combat apostasy — not just this particular apostasy, but any kind of error. We might expect him to recommend extensive preparation for a complicated plan of attack and then a long, hard-fought campaign against error. Instead, he sets out an uncomplicated strategy. A "good servant of Jesus Christ" consistently and faithfully identifies false teaching and confronts false teachers with the truth. Spiritual leaders call a spade a spade. They speak the truth. They correct false teaching with Scripture and reinforce sound doctrine. No need for politics or power plays. Faithful shepherds simply shine the light of truth on darkness (Matt. 10:27–28; Eph. 5:11) and then remove predators from the flock (Rom. 16:17–18; Titus 3:10–11; 2 John 10).

Many young ministers take on their roles expecting to change the world — or at least their little corner of it. New pastors carry visions of a socially vibrant, spiritually enthusiastic, emotionally healthy congregation locking arms to transform their community. They prepare nourishing lessons and challenging sermons; they lead committees and counsel individuals; they organize, systematize, and strategize, all the while struggling to manage a growing frustration with a lack of significant progress. No matter what they do, evil continues to oppress and undermine the church. If something doesn't change, a young minister's fire can quickly flame out.

Seasoned pastors, however, never lose their youthful idealism; they merely change their definition of a "successful ministry." While they never stop pressing for the ideal, they never lower their expectations. They do, however, accept the fact that no ministry can fully rid itself of evil until Christ returns. Experience eventually teaches them that "success" is best described as "faithful," "vigilant," or "consistent."

At a critical moment in Timothy's pastorate in Ephesus, Paul introduces a healthy dose of realism to temper the younger man's expectations. The presence of evil in the church is not the result of anyone's failure; it's to be expected. Apostasy remains a constant threat within even the most theologically sound churches, organizations, and institutions. The apostle says, in effect, "No sermon series will ever inoculate a congregation against depravity, so expect sin to remain a continual source of frustration; no church program will ever shield leaders from false teaching, so diligently confront apostasy."

While we must never tolerate overt acts of evil within the church, we should not allow ourselves to be surprised when we discover it lurking in unexpected corners.

Application

Ministering amidst the Crazies

I would have loved to minister in a church without problems. Unfortunately, the only churches I could find that didn't have challenges were empty! As soon as you add people, you add problems. As numbers grow, problems proliferate. *All* churches struggle to overcome the negative impact of difficult people, including the most deadly difficulty of all: false teaching. In light of the passage we have just considered together, let me make three practical observations concerning the problem of apostasy.

First, *the constant threat of apostasy should be a constant reminder that we are living in the last days.* The rise of false teaching and its general acceptance by many who call themselves Christian shouldn't come as a surprise because we have been warned. The end of days will be marked by false teaching that leads to behavior the Bible condemns.

We might be tempted to interpret the presence of false teaching as failure on our part. But instead of wondering what we're doing wrong, we should expect apostasy to invade the church as surely as weeds attack gardens. Not infrequently, the faithful declaration of God's truth intensifies the Adversary's attacks.

Second, *Satan is the source of all lies, and he's very good at what he does.* Credible-sounding people with excellent credentials, impeccable Christian pedigrees, and trustworthy demeanors will claim to have received new information by the Spirit of God or through a dream or from this vision or that miracle.

We might be tempted to allow style to divert our attention away from substance. But despite the impressive appearance of false teachers, we must compare their doctrine to the truth already received in the sixty-six books of the Bible.

Third, *movements fueled by false teaching are difficult to resist.* Satan's spokespeople outnumber men and women of God, and they possess incredible gifts of persuasion. Few can resist their charisma, so many will be swept up in their movements. To make the problem more frustrating, false teachers often have an abundance of money and great charm. Many of them inspire such unquestioned devotion that biblical truth appears dull or tedious by comparison.

We might feel tempted to expose the hypocrisy of false teachers, drawing attention to their appalling lack of character. But too much of that will only reflect poorly on the champions of truth. Instead, we must focus on the content of their teaching, exposing how contrary to Scripture it really is.

Paul outlines an uncomplicated, straightforward strategy for counterattack when apostasy invades the church. We simply "point out these things to the brethren." That is, we consistently proclaim the truth, highlighting every disparity between apostasy and God's Word.

The Dos and Don'ts of a Healthy Ministry (1 Timothy 4:7–16)

---

[7]But have nothing to do with worldly fables fit only for old women. On the other hand, discipline yourself for the purpose of godliness; [8]for bodily discipline is only of little profit, but godliness is profitable for all things, since it holds promise for the present life and *also* for the *life* to come. [9]It is a trustworthy statement deserving full acceptance. [10]For it is for this we labor and strive, because we have fixed our hope on the living God, who is the Savior of all men, especially of believers.

[11]Prescribe and teach these things. [12]Let no one look down on your youthfulness, but *rather* in speech, conduct, love, faith *and* purity, show yourself an example of those who believe. [13]Until I come, give attention

to the *public* reading *of Scripture,* to exhortation and teaching. ¹⁴Do not neglect the spiritual gift within you, which was bestowed on you through prophetic utterance with the laying on of hands by the presbytery. ¹⁵Take pains with these things; be *absorbed* in them, so that your progress will be evident to all. ¹⁶Pay close attention to yourself and to your teaching; persevere in these things, for as you do this you will ensure salvation both for yourself and for those who hear you.

I cannot overstate the value of mentors. The patient, practical influence of several godly men continues to influence my decisions and prompt my actions. A couple of discerning deacons started me on a Scripture memory program as a teen. Ray Stedman taught this young Marine stationed in San Francisco my earliest understanding of a healthy pastoral ministry, even as I planned to continue my training as a mechanical engineer. I later returned and served as an intern at Peninsula Bible Fellowship, just to gain more practical wisdom from Ray. While stationed on the far-off island of Okinawa, Bob Newkirk, with The Navigators, whetted my appetite for the Word and helped me discover and confirm God's call to ministry.

Shortly after my discharge, I enrolled at Dallas Theological Seminary, where I encountered three mentors who have continued to influence me throughout my years in ministry: Drs. Howard Hendricks, Dwight Pentecost, and Stan Toussaint. In addition to teaching, correcting, and encouraging me, they offered practical advice based on their own successes and failures. I learned how to run an effective elders meeting, how to use proper etiquette in hospital visits, how to confront false teachers and deal directly with sin, and even now to baptize a large man by immersion without drowning him (or me!). My mentors exposed me to many of the challenges I would eventually face on my own, and they equipped me to meet them successfully. That explains why I wrote that I cannot overstate the value of my mentors. Their influence in my life cannot be measured.

Timothy had, of course, ministered side-by-side with Paul since the beginning of his second missionary journey. But flying with an instructor and flying solo are different matters! As false teachers tugged the Ephesian believers in multiple directions, pagan oppression continually undermined confidence, wealth lured members away, and the forces of darkness infiltrated leadership, Timothy needed practical guidance from a seasoned and strong spiritual leader.

Paul has already reminded Timothy of his primary responsibility: to be "a good servant of Jesus Christ" (4:6). The pastor is not enslaved to people, so he should neither feel intimidation nor try to manipulate or control others. He is a servant of

Christ, not beholden to the unrealistic expectations of people. Moreover, the servant of Jesus Christ isn't an unthinking go-between; he's an emissary of the King, trained and equipped to lead God's people in all truth. Yet the servant of Jesus Christ is not a celebrity deserving any superior status or special recognition beyond that of any member of the church. He is a servant among servants.

So, how does a servant of Jesus Christ serve? Paul gives his protégé practical, realistic instructions in a list of specific "dos and don'ts," positive and negative commands to help him stay on target.

Negative Commands	Positive Commands
Have nothing to do with worldly fables. (v. 7a)	Discipline yourself for the purpose of godliness; (v. 7b) prescribe and teach these things. (v. 11)
Let no one look down on your youthfulness. (v. 12a)	Show yourself an example of those who believe. (v. 12b)
	Give attention to the public reading of Scripture, to exhortation and teaching. (v. 13)
Do not neglect the spiritual gift within you. (v. 14)	Pay close attention to yourself and to your teaching. (v. 16)

— 4:7 —

The Greek phrase translated "worldly fables fit only for old women" might be rendered better "common talk and old wives' tales." I especially like the NET Bible's rendering, "myths fit only for the godless and gullible." Today, we would encourage pastors to avoid urban legends and folk theology (cf. 1:4; 6:20; 2 Ti. 2:16; 4:4; Titus 1:14).

Instead, Paul urges Timothy to get himself into the spiritual gymnasium. The Greek word for "discipline" is *gymnazō*, which pictures an athlete preparing his body for a competition. He lifts weights, works on endurance, practices elements of his sport, concentrates on the fundamentals, spars, scrimmages, sweats, and rehearses. He disciplines himself for the day of testing. Only for Timothy, the training is spiritual, not physical, and his purpose is "godliness," not physical fitness. The root term is *sebomai*, which originally meant "to fall back before" or "shrink from," as one would do in the presence of a deity. By the time of Paul, the word described a general attitude of reverence or worship. Perhaps the best definition is "taking God seriously."

Interestingly, an attitude of worship does not occur naturally for a believer ... or even one called into ministry. Godliness is never automatic. It requires training, just as athletic competition requires physical discipline.

— **4:8–9** —

Western culture, especially in the United States, has become obsessive about the body. Diet plans flood the market, health clubs proliferate, nutritional supplements vie for advertising space, organic foods attract record numbers of customers, and plastic surgery has become commonplace. Ironically, our obsession with the body has done little to curb steadily worsening obesity statistics.

Paul doesn't discount the value of physical fitness. The NASB renders the phrase with the word "only," which is not present in Greek. He acknowledges the benefit of physical training to keep the body healthy; he merely points out the temporal value of physical exercise compared to the eternal value of spiritual training. In his letter to the believers in Corinth, host of the Isthmian Games, Paul mentioned "a perishable wreath" (1 Cor. 9:24–27). The victor received a crown made of woven pine fronds, but that's not all. Victors also received royal treatment at the games and in their hometowns. City officials would break a large opening in the city wall and then cover it with a brass plate bearing the engraved name of the winner. A particularly successful athlete might even enjoy tax-free status for the rest of his life and receive a lifetime supply of food from the city. He could literally rest on his laurels.

For all the fame and money a star athlete could win, his wreath withered, his fame vanished, his bank account dwindled, and he eventually rotted in a grave long covered by the dust and debris of time. At the end of life, the body decayed and turned to nothing. Physical fitness and laurel crowns cannot compare to the eternal rewards for which we strive. We train for a prize called "godliness," which we will carry with us to heaven and lay before the feet of our King.

Whenever Paul uses the phrase "a trustworthy statement deserving full acceptance," he means to add extra emphasis to a particular teaching (cf. 1 Tim. 1:15; 3:1; 2 Tim. 2:11; Titus 3:8). In this case, the "trustworthy statement" is the eternal worth of godliness over the temporal worth of physical fitness.

— **4:10–11** —

Paul continues to stress the value of godliness using two athletic terms: *kopiaō*, which means "to wear out," and *agōnizomai*, which means "to strive for victory." We get our word "agony" from the Greek concept of giving all of oneself to reach a goal. That goal is not salvation, nor is it godliness, although an attitude of worship is the reason for our striving. Just as a runner fixes his or her eyes on the finish line, we focus our spiritual eyes on "the living God." The Lord is our goal. We are running toward Him. Why? Because He has rescued us!

Paul combines two phrases, "who is the Savior of all men" and "especially of believers," to convey some important truths.

First, while we "labor and strive," salvation is *not* our goal. Believers "labor and strive" *because* we are saved, not to in order to be saved. God is the Savior; He does the saving, not us.

Second, God is the Savior of *all* people, not just the elect (cf. 1 John 2:2). Jesus came to save the world and He died for the sins of all.

Third, while God is the Savior of all people, not everyone will be saved. All people have life and breath in this life because of Him, but not all will receive eternal life. Paul adds the last phrase to clarify his meaning. In the eternal sense, God is the potential Savior of all, but the effective Savior of some. The difference is belief—hence Paul's use of the term "believers."

Paul reinforces and extends the earlier command, "discipline yourself," by instructing Timothy to reproduce his own godliness in the lives of the congregation. "Prescribe" is another rendering of the same verb Paul uses in 1:3 ("instruct"), 5:7 ("prescribe"), and 6:17 ("instruct"). Unfortunately, "prescribe" and "instruct" do not capture the authoritative flavor of the Greek verb. He expects the pastor to use his authority to "command" or "order" church members to discipline themselves for godliness.

— **4:12** —

Paul's urging Timothy to "command" or "order" the Ephesian believers to respond a certain way should be seen in its context. He does not intend for Timothy to behave disrespectfully or to adopt an authoritarian, autocratic leadership style. He merely expects him to adopt a confident demeanor and lead the people with strength of conviction. Timid leaders give followers an uneasy feeling, causing them to wonder if the leader doubts his or her own direction.

Apparently, Timothy struggled to maintain credibility (cf. 1 Cor. 16:10–11). Some expositors suspect his youth undermined the respect of older believers, but Timothy would have been close to forty years of age by the time of this writing. He may have been "youthful" compared to some, but he would not have been considered a youth.

Others have theorized that Timothy's soft-spoken, sensitive personality (2 Tim. 1:4) accompanied a passive disposition. I think this accurately describes the younger minister, but Paul writes something similar to Titus (Titus 2:15), which suggests another explanation. The apostle undoubtedly casts a long shadow, such that *all* of his students struggled to earn respect, especially in the churches he personally established. This put anyone but Paul at a distinct disadvantage.

Regardless, Paul observes that people don't mind youth or even youthfulness in their leaders; they do, however, resent immaturity. Paul encourages Timothy to let his outward behavior reveal his inner wisdom, which would inevitably gain the church's respect. Furthermore, he expects his understudy to lead by personal example.

— **4:13** —

Paul's third positive command involves "giving attention" (the opposite command to what is cited in 1:4 and 4:1) to three community activities. First, the public reading of Scripture. The actual Greek phrase omits the word, "Scripture," but this is clearly implied. Whereas most Jewish men and some women learned how to read in their local synagogues, only the wealthiest Gentiles were literate. Furthermore, the cost to reproduce documents made it next to impossible for the average person to own a copy of the Scriptures. People, therefore, depended on public readings to hear God's Word.

I think hearing divinely inspired words read aloud adds an extra dimension to private devotion time. I regularly read passages of Scripture aloud to myself in my study. Not only does it block out any distractions, I gain the benefit of added senses. I also pay more attention to inflection and the rhythm of the words as I take care to enunciate each syllable. An added benefit is that I can't gloss over anything. Reading aloud forces me to slow down and allow the truth to soak in.

Second, "exhortation" (*paraklēsis*) is related to the verb *parakaleō* ("to exhort"), from which we get "Paraclete," a term referring to the Holy Spirit. The best modern definition I can think of would be "to coach," at least when used in the context of a relationship between individuals. In this context, the public nature of "reading" carries forward to include both "exhortation" and "teaching." Public exhortation is nothing other than preaching.

Both preaching and teaching involve instruction and a call to action. Preaching differs from teaching, however, in both style and emphasis. Whereas teaching emphasizes the transmission of information for the sake of instruction, preaching instructs for the sake of motivation. Preaching rallies or exhorts the congregation to act on the information they hear. Unfortunately, much of what passes for expository preaching is really teaching from the pulpit. Lots of great information passed along, but no application, no challenge, no exhortation.

Third, "teaching." When I preach to an unfamiliar group of people, I can tell when they have been well-taught. The difference is like striking a bell versus a brick. One resonates, the other thuds. With its emphasis on exhortation, a sermon resonates loud and clear with a knowledgeable audience, but does little to stir the ignorant.

Teaching, therefore, must take place in addition to preaching. It's a different kind of gift, requiring a specific set of skills. Teaching also utilizes methods that help build community and mutual accountability. It's usually in a teaching context that error surfaces, providing mature believers the opportunity to confront gently and correct thoroughly.

— 4:14–15 —

Back on the negative side of the column, Paul offers Timothy (and all ministers) a final "don't." He writes, in effect, "Don't let your spiritual gift go to waste." Paul recalls Timothy's ordination again (1:18) for the benefit of the congregation in Ephesus. Prophets had revealed God's commissioning of Timothy as a shepherd, and the elders — most likely in Jerusalem (Acts 11:30) — had affirmed his calling.

The practice of "laying on of hands" dates back to the earliest days of the Hebrew people. The gesture symbolizes the passing of something intangible from one person to another, such as blessing (Gen. 48:14; Matt. 19:14–15), guilt (Ex. 29:10), judgment (Lev. 24:14), authority (Num. 27:18–20; Acts 6:5–6), or identity (Acts 8:17–20). The New Testament church commonly used this practice to commission someone officially to carry out a specific task (Acts 6:5–6; 9:17; 13:3).

"Take pains with ..." translates a single Greek term typically referring to meditation or devising a detailed plot. An effective, healthy ministry doesn't just happen. Paul urges Timothy to plan well, communicate his plans, and then follow through on them. A congregation cannot help but learn to respect a man who is making progress in his Scripture reading, preaching, and teaching. Such public expressions endear the shepherd to his flock.

— 4:16 —

Paul concludes his list of dos and don'ts with perhaps the most helpful positive command a young minister could receive. "Pay close attention to" derives from a Greek word meaning "to hold upon, fasten attention on," although Paul doesn't mean for Timothy to become self-absorbed. He urges Timothy to shift his perspective away from results, which can be fickle, to concentrate on what he can control: himself and his teaching.

Leading a church is not like running a business. A good entrepreneur constantly monitors success in order to determine what should be done next. Good results? Do more of the same. Bad results? Discover problems and implement change. Ministry methods, however, don't change. Ministers do as they have been commanded: set a godly example (3:7–12), preach and teach Scripture (3:13), and do both with unfailing consistency (3:14–16).

Poor results over a long period of time may require serious soul-searching, leading to difficult decisions. However, I have found that nothing good can come from concentrating on results, such as efforts to enlarge attendance, emphasizing the number of conversions, or referring often to weekly receipts. Good results can puff me up; bad results can make me feel like a failure. If, however, I leave those concerns to the elders and other fellow-servants in ministry and stay focused on faithfully, diligently, consistently doing what I know to be right, results take care of themselves. Remember Paul's words to the Corinthians: "I planted, Apollos watered, but God was causing the growth" (1 Cor. 3:6).

The key to successful ministry, in a word, is perseverance. In fact, perseverance *is* ministry success; the only way to fail in ministry is to back off and give up. Therefore, it should come as no surprise that perseverance is also the minister's greatest challenge. Discouragement seemingly comes from nowhere to knock us flat. Criticism makes us wonder why we should stay at it. Laziness promises the work will be easier tomorrow. Greed looks for greener grass in another occupation. Idealism wearily wrestles with futility. Hope barely staves off fatigue. Determination eventually overcomes doubt. And if the minister isn't seeing results or receiving encouragement from the congregation, resignation will likely follow. Faithful expositors need few things to keep them going ... but encouragement is one of them.

Application

Five Lessons for Young Ministers

I have the distinct pleasure and privilege of teaching pastors in preparation, including a doctoral seminar on church ministry. Imagine for a moment you have slipped into the room during one of our class sessions. A young man asks, "Based on your understanding of Paul's advice to Timothy and your own experience as a pastor, what do we need to know as we enter full-time Christian ministry?" This actually occurred, which led me to think through and record my answer.

I have five lessons worth remembering.

First, *there is no higher goal in ministry than servanthood.* If you really want to aspire to greatness in ministry, don't try to become a leader; instead, seek opportunities to serve. Don't aim high; lie low. Look for ways to make someone else's job easier or more pleasant. Rather than distinguish yourself as the smartest one in the room, call attention to someone else. Instead of trying to impress others, highlight the accomplishments of another. If you're meant to be a leader, God will make it happen. He found Moses. He found David. He found Elijah. He found Esther. He will find you as you serve others ... and He will use you in His time.

Second, *there's no greater temptation in ministry than extremism.* Ministers frequently gravitate to those areas of ministry or spirituality that come naturally. If they aren't careful, their aptitude can dictate their priorities instead of the needs of the congregation. Fulltime vocational service to God requires balance. Devotion to people and dedication to truth. Theory and application. Self-awareness and selflessness. Prayer and action. Teaching and fellowship. Stay balanced ... guard against extremes.

Third, *there's no more important responsibility in ministry than exposition—the reading and explanation of Scripture, followed by application and exhortation.* While this is especially true for the role of senior pastor, the same is true of every ministry position, including executive pastor, counselor, minister of music, children's ministry, home fellowship coordinator, hospitality, even the leader of the parking attendants. Scripture is the basis of everything we do in church and has something vital to teach every role and responsibility. Cling tightly to the Word of God!

Fourth, *there's no more effective means of spiritual leadership than a growing minister.* Paul urges Timothy to show himself an example (4:12) and to let his progress be evident to all (4:15). When a pastor or other Christian minister becomes steeped in biblical truth and grows in wisdom and godliness, people notice. Authenticity is observed and respected. Eventually, they begin to believe they can experience the same transformation. Keep growing in your walk. As you grow older, grow deeper.

Fifth, *there's no better proof of an authentic ministry than perseverance.* Ministers don't succeed in ministry because of brains, talent, charisma, or interpersonal skills. Ministers succeed by hanging tough through difficult seasons. (Expect them.) They persevere through disappointment. (Hang tough.) They don't let dirty politics get the best of them. They refuse to quit when people criticize or run after false teaching. Success for the minister is faithfully carrying out the duties of ministry, day in and day out, in season and out of season, year after year, regardless of the results.

Respecting and Rebuking the Saints
(1 Timothy 5:1–2)

---

¹Do not sharply rebuke an older man, but *rather* appeal to *him* as a father, *to* the younger men as brothers, ²the older women as mothers, *and* the younger women as sisters, in all purity.

Down through the years we've been told that it was the prophet's job to comfort the afflicted and afflict the comfortable. I think that is the pastor's job as well. To fulfill both of those mandates, a pastor—or any minister, for that matter—must learn how to handle people as well as he does Scripture. Most of the people I know who have struggled in ministry didn't misdirect building programs, or misuse church funds, or even mishandle Scripture or theology. Most ministers who fail meet their end because they don't know how to relate to or interact with people. For all their intellect and giftedness, they lack social skills and emotional savvy.

A pastor-shepherd must enjoy interacting with people as much as he loves studying and expositing God's Word. And he must do both of these *well*. In my experience, those two qualities are rare among people in general and tragically rare in pulpit ministry. Some take on the role of shepherd because they love people and derive great satisfaction from serving them. They possess wonderful skills interacting with the public—often, though, at the expense of teaching and preaching the truth.

More often in conservative circles, men become shepherds because they love the Scriptures and have a gift for public speaking. Unfortunately, as they deepen their understanding of God's Word (usually in seminary), they become more reclusive, even cynical. They continue to remain aloof and isolated, glued to their books and growing deeper in knowledge. Soon all that Bible knowledge goes to waste because they've alienated everyone but the most thick-skinned. Their lack of self-awareness becomes palpable.

Paul, of course, recognizes this danger. After his discourse on doctrinal purity and his command to "give attention to the public reading of Scripture, to exhortation and teaching" (4:13), the apostle turns to the pastor's responsibility to maintain good relationships among the congregation. In 1 Timothy 5, Paul examines the needs of six distinct groups within the church:

- older men (v. 1a)
- younger men (v. 1b)
- older women (v. 2a)

- younger women (v. 2b)
- widows (vv. 3–16)
- elders (vv. 17–25)

Paul devotes only a couple of sentences to Timothy's interaction with the general population, but he manages to say a lot in a short space. We'll consider his insights in these first two verses of chapter 5 before examining his specific counsel regarding "widows" and "elders."

— **5:1** —

The Greek term *presbyteros* can be translated "older man" or "elder." Ancient cultures regarded age without wisdom to be a sad abnormality. Ideally, older men should be wise leaders. Nevertheless, Paul maintains a distinction between "older men" and the church office of "elder"; context tells us how to translate it. In this case, we know Paul is referring to men of advanced age and not the church office of elder or "overseer" because they are his focus in verses 17–25. Similarly, "older women" and "widows" refer to two different groups.

Paul counsels Timothy to exercise the authority of leadership in all cases, including the occasional need to correct a member. The adverb "sharply" doesn't appear in the original Greek, which uses only the term for "rebuke." Many translators infer the additional qualification, "sharply" or "harshly," for two reasons. First, Paul later charges Timothy with responsibility to "reprove, rebuke [same Greek term], exhort, with great patience and instruction" (2 Tim. 4:2). Therefore, the act of rebuking is not inappropriate on its own. Second, the rest of the command, "but rather appeal to him as a father," affirms the need for confrontation, only with a softer approach.

In the case of older men, Paul recommends an "appeal," using the familiar word *parakaleō*, "to exhort, comfort, instruct, encourage, advocate." Rather than take an older man by the shoulders and shake him, that is, rather than treat him harshly, Paul expects Timothy to address an older man as he *should* his own father, with due dignity, respect, and high honor.

I use "should" deliberately and with emphasis. Times have changed since Paul penned these words. Ancient cultures, though immoral in many cases, nonetheless thought of the family as a miniature kingdom over which the patriarch presided as a just and wise king. They afforded their father the same dignity and submission owed to a king. Sadly for our day and time, many fathers do not manage their households with dignity, respect, and high honor, and children are not likely to offer unearned respect. So, the advice, "appeal to him as a father," might not resonate in today's culture as well as it did in Timothy's. Perhaps we might adapt it slightly to say, "appeal to him as a highly respected king, president, or prime minister."

Bottom line: firm is acceptable; abrasive is forbidden.

Confronting a peer, however, calls for less formality; the standards relax a little. When a man confronts or rebukes a brother with whom he has shared a common upbringing, he can afford to be a little more abrupt; he can get straight to the point with less formality and dignity than when addressing his father. Therefore, a pastor should address a man of the same age or younger with concise, forthright truth, yet without robbing him of his dignity. Gentleness wears well, regardless of age or office.

— 5:2 —

In regard to confronting older women, Paul returns to his family analogy. A pastor must not harshly rebuke an older woman, but appeal (*parakaleō* is understood from the context) to her as one should his mother (again, I stress the word "should"). Whereas the key word for confronting a father is "respect," for a mother it is "tenderness." A pastor must treat all older women with gentle kindness, especially in the midst of a difficult conversation.

Curiously, Paul reinforces the idea of confronting younger women as sisters with the phrase "in all purity." His choice of Greek terms most often refers to ritual purity, such as the washing and setting aside of temple instruments, but here he has "innocence" in mind. The rapport a man cultivates with his sister is unlike any other relationship. He remains mindful of her femininity, yet without the slightest hint of sexuality. This seasoned minister expects Timothy—and all who follow in his steps—to cultivate this same unconsciously innocent rapport with women.

Paul doesn't choose his analogies haphazardly. His references to family do more than illustrate how a pastor should interact with various members of his congregation. He purposely avoids using terms from business or government because the church is neither. Many business practices can be useful in church operations, but the people in congregations are not personnel. All churches need orderly government, but God's sheep are not subjects. Church members share a common Father, look to Christ as the eldest brother, and live in a household with extended family, as it were. Therefore, we should regard one another as brothers and sisters, some older and some younger, but as family nonetheless. A corporate mentality is lethal in the church.

With this general principle established, Paul goes on to address the concerns of specific groups within the church and how Timothy—and all pastors—should minister to their unique needs.

Application

Six Words of Warning for Ministers

Few things grieve me more than hearing about another fallen minister. I hate it for the man or woman who sinned, I hate it for their families and their congregations, and I hate it for the damage done to the gospel. Tragedy can be avoided. No one fails without multiple warnings; they simply decide to ignore them. No one suddenly becomes a shipwreck.

So that you will not become another heartbreaking statistic, let me offer six words of warning. I have written these specifically for people serving in full-time Christian ministry, but they can be adapted to fit any vocation.

Warning 1: Authoritarianism. As trust for a minister grows among a congregation and they begin heeding his or her words, pride can set in. In subtle ways this opens the door to an autocratic, authoritarian style of leadership. He can easily begin to think his methods are superior and demand things be done his way when other approaches might work. She can become inflexible, dictatorial, oppressive, or even tyrannical. When a formerly teachable minister begins barking dogmatic orders instead of making gracious and gentle requests, he or she has exchanged leadership for dictatorship.

Warning 2: Exclusivity. As a minister spends more and more time studying every nuance of God's Word, he can begin to believe he has a unique corner on truth. She begins to think, *I have it right and everyone else is mistaken.* But I know of only one Person who needed no one's help discerning truth, and He's not physically on earth right now. The rest of us need one another to challenge our thinking as we read, interpret, understand, and apply Scripture.

The same holds true of a community of believers. When exclusivity replaces humility, a group can turn cultish and paranoid, defining truth not by God's Word but by association with a particular person or crowd.

Warning 3: Greed. The dictionary defines greed as the desire for more money than one actually needs. But how much money does a minister need? The erosion of contentment can quickly transform wants into needs, turning the minister's soul into a breeding ground for temptation. Because the rise of greed can occur gradually and subtly, I maintain a strict hands-off policy with regard to money. I don't accept cash given to me, I don't handle donations, I don't count the offering, and I don't determine how funds should be distributed. In fact, I don't even know who gives what in the church I serve. (I don't even know who counts the offering.) But I am confident of this: whoever does can be trusted, since all positions of responsibility are filled by people of integrity.

Warning 4: Rationalization. One can maintain righteousness in one's own eyes in one of two ways: by rising to the occasion or by lowering the standard. Rationalization is lowering the standard by justifying or minimizing wrong. Rationalization twists facts or skews Scripture in order to call an evil deed righteous.

Many years ago, I knew a pastor who began meeting with female members of the congregation. To avoid accountability, he began to preach what he called the "doctrine of privacy." He cleverly arranged Scripture with sleight-of-hand reasoning to make the "doctrine of privacy" a major theme of his preaching. This kept his congregation off-balance long enough to enable him to pursue a sensuous lifestyle for many years.

Not all rationalizations are this patently evil, however. Because ministers care so much about accomplishing good, they can adopt an "end-justifies-the-means" perspective and fall into this trap for the good of the church. For example, the church secretary receives a sizable check earmarked for missions, but the payroll account is short with payday just around the corner. The pastor could rationalize, *If I use a portion of the check to pay staff salaries this week, I can repay the "loan" from the missions account with payroll next week. No problem; it's all God's money anyway.*

An executive pastor I admire used the expression "clean and clear" whenever we faced the temptation to rationalize any poor decision. In all the difficult decisions I've made as a pastor, I've never regretted the ones that were "clean and clear."

Warning 5: Sensuality. Ministers do not suddenly become asexual beings once they decide to serve God full time. Nevertheless, moral purity is nonnegotiable. A man or woman serving the needs of wounded, emotionally vulnerable people can easily cross a moral line. A reassuring hug can quickly become a lingering embrace. After several months of criticism, a wounded self-esteem can find comfort in illicit sensuality.

I recommend writing a strict code of conduct, a set of rules to obey. For example:

I will never meet privately with a person of the opposite sex without a third person present.
I will avoid touching a person of the opposite sex anywhere but the hands.
I will install accountability software on any computer I use regularly.
I will not be in an automobile alone with a person of the opposite sex.
I will not eat at a restaurant alone with a person of the opposite sex.
I will...

Then, I recommend sharing your list with a trusted colleague for the sake of accountability.

Warning 6: Unaccountability. No one is immune to temptation. Accountability provides a secure backup to one's personal resolve to avoid falling into serious sin. All leaders must remain accountable to someone in a chain of command, all the way up to the senior pastor, who must remain accountable to fellow elders. And rather than resent oversight or routine checking in, we must invite it.

Frankly, I find great comfort in accountability. I like knowing that if I do something wrong, I will be caught. That strengthens my resolve to do what is right and to steer a wide berth around temptation.

What about Widows? (1 Timothy 5:3–16)

³Honor widows who are widows indeed; ⁴but if any widow has children or grandchildren, they must first learn to practice piety in regard to their own family and to make some return to their parents; for this is acceptable in the sight of God. ⁵Now she who is a widow indeed and who has been left alone, has fixed her hope on God and continues in entreaties and prayers night and day. ⁶But she who gives herself to wanton pleasure is dead even while she lives. ⁷Prescribe these things as well, so that they may be above reproach. ⁸But if anyone does not provide for his own, and especially for those of his household, he has denied the faith and is worse than an unbeliever.

⁹A widow is to be put on the list only if she is not less than sixty years old, *having been* the wife of one man, ¹⁰having a reputation for good works; *and* if she has brought up children, if she has shown hospitality to strangers, if she has washed the saints' feet, if she has assisted those in distress, *and* if she has devoted herself to every good work. ¹¹But refuse *to put* younger widows *on the list*, for when they feel sensual desires in disregard of Christ, they want to get married, ¹²*thus* incurring condemnation, because they have set aside their previous pledge. ¹³At the same time they also learn *to be* idle, as they go around from house to house; and not merely idle, but also gossips and busybodies, talking about things not proper *to mention*. ¹⁴Therefore, I want younger *widows* to get married, bear children, keep house, *and* give the enemy no occasion for reproach; ¹⁵for some have already turned aside to follow Satan. ¹⁶If any woman who is a believer has *dependent* widows, she must assist them and the church must not be burdened, so that it may assist those who are widows indeed.

People who don't know Paul's writings very well often consider him a woman-hater. I once taught a class on Monday mornings to a group of women who had only superficial knowledge of the Bible. Their opinions took me by surprise. The hostility toward the Bible created by the women's revolution of the 1970s has cooled a little, but many continue to think that Paul simply didn't like women. The ladies in my class, therefore, decided to take all of Paul's teaching with a grain of salt. It was an uphill climb to correct and change their perspective.

A cursory review of Paul's teaching might appear harsh, but only if you read them in isolation. All of his writings concerning women should be read through the lens of Galatians 3:28, which says, "There is neither Jew nor Greek, there is neither slave nor free man, there is neither male nor female; for you are all one in Christ Jesus." Furthermore, except for passages intended for other specific groups, he directed all of his teaching to men and women generally.

Women in Paul's Letters	
1 Cor. 7:25–26	Advice to unmarried women
1 Cor. 11:2–16	Women in church
1 Cor. 14:33–36	Women in worship services
Galatians 3:26–28	Equality of women
Eph. 5:22–24	Advice to wives
1 Tim. 2:9–15	Women in worship services
1 Tim. 3:11	Women deacons (?)
Titus 2:3–5	Responsibility of young wives

First-century Western civilization was not kind to women. Pagan cultures tended to view all people in terms of their usefulness, to family first and then to the state. They prized healthy, newborn sons because they extended the family's wealth and power and gave stability to kingdoms. Newborn daughters and unhealthy baby boys, however, often were left to the elements—a practice called "exposure"—because they were deemed too burdensome to rear.

Similarly, ancient civilization valued women primarily for their ability to produce heirs. Therefore, a woman without a man or tragically bereft of other family members found herself utterly helpless to survive on her own. While Greek and Roman customs expected families to care for their own, public assistance didn't exist outside Hebrew culture. Gentile women without the protection and provision of a man usually had to choose between prostitution and starvation.

Surprising as it may seem to many today (especially women), Paul's instructions to Timothy represent a giant leap *forward* for women in the first century. He drew on his Hebrew heritage, which valued *all* people as bearers of God's image and, therefore, worthy of dignity. Moreover, Christ died for all people as a gift of grace, not for what any recipient of salvation can do in return. Because Jesus values people simply because He made them, the church must care for people regardless of their "usefulness."

The apostle opens his discourse on the treatment of widows with the simple command to "honor" or "assign high value" to them (cf. Rom. 12:10; 13:7). He then divides widows into three distinct categories, only one of which is to be added to "the list."

- widows with living relatives (vv. 4–8)
- "widows indeed" (vv. 9–10, 16)
- widows likely to remarry (11–15)

This "list" isn't mentioned elsewhere in Scripture; nevertheless, we can discern its purpose from the context. The church maintained an official roster of people—widows mostly, but not limited to them—who were eligible to receive tangible assistance. Then, just like today, the church needed an official policy stating who may receive what.

— **5:3** —

The Greek word for "to honor" (*timaō*) is the same as Peter's choice in 1 Peter 2:17, when he commanded Christians to "honor the king." The church shines brightest when it gives royal treatment to people who have suffered greatly yet remain faithful. Furthermore, the tense of the verb indicates ongoing or continual action: "Keep on honoring."

The term also means "to set a price," strongly suggesting this "honor" was to be given tangible expression in the form of money; after all, we financially take care of the people we value. This probably took the form of a stipend in return for required service to the church (cf. 5:17–18). We would call it an honorarium today. Supporting this view is the fact that the "honor" was conditional, unlike charity, which is not. Paul reserves this honor for true widows or "widows indeed." He defines this special group in verses 4–15.

— **5:4–5** —

Paul distinguishes "widows indeed" from women whose husbands have died, yet who have living children or grandchildren. He charges the family with the care of such widows, based on two principles: righteousness and gratitude.

From My Journal

Honor, with a Personal Touch

Not long after my mother died, my dad came to live with us—Cynthia, me, and our four children. We tried to prepare ourselves and the house to give him the best possible care, but we had no idea what to expect. I'm glad to say the first couple of years were relatively uneventful. Other families complain about interference when parents move in, but Dad preferred his solitude, so it proved more of a struggle to draw him out of his room and have him engage with the family.

Toward the end of his life, however, his physical problems became severe. A few touch-and-go moments eventually led to the need for around-the-clock nursing. While my wife and I wanted to provide personal care and were dedicated to making any necessary adjustments, we simply lacked the required time and training. (I'll not go into the issues; trust me, they were significant.) As we wrestled with a difficult decision, we also wrestled with guilt. But after much discussion, lots of prayer, and carefully weighing of Scripture, we realized that honoring my father didn't require us to provide his medical care *personally*. In fact, he was more comfortable with a professional taking care of the medical details while we (and my sister, Luci) remained personally involved. All the way to his death, he was treated with honor and respect. We did our best to keep him from feeling abandoned.

Aging parents deserve our honoring them. We can entrust their physical care to professionals, but we must never abandon them.

Paul calls on the families of widows to "practice piety," drawing on the verb form of the adjective "godly," a supremely important word throughout this letter (2:2; 3:16; 4:7–8; 6:3, 5–6, 11). The purpose of pastoral ministry and the work of the church are to help its members lead godly lives (1:5), not the least of which is taking care of their own.

Paul also appeals to them on the basis of gratitude. Children and grandchildren owe their very existence to their parents' willingness to sacrifice comfort in order to provide for them and protect them. Their mothers, especially, bore them in her body and then delivered them through incredible discomfort and pain at childbirth. If the desire to be righteous were not enough, gratitude alone should prompt children to care for their widowed mothers.

— **5:5–7** —

Expositors differ over the best interpretation of these verses. One's interpretation depends on the answers to two questions. First, to whom is Timothy supposed to "prescribe these things" in verse 7? The widows, or their families via the church-at-large? Second, what does "give herself to wanton pleasure" mean? Most expositors suggest it describes seeking her own pleasure by pursuing sin. A few see this as Paul's euphemism for prostitution, such that she makes herself the object of "wanton pleasure" to earn a living.

The key to understanding lies in an accurate grasp of the full context of verse 6. Paul opens and closes the discussion with the issue of provision (vv. 4, 8). I also find it difficult to believe a great number of destitute widows would pursue sin for the mere sake of fun (i.e., their own "wanton pleasure"). On the contrary, prostitution historically has been the only alternative to starvation for widows throughout the centuries until the advent of public assistance. Viewing "wanton pleasure" as a means of provision also makes the best sense of the contrast between verses 5 and 6.

A widow with no surviving family must cast herself on the goodness of God to meet her needs; continued life becomes a matter of faith. A widow who casts off faith, exchanging the uncertain provision of God for the certainty of provision through prostitution, "is dead even while she lives." Paul's irony is rich. The godly widow places her hope in God and struggles daily to survive by faith; the ungodly widow places her trust in prostitution, only to receive a kind of walking death.

If verse 6 refers to prostitution, then Paul addresses verse 7 to the families of widows via the church-at-large. He implies that family members who fail to care for their widowed mothers will be morally complicit in the sin of prostitution. No one can be held responsible for the sinful choices of another, but neither are they above reproach when they fail to encourage godliness by whatever means possible. Therefore, Paul urges Timothy to "prescribe" (translated "instruct" or "command" in 1:3, 18; 4:11; 5:7; 6:2) families to care for their widowed mothers.

— 5:8 —

Paul agues for family support of widows from the positive angle in verse 4 — "practice piety" and "make some return" — and then from the negative in verse 8. Whereas care for one's widowed family member constitutes righteousness, failure to do this proves one's utter lack of moral worth. Even pagan, debauched Greeks and Romans took care of their own families. Paul cannot imagine a genuine Christian refusing to behave at least as decently as unbelieving neighbors.

Take note of the contrast between "they" in verse 7 and "anyone who does not provide" in verse 8. This is further indication that "they" refers to the families of widows, not the widows themselves, and that faithfully caring for one's own renders the family members above reproach (v. 7).

— 5:9–10 —

Having argued against church support for widows with living relatives (vv. 4–8), Paul argues against church support for young widows (vv. 11–15), again by contrasting their circumstances. He set the standard here for widows who are to be "put on the list" before stating the reasons for denying long-term support for younger women whose husbands have died.

I insert the qualifier "long-term" for two reasons. First, Paul would not have argued against helping a younger widow in short-term need of food, clothing, or shelter. His purpose is not to be legalistic or callous toward anyone in need, least of all a young woman suddenly left without a husband. Second, verse 11 indicates that names added to "the list" should not be removed, that one's enrollment marked a permanent transition to a new stage of life marked by singular devotion to serving God through the church (5:5; cf. Luke 2:37). He deems it unseemly for a woman to devote herself to the service of God, only to renege after meeting a man.

The apostle specifies three requirements for a widow to be put on the list, one objective and two subjective.

Not less than sixty years of age. According to the Mishnah, a Jewish document compiled around AD 200 recording rabbinic oral tradition, the age of sixty marked

From My Journal

Aunt Mae

During our days in seminary, Cynthia and I grew to love a widow supported by our home church in Houston, Texas. I cannot remember her last name because we—and a few other ministry couples—knew her only as Aunt Mae.

Unlike most people who glibly say, "We're prayin' for you!" Aunt Mae meant it. She asked us about our needs and carefully made note of each one. Then she'd say, "You're accountable to me, now. I'm praying, so I need to know how you're doing."

After several months of studying in Dallas, I always felt a sense of obligation to check in with Aunt Mae upon our return. She'd pull out her prayer list—always a little worn with use—and run down the list. "Now, Chuck, the last time we were together, you mentioned this need; how'd that work out?"

"Well, pretty good," we might reply. Aunt Mae would take her pen and scratch that item off the list.

"What about this one?"

I'd say, "We still need help in that area." And she'd keep it on the list.

Aunt Mae kept in regular contact with us throughout my years in seminary, and she faithfully talked with the Lord on our behalf. I sometimes wonder how different our experience would have been if she hadn't prayed so faithfully. A lot worse, I suspect.

the official beginning of old age at which a man could be considered an "elder" (Mishnah *Avot* 5:24).

A "one-man woman" (lit. translation). The construction of this phrase matches "one-woman man" in the list of qualifications for overseer and deacon (3:2, 12; Titus 1:6). Like these other lists, the qualification has more to do with the person's character than with how many times he or she has been married. Scripture never condemns someone for remarriage after the death of a spouse or falling victim to an unjust divorce (1 Cor. 7).

A reputation for good works. The Pastoral Epistles—especially Titus—concern themselves with good works almost to the point of obsession. That's because Paul, drawing on the very best Jewish theology, looks to good works as the fruit of righteousness. Godliness that fails to produce good works is as pointless and as useless as a fig tree that fails to yield figs (Luke 6:43–44; 13:7) or a vineyard devoid of grapes (Isa. 5:1–7; Ezek. 15:1–5; John 15:1–11).

The next five qualifications are not independent requirements, but five specific examples of "good works." Unlike the first three qualifications, these examples appear as five conditional "if" clauses, subordinate to "having a reputation for good works":

- having reared children, demonstrating a whole range of emotional and spiritual maturity
- having shown hospitality to strangers, the quintessential mark of decency recognized by all Ancient Near Eastern cultures
- having washed the saints' feet, the quintessential mark of humility and godliness, unique to Christianity (John 13:5)
- having assisted those in distress, displaying not only the quality of mercy but of obedience (Luke 10:25–37)
- having devoted herself to good works, which means she didn't wait for opportunities to do good deeds; rather, she looked for and participated in them

That's quite a list of qualifications! It's certainly no less stringent than the qualifications for overseer or deacon. This offers strong evidence to support the official office of "widow" in the church, complete with qualifications, duties, and remuneration for service. In fact, several early church fathers mention the office of "widow," complete with "ordination":

- Ignatius, *The Epistle of Ignatius to the Philippians* 15
- Clement of Alexandria, *The Instructor* 3.12.[3]
- Tertullian, *On the Veiling of Virgins* 9

—5:11–13—

In his argument to exclude young widows from "the list," Paul cites two primary reasons. First, their natural inclinations for love and sex will likely prove too much to overcome and they will eventually pledge themselves to a husband in violation of their vow to forfeit remarriage in favor of serving the church. The "condemnation" they incur is not the loss of salvation or even the displeasure of God, but the derision of outsiders from the resulting scandal. Remarriage is not sinful by itself—only when it violates a solemn vow to remain single in service to God.

The second reason is the relative immaturity of young widows. They learn to be "idle," which could mean "lazy" (Titus 1:12) or ineffective (2 Peter 1:8). The latter fits the context better. Paul doesn't accuse younger women of being lazy, but of being undiscerning. Since they lack mature wisdom, younger women will likely mishandle the information they hear. Instead of helping and maintaining discretion, they will unwittingly indulge in gossip and create drama.

—5:14–15—

Rather than have young widows struggle against their natural inclinations, Paul encourages them to remarry, enjoy lovemaking with a husband who loves them, and relish the blessings of family life. In other words, young widows should act their age and enjoy their youth rather than make a pledge they will struggle to keep and might even come to resent. To be certain, idleness will never become a problem, especially in the "lazy" sense of the word. (I don't know too many idle mothers.)

—5:16—

Paul concludes his teaching on the topic of widows with a final instruction concerning their provision. Verse 8 calls on men who are heads of households to provide care and protection for their widowed mothers and grandmothers. Some single or widowed women, however, enjoyed considerable means. He encourages them to step forward and adopt, as it were, a less fortunate widow. Paul, the seasoned minister, knows that ministry funds can be stretched only so far before programs lose their effectiveness. He would rather have a significant impact on a few people instead of giving a pittance to a multitude.

Application

Practical Help for the Helpless

Paul's teaching on the topic of widows, young and old, offers no less than four principles that can be applied to other groups of people in need.

First, *church charity is not a substitute for personal responsibility* (v. 4). Paul alludes to biblical and cultural principles that were so well-known to his readers that he doesn't bother to quote them. The Lord commanded parents to provide for their children in their youth (Prov. 19:14; 2 Cor. 12:14), and He commanded adult children to "honor" their parents (Ex. 20:12). As we have seen from the exposition of 1 Timothy 5:3–16, to "honor" someone includes financial provision for their needs. Therefore, children and grandchildren are to care for their widowed mother and not expect the church to relieve them of their personal responsibility.

In a broad sense, we must not rely on the church to do what we, as individuals, can and should do ourselves. We can work in cooperation with the church, but we need not wait on the church, and we must not blame the church for not taking action. If you see a need in the world, get busy!

Second, *suffering and grief do not automatically produce godliness* (vv. 5–6, 11–12). Paul worries that the deep pangs of grief suffered by younger widows and their need for provision will prompt them to sin rather than endure their anguish with patience and trust the Lord for help. Suffering merely offers us the opportunity to draw closer to the Lord and to experience spiritual growth, but we can just as easily attempt to shut off the pain through sin. That's why the members of God's family must minister to those who grieve, to help them fill the vacuum left by loss.

One effective means of meeting the needs of grieving believers is to mobilize volunteers through a training program designed to equip them for care. This is not psychological training or merely a lay counseling program, but a course in chaplaincy for the typical Christian.

Third, *the church cannot support everyone in need, nor should we expect it to* (vv. 9–10). The apostle carefully describes which widows should be added to "the list" and, just as important, which should not. Financial assistance, especially long-term care, must never be given indiscriminately. The community will always have more needs than the local assembly can meet; resources are limited. Therefore, the church must use discernment and respond wisely.

Many churches set aside a portion of their offering in a "benevolence fund," to be administered by a small committee of deacons and other trusted, seasoned members of the fellowship.

Fourth, *a full, active life is much more likely to remain godly than an idle, uninvolved one* (vv. 13–14). This can be taken to extremes, of course. Too busy a life can become a liability—a distraction to growth in godliness. Nevertheless, generally speaking, a house full of kids and a life engaged in conquering the demands of career tend to be much safer than an empty home with time on one's hands. If circumstances have left you with no one to care for and no aspirations, let me encourage you to invest yourself in something significant. The world is filled with needy people and causes that need champions. So, stay involved ... volunteer!

A Prescription for Pastoral Health (1 Timothy 5:17–25)

> ¹⁷The elders who rule well are to be considered worthy of double honor, especially those who work hard at preaching and teaching. ¹⁸For the Scripture says, "You shall not muzzle the ox while he is threshing," and "The laborer is worthy of his wages." ¹⁹Do not receive an accusation against an elder except on the basis of two or three witnesses. ²⁰Those who continue in sin, rebuke in the presence of all, so that the rest also will be fearful *of sinning.* ²¹I solemnly charge you in the presence of God and of Christ Jesus and of *His* chosen angels, to maintain these *principles* without bias, doing nothing in a *spirit of* partiality. ²²Do not lay hands upon anyone *too* hastily and thereby share *responsibility for* the sins of others; keep yourself free from sin.
>
> ²³No longer drink water *exclusively,* but use a little wine for the sake of your stomach and your frequent ailments.
>
> ²⁴The sins of some men are quite evident, going before them to judgment; for others, their *sins* follow after. ²⁵Likewise also, deeds that are good are quite evident, and those which are otherwise cannot be concealed.

"The elders who rule well are to be considered worthy of double honor." How true that is. Finding such a man, however, can be like panning for gold. I don't mean to compare people to silt; I merely desire to emphasize the need for keen observation. As a prospector swirls a slurry of river silt and water in his pan, he looks for the glint of tiny gold specks, usually no larger than the head of a pin. Similarly, men well-suited for spiritual leadership usually don't draw attention to themselves; they quietly and unobtrusively move among the congregation, serving and leading without fanfare. Precious and rare, they shine for brief moments, and no more, so it takes a trained eye to locate them and select them for leadership.

Paul spent much of his travels panning for gold. As he evangelized the Roman Empire between Antioch and Athens, founding churches and training leaders, he gradually added choice men to his entourage. He plucked Titus from his home base of Antioch (Gal. 2:1–3), Timothy from the city of Lystra (Acts 16:1–3), Tychicus from Ephesus or Colossae (Acts 20:4), Trophimus from Ephesus (Acts 21:29), and Gaius and Aristarchus from Macedonia (Acts 19:29), just to name a few. Then, near the end of his ministry, Paul deployed them in key churches to continue the work he had begun.

Now, having posted Timothy in the dizzying, distorted city of Ephesus, Paul encouraged his choice assistant to find other worthy men capable of "ruling well."

— 5:17–18 —

It's difficult to determine the difference between "overseers" (*episkopoi*) and "elders" (*presbyteroi*) in Paul's writings. He uses the terms interchangeably when listing their qualifications (3:1–7; Titus 1:5–9); both have a responsibility to "rule," and both should be able to teach and preach. Therefore, "overseers" and "elders" describe the same role within the church. And, like widows on "the list," they are to receive a stipend for their service.

Paul calls for a double honor, or twice the regular stipend, for elders who lead the affairs of the church effectively, and especially those who teach and preach. The literal Greek reads, "especially the hard-working ones in Word and teaching." The term "Word" (*logos*) in this context can mean only the exposition of the Scriptures. It artfully combines the common expression for the Bible with the expected meaning, "to speak publicly." Note that not all elders were responsible for the tasks of teaching and preaching. All should be able, but the responsibility to do it fell to some and not others.

To give added weight to his recommendation, Paul cites two Old Testament passages. Deuteronomy 25:4 had become an idiom by the first century, drawing on the ancient, familiar image of an ox dragging a threshing board over cut grain to separate the kernel from the husks. As the ox worked, it was allowed to eat some of the grain. Mosaic law declared this only fair (cf. 1 Cor. 9:9). If the farmer gains from the work of the ox, he should allow the animal to sustain itself.

Paul also quotes Jesus (Matt. 10:10; Luke 10:7), who had alluded to the Old Testament (Lev. 19:13; Deut. 24:15). Not even pagans would expect work from someone without paying a fair wage. Elders, especially those who bear the extra burden of teaching and preaching, provide a valuable service to the congregation, and they do this at the expense of earning a living elsewhere. If a church values excellent teaching, strong preaching, and spiritual leadership, the congregation should give its leaders sufficient financial provision to devote a normal work week to the church's ministries.

— **5:19** —

Most elders and/or pastors are worthy of their wages, but not all. Some begin well and then overshadow their great accomplishments by sinning in shocking, grandiose fashion. I am always saddened to hear about a fallen minister or elder. Nevertheless, it is a reality that all spiritual leaders inevitably encounter. Paul prepares Timothy for the inevitable with three specific recommendations:

- Investigate thoroughly (v. 19).
- Discipline publicly (v. 20).
- Administrate impartially (v. 21).

The primary concern for Paul — and all ministers who follow in his vocation — is the integrity of the church. Not merely its reputation, which is a PR concern. God commissions and empowers the church to be a conduit of His blessing, a

Artwork originally published in 1884 in *Earthly Footsteps of the Man of Galilee* by Bishop John H. Vincent, N.D. Thompson Publishing Co.

Ancient farmers used this crude, yet effective, method to separate kernels of grain from their husks. Oxen dragged a threshing board over cut stalks of grain. Muzzling the oxen kept them from eating the grain they helped to harvest, but the Lord considered this practice unworthy of His people (Deut. 25:4).

means of His grace, and a custodian of divine truth; therefore, it must remain pure. No one wants to drink water from a contaminated faucet, and no one trusts the Word of God to a polluted mouthpiece.

Investigate thoroughly. Paul's first recommendation protects the church from false accusations. Put bluntly, some churches are pastor killers. They have a habit of calling the very finest men and, for the first six months, behave like a model church. Then they turn. They don't want to be led; they want to lead. First, they doubt the leader they once hailed as their salvation and they start to question his ability to lead. When he remains steadfast, they undermine his authority by challenging his suitability to lead. Eventually, if he persists in telling them what they do not want to hear, they drum up a list of sins or seize on a convenient accusation to impugn his moral qualification to lead.

After a brutal bloodletting, they cycle through a few interim pastors before starting the cycle again. Pastor-killing churches rarely change. Thankfully, some do. Invariably, those who do, remove from their midst the leaders who contaminated the church with their carnality.

Timothy might have had a pocket of pastor killers in Ephesus. Paul wisely says, in effect, "Don't listen to every whim of criticism; investigate any accusation thoroughly to test its merit before taking any action." We must not interpret Paul's words too woodenly. He quotes Deuteronomy 19:15 (cf. Deut. 17:6) because that was the best standard of veracity in his day. In other words, we need not limit our investigation to eyewitness testimony. Other hard evidence may prove multiple witnesses to be mistaken or confirm the accusation of only one. In one tragic case I can recall, inappropriate emails between a staff member and his mistress exposed their sin.

— **5:20** —

Discipline publicly. The NASB rendering, "those who continue to sin," is not the best translation of the Greek text. It suggests that the instruction to follow applies only to ministers who refuse to repent and stubbornly persist in their sin. Paul uses a plural participle of the verb "to sin." The literal translation would be "the sinning ones" or "the sinners." Unlike church discipline applied to a member not in leadership (Matt. 18:15–17; 1 Cor. 5), repentance has no bearing on the censure of a pastor or elder. His repentance should be met with a plan for eventual restoration sometime in the distant future, but his ordination places the pastor or elder in a unique category within the church. His public stature and his purporting to

From My Journal

Admire Your Mentors, but Follow Christ Alone

Find worthy mentors and cultivate close relationships with them, but don't become a devotee of anyone but Christ.

The most disillusioning experience of my entire spiritual adolescence came when the man I admired and had devotedly followed ultimately drifted into a cultlike leader. It was a disillusioning experience, regaining my equilibrium after my faith nearly spun off its axis. But I learned a valuable lesson. I never should have placed anyone but the Lord at the center of my faith.

The church is full of great, godly men and women who will make wonderful mentors. Let some of them disciple you. Learn from them and imitate their positive qualities. But never allow anyone to become an earthly god—not unless you want everything you believe to come crashing down. You can rest assured that even the most godly mentors will occasionally disappoint you. Keep Christ—and Christ alone—in central focus. He never disappoints!

represent the Word of God require public censure by the church in an official and orderly manner.

Once a pastor or elder's guilt has been confirmed, he must be confronted with the evidence and given an opportunity to answer. Furthermore, he must be afforded the dignity of facing his accusers and reviewing the evidence against him. This is not a trial. Nevertheless, it is his opportunity to clear his name or accept responsibility for wrongdoing. Because the evidence should be conclusive in the first place, the primary purpose for the confrontation is to establish the man's guilt and inform him of the consequences. It is to be hoped that he will humbly offer a letter of resignation that acknowledges his sin and apologizes to the congregation. Regardless, Paul prescribes the next step.

The sinning pastor or elder must be "rebuked." Outside the New Testament, the Greek verb used here has a broad range of meanings, including "to shame," "to blame," "to expose," "to punish," "to condemn or convict," or "to resist." Strong words, each implying serious consequences. Within the New Testament, however, the term used in this particular construction[4] always means "to show people their sins and summon them to repentance."[5]

Furthermore, the rebuke must take place "before all" or "in the sight of all" in the local congregation. This is not to humiliate the individual—although shame is inevitable—but to remain transparent and truthful as a church. Dealing with particularly grievous sins in secretive, hushed tones, or back rooms brings the church under suspicion. An authentic church holds itself accountable in plain sight, even as it raises the standard of righteousness before a watching world.

— **5:21** —

Administrate impartially. Paul's charge to Timothy could not have been more sobering. He calls on every divine judge in the realm of heaven—the Father, the Son, and His divine messengers (Matt. 25:31; Mark 8:38; Luke 9:26; Rev. 14:10)—to hold the younger man accountable in one respect above all others: to remain utterly impartial when hearing and investigating accusations, discerning the truth of a matter, and then holding pastors and elders to a high standard of moral purity.

Paul does not specify a direct object for the verb *phylassō* ("to protect, watch, guard, care for, keep"). My literal, inelegant rendering would be, "I solemnly charge you ... in order that these you might guard ..." The definite reference of "these" remains ambiguous. Therefore, most translations insert "principles" (NASB), "commands" (NET), or "instructions" (NIV). Most likely, "these" refers to the duties outlined in verses 19 and 20. He expects Timothy to investigate thoroughly and, when necessary, discipline publicly without prejudice (lit., prejudging). He must not judge ahead of time or make up his mind before the fact. Nor should he carry out his duties with any particular leanings.

The most popular symbol of justice in Western court systems is a statue of the Roman goddess Justitia (known to the Greeks as *Dikē*, pronounced *dee-kay*). She wears a blindfold to avoid prejudice. She holds up a balance scale, ready to weigh evidence objectively. And she wields a sword in her right hand, ready to carry out justice. Paul solemnly charges Timothy to maintain these ideals of justice within the church.

— **5:22** —

To "lay hands" on someone in the context of ministry is to ordain and endorse that person to serve the congregation and to represent the church in an official capacity. Paul warns Timothy to avoid ordaining a man too quickly. This can be taken one of two ways. First, a church should not ordain a man without first seeing a consistent track record of maturity and integrity (cf. 3:6). Second, the church should not restore any fallen minister to any position without assurances that he has given sufficient time and attention to allow the Lord to reform his character.

While I favor the latter view, the principle is the same either way. We do not look for perfection in our elders or pastors. No man comes to the office without a sin-stained past. Paul himself has affirmed this (1:12 – 14). But has a fallen minister demonstrated consistent growth in maturity and integrity? Is he free from addictions, compulsions, moral and ethical corruption, or ugly habits? Does he remain accountable to some and transparent to all?

Paul warns that failure in due diligence will result in Timothy's "sharing" in the sin of others. The Greek word is *koinōneō*. We transliterate the noun form as *koinōnia*, a favorite New Testament word for the unique, supernatural bond of fellowship between Christians. Only in this case, Paul turns the term around. To ordain a man in haste, only to have him disgrace the church with his sin, is to share a bond of shame rather than joy. Moreover, apathetic leaders who think so little of the church as to ordain unworthy men become complicit in their sin.

Again, the church is a family. When a daughter chooses a mate to share in all in the rights, prerogatives, and privileges of her family, her relatives want to be certain the man can be trusted. The parents have invested years into rearing a daughter, nurturing, providing, protecting, spending hours in prevailing prayer. Naturally, her family hopes she will not rush into anything, but will give careful consideration and adequate time to knowing her future mate well before committing herself to him. After all, if he fails morally, the entire family suffers.

The older minister urges the younger man to keep himself "free from sin." The term actually means "ritually pure" or "ceremonially clean." In the Old Testament, a priest kept himself ritually undefiled and then observed cleansing rites to remain ceremonially pure. Otherwise, he could not fulfill his priestly duties of leading worship, sacrificing on behalf of the people, and teaching the Scriptures. Furthermore, the word order emphasizes "yourself" in the sentence, implying a sharp contrast from the previous warning.

I would render verse 22 this way: "Lay hands on no one hastily and [as a result] do not share in the sins of others — yourself keep pure."

—5:23—

I must be candid. The placement of this verse perplexes me! It reminds me of the time my wife and I sat down to enjoy a meal together in a restaurant in Massachusetts, where I noticed some decorative printing on the cover of the wine list. It read, "Drink no longer water, but use a little wine." Frankly, the words appear just as out-of-joint here as it did in that restaurant.

I am not alone in that feeling, apparently. Most of my commentaries struggle in vain to link this verse to the rest of the discussion. Many venture a speculation about the influence of ascetics and the possibility that Timothy had been avoiding wine so that criticism would not become a distraction. That may have been the case. Apart from an obvious — or even reasonable — tie-in with the argument, it's best to view this as a parenthetical comment, perhaps triggered by Paul's command to remain pure.

Timothy often became ill, apparently due to stomach problems. Paul writes, simply, "No longer water-drink." The single Greek verb combines the ideas of drinking and water. Translators insert "exclusively" (NASB) or "only" (NIV) because it's a reasonable interpretation, given the context. Nevertheless, Paul's prescription calls for Timothy to stop drinking water. While Ephesus boasted a rather sophisticated municipal water system, including cisterns for storage and a network of terracotta pipes for distribution, even a sewer system to flush waste out to sea, sanitation was undoubtedly not up to modern standards. Fermented wine in moderation, on the other hand, would have been safer to drink.

—5:24–25—

Paul concludes his advice on the administration of elders with a cautionary comment. His observation holds true for people in general, but it's offered here in the context of choosing elders, rewarding those who rule well and confronting those guilty of sin. Some men sin openly so that their true character will take no one by surprise at the final judgment. Others, however, project such an impressive, pious image that everyone will be shocked when the final judgment reveals all secrets.

Deeds, however, speak for themselves. Good deeds are just as evident as the sins of the open sinner, and evil deeds eventually find their way out of the shadows. We cannot see into a man's soul to assess his character; we can observe only deeds. A healthy spirit—one marked by maturity and integrity—cannot help but do good. Follow the trail of good deeds to their source, and you will have found a worthy elder.

In nearly fifty years of pastoral ministry, I recall few weak, unqualified elders or staff, and many faithful, qualified partners in ministry. But early in my vocation, I learned the inestimable worth of a truly excellent elder or pastor. Plan all the programs you want, fund all the ministries you can afford, dream all the great dreams you dare, but without the right people in leadership, those things will all come to nothing. But if you find an elder or staff member who leads well—a genuine, devoted follower of Christ and servant to the people—the work of the church will stay healthy and, in fact, flourish.

Application

Hope for Fallen Spiritual Leaders

One of the saddest days in the life of a senior pastor occurs when he must confront a fallen elder or a member of the pastoral staff who has disgraced himself (or herself) with sin. Because of his high-profile position of spiritual leadership, his case requires special handling. God has made Himself clear on the matter. The sin must be exposed and the guilty person reproved "in the presence of all, so that the rest also will be fearful of sinning" (v. 20). Lest that policy seem unnecessarily harsh—I have been tempted to bypass this part when removing a fallen minister from his position—we must keep three truths in mind.

First, *we must remember that the integrity of the entire church is at stake, not just the feelings of one person.* While I sometimes struggle to carry out this scriptural mandate, I have come to appreciate the wisdom in it. In the days following a terrible event like this, a somber quiet settles over the church congregation and the other ministers. Pastors reflect on the holiness of their calling as other ministers redouble their commitment to personal purity. Imagine the effect if the sin were simply brushed aside and the man quietly given his walking papers.

Second, *we must remember that the church has a responsibility to maintain a consistent example of obedience to God's Word.* Before experience taught me better, I thought the public rebuke of a ministry leader would shake the congregation's trust and fan the flames of suspicion in the surrounding community. On the contrary, everyone feels reassured. As shock and sadness wear off, a peaceful assurance of confidence settles in.

Third, *we must remember that the purpose for exercising church discipline is not to punish but to restore.* Paul's instruction in verse 22 allows for the reinstatement of the man after he has repented, reformed, and demonstrated a pattern of righteousness. While the church needs mature, godly leaders, it is held together and built up by grace.

I once supported a pastor friend as he faithfully carried out the public discipline of a once-trustworthy leader in his church. It was dreadful. The fallen leader had been a well-known Christian figure in the community, so his sin made the news. After the pastor rebuked his friend publicly and removed him from his leadership post, the man walked away from God. He remained angry with the Lord and bitter toward the church for several years. Then, he turned. He wrote a letter of apology to the church and admitted to his pastor friend, "You were right. I was in sin. You called me on it and, instead of repenting, I rebelled." He fully repented.

I'm glad to say the church received the man with open arms. In fact, they threw a party for the express purpose of welcoming their brother back into the fellowship. It was a wonderful evening of praise. And that made the news, too.

Responding Correctly to Authority (1 Timothy 6:1–6)

---

¹All who are under the yoke as slaves are to regard their own masters as worthy of all honor so that the name of God and *our* doctrine will not be spoken against. ²Those who have believers as their masters must not be disrespectful to them because they are brethren, but must serve them all the more, because those who partake of the benefit are believers and beloved. Teach and preach these *principles.*

³If anyone advocates a different doctrine and does not agree with sound words, those of our Lord Jesus Christ, and with the doctrine conforming to godliness, ⁴he is conceited *and* understands nothing; but he has a morbid interest in controversial questions and disputes about words, out of which arise envy, strife, abusive language, evil suspicions, ⁵and constant friction between men of depraved mind and deprived of the truth, who suppose that godliness is a means of gain. ⁶But godliness *actually* is a means of great gain when accompanied by contentment.

Everyone is subject to authority. Children have parents. Employees have bosses. Bosses have their superiors. Citizens have governments. Governments have checks and balances (I hope!). The wealthy have financial advisors. Even those few who have managed to rise above all human accountability must ultimately answer to God. Everyone answers to someone. Therefore, all people must come to terms with four fundamental truths:

First, *people do not naturally submit to authority*. Our sinful nature rebels when it doesn't get its way. Resistance feels a lot more gratifying than submission. The human heart, like cursed ground (Gen. 3:17–19), prefers weeds and resists cultivation. We are, by nature, independent, stubborn, self-reliant people who want to do things *our* way and in *our* time.

Second, *relationships with authority are usually complex and rarely painless*. Many of us have deep-seated resistance to authority stemming from painful experiences with someone who abused his or her authority. Their wounds left indelible scars that cannot be erased by platitudes and positive thinking. Moreover, a few brief encounters with divinely inspired truth will not suddenly make everything better. Supernatural transformation is needed, and that rarely happens instantaneously. Transformation is a process that God directs, but it requires our submission and goes smoother with our participation.

Third, *many in authority have not earned our respect*. I recall my days in the Marine Corps. I saluted a lot of high-ranking uniforms, but on some occasions I didn't salute the men inside them. I knew their lifestyles; I knew where they went and what they did off-base, during leave. And, to be completely candid, I saluted as a matter of survival. I didn't want to bear the consequences of insubordination.

You did not elect most of the people who hold authority over you. Let's face it; some don't even deserve their positions of power. In those cases, you would place other, more worthy people, in those positions. Unfortunately, that prerogative is not yours, so you must learn to live with it.

Fourth, *resisting authority is not always wrong*. Sometimes earthly authorities press subordinates to violate the laws of God. Acts 5:40–42 describes the attempts of the religious authorities in Jerusalem to suppress the gospel. They arrested and flogged the apostles, commanding them to remain silent. But "they kept right on teaching and preaching Jesus as the Christ" (v. 42).

Submitting to authority can sometimes be wrong. Nevertheless, we must use discernment when choosing passive resistance, active subversion, or outright rebellion against an ungodly authority.

The issue of authority under the rule of Rome in the first century presents Paul with a thorny theological problem. Slavery had become a centerpiece of Roman culture, both inside the capital city and throughout the empire. One respected author estimated that "there existed, in the time of Claudius, about twice as many provincials as there were citizens, of either sex, and of every age; and that the slaves were at least equal in number to the free inhabitants of the Roman world."[6] Because slaves were not chosen based on race, they looked indistinguishable from Romans in the capital city, so the senate considered a plan to make slaves easily identifiable at a glance. They decided against the plan because the slaves might see their superior numbers and feel confident in staging a revolt.

The believers in Ephesus spanned the cultural spectrum. Wealthy elites mingled with common folk. Men and women stood or sat together in worship. Intellectuals and workmen, new believers and elders, Jews and Gentiles, all embraced the gospel and became one people under the cross. This included slaves and perhaps even their owners. Paul, having addressed the topics of older men, younger men, older women, younger women, elders, widows, husbands, and wives, eventually comes to the unsettling issue of slaves. Unsettling from our point of view, at least. To the disappointment and confusion of many—in our day, not his—Paul did not set his sights on social reform, beginning with the abolition of slavery.

As a result, modern critics have accused him of giving tacit approval to the practice. Pro-slavery expositors in the American South even used his letters to argue against abolition. And I admit, my initial question was probably the same as yours: "So, why didn't Paul take a stronger stand and condemn slavery?" After giving that further thought, perhaps a better question would be, "How should a fledgling movement utterly opposed to human bondage begin to address such a formidable institution?"

Paul chose a uniquely Christian approach. It was so brilliant that it could have come only from God. In these six verses, Paul not only gives practical advice to slaves in the present, before the eventual undoing of slavery, he also advances the gospel as a means of world change. Activism can reform a society, but only when the time is ripe. Revolutions—the bloodless kind—begin with transformed hearts, which then transform institutions. And the results speak for themselves. Two thousand years later, Western societies—Christian in their origin—have rejected slavery. Today, even unbelievers give no quarter to the thought of human bondage.

Slavery is a relic of a more primitive history. Nevertheless, Paul's words to Timothy have much to teach us about authority and submission. No, we do not have masters. We do, however, have bosses, and government officials, and police officers, and parents, and church elders. The institutions have changed, but the challenges of authority and our love for autonomy remain the same.

The first six verses of chapter six can be divided into three distinct parts:

- submission to a non-Christian authority (v. 1)
- submission to a Christian authority (v. 2)
- submission to the authority of God's Word (vv. 3–6)

— 6:1 (Submission to a non-Christian Authority) —

The "yoke" was a powerful symbol of subjugation. Farmers laid a carved wooden beam across the shoulders of a beast of burden, cinched it tight with leather straps, and harnessed it to a plow or some other kind of implement. Teachers sometimes used the image to inspire students to submit to the difficult task of learning. In the context of slavery, however, the yoke illustrated dehumanizing servitude. Slaves were human tools, subject to the whims of their masters. Whereas citizens of the empire enjoyed remarkable protections and Roman subjects lived in relative harmony with their government, slaves had few rights.

Paul calls on slaves to "regard"—that is, "to lead, think, believe"—their owners "worthy of honor." This is to be a choice on the part of the slave, a decision sourced within his or her will. Regardless of outside circumstances, slaves are encouraged to alter their thinking to accept that their masters are better than they actually behave. The word for "honor" is the same as 5:3 and 5:17. Widows should receive honor, elders should receive "double honor," and the unbelieving slave owner should receive from their Christian slaves "all honor." In this case, of course, the honor is not monetary, but in the form of respect.

Take note of the apostle's reason for commanding this admittedly difficult attitude: to avoid giving influential non-Christians any reason to defame the Lord or to discredit the gospel. Subversion is not the answer; godly influence is the best means of undermining the practice of slavery. The institution of slavery may persist throughout the world, but if one's own master becomes a brother, then in a practical sense, the goal has been reached.

— 6:2 (Submission to a Christian Authority) —

This verse begins with the Greek contrasting conjunction *de* ("but"), turning from the issue of slaves with non-Christian masters to that of Christian slave owners. Paul's advice could be considered the most difficult to understand in the passage. One might expect him to have written, "Christian masters, do what is right and set your slaves free immediately!" But he didn't for at least three reasons.

SLAVERY IN THE ROMAN EMPIRE

By the time of Paul, slavery had been around a long time, dating back as far as recorded human history. But the Athenians and Romans had transformed the practice into a state-sponsored institution, complete with detailed legal codes, sophisticated economic procedures, and complex social customs. The institution of slavery in the Roman Empire, while sometimes brutal, bore little resemblance to the slavery of seventeenth, eighteenth, and nineteenth century England and America.

Slaves came under bondage in one of four primary ways:

(1) Prior to the death of Augustus and the end of Rome's foreign expansion, slaves were either captured in war or kidnapped by pirates and then sold at auction. Paul listed this kind of slavery, *andrapodistēs* or "man-stealing," among other detestable practices, such as sexual immorality, homosexuality, and perjury (cf. 1 Tim. 1:10; Ex 21:16).

(2) After the death of Augustus, breeding became the primary source of slavery. According to Roman law, children of enslaved women were bound to their masters as well.

(3) An extremely common means of escaping the hardscrabble life of freeborn poverty was to sell oneself into slavery. Many non-Romans chose voluntary indenture as a way to gain work skills, climb socially, earn citizenship after manumission — a reasonable expectation, according to Roman law — and even serve in public office. Many believe this had been the path chosen by Erastus (Rom. 16:23), the city manager of Corinth. (More on the rights of slaves in a moment.)

(4) A common method of dealing with an unwanted pregnancy was to bear the infant and then abandon him or her to the elements, a practice called "exposure." Infants found alive often were raised as slaves. Extremely poor parents might elect to sell their child into slavery instead — not for the money, necessarily, but as a crude form of adoption.

Roman law considered slaves to be property. A slave could be owned, traded, or sold like a beast of burden. A slave could not legally marry, bring a suit against someone in court, inherit property or money, or do anything without his or her master's consent. While slaves received more severe punishment for crimes than their freed counterparts, they did enjoy some legal protection from excessive abuse, not unlike our laws against animal cruelty. Enforcement, however, was inconsistent.

On the bright side, slaves could own property, which they legally controlled without interference from their masters. Some even acquired their own slaves, whom they sold for a profit. Slaves also could accumulate wealth and then use it to purchase their freedom, a common method of wiping out debt and reentering life with advanced social status.

Legally, slaves occupied a decidedly subordinate status in Roman society, but socially, they often rose to relatively high ranks. In fact, few could distinguish slaves from freeborn workers-for-hire, who carried out the same kinds of duties.

> In Greco-Roman households slaves served not only as cooks, cleaners, and personal attendants, but also as tutors of persons of all ages, physicians, nurses, close companions, and managers of the household. In the business world, slaves were not only janitors and delivery boys; they were managers of estates, shops, and ships, as well as salesmen and contracting agents. In the civil service slaves were not only used in street-paving and sewer-cleaning gangs, but also as administrators of funds and personnel and as executives with decision-making powers ... As such, in stark contrast to New World slavery in the 17th–19th centuries, Greco-Roman slavery functioned as a process rather than a permanent condition, as a temporary phase of life by means of which an outsider obtained a place within a society.[7]

Most slaves could expect to be freed by the age of thirty, or even sooner, as many owners set all their slaves free as a part of their final testaments.

First, *the circumstances of slavery varied.* Some slaves had been captured from conquered nations and sold on the block as chattel. Paul, reflecting Old Testament law (Ex. 21:16), expressly forbade this, counting "man-stealers" among other detestable sinners (1 Tim. 1:10). Many people sold themselves into slavery to pay off debt or accepted indenture in exchange for the assurance of room and board. Others bound themselves voluntarily to a family out of devotion (cf. Ex. 21:5 – 6). For Paul, the issue of submission didn't change based on the circumstances.

Second, *Paul addresses the issue from the slave's perspective, not the slave owner's.* Elsewhere, he commands believing slave owners to grant their slaves "justice and equality" (Col. 4:1;[8] Philem. 16), which essentially translates to freedom without unraveling any financial contracts that might exist. Note he does not characterize the slaves of a Christian master as "under the yoke," perhaps because he presupposed their fair treatment.

Third, *the topic here is submission to authority, not the morality of slavery.* Christian principles might revolutionize human institutions eventually, but not before changing their character first.

Paul calls slaves to offer their Christian masters respect and to serve them all the more, not to avoid punishment, but to accept the circumstance as an opportunity to love a brother. Service, after all, is the cornerstone of Christian virtue (Matt. 20:26 – 28; John 13:4 – 17). He says, in effect, "Use your position as an opportunity to shower a Christian brother with blessing. Do your work as a gift of service to a fellow believer."

— 6:3 – 5 (Submission to the Authority of God's Word) —

The issue of authority is a golden thread running through this entire section, beginning in 4:1. Throughout the section, Paul addresses the attitudes and responsibilities of a minister, who must exercise authority in regard to apostasy (4:1 – 6), the congregation at large (4:7 – 16), church members in error (5:1 – 2), widows (5:3 – 16), elders and pastors (5:17 – 25), and finally slaves (6:1 – 2). He has been clear that the pastor does not stand on his own authority, but on the bedrock truth of God's Word. All must submit to the authority of the original and pure teaching of the Lord Jesus Christ. In Paul's day, believers received this teaching from the apostles, the Lord's appointed emissaries, both verbally and in writing; today we have God-breathed words preserved for us in the sixty-six books of the Bible.

Paul strongly condemns anyone who teaches something contrary to this orthodox teaching of Christ. The Greek word is a compound of *heteros* ("different, another, foreign") and *didaskō* ("to teach"). Paul has used the phrases "sound words" and "sound teaching/doctrine" (1:10; 4:6; 2 Tim. 4:3; Titus 1:9, 13; 2:1, 2) in a technical sense to mean "orthodox teaching from Christ through the apostles." Here he is not referring to someone who merely differs from the pastor on a minor point of doctrine, or even one who advocates a different ministry method. Paul has in mind someone who has strayed from God's Word in forming his or her beliefs. One test for sound doctrine is its conformity to godliness. If someone's doctrine does not lead to good deeds, then it fails the first test of orthodoxy.

The apostle doesn't mince his words in describing those who do not submit to the authority of Scripture. He names three negative characteristics and five church-killing effects of their influence.

Those who reject the authority of Scripture are "conceited." This is the same term Paul uses of a new convert given too much authority too quickly (3:6). The word means "wrapped in smoke" or "head-in-the-clouds," describing someone whose lofty view of himself and his own ideas towers above everything and everyone else.

Despite the heretic's lofty view of himself, he "understands nothing." We transliterate the Greek term used here (*epistamai*) to form our word "epistemology," which is the study of knowledge. It refers to knowledge gained through formal education and personal study. Paul uses the participle form, which would translate literally: "he's a know-nothing."

Paul's use of Greek (the rare and dramatic contrasting conjunction, *alla*) highlights the irony of a conceited know-nothing trying to unravel the mysteries of philosophy. "Controversial questions" translates a word meaning "philosophical investigation," for which Ephesus had become renowned. "Disputes about words" comes from a rare compound word meaning (lit.) "word-fight." One Greek satirist described the debate between Stoics and Epicureans as a "word-fight,"[9] deliberately using the term to make them look silly.

The apostle lists five church-killing effects of a heretic's activities, many of which he elsewhere included among the worst qualities of depraved humanity (cf. Rom. 1:29). The fifth, and most serious, tears Christian unity into pieces. The issues at the core of their "constant friction" have changed over the years, but these depraved, ignorant men have a singular motive behind their word-fighting and philosophical prattle: personal, monetary gain. These arrogant know-nothings plagued the church in Ephesus, and Crete (Titus 1:11), and Corinth (2 Cor. 2:17), and Macedonia (1 Thess. 2:5), and virtually every church in the first century (2 Peter 2:14; Jude 16). Make no mistake: they continue today in the form of smarmy prosperity prophets and smiling peddlers of health-and-wealth greed ... all done under religious guise.

Such false teachers do not recognize the authority of Scripture; instead, they conform God's Word to support their own self-serving theological perversions. Moreover, they avoid accountability to others at all costs because they are an authority unto themselves, and we can be sure they have something to hide.

— **6:6** —

Ironically, genuine godliness (the same word is found 2:2, 10; 3:16; 4:7–8, 6:11) does lead to great gain. Although Paul does not have making a financial profit in mind, I don't think he means to exclude material wealth or to focus on intangible blessings only. He merely highlights the essential quality of "contentment." Thayer defines the Greek term as "a perfect condition of life, in which no aid or support is needed."[10] Colton wrote, "True contentment depends not upon what we have; a tub was large enough for Diogenes, but a world was too little for Alexander."[11] The issue is attitude, not circumstances (Phil. 4:11).

In 1852, Harriet Beecher Stowe published a book that many believe sparked the abolitionist movement in the United States. *Uncle Tom's Cabin* told the story of a longsuffering slave "sold down the river" to a despicably cruel master, Simon Legree. When Tom refused to whip a fellow slave, Legree resolved to beat his faith in Christ out of him. Tom almost succumbed to his master's cruelty, but a vision of Jesus strengthened his resolve. His contentment despite the brutal conditions prompted Legree to beat him all the more.

> But the blows fell only on the outer man and not, as before, on the heart. Tom stood perfectly submissive; and yet Legree could not hide from himself that his power over his bond thrall was somehow gone. And, as Tom disappeared in his cabin, and he wheeled his horse suddenly round, there passed through his mind one of those vivid flashes that often send the lightning of conscience across the dark and wicked soul. He understood full well that it was God who was standing between him and his victim, and he blasphemed him. That submissive and silent man, whom taunts, nor threats, nor stripes, nor cruelties, could disturb, roused a voice within him.[12]

We will forever be tormented by the injustice of the world and the unworthiness of our authorities until we come to terms with our predicament. We live in a world dominated by evil, and those without Christ *cannot* be Christlike. Even if they try with their whole heart, it's impossible. They need Christ! Nevertheless, we have been given a genuine stake in God's plan to change the world. Activism and resistance have their places and times, but until enough hearts are transformed, little can change. In the meantime, the Lord calls us—actually, He *commands* us—to submit to authorities (godless though they may be) so that we might leave them no reason to question our faith or doubt our God.

Application

At Your Service

Slavery is not the norm these days, at least not the brutal kind experienced in the first century. Nevertheless, the principles outlined by Paul do have application for anyone drawing a paycheck. So, let me note just two and then suggest ways to apply them specifically in the workplace.

First, *submission to authority at work is our best means of evangelism.* Perhaps you work for a non-Christian employer and you answer to a nonbeliever. Furthermore, you find that as a Christian you would make different decisions or adopt a different leadership style. But you're not in charge, and no one has asked for your opinions or suggestions. Therefore, as long as you have not been asked to do something illegal or immoral, you should do as you're told, and do it with a positive attitude "so that the name of God and our doctrine will not be spoken against" (6:1).

Too many Christians view their work primarily as the place to do evangelism. Too many Christians have the idea that our basic assignment on the job is to present the gospel to everyone on the payroll. Inevitably, they earn a poor reputation as a distraction, and instead of bringing glory to the name of Christ, they bring reproach.

Naturally, we want to introduce others to Christ and to offer them good news. That's our driving force and our hope of glory. If, however, we are hired out to do a job, then as a matter of integrity, we need to do it with diligence and excellence. Then, amazingly, our faithfulness and integrity earn unexpected opportunities to make Christ known to coworkers and even supervisors. In other words, when we are working for a non-Christian superior, let's leave him or her no reason to question our faith, no reason to wonder if our belief in Christ will be a hindrance to accomplishing company goals.

Second, *Christian supervisors deserve our submission just as much, if not more than, non-Christian bosses.* The Babylonian Talmud[13] quips, "Whenever [a Hebrew] acquires a Hebrew slave he acquires a master" (*Qiddushin* 22a). Paul notes the same tendency among Christians, which survives today. The likelihood of unfairness and the fear of mistreatment keep us on our toes in the dog-eat-dog world of secular employment, so with less fear, some believers take advantage of their boss's patience and goodwill. Believers often choose to work for other believers because they share the same basic values, they play by the same rulebook, and they answer to the same God. Consequently, when some believers work for Christian organizations, they tend to relax their work ethic, they watch the clock, or they expect special favors.

Paul encourages believing slaves of Christian owners to "serve them all the more" (6:2). Without fear of unfairness as a negative motivation, Christians have the opportunity to pursue a wonderfully positive motivation: love for fellow believers. Why not work all the more diligently to benefit a brother or sister in Christ?

At the same time, however, Christian employers need to keep their expectations reasonable and fair. Some believers take advantage of Christian employees, appealing to their mutual faith and holding them to a higher standard of conduct and performance than for non-Christians. So, the idea of respect works both ways.

The Missteps of Malcontent Ministers (1 Timothy 6:7–10)

> [7]For we have brought nothing into the world, so we cannot take anything out of it either. [8]If we have food and covering, with these we shall be content. [9]But those who want to get rich fall into temptation and a snare and many foolish and harmful desires which plunge men into ruin and destruction. [10]For the love of money is a root of all sorts of evil, and some by longing for it have wandered away from the faith and pierced themselves with many griefs.

There's a fine line between contentment and complacency. Merriam-Webster's definitions are telling:

> Contented: "feeling or showing satisfaction with one's possessions, status, or situation."
> Complacency: "self-satisfaction, esp. when accompanied by unawareness of actual dangers or deficiencies."

Both find rest. Both experience satisfaction. Both enjoy their status in life. Two crucial differences, however, separate them. First, whereas contentment thanks God for everything, complacency congratulates self. Second, whereas complacency rests on its accomplishments, contentment passionately pursues excellence. Paul enjoyed contentment in every circumstance (Phil. 4:11–12), yet he refused to remain idle or become passively indifferent. Take note of his restless striving to know Christ:

More than that, I count all things to be loss in view of the surpassing value of knowing Christ Jesus my Lord, for whom I have suffered the loss of all things, and count them but rubbish so that I may gain Christ, and may be found in Him, not having a righteousness of my own derived from the Law, but that which is through faith in Christ, the righteousness which comes from God on the basis of faith, that I may know Him and the power of His resurrection and the fellowship of His sufferings, being conformed to His death; in order that I may attain to the resurrection from the dead. (Phil. 3:8–11)

No complacency there! The healthy Christian life doesn't waste time on self-satisfaction. On the contrary, Paul considered this contented striving the mark of a successful minister. Toward the end of his first letter to Timothy, he encourages the younger pastor to find contentment in Christ rather than in the world (6:7–10), to let that satisfaction fuel his striving for excellence (6:11–16), and then to reproduce his contented striving in others (6:17–19). This is the joy at the core of Christian ministry.

Many people in ministry never experience this joy. They pursue a different path because they lack contentment. Paul's description of these ministerial misfits actually begins with verse 3, where he landed with both feet on false teachers who "advocate a different doctrine" — conceited, know-nothing men who dally in empty philosophies for the sake of material gain. True godliness, according to this seasoned minister, turns away from material gain in the temporal dimension to seek spiritual gain in the eternal (v. 6). This is genuine contentment and the foundation on which a believer builds a joyful life. Kenneth Wuest writes, "Paul's teaching here is that the possession of a godly piety makes a person independent of outward circumstances, and self-sufficient, enabling him to maintain a spiritual equilibrium in the midst of both favorable circumstances and those which are adverse."[14]

In 6:7–10, Paul defends his point of view and explains how a minister — and any Christian — who lacks contentment will eventually pursue his own destruction. He says, in effect, "Show me an individual who enters ministry for what he or she is going to get out of it, and I'll show you a shipwreck waiting to happen."

— **6:7–8** —

The Talmud observes, "Man is born with his hands clenched; he dies with his hands wide open. Entering life he desires to grasp everything; leaving the world, all that he possessed has slipped away."[15] Job said, "Naked I came from my mother's womb, and naked I shall return there" (Job 1:21). Solomon wrote, "As he had come naked from his mother's womb, so will he return as he came. He will take nothing from the fruit of his labor that he can carry in his hand" (Eccl. 5:15). A more recent sage quipped, "You'll never see a hearse pulling a U-Haul."

Paul defends his definition of contentment by accepting an undeniable truth. Everything material is fleeting. Material wealth has value; it helps us sustain life and accomplish good while on earth, but it's temporary nonetheless. He mentions "food and covering," an unusual choice of terms undoubtedly intended to emphasize the basic functions of clothing and shelter.

A contented attitude gratefully receives the basic necessities of life instead of demanding steak and chateaubriand or designer clothing or a 55-foot yacht or a nine-bedroom home with a seventeen-mile driveway in Monterey. This is not to suggest that one shouldn't have those things if he can afford them, only that they shouldn't be expected or demanded. Furthermore, people who expect these things will never experience contentment.

— 6:9 —

Paul chooses his words carefully as the Holy Spirit supernaturally steers his mind. Note he does not write, "Those who are rich fall into temptation …" The Bible never condemns the rich for their abundance. God never calls money or wealth evil. Again, contentment has nothing to do with circumstances and everything to do with attitude. The fundamental question is not, "What do you have?" but "What do you *want?*"

The apostle could have chosen one of two Greek terms for "want," *thelō* or *boulomai.* By the time of the New Testament, *thelō* had become more common and was the stronger of the two, so that *thelō* indicates the *exercise* of the will, while *boulomai* describes its natural *tendency.* Paul's word choice suggests that humanity naturally tends to pursue material wealth, so an individual must exercise his or her will to choose otherwise. Those who follow their inclinations toward temporal comforts fall into a four-step decline.

Step 1: "Temptation." The Greek noun for "temptation" is based on the verb meaning "to test, attempt, examine." The idea of temptation is to determine the true nature of something by putting it to the test. Temptations try men's souls and frequently prove them weak. Therefore, the Bible doesn't command us to resist temptation; it instructs us to *flee* temptation (1 Cor. 6:18; 10:14; 2 Tim. 2:22). People with an unchecked desire for greater wealth or more money will find themselves facing one moral dilemma after another until they finally succumb.

Step 2: "A snare." The term *pagis* has the straightforward meaning, "trap." In Greek literature, the Trojan Horse was called a wooden *pagis.*[16] Just as one lie leads to a web of lies, so one compromise leads to the wholesale loss of integrity, bit by bit.

Step 3: "Foolish and harmful desires." The Greek term translated "foolish" is the word for "mind" or "think" with the negative prefix, *a-*. Literally, it's "non-thinking." "Desires" is better rendered "passions" or "lusts." Secular Greek uses the term most often in conjunction with food or sex. Again, Paul emphasizes the desires, not the things pursued. *Anything* pursued for the wrong reasons leads to immediate gratification followed by a more desperate longing than before. Non-thinking passions lead to treacherous destinations.

Step 4: "Ruin and destruction." These two terms picture corruption or internal corrosion, followed by utter destruction. The New Testament frequently uses the latter word to mean eternal damnation (Matt. 7:13; John 17:12; Rom. 9:22; Phil. 1:28; 2 Thess. 2:3; 2 Peter 2:1; Rev. 17:8, 11).

— **6:10** —

In perhaps the most misquoted verse in the New Testament, Paul gives the reason for the four-step descent into eternal destruction: the *love* of money. Not money itself, but an attitude described by a compound Greek word that means (lit.) "love-for-silver." The excessive desire to build wealth is the taproot that feeds an endless network of evil.

The love of money eventually causes a person to exchange his or her faith in a limitless, loving God to seek satisfaction and safety in wealth. This, in turn, leaves the hapless victim open to "many griefs." Health fails. Contentment flees. Marriages come unraveled. Children rebel. Addictions take over. Economic collapse happens. Desperation follows. The word order in this sentence places emphasis on the pronoun "themselves." The unwise choices of people cause their many sorrows, beginning with the haphazard decision to love the wrong objects. Therefore, in the end, they have only themselves to blame.

While Paul's sober warning applies to all believers, he directs these words to Timothy in regard to ministry. Those who "advocate a different doctrine" (v. 3) do so to justify their pursuit of wealth and creature comforts because they lack contentment (vv. 5–6). Consequently, they abandon the faith in pursuit of temporal satisfaction, and they suffer for their foolishness. The lesson: malcontented ministers are a dangerous lot.

Like you, perhaps, I have encountered my share of joyless ministers. Many Christian workers slump around with basset hound eyes and rounded shoulders, bemoaning the burdens of ministry. Unfortunately, they do more harm than good among God's people. My advice? They should find another vocation as soon as possible. Vocational Christian service, like everything in life, has its ups and its downs, but if you have answered a genuine call of God, nothing will give you greater satisfaction. In fact, I offer a simple test when people tell me they're considering ministry as a vocation — and I mean this in all sincerity. I urge them, "If you can be happy doing anything else, do *that*." In my experience, those who have been called of God *know* they will never find contentment in any other pursuit.

Application

Contentment, and How to Miss It

Our fast-paced, consumer-oriented culture would have us believe that contentment is the cardinal sin of capitalism. Few products are built to last because, in just a couple of years, they will be obsolete, which keeps marketing gurus working overtime to convince us that we desperately need the latest updates. Don't get me wrong; I'll take capitalism over communism any day, and there's nothing wrong with product improvement. The problem is not on the supply side of the consumer equation; it's on the demand side. It's not up to Madison Avenue to tell us what will make us happy; that's our own, independent responsibility.

The truth is, we will never find happiness in the acquisition of more, more, more. On the contrary, contentment is not something we find; it's something we *decide*. And when we make the choice to be content, we receive three priceless gifts.

First, *current enjoyment instead of constant striving.* At some point in the past, you decided that the acquisition of what you have today would be fulfilling. When you choose contentment, it is! But if you are always seeking fulfillment from the future, you will never find it, you will never be satisfied, you will never enjoy what you have. Enough will never be enough.

Second, *complete freedom to recognize and applaud another's achievement without envy.* When I choose to enjoy what I currently have, envy finds no place in my life. As a result, I multiply my joy. I'm happy with my own lot in life and I genuinely delight in the good fortune of those around me. Furthermore, when I choose contentment, I never view the advancement of another as something taken from me. Contentment drains the fuel from my tank of competition, allowing me to rejoice with those who rejoice.

Third, *the cultivation of a genuinely grateful spirit.* When we choose contentment, anything we receive in the future becomes an unexpected gift. This allows us to live in a constant state of surprise, finding delight in the smallest of blessings.

For those who prefer continual dissatisfaction and constant unrest, let me offer three sure-fire ways to avoid contentment.

First, *decide to make something essential beyond the need for food, clothing, and shelter.* That doesn't mean you can't desire more and then set out to acquire more.

There's nothing wrong with wanting to improve your lot. But beware the gradual shift in perspective. When you begin to perceive something other than food, clothing, or shelter as essential, you become its slave.

Second, *decide to make increased income the primary focus of your vocation.* If you begin to base career decisions on the prospect of increasing your income, you will become ineffective in your current vocation. Your decreasing income will reflect that ineffectiveness, pushing contentment just that much further out of reach.

Third, *decide to devote more energy to keeping money and possessions instead of releasing them.* When you look for opportunities to give away money or property to feed, clothe, or shelter those who lack these essentials, contentment becomes an easy decision. But the tighter you clutch your possessions, the greater hold they have on you.

To express all of this more positively, I encourage you to adopt three short statements and then resolve to make them true:

- I'm grateful for what I have.
- I'm satisfied with what I earn.
- I'm generous to those in need.

Clear Commandments of Godliness (1 Timothy 6:11–19)

---

[11]But flee from these things, you man of God, and pursue righteousness, godliness, faith, love, perseverance *and* gentleness. [12]Fight the good fight of faith; take hold of the eternal life to which you were called, and you made the good confession in the presence of many witnesses. [13]I charge you in the presence of God, who gives life to all things, and of Christ Jesus, who testified the good confession before Pontius Pilate, [14]that you keep the commandment without stain or reproach until the appearing of our Lord Jesus Christ, [15]which He will bring about at the proper time — He who is the blessed and only Sovereign, the King of kings and Lord of lords, [16]who alone possesses immortality and dwells in unapproachable light, whom no man has seen or can see. To Him *be* honor and eternal dominion! Amen.

[17]Instruct those who are rich in this present world not to be conceited or to fix their hope on the uncertainty of riches, but on God, who richly supplies us with all things to enjoy. [18]*Instruct them* to do good, to be rich in good works, to be generous and ready to share, [19]storing up for themselves the treasure of a good foundation for the future, so that they may take hold of that which is life indeed.

You may not have thought of it this way before, but there are two kinds of road signs. Some offer helpful advice or general principles. For example, "Watch for Ice on Bridge," "School Zone," or "Pass with Care." In response, the driver must observe the circumstances, draw on his or her experience, make appropriate decisions, and then apply the sign's principle accordingly. In a matter of moments, the driver must account for the season, the weather, the time of day, or the traffic conditions, and then having done so, exercise wisdom.

Other signs don't require any complex reasoning. They declare hard-and-fast rules and demand unquestioning obedience. "Speed Limit 45." "Do Not Enter." "Stop." You simply do as the sign instructs or a law enforcement officer will give you a little added incentive to help you remember the next time.

Scripture is much like that. Generally speaking, the Bible offers two kinds of instruction: principles and precepts. Principles are *nonspecific and require wisdom* to apply. The Lord gives us principles to prepare us for the ever-changing landscape of culture and a variety of circumstances. Principles equip us to behave wisely in a broad spectrum of situations. For example, Philippians 2:3 calls for Christians to "do nothing from selfishness or empty conceit, but with humility of mind regard one another as more important than yourselves." We're not told specifically where humility stops and pride starts. We must discern how to behave unselfishly when we find ourselves in any given situation.

Precepts, on the other hand, are *specific and require little if any thinking* to apply. God expects us to obey precepts, no questions asked. First Thessalonians 4:3 is a good example: "Abstain from sexual immorality." That doesn't require much interpretation. You don't have to observe the conditions and then adapt your response. Rather, simply avoid all circumstances that might make sexual immorality available. Furthermore, whenever sexual immorality presents itself, follow the example of Joseph, the Old Testament patriarch. *Run!* (Gen. 39:12).

Throughout this section, Paul has given Timothy several principles to apply concerning authority (6:1 – 2), false teachers (6:3 – 6), and contentment (6:7 – 10). Then, suddenly, his tone changes. He aims his pen directly at Timothy and fires off several precepts. The Greek verbs change from the more common "indicative mood" to the relatively rare "imperative mood."[17]

While Paul issues these specifically for Timothy, the Holy Spirit intends them for all believers in all circumstances, and especially for all ministers of the gospel. Whatever your circumstance, wherever you serve in God's kingdom, whether you are a vocational minister or a volunteer, read the passage again slowly. Only this time, imagine your shoulders gripped by Paul's battle-scarred hands—gnarled from beatings and hardened by weather. Imagine his eyes, flashing with keen intellect yet softened by suffering, staring intently into yours. These commands—these precepts—are for you and for me.

—6:11—

The Greek language uses word order as a means of emphasis. In this case, Paul marks a dramatic shift in tone by placing the personal pronoun "you" at the front of the sentence. This sets Timothy apart from the faithless, apostate teachers described in 6:3–10. Paul further emphasizes Timothy as his intended target with the vocative expression, "O man of God" (lit.), a familiar Old Testament title reserved for prophets. He writes, in effect, "But *you*—O man of God, unlike those who are not—you don't advocate a different doctrine (6:3), you understand what God says (6:4), you don't use the role of minister as a means of getting rich (6:5), you *are* content with God's provision (6:6–8). Unlike those who pursue self-serving ministry to their own destruction, *flee!*"

The first of Paul's commands uses the Greek verb *pheugō*, from which we derive the English word "fugitive." He commands Timothy to become, as it were, a fugitive. He is to flee "these things," a common Greek phrase intended to encapsulate everything an author had just expressed. In this case, "these things" refers to everything related to apostate or misguided ministers: their motivation, their ignorance, their behavior, and especially their fate.

Paul goes on to command Timothy to "pursue" something else instead. In a clever bit of wordplay, he chooses a verb frequently used to describe the role of a persecutor or pursuer on the trail of a fugitive. It carries the idea of becoming a dogged, relentless hunter in search of something. He then places six things on Timothy's list of prey:

- *righteousness*, a state of the heart and mind that operates in harmony with the mind of God as expressed in His Word
- *godliness*, the authentic and abiding desire to glorify God through every thought, every reaction, every word, and every deed
- *faith*, resting in God's promise to provide, protect, empower, and guide; choosing to be content with what the Lord provides, directs, or permits
- *love*, seeking the highest, greatest good of other people, especially those a minister has been called to serve
- *perseverance*, a deliberate, steadfast obedience despite pressures, difficulties, or temptations
- *gentleness*, a controlled, confident, firm strength that offers reassurance to weak or wounded people

— 6:12 —

Paul's third command, "fight," sounds antagonistic, especially after condemning the behavior of false teachers. Unlike 1:18, which reads (lit.) "war the good warfare," this command uses the Greek verb *agōnizomai*, from which we get our word "agony." This has more to do with athletic struggle than warlike conflict. The enemy is the event itself, over which the competitor must agonize to win. In this case, the event is faith. Faith is an endurance race that tests the runner's determination to keep going, despite the cry of every cell in his body to slacken or to quit.

In a fourth imperative, the apostle commanded Timothy to "seize upon" or "grasp" eternal life, not because it might slip away or because obtaining eternal life depends on his effort. Unlike the earlier imperative verbs, which are present tense describing continual action — keep on fleeing, keep on pursuing, keep on fighting — "take hold" uses a tense that implies culmination. He urges the younger minister to grab eternal life and hold it tightly because it belongs to him. He assures Timothy that he has agonized in a competition he is predestined to win; the trophy called "eternal life" has his name permanently engraved on it before the starting gun sounded.

Two clauses modify the phrase "eternal life."

The first, "to which you were called," uses what linguists call a "divine passive" because it strongly suggests that God did the calling. This clause reminds Timothy that the Lord has called him to receive eternal life and that God's decrees never fail. The second, "[to which] you made the good confession," reminds Timothy that he acknowledged the Lord's calling him to eternal life by claiming the gospel publicly, probably at his baptism. These two clauses add both the assurance of victory and the gravity of an oath to Timothy's endurance race called "faith."

— 6:13–14 —

Paul follows his four imperatives — flee, pursue, fight, take hold — with a solemn charge (cf. 5:21; 2 Tim. 4:1): "keep the commandment." In Greek, when no specific edict has been described, the term rendered "commandment" usually refers to a government official's appointment or a soldier's commission. Therefore, in this context, "guard the commission" makes the best sense. Furthermore, Paul's other charges (cf. 1:18–19; 5:21) appear to have the pastor's role in view rather than one specific duty.

It has been my observation that when people in ministry compromise their calling by pursuing sin, they bring "stain" and "reproach" on themselves, the family, the church, the vocation of ministry, and even the name of their Savior. As a result, something is lost that is seldom regained. A congregation's trust hangs on a thin wire, so a pastor's sin not only undermines their confidence in the gospel, it makes the job of other ministers so much more difficult.

The apostle reminds his protégé that he stands on divine authority in issuing this charge. He speaks on behalf of God the Father, to whom everyone owes his or her life, and God the Son, who became the pastor's ultimate example when He stood before Pontius Pilate. Note the link between the "good confession" of Timothy and that of Jesus. The expression "good confession" is probably an idiom for one's public declaration of the gospel (cf. 2 Cor. 9:13), especially on the pain of death. Pastors must follow the example of Christ when He declared divine truth before a hostile audience, regardless of the consequences.

—6:15–16—

On a future day declared perfect by the Father, the Son will return to earth. Not spiritually. Not metaphorically. Not in reincarnation. Not in dreams or visions. And not in the form of any other man or beast. He will return bodily, in person. When He does return, it will not be as the lowly lamb destined for sacrifice, but as the warring lion reclaiming His throne from evil (Rev. 5:5; 17:14). While the custom of many empires has been to call their rulers "king of kings," the Old Testament reserves this title for God (Deut. 10:17; Ps. 136:2–3). Nevertheless, Christ shares the title as the Son of God, the only man worthy to bear it (Rev. 17:14; 19:16).

Paul can barely contain his excitement at the thought of the Lord's return to exercise complete dominion over all creation in person. This, after all, is the consummation of ministry. Pastors merely fill the role of undershepherd during the Lord's physical absence from the earth. Pastors and all ministers work together in various capacities to establish God's kingdom in the hearts of men and women in advance of His Son's coming in person, yet with limited success. Our job will not be complete until the Lord comes to complete it Himself.

The thought of this thrills the apostle, which he expresses in a great closing hymn to God, which, of course, includes Father, Son, and Holy Spirit. He is immortal; He cannot cease to be (1:17). He dwells in "light," a literary archetype for truth (1 John 1:5). And no human has ever seen God, except in the person of Jesus Christ, who is God in human flesh (John 1:14, 18).

—6:17—

As Paul draws his letter to a close, he returns to the topic of temporal wealth. He forcefully warns Timothy to remain content with God's provision and protection and to avoid the futile pursuit of wealth. Discontent and ministry cannot coexist in a minister's heart without soon leading to trouble. This is not to suggest that money is bad, however, or that all wealthy people have been corrupted by it. On the contrary, for those who work hard and are fortunate enough to receive material abundance, I say, "Praise the Lord!"

Throughout my years in ministry, I have been humbled by the unselfish generosity of wealthy Christians, who see their monetary fortunes mainly as a means of advancing God's work around the globe. More than once, someone has handed me a seven-figure check made out to a Christian organization, a church, or a school on the condition that I keep the giver's name confidential. These godly, openhanded people didn't want any reward except the pleasure of their heavenly Father.

Money is not evil, and not all people allow money to corrupt them. But the potential remains. Therefore, Paul issues four imperatives, two negative (v. 17) and two positive (vv. 18 – 19).

First, *don't be conceited.* Reject the notion that talent and hard work necessarily reap financial rewards. They don't. Smart, hard-working, honest people apply themselves with diligence and wisdom, day in and day out, only to suffer constant financial setbacks. They struggle against a world that rewards evil and punishes good, more often than not. By contrast, many people with relatively little talent put in fewer hours and find great monetary success.

Wealthy people must neither believe their efforts are solely responsible for their riches, nor see the misfortune of others as a reflection of God's attitude toward them. The Lord sovereignly gives to each person whatever is needed to cultivate a heart of righteousness.

Second, *don't fix your hope on the uncertainty of riches.* When you're out of money—and trust me, I've been there!—the world feels horrifically unsafe, like walking through a gauntlet of tricks and traps, just waiting to knock you unconscious or bring you to your end. And when you have an ample monetary cushion, you feel more secure. Those are good reasons to plan well and to sacrifice what you must to maintain a savings account. We exercise discipline, however, and rise above our natural inclinations. We must never look to money as the source our security. Money can be the means of God's provision and protection, but it is only one. He is our safety and our strength (Ps. 91) . . . and He never runs out of surprises.

— **6:18–19** —

Having issued two "don'ts," the apostle encourages the wealthy (through Timothy) with two positive imperatives. First, *become rich in good works.* Paul draws on the same banking imagery Jesus used in His sermons.

> Do not store up for yourselves treasures on earth, where moth and rust destroy, and where thieves break in and steal. But store up for yourselves treasures in heaven, where neither moth nor rust destroys, and where thieves do not break in or steal; for where your treasure is, there your heart will be also. (Matt. 6:19–21)

Second, *be generous and ready to share.* After all, we can afford it! We have God as our advocate, not a bank account. He can easily replenish a dwindling portfolio.

The banking analogy used by Jesus and Paul doesn't teach that doing good deeds will earn protection, either directly nor indirectly. They don't suggest that a bankroll of good works stored up in heaven will offer the same or even better protection from harm on earth. The kingdom of God is not an emergency savings plan; it's an investment opportunity. We are invited to cast all that we are and all that we own into the Lord's grand venture, and as full partners, we have complete access to everything that belongs to Him.

Beginning with the words, "But you, O man of God . . ." (lit. rendered), Paul has intended to cut Timothy loose from the entanglements of people-pleasing worries and temporal concerns. A pastor cannot effectively preach or teach, admonish or lead if he lives in constant fear of a resentful congregation cutting off his income. On the contrary, "the blessed and only Sovereign" will see to the health and sustenance of His servants. Therefore, ministers must rest in the contentment of His provision, not the church salary, and must faithfully guard their commissions "without stain or reproach until the appearing of our Lord Jesus Christ" (v. 14).

Application

Trust and Obey

In the New Testament, God's precepts are fewer in number than His principles. That's a huge change from the old covenant. Nevertheless, He has issued several that we dare not overlook. Here are four truths to keep in mind as you keep your eyes open for them.

First, *commands are usually brief, simple, and clear.* The Lord doesn't disguise His will; He makes His commands easy to find and simple to follow.

Second, *commands call for one response: obedience.* Unlike principles, precepts are given without much explanation; therefore, obedience requires almost no critical thinking. The required response is easy to identify, but difficult to do.

Third, *commands carry grave consequences when disobeyed.* Whenever I fail to obey God's precepts, I lose something. Sometimes, the loss involves something I can never regain.

Fourth, *commands are for our good and God's glory*. The Lord doesn't issue precepts because He wants to take away our fun. On the contrary, His precepts steer us away from danger and guide us toward greater opportunities for joy.

Our sinful natures do not like commands. They much prefer to find wobble room in principles. Therefore, we must monitor our attitudes as we apply the Lord's precepts. Otherwise, we will likely become dour, joyless automatons, gritting our teeth as we grind out obedience. Paul could foresee this danger, so he calls for Timothy to adopt three helpful attitudes.

In verses 11 – 12, he called for *gratitude*—obedience inspired by the free gift of eternal life. This is not a quid pro quo relationship in which the believer must check off a to-do list in order to receive God's blessing. Heaven isn't a reward for good behavior; it's a promised gift. If we truly appreciate the immensity of this gift, obedience becomes a pleasure.

In verses 13 – 14, he called for *unswerving devotion* to a person, Jesus Christ, not blind acceptance of an impersonal ideal. Internal fortitude—resolving to obey God's commands just because it's the right thing to do—won't get us very far. Let us, instead, obey these precepts as a part of our ongoing relationship with Jesus Christ, who continues to demonstrate unswerving devotion to us!

In verses 15 – 16, he called for *genuine humility*. Because God is all-knowing and we are pitifully ignorant, because God is truth and sin draws us like flies to honey, we must admit our continuing need for guidance.

A Treasure Worth Guarding (1 Timothy 6:20 – 21)

²⁰O Timothy, guard what has been entrusted to you, avoiding worldly *and* empty chatter *and* the opposing arguments of what is falsely called "knowledge" — ²¹which some have professed and thus gone astray from the faith.
        Grace be with you.

I had spent the better part of a week ministering to four hundred victims of starvation. You couldn't tell by looking, though. They appeared to be well-nourished. They arrived in luxury cars, clad in trendy clothes, perfumed and coiffed to elegant perfection. Most had earned at least a master's degree and I addressed many of them as "Doctor." And even though some were overweight, they suffered from malnutrition, nonetheless.

I opened my talk on the first night by declaring the obvious. "I will send a famine on the land. 'Not a famine for bread or a thirst for water, but rather for hearing the words of the LORD'" (Amos 8:11). That was their first morsel of food after a long time of starvation. And with that first taste, the famished congregation recognized their need and then eagerly received what I had prepared.

It grieves me to see churches suffer such famine in lands that flow with the milk and honey of God's Word. Bookstores sell Bibles in every major language, in every possible size, and in every conceivable print, font, and format. Unprecedented numbers of people can read the Scriptures without the aid of clergy, which was not generally true as recently as one hundred years ago. The internet teems with modern translations of the Scriptures along with Bible study resources—most of them free. Electronic handheld devices contain every verse found in the Holy Scriptures. Never in the history of humanity have so many people enjoyed such ready access to the Bible, yet many Christians continue to starve. Why? Because, in most churches, someone has failed to guard the treasure. Thieves have broken through or simply slipped past the guard unnoticed, and they have robbed local churches of their only asset: sound doctrine based on the teaching and preaching of the Word of God.

The danger is not new, however. Robbers have always lurked around the doorways of churches, waiting for their appointed guardians to relax their vigil or abandon their posts. The church in Ephesus struggled to expose and remove false teachers, who nearly succeeded in overwhelming timid Timothy. Fortunately, Paul's letter arrived in time to encourage the reluctant and beleaguered pastor. Throughout the letter of 1 Timothy, we find Paul urging him to stand firm and to counter false teaching with the truth of God's Word.

> As I urged you upon my departure for Macedonia, remain on at Ephesus so that you may instruct certain men not to teach strange doctrines, nor to pay attention to myths and endless genealogies, which give rise to mere speculation rather than furthering the administration of God which is by faith. (1:3–4)
>
> This command I entrust to you, Timothy, my son, in accordance with the prophecies previously made concerning you, that by them you fight the good fight, keeping faith and a good conscience, which some have rejected and suffered shipwreck in regard to their faith. (1:18–19)
>
> I am writing these things to you, hoping to come to you before long; but in case I am delayed, I write so that you will know how one ought to conduct himself in the household of God, which is the church of the living God, the pillar and support of the truth. (3:14–15)
>
> Pay close attention to yourself and to your teaching; persevere in these things, for as you do this you will ensure salvation both for yourself and for those who hear you. (4:16)

I charge you in the presence of God, who gives life to all things, and of Christ Jesus, who testified the good confession before Pontius Pilate, that you keep the commandment without stain or reproach until the appearing of our Lord Jesus Christ. (6:13–14)

The apostle then closes the letter as he had begun, with a solemn charge to guard the inerrant, inspired treasure: the truth of God's Word.

— **6:20** —

Paul typically closed his letters with a few lines of personal greeting, and they usually express a cheerful tone. But not this time. If anything, the apostle conveys an even deeper sense of gravity, beginning with an interjection, "O." The apostle rarely uses this expression of deep emotion in a personal context;[18] once when lamenting the foolishness of the Galatians (Gal. 3:1) and twice when charging Timothy (6:11, 20). This only magnifies the solemnity of his next command.

Secular Greek literature used the verb translated "guard" to describe military sentry duty or the role of a prison guard. The object, "what has been entrusted to you," derives from a technical, legal verb meaning "to leave an object in another's keeping, with strict penalties for embezzlement."[19] Put these three elements together—the interjection, "O," along with the apostle's choice of verb and direct object—and we have an almost menacing charge (cf. James 3:1). He wrote, in today's terms, "You, Timothy, have been entrusted with *the* most important and valuable commodity on the planet. *Don't blow it!*"

The next two phrases explain how Paul expects the pastor to "guard" his precious deposit. First, he is to "turn away from" or "avoid" using philosophy as a means of gaining spiritual insight. Paul uses the expressions "worldly and empty chatter" (cf. 2 Tim. 2:16) and "worldly fables fit only for old women" (1 Tim. 4:7) to characterize philosophy, humanity's attempt to understand spiritual truths through reason alone. Because we are limited to our five senses, it's absurd to think we could know anything beyond the tangible realm unless Someone from that realm reveals it to us. He did this in the person of Jesus Christ, and He did this by giving us Scripture.

This is not to say that Christians shouldn't study philosophy. Neither does Paul mean for believers to avoid intelligent discussion in evangelism. Paul displayed amazing command of Greek philosophy in Athens (Acts 17:16–34). He did, however, forbid using philosophy as a means of gaining spiritual understanding. We have the Bible for that.

From My Journal

Our Poverty of Truth

Back when I ministered in New England, I took time to visit the Harvard University campus on a number of occasions. One wintry afternoon, I stood in the snow, staring at the statue of John Harvard, majestically seated with a book in his lap, watching over the campus he helped to build. The young minister became the school's first donor upon his death, giving his library and half his estate to the newly chartered college, which was renamed in his honor. The original school "Rules and Precepts" set the standard for admission and study.

> Precept #2: Let every student be plainly instructed, and earnestly pressed to consider well, the maine end of his life and studies is, *to know God and Jesus Christ which is eternall life*, Joh. xvii. 3. and therefore to lay Christ in the bottome, as the only foundation of all sound knowledge and learning.[20]

Harvard's original seal bore the Latin motto, *Veritas Christo et Ecclesiae*, "Truth for Christ and the Church."

Back then, as I studied the bronze statue, I wondered what John Harvard might think of the school today if he were to wander the campus, talk to students, attend a few lectures, and see how far it has wandered from its original purpose. But as it turns out, the statue I admired is a more fitting symbol of the school today than when it was first established. I was disappointed to discover that tour guides refer to the bronze image I admired as the "Statue of Three Lies" because of the misleading inscription: "John Harvard, Founder, 1638." The figure is not John Harvard, but a model. The real John Harvard left no likeness of himself. "1638" records the year of his gift to the school, not the date of its official inception in 1636. And, strictly speaking, he didn't found the college. It was formed by the Great and General Court of the Massachusetts Bay Colony.

Today, most people don't know that Harvard was established to train ministers for the gospel. The motto has been truncated in popular use to simply, *Veritas*, "Truth." And postmodernism has reduced even that to less than nothing.

Years ago, someone failed to guard the treasury.

—6:21—

Paul laments the fact that some claim to possess spiritual knowledge that cannot be gained from Scripture. Instead of teaching doctrine consistent with "the faith"—that is, Christianity as defined by Jesus and His apostles—these men have "swerved" or "missed the mark." They did the very opposite of "guarding what had been entrusted to them." Instead, they abandoned the truth they had received from God to find truth among godless pagans.

To be sure, the work of ministry challenges those who take up the pastor's mantle as they never imagined possible. They must be prepared to be misunderstood, maligned, criticized, taken for granted, and often isolated. Such are the occupational hazards of the awesome responsibility to guard the treasure of God's Word. For sure, it's not for everyone.

Nevertheless, the rewards cannot be calculated. I wouldn't trade anything for the intimacy I share with the Almighty as a result of countless hours in Scripture, untold experiences of His love overcoming evil, inexpressible wisdom gained through challenges in ministry, and overwhelming gifts of grace from His dear people. I live my life continually surprised by the goodness I receive on an almost-daily basis as a result of saying yes to God's call fifty years ago. And I cannot imagine leaving my post for something as boring as retirement.

NOTES:

1. Kittel and Friedrich, eds., *Theological Dictionary of the New Testament: Abridged in One Volume*, 404.
2. Ibid., 1236.
3. Clement also mentions his treatise, *On the Offices of Bishops, Presbyters, Deacons, and Widows*, but it is apparently lost to history.
4. The verb *elenchō* followed by the accusative of person.
5. Kittel and Friedrich, eds., *Theological Dictionary of the New Testament: Abridged in One Volume*, 222.
6. Edward Gibbon, *History of the Decline and Fall of the Roman Empire* (Cincinnati: J.A. James, 1840), 1:27.
7. Geoffrey W. Bromiley, *The International Standard Bible Encyclopedia*, rev. ed. (Grand Rapids: Eerdmans, 1988), 4:544.
8. The term translated "fairness" in the NASB is the Greek term *isotēs*, which means "equality" or "equal standing."
9. Gerhard Kittel, ed., *Theological Dictionary of the New Testament*, trans. G. F. Bromiley (Grand Rapids: Eerdmans, 1978), 4:143.
10. Joseph Henry Thayer, ed. and trans., *A Greek-English Lexicon of the New Testament*, (New York: Harper & Brothers, 1887), 84.

11. Charles Caleb Colton, quoted in *Onward to Fame and Fortune* by William M. Thayer (New York: Christian Herald, 1897), 242.

12. Harriet Beecher Stowe, *Uncle Tom's Cabin* (Boston: John P. Jewett & Company, 1852), 2:247–48.

13. A book recording the oral traditions and teachings of Jewish rabbis, collected over centuries and then compiled in the fifth century AD.

14. Kenneth S. Wuest, *Wuest's Word Studies from the Greek New Testament: For the English Reader* (Grand Rapids: Eerdmans, 1984), see 1 Timothy 6:6.

15. From the "Rabbinical Ana." See *Translations from The Talmud, Midrashim, and Kabbala* (M. Walter Dunne, 1901), 313.

16. *Anthologia Palatina*, 9:152.

17. The mood of a verb is the manner in which the action is intended by the author. English has three moods. "Indicative," by far the most common, states a fact. "Imperative" states a command or request. "Subjunctive" expresses a desire, a potential, or a theoretical possibility.

18. Paul used the interjection "O" four times in Romans (Rom. 2:1, 3; 9:20; 11:33), usually in reference to humanity in general.

19. Kittel and Friedrich, eds., *Theological Dictionary of the New Testament: Abridged in One Volume*, 1179.

20. Benjamin Peirce, *A History of Harvard University, from Its Foundation, in the Year 1636, to the Period of the American Revolution* (Cambridge: Brown, Shattuck, and Company, 1833), appendix p. 5.

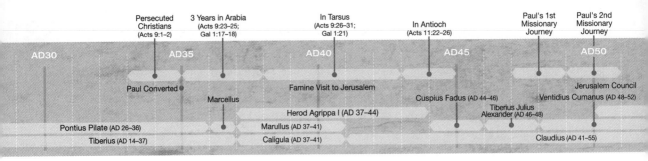

Persecuted
Christians
(Acts 9:1–2)

3 Years in Arabia
(Acts 9:23–25;
Gal 1:17–18)

In Tarsus
(Acts 9:26–31;
Gal 1:21)

In Antioch
(Acts 11:22–26)

Paul's 1st
Missionary
Journey

Paul's 2nd
Missionary
Journey

| AD30 | | AD35 | | AD40 | | AD45 | | AD50 |

Paul Converted

Marcellus

Famine Visit to Jerusalem

Cuspius Fadus (AD 44–46)

Jerusalem Council

Ventidius Cumanus (AD 48–52)

Herod Agrippa I (AD 37–44)

Tiberius Julius
Alexander (AD 46–48)

Pontius Pilate (AD 26–36)

Marullus (AD 37–41)

Tiberius (AD 14–37)

Caligula (AD 37–41)

Claudius (AD 41–55)

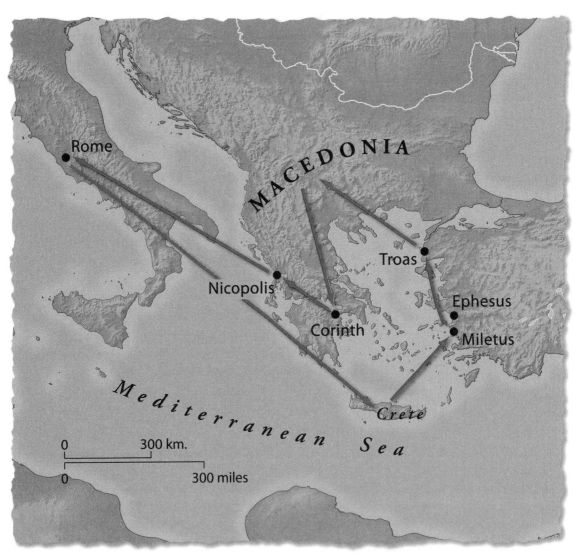

According to his letter to Titus, Paul planned to spend the winter in Nicopolis, a scenic, restful city across from Italy. He undoubtedly planned to begin a missionary journey toward Spain via Rome, in the Spring of A.D. 64.

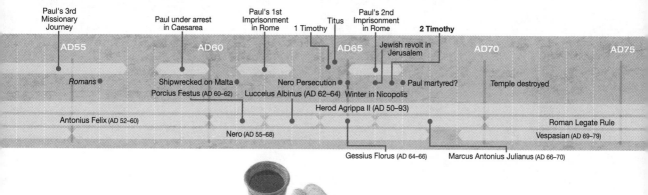

Paul's 3rd
Missionary
Journey

Paul under arrest
in Caesarea

Paul's 1st
Imprisonment
in Rome

1 Timothy

Titus

Paul's 2nd
Imprisonment
in Rome

2 Timothy

AD55

AD60

AD65

Jewish revolt in
Jerusalem

AD70

AD75

Romans ●

Shipwrecked on Malta ●
Porcius Festus (AD 60–62)

Nero Persecution ●
Lucceius Albinus (AD 62–64)

Winter in Nicopolis

● Paul martyred?

Temple destroyed

Herod Agrippa II (AD 50–93)

Antonius Felix (AD 52–60)

Nero (AD 55–68)

Gessius Florus (AD 64–66)

Marcus Antonius Julianus (AD 66–70)

Roman Legate Rule

Vespasian (AD 69–79)

2 TIMOTHY

Introduction

We ministers say yes to God's call, fully expecting to improve the world, or at least our little corner of it. For those of us who survive the devastating loss of idealism, humility settles in. Our desperate tug-of-war with pride ends with a kind of resignation; we learn to accept that nothing short of supernatural intervention can bring lasting change to the world — including our little corner.

Fortunately, the Lord doesn't leave us to wallow in gloomy despair; instead, He faithfully transforms the humbled minister. Resignation mellows into brokenness; brokenness results in surrender; surrender yields submission; submission endures to the end. And somewhere along the way, we accept a new definition of "success" in ministry. Men and women of God, seasoned by suffering, learn to take comfort in a difficult, yet reassuring, truth. We have not been called to change the world, or any part thereof. Instead, God calls us as ministers to be faithful; the Lord Himself will change the world in His own way and according to His predetermined schedule.

No one understood this better than Paul. By the time the apostle wrote his second letter to Timothy, he had engaged in a ministry of remarkable scope. In fifteen years his evangelistic zeal propelled three missionary journeys on which the tireless servant of God logged twenty thousand miles over land and sea. He had visited every major city in the eastern part of the Roman Empire, founded churches in most of them, trained dozens of choice men to water the seeds he had planted, and wrote a substantial portion of what would become the New Testament.

Paul's Swan Song
A Survey of Second Timothy

Guard the treasure!	Endure the hardship!
• Paul's personal greeting	• Passing on the truth
• Timothy's private life	• Illustrations of the truth *(Soldier, athlete, farmer, workman, vessel, servant)*
• God's sacred treasure	
• Others' varied reactions	• Suffering for the truth

	Guard the treasure!	Endure the hardship!
Perspective	The Past	The Present
Tone	Gratitude	Compassion
Key Verse	*Guard, through the Holy Spirit who dwells in us, the treasure which has been entrusted to you.* 2 Timothy 1:14	*Suffer hardship with me, as a good soldier of Christ Jesus.* 2 Timothy 2:3

Continue the journey!	Proclaim the word!
• Difficult times	• A Solemn charge
• Depraved people	• Reason for the charge
• Pressing on regardless	• Personal reflections
• Standing firm in the scriptures	• Urgent request

The Future	
Warning	Command
You, however, continue in the things you have learned and become convinced of, knowing from whom you have learnred them. *2 Tomothy 3:14*	*Preach the word; be ready in season and out of season; reprove, rebuke, exhort, with great patience and instruction.* *2 Timothy 4:2*

For the most part, politics in the capital city preserved the Pax Romana, the "peace of Rome." The empire's iron rule kept roads and shipping lanes free of robbery and piracy, subdued political unrest, and even tolerated religious diversity. But as Paul looked westward, planning a missionary journey through the western frontier as far as Spain (Rom. 15:28), the political winds shifted. The world was indeed changing, but not for the better.

"I SUFFER HARDSHIP EVEN TO IMPRISONMENT AS A CRIMINAL"

Paul's letter to Titus revealed the apostle's plan to spend the winter in Nicopolis, a delightful seaside refuge on the narrow isthmus between the Ionian Sea and the Gulf of Arta, just a short distance from the bottom of Italy's "boot." He undoubtedly set out for Rome in the spring of AD 64, intending to make good on his long-delayed plans (Rom. 15:28). When he arrived, however, he did not "find refreshing rest" (Rom. 15:32), but a city rumbling with civic strife. A few months later, in July of that same year, a massive fire raged for a week, devastating nearly half of Rome. To deflect rumors that Nero had set the fire himself, the demented despot rounded up Christians and tortured confessions out of them. He then positioned himself as the savior of Rome by funding its restoration personally, providing food and shelter for the victims and rebuilding the affected districts bigger and better than before. As the city slowly returned to normal, the madman began a horrific persecution against the church.

> To their death and torture were added the aggravations of cruel derision and sport; for, either they were disguised in the skins of savage beasts, and exposed to expire by the teeth of devouring dogs; or were hoisted up alive, and nailed to crosses; or wrapped in combustible vestments, and set up as torches, that, when the day set, they might be kindled to illuminate the night.[1]

Paul originally hoped to depart from Rome for Spain, having gathered provisions and an entourage of assistants, but Nero's persecution of Christians changed everything.[2] The apostle would not have left the church in Rome to suffer without his leadership, so it's reasonable to assume that Nero's accelerated campaign of hatred eventually enveloped him as well. Tradition holds that Paul languished in what came to be called the "Mamertine Prison," a subterranean structure consisting of two vaulted chambers, one above the other and connected by a small hole. Many believe the lower chamber originally served as a cistern. When converted into a prison, men were lowered through the hole and held in the lower chamber until their execution.

Paul may indeed have been placed there just prior to his martyrdom, but not likely before final sentencing. It would have been nearly impossible to receive visitors, much less make use of books and parchments (2 Tim. 4:13). Nevertheless, he didn't receive anything close to the preferential treatment given during his first imprisonment (Acts 28:30–31). Make no mistake, the language of 2 Timothy is dungeon-talk, the anguished words of a man suffering the maltreatment of a dank, rat-infested pit.

"COME BEFORE WINTER"

No more than two years after bidding farewell in Ephesus, Paul endured the hardships of prison in Rome. Isolated from other Christian prisoners because of his Roman citizenship and abandoned by most of his ministry companions, the weary apostle reached out to Timothy, whom he affectionately calls "my beloved son" (1:2).

The two men had ministered together since the beginning of Paul's second missionary journey. Their mentor-protégé relationship had progressed to the point that Paul felt comfortable sending the younger minister on long-term errands into difficult circumstances. Sometime during his first imprisonment in Rome, Paul

Todd Bolen/www.BiblePlaces.com

Many prisoners awaiting execution in Rome were transferred to the Mamertine Prison, an abandoned cistern, accessible only through the hole shown here in the center of this photo. The stairs were added later to allow tourists access to the lower chamber.

stationed Timothy in Ephesus to lead the church as its permanent pastor. The trainee had come of age. As often happens, though, the challenges of ministry in such a difficult region began to overwhelm Timothy and nearly put him to flight. Only a visit from Paul after his release—perhaps in Miletus on his way to Macedonia (1 Tim. 1:3)—kept the younger minister at his post. Even so, difficulties continued to plague Timothy's ministry, such that nothing short of a personal visit to Ephesus would suffice (1 Tim. 3:14; 4:13). Then, after a stay of unknown duration—perhaps no more than a couple of months—Paul left Timothy in charge, in all likelihood never expecting to see his face again.

Now the tables had turned. Instead of providing encouragement, Timothy's mentor very much needed it. In perhaps the most heartrending phrase ever penned by the apostle, he made a simple yet urgent request, "Come before winter" (2 Tim. 4:21).

"PREACH THE WORD"

Unlike Paul's first letter, which indirectly reveals Timothy's temperament and circumstances, this second letter allows us to see the apostle at his most vulnerable. Without the benefit of nearly two thousand years of history to review, Paul would have had every reason to feel like a failure. He founded numerous churches, only to see heretics lead them astray. Many of his trusted lieutenants abandoned the faith, while others tentatively struggled to "guard the treasure" of pure doctrine. And, perhaps most disappointing of all, he probably never completed his mission to Spain.

Moreover, the apostle fully expected to see, in his lifetime, the Lord's return to remove His people from this earth. *Every* generation should live in anticipation of this glorious event, yet evil continues to tighten its stranglehold on the world. Instead of joining his brothers and sisters in the clouds to meet Christ, Paul languished alone in a foul and filthy Roman dungeon. A less-than-ideal ending to a remarkable career—at least from a human point of view.

Nero's demented reign could have demoralized the apostle. Fortunately, Paul didn't view his ministry through human eyes. As we will see, he chose to see his life and work from a divine perspective. Paul's plea for Timothy to bring aid to Rome, though dripping with humanity, reveals the heart of a mature man of God. Even as he admitted his need for the encouragement of companionship, he affirmed the work of ministry and inspired Timothy to devote himself all the more to his calling.

- "Do not be ashamed of the testimony of our Lord" (1:8).
- "Guard . . . the treasure which has been entrusted to you" (1:14).
- "Be strong in the grace that is in Christ Jesus" (2:1).
- "Realize this, that in the last days difficult times will come" (3:1).

- "Continue in the things you have learned" (3:14).
- "Preach the word" (4:2).
- "Be sober in all things, endure hardship, do the work of an evangelist, fulfill your ministry" (4:5).

Even as he wrote, Paul felt the approach of death, and he knew the time to pass the torch had come. Scripture doesn't tell us what happened after this. Tradition says that Paul was beheaded in accordance with Roman law concerning citizens, not subjected to the humiliation endured by most Christians. I like to think that Timothy collected Paul's cloak and books in Troas, picked up Mark in some other city, and made it to Rome before his mentor was beheaded. We can't know for certain. Regardless, by virtue of this letter, the flame of divine truth passed like the torch of the Olympiad from the hand of Paul to the hand of Timothy ... and on to Titus, and then Tychicus, and then Luke, and Mark ... and Chuck ... and to your hand as well.

Hold it high. Guard it well. Pass it on.

NOTES:

1. Tacitus, *The Works of Tacitus* (London: Woodward and Peele, 1737), 2:698–99.
2. The testimony of church tradition suggests otherwise (Clement of Rome, *First Epistle to the Corinthians,* 1.5), but the time between his first and second letters to Timothy would not have permitted more than a cursory visit at best.

TENDER WORDS FROM A MENTOR (2 TIMOTHY 1:1–7)

¹Paul, an apostle of Christ Jesus by the will of God, according to the promise of life in Christ Jesus,

²To Timothy, my beloved son: Grace, mercy *and* peace from God the Father and Christ Jesus our Lord.

³I thank God, whom I serve with a clear conscience the way my forefathers did, as I constantly remember you in my prayers night and day, ⁴longing to see you, even as I recall your tears, so that I may be filled with joy. ⁵For I am mindful of the sincere faith within you, which first dwelt in your grandmother Lois and your mother Eunice, and I am sure that *it is* in you as well. ⁶For this reason I remind you to kindle afresh the gift of God which is in you through the laying on of my hands. ⁷For God has not given us a spirit of timidity, but of power and love and discipline.

Paul had written from captivity before, but never like this. He was no longer writing from the relative comfort of the Roman procurator's palace (Acts 24:27) or rented quarters under house arrest (Acts 28:30–31), but from a cold, dark, foul-smelling, overcrowded cell somewhere below ground. Unlike modern detention centers, ancient prisons provided barely enough food and water to survive. Prisoners depended on supplies brought to them from friends or family from the outside, who were given relatively free access as long as they satisfied the guards with gifts or money. Fortunately, Paul had Dr. Luke tending to his health and supplying him with pen and parchment (4:11). As the apostle awaited his final trial, he thought of his closest companion and began to write.

About 830 miles southeast of Paul's dungeon, across the Ionian Sea, past Greece, beyond the Aegean Sea, in a busy port city on the western coast of present-day Turkey, Timothy—now in his early forties—continued to lead the troubled congregation of Ephesus. Perhaps as the pastor prepared his sermon for the upcoming Lord's Day, sometime in late summer of AD 65, a knock came at his door. A courier. Tychicus (4:12)? A scroll bearing Paul's seal! Timothy surely felt a rush of excitement. He had known the apostle for nearly twenty years, traveling with him, binding his wounds after more than one stoning or beating, marveling at his miracles, memorizing the sermons he gave in each new city, observing his leadership.

The pastor of Ephesus no doubt had heard of Paul's arrest. Certainly, the letter gave him an overwhelming sense of relief. Paul was alive and well enough to write — or at least dictate his thoughts to Luke. Timothy hastily broke the seal and stared silently at the first line.

—1:1—

"Paulos . . ." How often Timothy must have uttered that name! Ironic that it should mean "little," for in the minds of most believers in the first century, he was anything but small. Nevertheless, the apostle much preferred it to his given name, Saul. He became a very different man after a vision of the risen Christ toppled him from his high horse on the road to Damascus. On that day, the greatest persecutor of Christians became little before his Master. No longer the messenger of death, the man from Tarsus trained as a Pharisee bore the title *apostolos*, "messenger" or "envoy."

Obviously, Timothy knew Paul intimately, so why the official title? Why such an authoritative opening line? Because Paul understood the importance of his final epistle. He wrote to Timothy, but not to him only. The apostle's writings were later read to the congregation, copied several times, and then distributed to other area churches for their edification. He undoubtedly knew that these final words would be preserved for the equipping of believers for many years to come, should the Lord delay His return.

Ironically, the validity of his apostleship had come under fire near the end of his life. Therefore, he now affirms the legitimacy of his office, not by self-proclamation (as some brazenly do today), but by the sovereign choosing of God (cf. "command of God," 1 Tim. 1:1) and by virtue of the message he carried. The "promise of life" is none other than the gospel.

—1:2—

Paul addresses the letter to Timothy, personally and individually, affectionately calling him "my beloved child" (lit. trans.). The Greek term refers to one's legitimate progeny. Paul had adopted him as his spiritual son, of course; Timothy was the son of a Greek father and a Jewish mother named Eunice. While the letter initially was written for the benefit of Timothy, the apostle intends to instruct everyone walking in Timothy's footsteps: pastors and ministers of all kinds.

Paul's threefold greeting, "grace, mercy, and peace," appears nowhere else in his letters except his salutation in 1 Timothy 1:2. Given his circumstances, he might have stated, "Pain, mistreatment, and misery accompany me." But rather than pity himself—the unfairness of his imprisonment, or his scarred, ailing body—he blessed his more fortunate disciple. When you are called by the will of God, your message is not about self. The gospel message is about grace, God's gift to the worthless. It's about mercy, God's ministry to the helpless. It's about peace, God's love for the restless.

— 1:3–4 —

Having concluded his salutation per his usual style—"From ...," "To ...," followed by a benediction—Paul gives his apprentice a threefold gift of encouragement. Before I outline them, take note of how the apostle could lift himself out of his circumstances to express such admiration.

First, *he adopts an attitude of gratitude*: "I thank God ..." Gratitude is the first prerequisite of genuine encouragement. A self-centered attitude cannot affirm others because encouragement can come only from a generous spirit. Show me a grateful person and I'll show you someone who spends a good deal of his or her time encouraging other people.

Second, *he cultivates a heart of worship*: "... whom I serve." The Septuagint, the Greek translation of the Old Testament, uses the term translated "serve" here to describe the activities of priests in the temple. The primary purpose of their service was worship. Attitude changes our perspective; worship directs our focus.

Third, *he maintains a clear conscience*: "... with a clear conscience." There is no better way to relieve anxiety than to do what is right, *always*. Whenever we violate our conscience, fear of God's wrath starts twisting our perspective and gives Satan the opportunity to drive a wedge between us. But when gratitude, worship, and a clear conscience combine, your mind is free to see the world as the Lord sees it. Furthermore, you are better able to empathize with others rather than worry about yourself.

As Paul reflected on his life and reviewed his current situation—waiting for the final verdict and the executioner's sword—nothing in his conduct caused him to second-guess his decisions or regret a particular failure. He never had to lament, *If only I hadn't committed that one terrible deed, perhaps I would be on my way to Spain right now.* He knew he has obeyed; therefore, his circumstances were perfectly aligned with the Lord's will. That doesn't mean Paul was morally perfect or that he never sinned. It means he kept short accounts of wrongdoing. He repented promptly, he learned from his mistakes, and he didn't repeat them.

Because Paul's conscience remained clear, he didn't waste time thinking about himself. He thought of what Timothy needed and gave him encouragement in three statements.

First, *"I constantly remember you in my prayers night and day."* I can think of few affirmations more meaningful than a busy person taking the needs of another before the throne of grace.

Second, *"[I long] to see you."* This told Timothy that he had value to Paul. His mentor didn't simply tolerate his presence; he enjoyed his presence and missed him when he was gone.

— 1:5 —

Third, *"I am mindful of the sincere faith within you."* Paul traveled with Timothy, observed his life up close, and found the younger man's faith to be genuine. What a compliment! How often we can lose respect for someone the more we get to know him or her. But Paul—being a man who had traveled widely and had encountered some great men and women in his time—affirmed Timothy's authenticity publicly in a letter to be read before the congregation.

Timothy came by his faith at an early age. John Calvin wrote, "It is as if Paul says, 'As you have been correctly instructed in the faith from your infancy, and having, so to speak, taken in sound teaching with your mother's milk.'"[1] His mother, Eunice, sang to him the songs of Zion and whispered the prayers of Moses. She instilled in her son the best attributes of Joshua, and David, and the prophets.

— 1:6 —

Paul turned his affirmation of Timothy's sincere faith into an opportunity to inspire him. The common expression "kindle afresh" pictures a man placing dry tinder on a glowing coal and then blowing on it to create a flame. Someone in every household in the first century woke up in the morning to coax fire from a dying ember, which then provided heat for cooking and warmth in winter.

The "gift of God" is both the ability and the privilege of preaching and teaching. Timothy had received the ability to carry out the duties of ministry, which Paul and the elders in Lystra affirmed in Timothy's ordination. Today, Paul might exhort a young preacher, "Keep studying. Don't go online and buy somebody else's sermon and then deliver it as though it's yours. Dig into the text on your own and get the message for yourself. Keep studying. Build your library. Work hard. Develop your skills."

—**1:7**—

Just in case Timothy wondered if he had what it took to be a competent minister, Paul sealed his affirmation and inspiration with a powerful truth that applies to everyone engaged in Christian ministry. Whatever our temperament, whatever our gifts or shortcomings, whatever our opinions of self, ministry is not about the minister; ministry is about the Word of God.

The "spirit" in this verse should be "Spirit," with a capital S. Paul's reference to the Holy Spirit in 1:14 strongly suggests the divine Spirit here, God-given courage emanating from a life submitted to and dependent on Him. In other words, competence for ministry never arises from the minister; it is always the result of God's Holy Spirit working in and through the man or woman He has chosen. We might be timid—as Timothy apparently was—but the Holy Spirit is bold. Our competence might falter, but the Spirit never fails. We might lack confidence, but the Spirit of God never disappoints and never suffers uncertainty.

Paul describes the qualities produced by the Holy Spirit in the man or woman who yields to His control:

- *dynamis*, "power," the supernatural ability to do the will of God
- *agapē*, "love," the distinctly Christian brand of love that begins with a decision, behaves unselfishly, seeks the highest and greatest good of another, and flows with deeply-felt godly emotion
- *sōphronismos*, "discipline," a rational, reasonable, sound-minded manner of thinking and behaving that reflects the orderly mind of God; it is seeing the world from His perspective

Paul began his letter to Timothy with a potent vote of confidence. This not only built up Timothy in the eyes of his congregation, giving them more reason to follow his leadership; it also prepared him for exhortation. And he was about to receive a *boatload* of exhortation. In this second letter to Timothy, the apostle used no less than thirty-three imperative verbs in twenty-seven commands. His time was growing short, and he had a lot of urgent information to tell his friend.

Application

Roles and Responsibilities of a Spiritual Leader

If you have taken on a leadership role at church, especially one involving teaching, someone should have told you about three additional roles that go along with the job. If you don't fulfill these additional responsibilities, your effectiveness will be limited, leaving you to wonder what's missing.

First, *the role of intercessor.* Spiritual leaders must pray for the people they teach and direct. I would suggest that you put together a prayer list that has a line in the middle with the name of the individual on the left side and the need of the individual on the right. Make it specific, record the date you add the item, and a date to the far right on which you will follow up for an update. Then, at least once per day, dedicate the time you would normally spend to watching a television program — thirty minutes to an hour — praying down your list.

Second, *the role of mentor.* Spiritual leaders select promising individuals and deliberately live their lives openly before them. We must live transparently before all people, but this is a deeper and closer level of authenticity. A mentoring relationship is informal, yet intentional. A mentoring relationship uses real life as a laboratory, inviting a disciple to learn by example.

Think of another individual, preferably younger or less experienced in some respect. This would be someone of the same gender as you who might someday make a suitable replacement for you in your current role. Begin inviting that person to join you as you carry out the duties associated with your position. Ask for his or her help, even if you don't actually need it, and allow the person to complete some of your tasks. Include this person in planning sessions and pray together regularly.

Then, once you have this relationship established and running smoothly, choose another individual and repeat the process. I recommend limiting yourself to no more than five mentoring relationships; any more than that gets complicated.

Third, *the role of encourager.* Generally speaking, people do not receive nearly enough affirmation. It's a wonder they keep doing a good job, considering how little appreciation they receive. Nevertheless, encouragement is the simplest, most rewarding task of a spiritual leader, and it's amazingly effective as a motivator. Furthermore, it's easy! Simply catch people doing something right and then call attention to it. The most difficult part of this role is remembering to fulfill it.

The secret is to make observation a habit. Start by setting a goal for yourself: three comments of encouragement per day. When you're at the grocery store, look for a way to affirm the clerk or the bag boy. When you pick up your dry cleaning, take note of the person's attitude. Traveling? It's all too easy to notice what goes wrong; look for someone working hard to move passengers along efficiently. Be the one traveler in line who makes eye contact, smiles, notices the name tag, calls the agent by name, and briefly says something positive.

If you make encouragement a habit, you will be surprised by the response of the people you lead.

Whether you preach, teach, lead a small group, chair a committee, organize a function, or head up a task force, your position carries three additional roles: intercessor, mentor, and encourager. Fulfill them faithfully, and the responses will be remarkable! Those you lead will accomplish more than you ever thought possible.

NOTES:

1. John Calvin, *1 & 2 Timothy & Titus* (Wheaton: Crossway, 1998), 72–73.

THE PAST AND PRESENT
(2 TIMOTHY 1:8 – 2:26)

For the next few moments, imagine yourself in a place you probably never have been before. Imagine yourself imprisoned in a dungeon. There is no escape. There is no relief. Your captors have the power of life and death over you. They can torture you. They can interrogate you. They can kill you without consequence. You might exist for months or even years in this dark abyss, or you might be killed tomorrow. Each night you go to sleep unsure; each morning you wake to either another dismal day of abuse or your last day on earth.

Most of us cannot imagine what Paul experienced as he wrote these words from that awful dungeon. A few of us can. My friend Congressman Sam Johnson reads Paul's second letter to Timothy with a sad, knowing smile and a tear in his eye. Long before running for Congress, Sam flew over Vietnam in an F–4 Phantom jet. On April 16, 1966, while flying his twenty-fifth mission, he was shot down over North Vietnam, suffered a broken arm, dislocated shoulder, and broken back, which his captors used to torture him for information.

> I struggled to think cohesive thoughts. Memories became all-absorbing. In that dark cave of a cell, surrounded by the stench of death, the present was unbearable and the future almost unthinkable. Only the past had meaning. I brooded on memories. I recalled events from my past that I did not know I remembered. I dug back into my childhood for memories long ago dismissed as trivial. They suddenly had great significance ...
>
> I turned my attention toward God. When the guards increased their patrols and their vigilance and my talks with Howie had to be stopped, I could still talk freely to God. I knew with certainty that He was present in that dark, cramped closet of a cell. He listened when I prayed — this I knew without a doubt. He answered me. When Bible stories and verses of comfort came into my thoughts, I knew He placed them there. I was comforted and encouraged. And I began to know my Creator in a way I had never known Him before. I now know, in retrospect, that God's intimate interaction with me in the Mint strengthened me and built my faith, so that I would be able to trust Him in the darkness of the terrible days that still lay ahead for me.[1]

The crucible experiences of life have the capacity to bring out the very best or the very worst in a person. In the case of Paul, the very best emerged, in part through this letter to a longtime friend. We read not one word of bitterness or

KEY TERMS

διαμαρτύρομαι [*diamartyromai*] (1263) "to solemnly charge, declare emphatically"

Based on the verb μαρτυρέω [*martyreō*], "to bear witness, testify," this emphatic verb carries the idea of stating something firmly or with absolute assurance. When used as an imperative, the verb takes on the character of a charge, a solemn assignment of responsibility.

ἐπαισχύνομαι [*epaischynomai*] (1870) "to be very ashamed, be embarrassed by"

The main point of the root word is not as much the feeling of shame or embarrassment as being disgraced in public. Paul uses this term four times in this short letter, suggesting that pride had become a widespread problem. Not only did Christians distance themselves from the gospel to avoid death, they apparently couldn't stand the pressure of public opinion.

πάσχω [*paschō*] (3958) "to suffer, experience something from the outside"

Paul uses a form of this word five times throughout 2 Timothy. In the broadest sense, it means "to experience something from the outside," but it is almost always used in a negative context, so that the idea of suffering is assumed. In some places, Paul combines the word with κακός [*kakos*], "evil, bad," to emphasize the pain of his experience.

πιστεύω [*pisteuō*] (4100) "to entrust, trust, believe in"

The verb form of πίστις [*pistis*], "faith, trust," means to place faith or trust in something or someone. Paul uses this verb in various forms in his letter and in several contexts. Most often, he writes of the faith we have in Christ, but in a few instances, he refers to the treasure "entrusted" to Timothy, presumably by God.

blame. No complaints. In fact, we frequently encounter expressions of joy and even statements of gratitude, often mingled with praise for his God. We also find the apostle immersed in his memories, recalling cherished moments with his friends, especially Timothy. Unfortunately, some of these memories reminded him that some friends had abandoned not only him personally, but also the pure doctrines for which he was willing to die.

Fortunately, all was not lost. While Timothy struggled to minister in Ephesus, he remained faithful to the gospel. Now, if only he would remain engaged in the "good fight" against apostasy, Paul felt he could die in peace.

Straight Talk to the Timid and Reluctant (2 Timothy 1:8–12)

---

[8]Therefore do not be ashamed of the testimony of our Lord or of me His prisoner, but join with *me* in suffering for the gospel according to the power of God, [9]who has saved us and called us with a holy calling, not according to our works, but according to His own purpose and grace which was granted us in Christ Jesus from all eternity, [10]but now has been revealed by the appearing of our Savior Christ Jesus, who abolished death and brought life and immortality to light through the gospel, [11]for which I was appointed a preacher and an apostle and a teacher. [12]For this reason I also suffer these things, but I am not ashamed; for I know whom I have believed and I am convinced that He is able to guard what I have entrusted to Him until that day.

Paul's message to Timothy in this segment of his letter can be summarized in just three words: *Strengthen your resolve.* Once young ministers have completed their seminary training and stand ready to serve the Lord in fulltime Christian ministry, I want those three words ringing in their ears. They need to be ready for difficulty and discouragement. Satan isn't going to let them teach or preach the gospel without resistance. A fight is inevitable. Paul didn't write these words, however, as a motivational pamphlet. "Strengthen your resolve" is not a pull-yourself-up-by-your-own-bootstraps rallying cry.

When called upon to recite a poem in my graduation from high school, I chose the soul-stirring "Invictus," by William Ernest Henley:

Out of the night that covers me,
Black as the Pit from pole to pole,
I thank whatever gods may be
For my unconquerable soul.

In the fell clutch of circumstance
I have not winced nor cried aloud.
Under the bludgeonings of chance
My head is bloody, but unbowed.

Beyond this place of wrath and tears
Looms but the Horror of the shade,
And yet the menace of the years
Finds, and shall find, me unafraid.

It matters not how strait the gate,
How charged with punishments the scroll,

I am the master of my fate:
I am the captain of my soul.[2]

Heady stuff for a brash, young man with no life experience, ready to break out of Houston, Texas. We were taught to believe those words and to claim them as our mandate upon graduation. Paul, however, describes this kind of attitude using a rare Greek term: *hogwash!* Nobody is the master of his fate or the captain of her soul. That belief is but the doorway to a very long drop. No one is invincible. No one is indestructible. And no one is irreplaceable.

The call to "strengthen your resolve" is not about drawing upon your own might or whipping your enthusiasm into a can-do frenzy. It is, instead, a solemn urging to let the Spirit of God work through you and to carry out God's purposes, in God's way, on God's time, and for God's glory. From a human perspective, the purposes, methods, and timing of God can be painful and confusing. Nevertheless, that is the Lord's command to all who would serve Him.

That was Paul's challenge to Timothy, and his challenge to all who follow in the younger minister's footsteps.

— 1:8 —

"Therefore" draws on the thought expressed in the preceding lines. Paul has just encouraged Timothy to kindle his ministry afresh (1:6). Why? "Because," the apostle declared, "God has not given us a spirit of timidity, but of power and love and discipline" (1:7).

As noted above, "spirit" in 1:7 should be "Spirit. Fortunately, you don't have to pray for the Spirit of God to take up residence within you or for Him to empower you. No believer must wait for a second gift of the Spirit or work hard in order to become worthy of the Lord's indwelling presence. God has *given* us His Spirit. Past tense for those who are in Christ. Neither earned nor deserved, any more than salvation (Eph. 2:8 – 9). Make no mistake here: Christ is the Master of my fate; the Holy Spirit is the captain of my soul.

So, how do we "strengthen our resolve," if we don't become our own masters and captains? Paul here gives Timothy four action steps in these verses.

First step: *"Do not be ashamed of the testimony of our Lord"* (v. 8a). The Greek term *martyrion* means "testimony" or "objective proof." It didn't gain the additional nuance of death for the sake of one's belief (i.e., being a martyr) until the late second century. Christ's "testimony" includes His teachings, His life, His death on a cross — then considered a shameful, humiliating death — and most importantly, His resurrection.

In first-century Ephesus, the epicenter of Greek philosophy in the East, the idea of resurrection would have been far more "shameful" than death on a cross. To the Greek way of thinking, all tangible matter was detestable. This realm of substance we inhabit on earth was but a substandard shadow of the perfect realm of pure idea or thought. Humans, then, were divine sparks trapped within prisons of fleshy matter, and death was liberation. Freed from its captivity in the realm of substance, the mind could fly to its true home in the realm of idea. Therefore, to the Greek mind, resurrection—the reunion of mind with body—was an absurd hope (cf. Acts 17:30–32). More like a curse. Incarceration repeated. "Why," they wondered, "would anyone *want* that?"

Regardless, Paul boldly taught the truth of the gospel, including the unpopular notion of resurrection. This could not have been easy for anyone, least of all for Timothy, who lacked Paul's iron constitution. Most likely, Timothy was physically fragile and emotionally timid; therefore, he held back. Nevertheless, the apostle here encourages Timothy to proclaim the truth of Christ's promise boldly, to preach the "disgraceful" cross and the "absurd" resurrection without shame in the hearing of everyone in Ephesus, including the sneering doctors of philosophy. Moreover, he invites Timothy to join him in suffering for the gospel, which undoubtedly chased away any remnants of self-pity. Paul is writing from a dungeon; Timothy enjoys freedom. Paul faces beheading for the sake of the gospel; Timothy, little more than ridicule.

Second step: *Do not be ashamed of the people of God* (v. 8b). Paul included the phrase, "or of me, His prisoner," which may have stung the younger minister, but cut to the heart of our fallen nature. Despite how much we might love someone, we love ourselves more. The flesh will do almost anything, sacrifice anyone, to protect itself. Paul is sitting alone in a prison cell, surrounded by other abandoned souls, because no one except Luke dares to be close to him for fear of arrest and persecution.

We strengthen our resolve when we stop caring about what others think and we set aside our fear of consequences as we bear the gospel openly.

Third step: *Be willing to suffer for the sake of the gospel* (v. 8c). Paul didn't consider himself a prisoner of Nero. He called himself a prisoner of Christ. Jesus is our Sovereign, not Nero or Rome or Washington or Parliament or the Vatican or any other man-made authority. So far as Paul was concerned, he remained in a dungeon because the King of kings wanted him there in service to the kingdom of God. He didn't seek suffering. He didn't volunteer for imprisonment or petition for the execution. I have no doubt Paul would have gladly received acquittal and release with a huge sigh of relief and then resumed his plans for Spain. Yet he never would have considered denying Christ or distancing himself from the gospel to secure his release.

Paul didn't invite persecution so he could wear it as a badge of honor; but he did expect it (3:12).

— **1:9** —

Fourth step: *Anchor your life in the Lord's sovereign grace* (vv. 9 – 11). Let's face it; we like grace, so long as it's on our terms. We want grace without humility. We want grace without suffering. We want grace that brings us happiness and comfort. We want grace in the time and manner of our own choosing. We want it here and now, in this realm, as well as in the life to come. And we want grace in return for faithfulness.

Paul's perspective on grace differed in two respects. First, he saw grace as an eternal gift that puts us at odds with Satan's world system; therefore, it invites suffering so long as we live in this sin-cursed creation. Second, he rejected any sense of entitlement regarding grace. We deserve eternal torment in hell; therefore, anything better is an undeserved blessing from the goodness and mercy of God. This utterly humble attitude allowed the apostle to rest in the sovereignty and goodness of God, resulting in a peace beyond human understanding.

Paul considered himself Christ's prisoner, not Nero's. He was suffering "for the gospel *according to the power of God*" (v. 8, emphasis mine). The Greek preposition *kata*, translated "according to," is deliberately ambiguous in this case. It can be "in accordance with" or "in the manner of" or "corresponding with" or "for the purpose of."[3] For Paul, Christian suffering falls under the authority of God. The Lord is not the source of evil (Jas. 1:13; 1 John 1:5). Evil is perpetuated by Satan, the sinful world he rules, and those who live according to the sin-cursed world order. Nevertheless, God has promised to use evil to accomplish good purposes, not only within the person affected by evil (Rom. 8:28 – 39), but also for the good of the world through that person's submission to His authority (2 Cor. 12:9 – 10). Paul, therefore, considered the "evil" he was suffering through his imprisonment and impending execution as a part of God's sovereign grace.

The aging apostle saw his suffering as a single event in a grand plan begun by God in eternity past to redeem humanity from sin and to give us grace throughout eternity future. In that ethereal existence before time or space came to be, the Father, Son, and Holy Spirit — the triune God — determined, as it were, "This will be the plan of salvation. It will accomplish My purpose. It will be based on My grace, given to people who trust in My Son, who will be the ones to communicate it to all of humanity."

— **1:10 – 11** —

Having reflected on the eternal scope of God's grace in His grand plan of salvation, Paul refocused Timothy's attention on their present circumstance. Jesus Christ had revealed the eternal redemptive plan of God through His teaching, death, burial, resurrection, and promised return. Paul affirmed his place in God's eternal plan, not only in his teaching ministry between Antioch and Athens, but also through his suffering in a Roman prison. He said, in effect, "Timothy, shore up your life anchored by sovereign grace. It didn't start with you; it doesn't end with you; it isn't about you. You're merely a link in the chain of God's plan. As it works its way out, it's not for your health and wealth, for your happiness and safety, or for your glory or power or significance. Before God created time and space and before He placed humanity within a pristine creation, He established His plan, based on grace alone, accomplished by Christ alone, to be received through faith alone. And we have the astonishing privilege of communicating it to the rest of humanity!"

Paul described his place in God's redemptive plan as being "appointed" (v. 11). The Greek verb means "to place," usually with a strategy in mind. It was used of foundations, investments, armies, votes, or appointments to political office. Paul used the passive voice; "I was appointed" strategically by God in the furtherance of His plan. He then claimed three titles that reinforced his sense of duty, even in the face of death.

- *Kērux*, "a herald, envoy, proclaimer." This term carries a special connotation for secular Greeks and Romans:

  > Since politics and religion are inseparable for the Greeks, heralds on foreign missions are regarded as under the protection not only of their country but also of the gods. To violate them is to bring down divine wrath. Even if their message is unwelcome, they must be hospitably received. They have a special sanctity which enables them to speak without fear or favor. For this reason they often accompany envoys. Even in war they may go to the enemy camp to open up negotiations for peace. Similarly, they may go to an enemy capital to declare war.[4]

- *Apostolos*, "one sent out, an envoy, messenger." Much like *kērux*, an apostle was sent to carry out the wishes of the sender, only this term emphasizes the concept of authorization. An apostle not only bore a message, he was authorized to make decisions on behalf of the sender. His word carried equal weight with that of the authority he represented.

- *Didaskalos*, "a teacher, instructor." Gentiles and Jews in the first century used this term to denote a learned person who passes knowledge on to his students. The men establishing schools in Ephesus around a particular philosophical system called themselves "teachers." Without equating Christianity to a philosophical system (e.g., Stoicism or Epicureanism), Paul claims equal standing, at least, with the teachers in Ephesus, Athens, Jerusalem, and Rome.

— **1:12** —

Having commanded Timothy, "Do not be ashamed" (v. 8), Paul personally declared, "I am not ashamed." He then explained the reason for his boldness, which the NASB has rendered, "He is able to guard what I have entrusted." The literal Greek reads "my entrustment," which can mean either "that with which I have been entrusted" or "that which I have entrusted to Him." Some expositors side with the former because it reflects the parallel statement in 1:14. But just as likely, Paul may have intended the reciprocal of his command to Timothy, "O Timothy, guard what has been entrusted to you" (1 Tim. 6:20), and "Guard, through the Holy Spirit who dwells in us, the treasure which has been entrusted to you" (2 Tim. 1:14). In other words, the Lord had entrusted His servants with the gospel, and Paul had entrusted his soul to the care of God.

It's also possible that Paul left the term ambiguous to form a double entendre. "My entrustment" may include both — the treasure God has entrusted with His servants, and the apostle's soul, which he has entrusted to God. The apostle invites Timothy to follow his example, and by virtue of the Holy Spirit's preserving these words through the centuries, he has invited us to do the same.

As Paul's suffering increased, he strengthened his resolve. Yes, he did employ the power of thinking positively, choosing to see his suffering through the lens of God's sovereign grace. Yes, he did draw on the spiritual strength he had gained through years of faithful service. Yes, he had been conditioned by a career fraught with danger and hardship. But none of those can account for his courage. Not entirely. Brave though he is, his courage does not arise from his own steely constitution. Instead, he submits to his Master, who has given him the resolve he lacks naturally.

Paul trusted his Master completely. No reservations. No hesitation. No hedging or contingency plans. He lept from this world into the eternal unseen without a parachute, fully expecting God to carry him into glory. He had placed his faith in a person, not merely a message. Therefore, he proclaimed the gospel relentlessly and impressively because it came from God, whom he trusted implicitly.

Application

A Question of Resolve

So, how does one go about strengthening his or her resolve? I think the most direct way to answer the question is, "Be convinced that God will vindicate your life." If you like the word "reward" better, put that in place of "vindicate." Either way, be convinced that God will vindicate your life.

Paul used the word "entrustment," which is another term for "investment." The Lord is able to take my investment and hold it securely, or I am able to take what He has entrusted to me and He ultimately will reward me for it. Consequently, every task is worth your best. Every person is worth at least a little of your time. Every responsibility is worth your best discipline. Be wise with your time and energy, but when called upon and you say yes, give it your all. Don't waste people's time with a poorly prepared talk, not even a brief devotional. Prepare carefully. Work diligently. God deserves your best; after all, you're investing it in Him, who will be faithful to reward you, "for God is not unjust so as to forget your work and the love which you have shown toward His name, in having ministered and in still ministering to the saints" (Heb. 6:10).

Take some time to consider and then answer this question. Simple, yet profound. Uncomplicated, yet it impacts the rest of your life. *Are you resolved to give Him your very best?*

Jonathan Edwards, at the tender age of nineteen, while preparing for ministry, answered that question in the affirmative and set down no less than seventy resolutions (!) to guide his daily activities. He wrote the first twenty-one in his diary in one sitting, and the rest before his twentieth birthday. Here are just a few you might find helpful.[5]

1. Resolved, that I will do whatsoever I think to be most to the glory of God and my own good, profit and pleasure, in the whole of my duration.
6. Resolved, to live with all my might, while I do live.
7. Resolved, never to do anything, which I should be afraid to do, if it were the last hour of my life.
14. Resolved, never to do anything out of Revenge.
28. Resolved, to study the Scriptures so steadily, constantly and frequently, as that I may find, and plainly perceive myself to grow in the knowledge of the same.
33. Resolved, to do, always, what I can towards making, maintaining and preserving peace, when it can be done without an overbalancing detriment in other respects.
41. Resolved, to ask myself at the end of every day, week, month and year, wherein I could possibly, in any respect, have done better.
56. Resolved, never to give over, nor in the least to slacken, my fight with my corruptions, however unsuccessful I may be.
57. Resolved, when I fear misfortunes and adversity, to examine whether I have done my duty, and resolve to do it, and let the event be just as Providence orders it. I will, as far as I can, be concerned about nothing but my duty, and my sin.

These were very personal to Jonathan Edwards, who later became known as America's most significant theologian and greatest intellectual. But his need may not be yours. If you dare, write at least five. Place them in a spot where you'll see them daily. Make them a matter of daily prayer, asking the Lord for ability beyond your own. I am positive you will find that this kind of mental and spiritual discipline will transform your life — all for the glory of God.

Two Eternal Investments (2 Timothy 1:13 – 18)

> [13]Retain the standard of sound words which you have heard from me, in the faith and love which are in Christ Jesus. [14]Guard, through the Holy Spirit who dwells in us, the treasure which has been entrusted to *you*.
>
> [15]You are aware of the fact that all who are in Asia turned away from me, among whom are Phygelus and Hermogenes. [16]The Lord grant mercy to the house of Onesiphorus, for he often refreshed me and was not ashamed of my chains; [17]but when he was in Rome, he eagerly searched for me and found me — [18]the Lord grant to him to find mercy from the Lord on that day — and you know very well what services he rendered at Ephesus.

Few things on earth will last forever. According to the Bible, they are limited to God's Word (Isa. 40:8; Matt. 24:35) and the souls of people — those who believe in Christ, destined for eternal glory, and those who reject Him, resulting in eternal torment (Matt. 25:31 – 46). At the end of days, the fire of God's judgment will consume everything else, at which time He will fashion a new creation (2 Peter 3:7, 10; Rev. 21 – 22).

As the apostle languished in the darkness of a Roman dungeon, undoubtedly aware of his impending death sentence, he naturally began to think of things eternal. He reflected here on the timeless treasure of God's Word (vv. 13 – 14) and pondered the immortal souls of people (vv. 15 – 18). Unfortunately, when Paul had turned to some people for help, most turned away. Persecution put their resolve to the test, revealing them to be weak ministers and fickle friends. But rather than becoming bitter, Paul cherished genuine friendships all the more, and he encouraged Timothy to do the same.

— 1:13 – 14 —

The first phrase, "standard of sound words," carries the idea of a template or a pattern for making copies. Paul didn't expect Timothy to regurgitate his teaching verbatim, but to retain principles of sound doctrine as the younger minister adapted their application to meet the changing needs of his congregation. Educators call this "internalization," which requires thorough understanding rather than rote memory.

Paul then restated his command, returning to the familiar imagery used in his first letter (1 Tim. 6:20): "Guard ... the treasure." Because God's Word has the power to determine where people spend eternity, Paul urged Timothy to guard it, just like one might protect a room full of treasure against pilfering thieves. While the apostle devoted much of his first letter to this exhortation, it might seem unnecessarily repetitive to us. But we must remember that two or three years, and a lot of New Testament history, passed between his first and second letters.

The term "guard" is translated from the Greek verb *phylassō*, which means "to protect by keeping careful watch." It was used of prison guards, city watchtowers, and shepherds. The object of this verb here is the term for a deposit or a trust (cf. v. 12). When you deposit a check at the bank, you entrust the entire banking system to keep your money safe from those who would take it illegally. In the ancient world, the guardian of a trust fulfilled a sacred duty.

Let's be honest. If a minister took this command seriously enough, he or she would feel overwhelmed. Imagine the President of the United States giving you the responsibility to guard the nation's gold reserves at Fort Knox. "Here's a rifle with a few clips of ammunition. Guard the treasure. It's all up to you!" Anyone in his right mind would be terrified. If, on the other hand, he said, "Guard the treasure. You have the entire military forces at your disposal," you would have better than a fighting chance.

In repeating his earlier command to guard the trust, Paul added a key phrase for emphasis: "through the Holy Spirit who dwells in us." The Lord will not leave Timothy, or any other minister, alone to protect the pure doctrine of God from marauders. We have the power of Almighty God living within us!

— **1:15** —

Without announcing a change of subject, Paul turned from the topic of God's eternal Word to address another eternal commodity: the souls of men and women. In this case, he described two categories of people, those who disappoint and those who remain faithful.

Paul refered first to "all who are in Asia" as people who had turned their backs on him when he needed support. "Asia" denotes the Roman province of which Ephesus was the chief city. Naturally, his indictment didn't include every single person in the region; in the very next statement, the apostle named some true friends. Rather, the expression described either a numerical majority or a representative set

From My Journal

Ready or Not, Here They Come!

One Sunday afternoon, the telephone rang in our Southern California home. When I answered, a familiar Texas drawl greeted me. "Swindoll, this is McGee!" (as in J. Vernon).

"I know who this is!" I said. "I'd know that voice anywhere."

"Hey, I've got good news and I've got bad news."

"Okay ... gimme the good news," I laughed.

"I'm sending you two couples from the Church of the Open Door, who live closer to you than to us. I've really encouraged them to go to your church, and they're gonna come. So, you'll have four more people next Sunday."

"Great," I replied with hesitation. "What's the bad news?"

"They're the pus-pocket of the church!" And then he laughed long and hard. "I'm *so* glad to enlarge your congregation!"

McGee wasn't exaggerating. Within weeks, and for many years thereafter, almost every controversy could be traced to these two couples and their troublemaking friends. As a young pastor, I wasn't prepared to deal with troublemakers like these. So, for too many years, the entire congregation suffered the toxic effects of those malcontented individuals.

of individuals Paul needed most. He specifically named Phygelus and Hermogenes, who are mentioned nowhere else in Scripture. For what it's worth, Phygelus means "fugitive" in Greek; Hermogenes means "born of Hermes" (the Greek messenger god). Other than their names, we have no way of knowing the significance of these two men or what they did to fail the apostle. Timothy knew them well enough. The mere mention of their names established his point: *They proved fickle to me; they'll do the same to you.*

—1:16–17—

By sharp contrast, Paul named Onesiphorus as a faithful friend. His name meant "profit-bringer." He describes the ministry received from his friend as "refreshment," using a Greek verb that means, literally, "to cool or refresh with a breath" or "to dry out."[6] In the oldest sense of the word, it describes the physical recovery one received at an *asclepeion*. These sacred healing centers provided clean water and a breezy atmosphere for sick or wounded patients. Paul probably meant "refreshment" in the general sense of food and other supplies.

Apparently, Onesiphorus sent supplies remotely from Ephesus for some time and then visited the apostle in person, going to great trouble and even risking personal danger in the process. During Nero's persecution, visiting a Christian in prison could result in arrest and martyrdom, but Onesiphorus didn't run scared of that. He earnestly and diligently searched for Paul, which must not have been an easy task, given the confusion of a burned-out city ruled by a scapegoating madman.

The faithfulness of Onesiphorus stood in stark contrast with the behavior of the fickle friends, Phygelus and Hermogenes. They not only left Paul to rot in prison without food or supplies, they put as much distance between themselves and Rome as needed to remain safe. The abrupt shift from verse 14 to verse 15 strongly suggests they also failed to "guard the treasure" entrusted to them. Still, we can't automatically assume the men were guilty of apostasy. Cowardice, for certain; dereliction, probably; but not necessarily wholesale abandonment of the faith.

—1:18—

Interestingly, Paul referred to "the house of Onesiphorus" in the present tense and Onesiphorus, himself, in the past tense. Why did he not write, "you know very well what services he *continues to render* at Ephesus"? This has led many expositors to suggest the man had died by the time of this letter. If so, Paul's blessing, "the Lord grant to him to find mercy from the Lord on that day," could be construed as a prayer for the dead. The Greek term rendered "mercy" equates to the Hebrew term *chesed*, meaning "grace" or "loving-kindness," and "that day" refers to the day of judgment (cf. 1:12; 4:8).

This is a stretch for two reasons. First, Paul's use of the past tense could just as easily reflect the past deeds of the man, prompting the apostle to bless his entire household. He did the same for Stephanas, who was very much alive (1 Cor. 16:15, 17). Furthermore, Paul's blessing of the man himself could have been prompted by the arrest and potential execution of Onesiphorus while in Rome. As long as we're speculating, this scenario is just as defensible as the other. Second, even if the man were dead at the time of Paul's blessing, his "prayer" could be a simple expression of gratitude, such as, "May God repay his kindness because I cannot."

All speculation aside, one fact remains clear. Onesiphorus proved to be a faithful friend of immense value to Paul, for whom the apostle expressed deep admiration and gratitude. Ministers *need* supporters like Onesiphorus, especially because critics tend to outnumber advocates by a wide margin.

After the dual commands, "retain the standard of sound words" and "guard the treasure," the contrast between fickle and faithful friends undoubtedly spoke volumes to Timothy. Without having to say so explicitly, the apostle has communicated some poignant messages. First, "don't abandon me like Phygelus and Hermogenes; remain faithful to me like Onesiphorus." Second, "fickle Christians are like cowardly hirelings; they leave the flock to be devoured by wolves." And third, "ministers need advocates; seek them diligently, treasure them continually, thank them personally, and praise them openly."

Application

You Can Take These Treasures with You

You have probably heard the expression, "A hearse never goes to the graveyard pulling a U-Haul." That's a clever way of restating Job's truism, "Naked I came from my mother's womb, and naked I shall return there" (Job 1:21). I have attended the deaths of many people in my years of pastoral ministry, and have had the opportunity to see what dying people reach for in their final days. I've never seen anyone clutch a bank statement to his breast or ask to be surrounded by priceless antiques. Without exception, they call loved ones to be near. And if they cling to any material possession, it's their well-worn copy of God's Word.

As the icy grip of death closes around Paul as he writes from his dark prison hole, he reflects on two treasures that have sustained him through many difficulties: his friends and the Scriptures. Judging by his letters and Luke's account of his life, the apostle acquired great wealth in both respects, riches he would continue to enjoy after the executioner's sword.

How about you? What treasures on earth do you collect? The kind that must be passed to another before leaving this realm for the next? The kind governments tax and thieves steal? Or do you stockpile riches you *can* take with you? Let me share a couple of ways to build wealth that will last an eternity.

First, *stockpile the treasure of God's Word.* My obvious advice is to begin your own personal Scripture memory program. As a teenager, I began storing away Bible verses with a system developed by The Navigators. Their "Topical Memory System" arranges Bible verses by practical life issues or by theological subjects, and I continue to find application for them every day. Often when confronted with a particular challenge, relevant verses I memorized more than fifty years ago leap to mind automatically, bringing comfort I cannot fully describe.

But memorization is only one means of storing away God's Word. In a real sense, you are doing this right now as you read Scripture and reflect on its meaning with the help of a commentary. Scripture memory does little good without Scripture comprehension. As you read the Bible with the help of study aids, understanding the meanings of words, reflecting on the circumstances surrounding the literature, discovering the timeless principles contained in its pages, and seeking ways to practically apply divine truth, you are storing divine truth in the marrow and sinews of your body.

Well done!

A second way to accumulate eternal wealth is to *invest yourself in Christian relationships.* All of Paul's letters begin and end with personal greetings. Taken together, the names he counts among his friends and fellow servants add up to a long list. So, when it became dangerous to remain Paul's friend and many deserted him, he still had several men he could count on. Luke, Mark, Timothy, and Onesiphorus were unafraid to risk their lives to give him aid in person.

Unfortunately, friendships are not always convenient. Sometimes they're costly, time-consuming, labor-intensive, and emotionally draining. Friendships sometimes get in the way of progress, such that one's career might not advance as quickly, or the paycheck may boast fewer numbers to the left of the decimal. Friendships also cause heartache from time to time, requiring us to forgive and then endure the painful process of restoring trust.

My point is not to talk you out of cultivating friendships, but to highlight an obvious point that's easy to overlook — at least when we're thinking about relationships. Most worthwhile things in life require sacrifice, a conscious decision to accept less of something in order to enjoy more of something else. We give up play time in order to earn money. We give up money in order to have food, clothing, and a home. We might even purchase a smaller home to afford a better school for the children. These are facts of life we readily accept in every arena except relationships. Somehow, those are supposed to happen automatically, in our spare time, with little or no conscious effort.

The truth is, nearly everything worthwhile involves a tradeoff. And so it is with friendships. Cultivating meaningful Christian relationships requires a significant investment. So, what are you willing to do in order to cultivate a meaningful friendship with another believer? Start with a phone call. You probably know who. Have your calendar handy as you dial.

Traveling a Rough and Rugged Road (2 Timothy 2:1–13)

¹You therefore, my son, be strong in the grace that is in Christ Jesus. ²The things which you have heard from me in the presence of many witnesses, entrust these to faithful men who will be able to teach others also. ³Suffer hardship with *me,* as a good soldier of Christ Jesus. ⁴No soldier in active service entangles himself in the affairs of everyday life, so that he may please the one who enlisted him as a soldier. ⁵Also if anyone competes as an athlete, he does not win the prize unless he competes according to the rules. ⁶The hard-working farmer ought to be the first to receive his share of the crops. ⁷Consider what I say, for the Lord will give you understanding in everything.

⁸Remember Jesus Christ, risen from the dead, descendant of David, according to my gospel, ⁹for which I suffer hardship even to imprisonment as a criminal; but the word of God is not imprisoned. ¹⁰For this reason I endure all things for the sake of those who are chosen, so that they also may obtain the salvation which is in Christ Jesus *and* with *it* eternal glory. ¹¹It is a trustworthy statement:

For if we died with Him, we will also live with Him;
¹² If we endure, we will also reign with Him;
If we deny Him, He also will deny us;
¹³ If we are faithless, He remains faithful, for He cannot deny Himself.

I'd like to set the record straight once and for all. Despite what you hear from many preachers on the radio or television, God's number one priority is *not* to make you feel good—not through health, wealth, or any other worldly means.

More than anything else, He wants to make you like His Son. His desire is not to make us comfortable; it's to help us grow up, and I've never heard anyone say that it is easy to grow up. That's because Satan and the world system continue to conspire against God's plan for us, and he will do everything possible to keep us from becoming mature believers. Therefore, we can expect life to present difficult challenges as the Christian walk follows a rough and rugged path.

Fortunately, the news is not all bad. In fact, it's incredibly good! While happiness flits about on the winds of circumstance, capriciously landing and flying away, the Christian life is a journey toward lasting joy. As the British theologian and author F. B. Meyer wrote:

> Think it not strange, child of God, concerning the fiery trial that tries thee, as though some strange thing had happened. Rejoice! For it is a sure sign that thou art on the right track. If in an unknown country, I am informed that I must pass through a valley where the sun is hidden, or over a stony bit of road, to reach my abiding place—when I come to it, each moment of shadow or jolt of the carriage tells me that I am on the right road. So when a child of God passes through affliction, he is not surprised.[7]

The Lord did not promise to keep us *from* suffering (John 17:15–16); He promised to sustain us *through* suffering (Rom. 8:28–39), so that every experience will become God's means of creating in us a greater capacity for joy with each passing day. While I cannot recommend Simone Weil as a credible theologian, I do agree with at least one of her observations: "The extreme greatness of Christianity lies in the fact that it does not seek a supernatural cure for suffering, but a supernatural use of it."[8] If you haven't discovered the Lord's supernatural use for suffering, you will continue to struggle with disillusionment, perhaps wondering who's at fault, you or God.

Today, I join with Paul to extend an invitation for a journey. It won't be easy. There are many thrills along the way, but it won't always be pleasant. To remain where you are might seem easier, but I can assure you, the comfort of the status quo won't last. Besides, you don't want to miss what God has for you, either along the way or at your destination.

— 2:1–2 —

While the Christian journey toward joy is, indeed, rough and rugged, we do not travel without help. We have within us a divine GPS device; the Holy Spirit continually gives us expert guidance toward our destination—if only we will listen and heed His instructions! We have in our hands a perfectly reliable map of the terrain in the form of sixty-six divinely inspired books, bound together as the Bible. And the Lord has called and equipped trustworthy guides to lead the way. These, we call "pastors."

Having reflected on the past, Paul now meets Timothy in the present for the express purpose of passing the responsibility of leadership to him. But before handing him the torch, the apostle grabs the younger pastor's attention with the emphatic use of the personal pronoun "you." Then, in two verses, he summarizes the two-part responsibility of a pastor: to grow strong in grace and to teach others to do the same.

The phrase rendered "be strong" derives from the passive imperative form of the verb *endynamoō*, "to empower." Furthermore, the imperative is present tense, which calls for an ongoing response. So the command is best translated, "keep on being empowered." Theologians call this kind of passive verb a "divine passive," because it strongly implies divine agency. In other words, God does the empowering, so our responsibility is to submit to His work and to cooperate with it. But, in case there is any doubt, Paul attaches two additional phrases identifying the source of the power: "Be empowered in the grace that is in Christ Jesus."

Christ is the source of the power, we receive that power from Him, and grace is the means by which it flows from Him to us. Moreover, this must be a continual, uninterrupted process. Just like electricity in your home, if the flow of power stops, nothing works.

But the command doesn't stop with Timothy's growing strong in grace. That's only the first of two pastoral responsibilities. Paul expects Timothy to pass on what he has learned through years of tutelage. Early in his second missionary journey, Paul invited Timothy to join his evangelistic entourage, intending to train the younger man for a role of Christian leadership. Of course, Timothy was just one of many men Paul recruited and trained, including people such as Titus, Tychicus, Trophimus, Tertius, Erastus, John Mark, and Luke.

This should not be confused with the Catholic doctrine of "apostolic succession," whereby the Pope receives apostolic, prophetic authority from a long lineage of successors going back to the original Twelve, or to Peter, specifically. John Stott has clarified this well:

> It is to be a succession of apostolic tradition than of apostolic ministry, authority or order, a transmission of the apostles' doctrine handed down unchanged from the apostles to subsequent generations, and passed from hand to hand like the Olympic torch. This apostolic tradition, "the good deposit," is now to be found in the New Testament.[9]

Paul's command to Timothy applies to all of the apostle's pupils, and it applies to Timothy's as well. Paul expected Timothy's students to teach the next generation of teachers, who would, in turn, teach the next. In other words, Paul "entrusted" the truth to Timothy, charged him with the responsibility to guard it, and then commanded him to "entrust" the truth to "faithful men[10] who would be able to teach others also." As a result, the role of pastor has come down to us through countless generations over two millennia, and it remains the same. A pastor is to be empowered continually in the grace that is in Christ Jesus and to lead his flock on the journey we call the Christian walk.

As Paul invited Timothy to follow him, he warned that the journey would not be easy. To illustrate, he chose three examples:

- a soldier (vv. 3–4)
- an athlete (v. 5)
- a farmer (v. 6)

He then returned to the idea of receiving power from Christ through grace (vv. 8–13). Because Paul used these word pictures before (1 Cor. 9:6–7, 24–27), they would be familiar to Timothy.

—2:3–4 (The Focus of a Soldier)—

Stephen Ambrose pulled the title of his modern classic, *Band of Brothers*, from Shakespeare's stirring "St. Crispen's Day Speech" in *Henry V.* As the British army prepared for battle—cut off from retreat, sick with dysentery, fatigued from marching, and outnumbered five to one—the King rallied his generals:

> And Crispin Crispian shall ne'er go by,
> From this day to the ending of the world,
> But we in it shall be remembered,
> We few, we happy few, we band of brothers;
> For he to-day that sheds his blood with me
> Shall be my brother.[11]

Soldiers form a special bond on the field of battle. Paul invited Timothy to become his brother-in-arms through mutual suffering and under the command of Jesus Christ. Moreover, he called Timothy to adopt the focus of a soldier. This is not merely the short-term concentration of a man under fire, but the long-term dedication of a warrior setting aside all other concerns to win a campaign. He was not concerned with the stock market. He was not distracted by entertainment or the latest sports scores. He did not entangle himself in local politics. He remained focused on victory. That's because a distracted soldier is a dead soldier.

Paul's choice of the verb for "entangled" combines the Greek prefix *en* with the same term used by Matthew, Mark, and John to describe the crown of thorns pressed onto the head of Jesus (*plekō*). The root term means "to weave something together." When combined and prefixed with *en*, the word means "to weave in" — that is, on purpose, by design, willingly.

A good soldier intentionally avoids entangling himself in distractions so he can focus all his energy on accomplishing the goal established by his commanding officer.

— 2:5 (The Dedication of an Athlete) —

In Paul's day, Olympic athletes were required to swear an oath before Zeus that they had dedicated themselves to rigorous training for no less than ten months. Failure to train resulted in immediate disqualification. Moreover, failure to abide by the rules of competition earned an athlete a stiff fine for smaller infractions and scourging for serious violations.

Many people define "grace" as the absence of rules. Nothing could be further from the truth. The Word of God is, among other things, a rule book, a guide for life. The Bible contains principles requiring discernment to apply, but it also contains specific precepts — hard-and-fast rules — that must be obeyed without question.

- "Abstain from sexual immorality" (1 Thess. 4:3).
- "Be kind to one another" (Eph. 4:32).
- "Husbands, love your wives" (Col. 3:19).
- "Love one another" (John 13:34).

Jesus, the Giver of grace, said, "If you love Me, you will keep My commandments" (John 14:15). This isn't legalism; this is how we stay on course throughout the journey.

— 2:6 (The Diligence of a Farmer) —

When I drive by farms and look out my vehicle window, I see just enough to know that I want to keep driving. It's sunup-to-sundown toil — fertilizing, plowing, planting, weeding, protecting, harvesting, storing, transporting, selling — and let's not forget constant prayer. Pests, disease, frost, drought, or flooding can ruin

How to Be a Convincing Jesus Freak

Cynthia and I sometimes lead cruises with Insight for Living, usually one each year. We generally take up half the ship, which carries about 1,800 passengers. So, imagine you're an unsaved passenger boarding the ship. You've saved your money, eagerly anticipating a week of fun and leisure on your dream vacation, only to find out the other 900 are a bunch of Christians! The last thing you expected on your big adventure was seven days of 900 people judging your behavior and preaching at you.

We've done this for twenty-five years, so I take a few moments during the first meeting to set the tone. I say something like, "Okay, everybody. Listen to me. God did not put us on this ship to be crusaders. You have not been divinely appointed to make the other passengers' trip miserable. Don't walk through the casino handing out tracts. They'll just think you're nuts and throw it away, anyhow. Instead, let's help make this their best vacation ever. Jesus was a winsome party guest and people couldn't resist the good news He brought. Because we are His followers, let's do the same. Take your name badges off when you're not in our meetings. Be good neighbors. Become friends with them. You might want to go on some excursions with your new friends."

Virtually every cruise, as we near the final port, I'll have a number of other guests and even a few members of the crew say, "We dreaded this trip once we heard about all you Christians being aboard, but it turned out to be the best trip we could have hoped for."

I've never heard of anybody insulted into coming to Christ. No one has ever been made to feel foolish and then say as a result, "I just have to believe in Jesus. Those obnoxious people helped me see the light!"

an entire season's work; therefore, a farmer's diligence doesn't guarantee a good return on his or her investment. Furthermore, farming is not an occupation for the impatient. Delayed gratification defines the farmer's existence.

The farmer's diligent personal investment earns him the right to be first in the field to enjoy its bounty—and no one will enjoy it more!

— 2:7 —

Paul then encouraged Timothy to reflect on his three ministry word pictures. A pastor must exercise the focus of a soldier, the dedication of an athlete, and the diligence of a farmer. Note that the Lord will give him understanding as he ponders what he had been taught.

— 2:8 – 10 —

Paul's illustrations are admittedly human-centered, placing a great deal of responsibility on Timothy to grow in grace: Be focused. Be dedicated. Be diligent. So, it should be no surprise to see Paul return his focus to the role of Christ. Yes, we participate in our growth in godliness, but Jesus is the source of grace and the One ultimately responsible for each believer's progress.

While we suffer hardship for the sake of the gospel and must travel a rough and rugged road, we follow in the steps of One who blazed the trail through a depth of suffering we cannot imagine. "Remember Jesus Christ" indeed! "Risen from the dead" because He experienced the death of all deaths. As the "descendant of David," He deserved a throne, not a cross; so, no one has the right to cry "injustice" more than He. And the Son of God did this to give messengers like Paul good news to tell.

Christ led the way; Paul counted imprisonment his privilege to follow Him to an unjust death of his own. The Lord died to make the good news possible; Paul anticipated death to see it proclaimed. In fact, because he had such confidence in Timothy and his other students, the apostle could celebrate the irony of Nero's injustice. The demented emperor killed Christians, but their message only spread farther and faster. He imprisoned Paul and other faithful believers, but the Word of God enjoyed even greater freedom.

— 2:11 —

When Paul wrote the words, "It is a trustworthy statement," he had just stated something profoundly important; you should prepare yourself for a significant truth. In this case, Paul prepared Timothy for a hymn, two pairs of epigrams expressing four paradoxical truths. He presented them as four conditional clauses, "if we . . . ," each one followed by a result.

Paradox 1: *"If we died with Him, we will also live with Him."* This is the foundational promise of the gospel. If we trust in Christ, receiving His gift of eternal life, we will live with Him forever. We do not need to suffer martyrdom to receive this gift. When we receive this gift by grace, through faith, we experience a mystical union with Him, so that His death is ours, His resurrection is ours, and His eternal life is ours (Rom. 6:1–23; 1 Thess. 5:9–10).

— **2:12** —

Paradox 2: *"If we endure, we will also reign with Him."* The conditional nature of "endurance" shouldn't be stressed too much. Genuine believers *will* endure, as the apostle assures in verse 13. The promise is that enduring injustice in this life will be vindicated in the next. We will reign over the new creation, just as those who persecuted us will endure torment. While we enjoy unending intimacy with the Father, all evil will have been cast into the pit.

Paradox 3: *"If we deny Him, He will also deny us."* Again, the conditional nature of "deny" shouldn't receive too much attention. Persecution has a way of separating genuine believers from interloping nonbelievers. Imposters will deny Christ and forsake the gospel before suffering for someone in whom they do not genuinely believe. Those who deny Him are not "in Christ" and never were. Therefore, those who are truly His need not worry about cracking under torture and then losing their place in heaven (John 10:27–29).

— **12:13** —

Paradox 4: *"If we are faithless, He remains faithful, for He cannot deny Himself."* If any of the previous three conditional statements causes undue stress, the fourth should restore all confidence. While the Bible repeatedly calls for Christians to endure to the end and warns against apostasy, the genuine believer can rest in the faithfulness of Christ. Where we fail, He will succeed. When we lose confidence, become disillusioned, falter in our walk, or fail morally, Jesus Christ will be faithful to carry us through to the end (cf. 1:12; 1 Thess. 5:23–24).

Paul sealed this assurance with an undeniable truth. When God promises to save someone and offers him or her assurance of eternal life, He cannot go back on His promise without violating His own nature. He is holy; He cannot lie or break a promise. A believer's endurance, therefore, becomes a matter of personal honor to Him.

While the Christian's road is a rough and rugged one, it nevertheless leads to a wonderful destination. Blessings beyond measure and Christlike maturity await us at the end of our journey. Our decision to forego happiness in the short term will be rewarded with everlasting joy. That's His promise, and we can cast everything we have and everything we are on His fulfilling it. We can say with Paul, "I know whom I have believed and I am convinced that He is able to guard what I have entrusted to Him until that day" (1:12).

Application

The Rules of the Road

The journey of the faithful follows a rough and rugged road. Bound for heaven, to be sure, but difficult because it runs contrary to the way of the world. So how do we stay on such a challenging road all the way to our destination? How do we keep from succumbing to constant pressure to deny Christ, forsake the gospel, and simply go with the worldly flow? How do we keep the dark nights from turning our thoughts dark?

I find in Paul's exhortation to Timothy two specific rules that, if followed, will keep us moving in the right direction.

Rule 1: *When you lack understanding, reflect on God's Word and "the Lord will give you understanding in everything" (v. 7).* The Greek word translated "understanding" means "a coming together, a merging, a confluence." It carries the idea of puzzle pieces falling into place to form an intelligible picture. When we suffer, this is usually what we need. So, we go in search of answers. "What did I do wrong?" "What if I try *this* solution, or *that* strategy; maybe my pain will end." "Why is God doing this to me?" Tragically, in the absence of satisfactory answers, we fill in the blanks with desperate conclusions, which lead to destructive choices. Lack of understanding leads to discouragement, and discouragement always makes sin appear attractive.

Instead of going on a futile search for cause-effect solutions, immerse yourself in Scripture. You don't have to complete detailed studies of passages and write a paper. Just read, then ponder. Do this often. I have found that my need for answers or solutions slowly fades into the background, and I begin to see things with a serene clarity that can come only from God.

Rule 2: *When you feel overwhelmed, cling to God's promises, knowing He has already fulfilled them in the not-too-distant-future (vv. 11 – 13).* Discernment is needed here. Be careful with books claiming to compile lists of God's promises from the Bible. First of all, many of the so-called promises are merely statements lifted out of their original context. For example, here is one from a volume claiming to list multiple thousands of Bible promises: "God has promised deliverance from fear: 'I sought the LORD, and He answered me; He delivered me from all my fears' (Psalm 34:4 NIV)."

Not a promise. The Bible gives us plenty of reasons we should take courage in God's loving care, but this is not a promise, per se.

Second, not every promise in Scripture belongs to you. For example, "Your descendants will also be like the dust of the earth, and you will spread out to the west and to the east and to the north and to the south; and in you and in your descendants shall all the families of the earth be blessed" (Gen. 28:14).

Not yours. That one belongs to Jacob.

The Bible does, however, contain many promises from God to you, and He thought of you when He made them. Here are just a few.

- Come to Me, all who are weary and heavy-laden, and I will give you rest. Take My yoke upon you and learn from Me, for I am gentle and humble in heart, and you will find rest for your souls (Matt. 11:28–29).
- But if God so clothes the grass of the field, which is alive today and tomorrow is thrown into the furnace, will He not much more clothe you? You of little faith! Do not worry then, saying, "What will we eat?" or "What will we drink?" or "What will we wear for clothing?" For the Gentiles eagerly seek all these things; for your heavenly Father knows that you need all these things. But seek first His kingdom and His righteousness, and all these things will be added to you (Matt. 6:30–33).
- Give, and it will be given to you. They will pour into your lap a good measure—pressed down, shaken together, and running over. For by your standard of measure it will be measured to you in return (Luke 6:38).
- For God so loved the world, that He gave His only begotten Son, that whoever believes in Him shall not perish, but have eternal life (John 3:16).
- My sheep hear My voice, and I know them, and they follow Me; and I give eternal life to them, and they will never perish; and no one will snatch them out of My hand. My Father, who has given them to Me, is greater than all; and no one is able to snatch them out of the Father's hand (John 10:27–29).
- In My Father's house are many dwelling places; if it were not so, I would have told you; for I go to prepare a place for you. If I go and prepare a place

for you, I will come again and receive you to Myself, that where I am, there you may be also (John 14:2–3).

- You will receive power when the Holy Spirit has come upon you; and you shall be My witnesses both in Jerusalem, and in all Judea and Samaria, and even to the remotest part of the earth (Acts 1:8).

- But if the Spirit of Him who raised Jesus from the dead dwells in you, He who raised Christ Jesus from the dead will also give life to your mortal bodies through His Spirit who dwells in you (Rom. 8:11).

- No temptation has overtaken you but such as is common to man; and God is faithful, who will not allow you to be tempted beyond what you are able, but with the temptation will provide the way of escape also, so that you will be able to endure it (1 Cor. 10:13).

- If any of you lacks wisdom, let him ask of God, who gives to all generously and without reproach, and it will be given to him (James 1:5).

- If we confess our sins, He is faithful and righteous to forgive us our sins and to cleanse us from all unrighteousness (1 John 1:9).

- For whatever is born of God overcomes the world; and this is the victory that has overcome the world—our faith. Who is the one who overcomes the world, but he who believes that Jesus is the Son of God? (1 John 5:4–5).

Accurately Handling the Word (2 Timothy 2:14–19)

14Remind *them* of these things, and solemnly charge *them* in the presence of God not to wrangle about words, which is useless *and leads* to the ruin of the hearers. 15Be diligent to present yourself approved to God as a workman who does not need to be ashamed, accurately handling the word of truth. 16But avoid worldly *and* empty chatter, for it will lead to further ungodliness, 17and their talk will spread like gangrene. Among them are Hymenaeus and Philetus, 18*men* who have gone astray from the truth saying that the resurrection has already taken place, and they upset the faith of some. 19Nevertheless, the firm foundation of God stands, having this seal, "The Lord knows those who are His," and, "Everyone who names the name of the Lord is to abstain from wickedness."

For as long as there has been truth to tell, charlatans and deceivers and liars have profited from cleverly twisting it. They present themselves as shining beacons of God's light, and they draw unsuspecting, overly trusting, desperately hurting people like moths to a flame. These peddlers of a toxic faith offer nothing and consume everything.

In his book *Toxic Faith*, Stephen Arterburn describes the effect these religious charlatans had on his grandmother and continue to have on the world:

> They took her money and spent it on themselves and their big plans, schemes that had nothing to do with my grandmother's desire to tell the world about God's love or to feed and clothe orphans. Some of those ministers that she so faithfully supported wound up in jail, divorced their wives, were arrested for indecent exposure, or fell into other public sin. They proclaimed a faith on television or over the radio, but they lived something else. They didn't shrink from asking my grandmother and others like her to sacrifice their food money so they could buy jet fuel to fly to Palm Springs for a weekend getaway. What they did was dishonest, unfair — and very human. The kind of faith they lived looked radically different from the one they proclaimed on the public airwaves ...
>
> They built big empires for themselves while my grandmother turned off her heater at night so she might be able to save a few dollars and therefore give more. Their faith was *toxic*. It poisoned many who trusted them, and it distorted the view of God held by many who watched as these media ministers fell from grace. As a result, many today believe *all* ministers are charlatans and out to fleece the flock. These cynics have derived a toxic, unhealthy view of faith from the toxic examples they saw in the media.[12]

Paul lamented the very same challenges less than one generation after the Lord commissioned His apostles to evangelize the world. Technology has amplified the voices of religious profiteers — duplicating and disseminating their lies with greater speed and efficiency — but little else has changed. Their perversions and methods remain the same. So, as the light began to fade in Paul's dungeon, the apostle wrote his timid friend in Ephesus, encouraging him to expose and confront peddlers of apostasy. Two thousand years later, his words continue to inspire and equip all defenders of truth.

— **2:14** —

Ever the practical preacher, Paul gave his protégé specific instructions for how to expose and confront charlatans, beginning with the obvious: Proclaim the truth!

The NASB and other versions supply the pronoun "them," because, unlike Greek, the English verb "remind" looks odd without a direct object. A literal rendering of Paul's command would be, "Remind of these things." Remind whom? Everyone. At every opportunity.

"These things" refers to the truths Paul celebrated in the hymn just cited:

If we died with Him, we will also live with Him;
If we endure, we will also reign with Him;
If we deny Him, He also will deny us;
If we are faithless, He remains faithful, for He cannot deny Himself. (2:11–13)

In addition to proclaiming the truth, Paul urged the pastor to forbid "wrangling about words." This phrase translates the same rare compound word that Paul used in his first letter (1 Tim. 6:4), which means (lit.) "word-fight." One Greek satirist described the debate between Stoics and Epicureans as a "word-fight,"[13] deliberately using the term to characterize the men as pathetic.

— 2:15–16 —

The order in which Paul presented his commands to Timothy intrigues me. Verse 14 commands the pastor to conduct a *public* ministry of proclaiming truth and forbidding word-fights. Verses 15 and 16 urged Timothy to dedicate himself to a *private* ministry of gaining personal mastery of truth and personally avoiding word-fights. Paul said, in effect, "Preach, and then practice what you preach."

One might expect the reverse order. Practice, then preach. But this would suggest that a pastor somehow arrives at a level of expertise and then becomes the resident expert in all things godly within a particular congregation. In truth, a pastor never "arrives"; he's always progressing, always growing. Furthermore, the pastor's authority to exhort doesn't come from being a perfect example; he stands on the authority of God's Word. A pastor's sermons are no less for him than anyone in the congregation. (I frequently find myself convicted by my own Sunday messages!)

Paul's order — preach, then practice — further implies that a pastor must regularly retreat from public ministry to stand before God for examination. Ministers *need* this, especially pastors. According to the results of a survey reported in a respected leadership journal, many leaders lack the quality of self-awareness. In fact, this common deficiency prompted management experts to devise a painfully accurate leadership assessment called the "360 Feedback Evaluation," which asks no less than six people — two superiors, two peers, and two subordinates — to complete a detailed, anonymous questionnaire about an individual. The report usually stuns leaders. How they see themselves and how their colleagues perceive them frequently differ by a wide margin.

Paul urges Timothy to engage in continual self-examination, something charlatans avoid at all costs. They distance themselves from self-reflection and reject accountability, and they dare not stand before God for inspection. If, however, a pastor passes the Lord's muster, he will live above reproach before the flock, and this is vital to encouraging healthy faith. Once members of a congregation have heard the pastor proclaim a particular truth from God's Word, you can be certain they will be watching to see if he lives out that truth.

Take special note of the phrase "accurately handling," a term that the King James Version renders "rightly dividing." This expression is better translated, "practically living out." In other words, Timothy must handle the word of truth accurately *in his conduct.* "He is superior to the false teachers, not because he can present the word better, nor because he offers it in a theologically legitimate form, but because he follows this word of truth aright in his own life, and thus confirms it."[14]

There can be no substitute for expository preaching—the diligent study, accurate interpretation, and effective communication of God's Word. This essential duty lies at the heart of pastoral ministry. But this is the *minimum* standard called for by Paul in this verse. In the Hebrew concept of wisdom—we must not forget that Paul spent the first half of his life steeped in Jewish culture and studying at the highest levels of rabbinic tradition—knowledge apart from practical living is meaningless.

Beware overweight nutritionists, attorneys serving prison sentences, physicians who chain smoke, bankrupt financial advisors, and preachers who live contrary to the Word of God!

— 2:17–18 —

After forbidding "worldly and empty chatter" (see comments on 1 Tim. 1:9; 6:20; Titus 3:9), Paul reminded his friend of the deadly consequences and then illustrated his point with negative examples Timothy undoubtedly knew well.

The English word "gangrene" comes directly from the Greek term. It carries the idea of spreading poison throughout a system, a dreaded medical condition in the days before the invention of antiseptics and before people understood the importance of careful hygiene. Because few of us have ever witnessed a case of gangrene, a more poignant illustration today would be cancer. "Worldly and empty chatter"— Paul's characterization of philosophy, humanity's attempt to understand spiritual truths apart from Scripture—must be cut out of the body or it will metastasize and kill. That's the idea.

To illustrate his point, Paul named two men he had "cut out" of the congregation—events Timothy probably witnessed. In years past, Hymenaeus joined the popular heretic Alexander (4:14; cf. Acts 19:33) in teaching that the gospel didn't require obedience (1 Tim. 1:18–20). Later, he joined Philetus to promote a twisted concept of resurrection, either that it was spiritual only (cf. 1 Cor. 4:8; 15:12) or that it had already occurred (cf. 2 Thess. 2:1–4). Because Greek philosophy, which permeated Ephesus, discounted bodily resurrection as absurd, false teachers probably adapted

EXCURSUS

The Meaning of *Orthotomeō* in 2 Timothy 2:15

For as long as I can remember, expositors have taken 2 Timothy 2:15 as their mandate to study the Scriptures in order to discern their precise meaning, and then to preach the Word accordingly. But that may not have been all that the apostle had in mind with this verse. Don't misunderstand; expository preaching — the diligent study, accurate interpretation, and effective communication of God's Word — lies at the heart of pastoral ministry. There can be no substitute. But Paul may have been driving toward a deeper aspect of pastoral ministry: personal integrity.

The Greek verb translated "accurately handling" is *orthotomeō*, which literally means "to cut straight," but it can have one of two possible metaphorical uses. The first, which most translations of 2 Timothy 2:15 prefer, is "to expertly and correctly handle." By application, this would mean "understanding the word of truth correctly and then preaching it properly." But the evidence for this interpretation is virtually nonexistent. The evidence is much stronger in support of another figurative meaning: "to put into practice" or "to make what is theoretical a practical reality."

Interestingly, the verb *orthotomeō* cannot be found anywhere else in any kind of Greek literature except two verses in the Greek translation of the Old Testament:

- "In all your ways acknowledge Him, and He will *make* your paths *straight*" (Prov. 3:6, key verb in italics).
- "The righteousness of the blameless will *smooth* his way, but the wicked will fall by his own wickedness" (Prov. 11:5, key verb in italics).

Either the Jewish scholars translating these Hebrew proverbs into Greek decided to coin a term,[15] or the Greek term was used orally within the Jewish community. In both instances, the verb takes as the direct object *hodos*, "road" or "way," thus drawing on the imagery of clearing debris and then leveling out hills and valleys. In this sense, a construction crew can be said to "cut a straight path" from one place to another.[16] Metaphorically, the expression carries the idea of transforming a desire into a practical possibility. So, Proverbs 11:5 declares that righteous behavior clears a road through life, allowing the righteous one to get where he wants to go.

Paul could have chosen any number of words or expressions when exhorting Timothy with respect to "the word of truth," but he chose a verb unique to two proverbs urging obedience as a means of journeying through life. Therefore, given the context of Paul's argument in this segment (2:14–19), it would appear a better way of understanding *orthotomeō* in verse 15 would be, "Be diligent to present yourself approved to God as a workman who does not need to be ashamed, *cutting a straight path* with the word of truth" (italics mine). Factoring in the metaphor, I would render the verse: "Be diligent to present yourself approved to God as a workman who does not need to be ashamed, *practically living out* the Word of truth."

Christian doctrine to ease the tension. Greeks would have found mere spiritual resurrection very much to their liking—not very different from their own beliefs, in fact.

Unfortunately, the world system will always find Christian doctrine either offensive or absurd. The issues change, but the tension remains. The "word of truth" demands a choice. Therefore, we must study Scripture more than any other discipline. That doesn't mean we shouldn't study science, math, government, literature, or even philosophy. As the saying goes, "All truth is God's truth." We must, however, submit all other knowledge to the authority of God's Word. When people try to bend Scripture to harmonize with science or philosophy, they promote a false gospel and therefore promote a toxic faith.

— **2:19** —

"Nevertheless . . ." Paul now drew a bold double line across the page, as it were, leading off the next sentence with a strong contrastive conjunction. Despite all the dangers of apostasy, despite the defection of influential leaders, despite their leading many souls astray, regardless of how much injury the church has suffered, God's foundation of truth remains strong and sure.

Don't forget Paul's personal circumstances as he penned these words. At a time when he should have been carrying the gospel westward, the apostle was suffering the outrageous injustice of a criminal's dungeon. When the church could have been adding many more thousands of souls to their number, a madman captured, humiliated, tortured, and murdered Christians, all for the sake of entertainment and to curry favor with his countrymen. Nevertheless . . .

Paul drew on the familiar imagery of a building cornerstone bearing an official seal. A seal carved into the stone protected the building against intrusion or destruction. It communicated an implicit warning to any potential violator, "Harm this building and you'll answer to me!" The seal on the foundation of truth bears two inscriptions. These two statements, brandished on the foundation of the church, speak to the issue of identity from different perspectives.

Inscription 1: *"The Lord knows those who are His"* (cf. John 10:14; Rom. 8:29; 1 Cor. 8:3). The true church consists of those who belong to the Lord Jesus Christ. They are the elect (Matt. 24:31; Rom. 8:33; Col. 3:12; 2 Tim. 2:10), those who have believed in Jesus Christ by placing their trust in Him as their sole hope of heaven (John 3:16; 11:25–26).

No one has to declare to the Lord, "I am Yours; don't overlook me!" He cannot be fooled by hypocrisy, and failure cannot render His own unrecognizable.

Whereas no one on earth can determine who is saved and who is lost—at least not for certain—God alone knows for certain.

Inscription #2: *"Everyone who names the name of the Lord is to abstain from wickedness"* (cf. John 14:15; 1 John 3:6, 9; 5:18). The true church is filled with those who doggedly reject sin. They are not sinless; in fact, many are terribly flawed. But they hate their sin, and they devote themselves to living above and beyond the pull of wrongdoing.

While God knows His own, believers should identify themselves to others through obedience. Those who claim to be God's own, yet continue to walk in sin, bring shame on the church and promote a toxic faith.

God's sovereignty doesn't negate human responsibility, but count on this: the foundation remains firm!

In 1775, at the ripe, young age of twenty-two, John Rippon began serving the congregation of Carter's Lane Baptist Church in London, a post he held for sixty-three years. Wanting to expand the role of music in church, he compiled what he called "An Appendix to Dr. Watts' Psalms and Hymns," which he published as *A Selection of Hymns from the Best Authors*. It became a runaway hit among churches throughout Great Britain, going through no less than fifteen editions. Eventually it became a staple music resource in the United States.

He included a hymn by an author known only as "K—," originally titled, "Exceedingly Great and Precious Promises." We know it today by the first four words of the first stanza.

> How firm a foundation, ye saints of the Lord,
> Is laid for your faith in His excellent Word!
> What more can He say than to you He hath said,
> You, who unto Jesus for refuge have fled?
>
> In every condition, in sickness, in health;
> In poverty's vale, or abounding in wealth;
> At home and abroad, on the land, on the sea,
> As thy days may demand, shall thy strength ever be.
>
> Fear not, I am with thee, O be not dismayed,
> For I am thy God and will still give thee aid;
> I'll strengthen and help thee, and cause thee to stand
> Upheld by My righteous, omnipotent hand.
>
> When through the deep waters I call thee to go,
> The rivers of woe shall not thee overflow;
> For I will be with thee, thy troubles to bless,
> And sanctify to thee thy deepest distress.

When through fiery trials thy pathways shall lie,
My grace, all sufficient, shall be thy supply;
The flame shall not hurt thee; I only design
Thy dross to consume, and thy gold to refine.

Even down to old age all My people shall prove
My sovereign, eternal, unchangeable love;
And when hoary hairs shall their temples adorn,
Like lambs they shall still in My bosom be borne.

The soul that on Jesus has leaned for repose,
I will not, I will not desert to its foes;
That soul, though all hell should endeavor to shake,
I'll never, no never, no never forsake.[17]

Application

My Weekly Sermon Preparation

There's a saying among pastors: "Sunday just keeps coming!" That usually prompts a knowing laugh. Whether you're gifted or not, regardless of whether the week is uneventful or full of surprises, despite the relentless badgering of details, Sunday morning approaches like a lumbering, unstoppable freight train. So, you must either prepare to preach or prepare to get out of the way!

Preaching is the most visible aspect of a senior pastor's role. Some churches require the pastor to prepare three different messages each week: Sunday morning, Sunday evening, and a midweek "prayer" service on Wednesday evening, which is essentially no different from the other two meeting times. Fortunately, our church takes a different approach, and many other strong shoulders share the burden of leadership with me. So I prepare one sermon each week, which I deliver twice on Sunday. (In the past, I have delivered as many as five sermons each Sunday!)

Over the years, I have developed a weekly routine that works well for me. Having a routine helps me manage this very visible aspect of pastoral ministry without neglecting the many duties almost no one sees. The schedule below describes how a sermon comes together for me throughout a typical week.

One great advantage of expository preaching is that I never have to wonder what I'm going to preach the next Sunday. It won't be a hot topic ripped from the headlines or a clever insight I stumbled upon or saw in a dream. I preach the passage that comes after the one I just exposited, and the passage itself tells me the subject. I merely tell the congregation what the Lord revealed to me in those verses. While

I do sometimes preach a series of messages around a particular subject, such as marriage or some doctrine of suffering, the preaching is still expository. I assemble passages that speak to the topic at hand and then explain and apply them.

When I preach through a book of the Bible, I generally read the entire work as a whole and then break it down into manageable segments. I don't share this with anyone, because I invariably adjust the plan along the way. But this helps me get a sense of how many Sundays it will require, including holidays and breaks, and it helps the rest of the staff (especially our pastor of worship and music) plan their activities.

Sunday Evening

Sunday evening, after lunch and a long afternoon nap (often in front of a football game!), I cannot resist the urge to read the next passage. But that's all I'll do. Once it's in my head, it becomes a part of all my thoughts, which helps immensely.

Monday

I really should take all of Monday off to rest or take care of things around the house. But the church needs an outline by Wednesday, so I need to have a sufficient grasp of the text and where it's leading by then. So, I'll devote some time during the day to reading the passage — always out loud — and to drafting a rough outline (which I'll refine later, of course).

Tuesday

Tuesday is a big day for study. I begin with observations in the original language, initially without the aid of any references except a couple of lexicons. I pay attention to key terms and take note of the syntax, although I don't parse every verb or diagram every sentence, like some expositors. If I see something unusual, intriguing, or significant, I'll examine it closely. Take, for example, Matthew 1:16: "Jacob was the father of Joseph the husband of Mary, by whom Jesus was born, who is called the Messiah." I immediately noticed that the relative personal pronoun "whom" is singular and feminine in Greek, which doesn't come through clearly in English. Matthew carefully crafted that sentence to assert that Jesus was the biological son of Mary alone. I won't bore the congregation with unnecessary word studies and lessons on Greek syntax, but that's information I'll be sure to include.

After I have observed the passage thoroughly, I begin the work of interpretation. What does the human author mean to communicate and for what purpose? I reference historical works to understand the circumstances surrounding the passage. I want to know as much about the human author as possible, his influences, his perspective, even the circumstances and location of his writing. I'll examine the situation prompting his work, including the needs of the original audience and their location, culture, influences, and circumstances. If the text includes figures of speech, metaphors, references to the Old Testament, or stories, I want to hear them from the perspective of their time and culture. Encyclopedias, history references, and commentaries can supply a lot of that information.

I also want to do the work of correlation, which examines how the passage fits within the context of the book itself, the Bible as a whole, and especially in light of other passages that speak to the same issues. Paul and John may have said different things about the same issue. Because they both wrote inerrant divine truth, we have to understand how their words correlate.

I try not to think too much about how I'll present the passage or how it will apply, but usually three crucial elements begin to take shape in my mind: potential applications, a title, and an introduction. I make note of them as I go, so I won't lose them, but I remain focused on studying the biblical text. Eventually, however, I feel compelled to work on them, beginning with an introduction.

Wednesday

Almost without exception, the application has solidified in my mind sometime the day before, although I haven't crafted the actual wording. A title also has taken shape. I may have started working on the introduction on Tuesday, but I will devote most of Wednesday to crafting it carefully. I already know where the sermon is going and I know which parts of the text I will highlight, so my opening becomes extremely important to me. It refines where I go with the message and clarifies how I'm going to move the congregation toward that destination. I usually have a pull page of notes devoted to the introduction alone. I'll often memorize my opening line, which gives the sermon a strong start.

I will complete the outline as it will appear in the worship folder for Sunday and send it to the folks in charge of printing.

Thursday

I will spend most of Thursday detailing the message. With the introduction written and the rough outline complete, it's just a matter of determining how much emphasis to give each point and how to explain some of the more technical aspects of the language or theology in a manner that informs without becoming pedantic. Whereas the applications came to me earlier, I'll wait until I've crafted the message before putting the principles together.

I think of the applications in terms of how they relate to other people's lives, though sometimes to my own. Illustrations often come from my own experiences, but I try to think of what individuals in the congregation need. Naturally, that means I must have some knowledge of that through personal interaction.

Whereas Tuesday and Wednesday involve a lot of study time, I can tolerate interruptions fairly easily. Thursday, however, I really need uninterrupted time to

ACCURATELY HANDLING THE WORD   AM/SCC/ 9/20/09
2 Timothy 2:14-19   (#6)

INTRO: Toxic religion has been around for a long, long time.

For as long as there has been truth to tell, there have been charlatans and liars. This has caused many to become skeptical of ALL who speak for God, even those who can be trusted. Even worse, this has also resulted in many who lack discernment to trust and support any and all who claim to speak for God --- even the spurious ...the phony.

Listen to one man's story

- Stephen Arterburn/Jack Felton
Toxic Faith. Waterbrook Press, 1991.(pp.1-3)

Believe-it-or-not...there were charlatans and liars back in the FIRST century! The apostle Paul stood against them during his ministry...and was still warning others of them when he wrote his last letter -- 2 Timothy. Knowing that Timothy would have to deal with them, Paul didn't hesitate to expose them as he alerted Tim. to the damage they cause.

I. SEEING THE BIG PICTURE

Before we jump into these six verses in Chap. 2, I'd like to have us step back and get the "big picture" of what he is writing:

It will help if you mentally set aside the 14th verse...and go first to the 15th, which sets the scene for this section.

① Positive & Clear Instruction   (start @ v.)

As we'll see, Paul is urging this young pastor: ● a) be a diligent workman
● b) make certain that you, yourself remain authentic..."tried & true"
● c) handle the word accurately/well
● d) now -- go back to v.14 ... stand...

= 2 =

II. EXPLAINING THE ROLE OF ACCURATE MESSENGERS

The pen portrait painted by Paul is a helpful one --- and it's one that ought to hang in the mental gallery of all who speak for God. All who teach, all who preach, all who do evangelistic work, all missionaries, and all who counsel!

== What Do "Accurate Messengers" Do?

① We first must pay attention to OURSELVES.
Make every effort--pay close attention to--YOUR OWN EXAMPLE...make sure you pass the test of God's careful inspection.   [SEE 1 TIM. 4:12-16 !]

The charlatan has long-since lost ANY interest in making an honest appraisal of himself! Accurate, faithful, reliable messengers of God can stand the scrutiny of God's examination. NO SECRET DOUBLE LIFE. NO SHAME. NO ULTER.MOTI

② Next we must "acc. handle the word of truth"
KJV "rightly dividing" Lit. this verb means "to cut straight."
GREEKS used this term 3 different ways:
1) driving a coach/chariot on a straight road across the country
2) plowing a straight furrow across a field
3) a stone mason cutting/squaring a stone along a straight line

A reliable messenger is an accurate, careful, precise communicator of word of truth (Scripture) No deviation...undiluted...staying true to the context, refusing to mis-interpret/misapply the text of Scripture.
PRIMARY QUESTION TO ASK OF EVERY MINISTER:
Does the individual accurately handle the truth
· Physicians who fail to do accurate work are guilty of MALPRACTICE
· Attorneys who fail to do accurate work acc. to the law are guilty of ILLEGALITIES
· Those in financial institutions who fail to do acc...
BUT ... of FRAUD/other crimes
REMAI...

"WORKMAN"   = 3 =

To do it right requires hard, hard work! What passes for preaching is embarrassing these days! Undisciplined habits...sloppy research, negligent attention to detail...inadequate time/effort, and homiletical sloth! We must give account before our God -- and we're urged to do so w/o shame!

The word picture in this text is a diligent WORKMAN who does his work well--down to the last detail--and presents it to his superior master without reluctance and without shame. ILLUS...

== What Are We NOT to Do? (vv.14 and 16)
· Godless others/warn them about WORD FIGHTS!
Word fights are time-consuming, ego-building intellectual-jockeying that lead to quarrels and controversial arguments --- verbal fighting that results in "the ruin of the hearers" as Paul says.

-- Avoid empty chatter...just meandering talk that goes nowhere, but make no mistake, it DOES NO GOOD. In fact, it's "godless" and "gangrenous"
Spreads poison ---

NOTE: When you are not hard at work in the text of Holy Scripture, it's easy to drift into this kind of useless/dangerous verbal disputing, that has debilitating effect on all so engaged.

The farther these kinds of people go in their "empty chatter," the farther the depart fmtr...

III. EXPOSING THE WRONGS OF FALSE TEACHERS
==What they do. They spread false informa...
False doctrine: "resurrection has happened!" We Not going to be some final, great day of res tion, but it's a "spiritual resurrec.!" We all the benefits of it now -- not later! A

But false teachers rely on their suger-co style of delivery, great salesmanship and in their influence over others. No hope of departed 1...
BUT LOOK AT vv. 16, 17, 18
① All that talks leads further/fur
② That kind of talk spreads like
③ When that's combined, it "upset

-- Why They Do it   (v.18)
THEY HAVE GONE ASTRAY FROM THE TRUT
(Paul named two -- about whom we kn else than what is mentioned here --
Their departure works like ANTHRAX i
ILLUS: PEOPLE LONG TO KNOW TRUTH!/Chu...

= 4 =   TOXIC FAITH CONTINUES

As long as there is truth on this planet, there will be those who question it...smear it...cast doubts on it...explain it away...lead others from it

HOWEVER or NEVERTHELESS

Human being will shift and change...drift off and erode...become indifferent and fascilating & soft.

NEVERTHELESS !!!!! What?

IV. STANDING STRONG ON FIRM FOUNDATION (v.19)

With everything in a state of flux...as we watch churches and many ministers goin g under, spreading questions & doubt & poison, NEVERTHELESS, there is one solid & sure foundation. We fall back on it often! God Himself. God's Word. God's Plan.

Paul writes of this, implying that it's the TRUE CHURCH THAT CHRIST IS BUILDING!

It has a twofold seal/inscription
① The first is kept secret/remains invisible ("the Lord knows tho-e who are His")
② The second is seen by the public/it's visible ("Let everyone who names the name of) Christ depart from iniquity")

THE TRUE CHURCH consists of those who belong to the Lord Jesus Christ. The elect. Those who have been called out...chosen...believed. == be sure of this: the Lord KNOWS each one-

THE TRUE CHURCH is filled with those who deliberately/intentionally abstain from wickedness. Not perfect -- but pursuing a righteous lifestyle. Not sinless -- but facing the right direction w/their lives.

God's sovereignty does not negate human responsibili

But count on this --- THE FOUNDATION IS SURE! Christ is building His church"and the gates of hades will not overpower/overthrow it!"

Conclusion: How comforting it is to know that we may tremble on the Rock -- but it never trembles under us! All the changes/shifts/doubts have not in ANY way affected the foundation beneath us. We stand, by faith, on the solid rock!

See attached illus

6

put everything together and to prepare my notes. So I protect Thursdays unlike I do any other day. By the end of the day, I have the sermon almost complete.

Friday

I devote Friday to other duties, but the sermon is never far from my mind. I mentally review it and let it soak. Occasionally, I'll move some things around or even type out a replacement page to refine a section. But the work is minimal at this point.

Saturday

I make the passage and the sermon a matter of prayer much of the day and I read through it several times. I often read the passage in a couple other versions. Sometimes, I'll come up with an even better introduction. If so, I type it up and place it in front of the old. I do keep the old introduction with my notes, however. It might be useful for another occasion.

When I read through the notes, I quietly talk out loud, which means I need solitude. I can't have anyone around, or my mind goes to him or her instead of my message.

Sunday

Time to preach! I resist the urge to make last minute adjustments, although some are necessary. Because I don't have much opportunity to go through my notes again on Sunday morning, the second service is usually better delivered than the first.

When it's all over, I file the notes in the order I preached them, keeping the illustrations with the notes. The downside is that I don't have ready access to the illustrations at another time because I don't take the time to make copies and keep them indexed. But when I preach the sermon again in another context, I have everything clipped together and ready to go.

Sunday, after lunch, I typically collapse in my recliner and sleep for several hours. The process of preaching leaves me absolutely drained. Satisfied, but worn out.

Christian Leadership 101 (2 Timothy 2:20–26)

20Now in a large house there are not only gold and silver vessels, but also vessels of wood and of earthenware, and some to honor and some to dishonor. 21Therefore, if anyone cleanses himself from these *things*, he will be a vessel for honor, sanctified, useful to the Master, prepared for every good work. 22Now flee from youthful lusts and pursue righteousness, faith, love *and* peace, with those who call on the Lord from a pure heart. ²³But refuse foolish and ignorant speculations, knowing that they produce quarrels. ²⁴The Lord's bond-servant must not be quarrelsome, but be kind to all, able to teach, patient when wronged, ²⁵with gentleness correcting those who are in opposition, if perhaps God may grant them repentance leading to the knowledge of the truth, ²⁶and they may come to their senses *and* *escape* from the snare of the devil, having been held captive by him to do his will.

Effective leaders — not just in church, but in every arena — must be generously endowed with competence *and* character.

Competence relates to what we do. To be competent, one must acquire the necessary knowledge and skills to carry out a given task, and then consistently perform his or her duties with excellence. Competence tends to be a public quality. People witness the results of someone's efforts and then judge him or her to be competent.

Character, however, is a more private matter, having more to do with inner qualities that are more difficult to see, such as honesty, trustworthiness, responsibility, or diligence. Whereas competence describes what we do, character reflects what we are.

Believe it or not, there are rare occasions when competence outweighs character in terms of qualifications. As I write this segment of commentary, a fellow pastor is recovering from a seven-hour surgical procedure to remove a brain tumor. To be perfectly honest, I care more about the skill of the neurosurgeon's hands than whether he's a good husband and father, or whether he cheats on his taxes, or if he's a malicious gossip. Don't get me wrong; I care about character. But before a physician begins cutting into a man's brain, I would scrutinize his surgical track record before probing his inner life.

In most cases, however, character affects competence. This is especially true of leadership in the secular realm, and it is inescapable in the sacred. But what if this talented, albeit morally deficient, surgeon expressed an interest in teaching a class in your church or presented himself as a candidate for deacon or elder? His skills in the operating room suddenly retreat to the background. In the role of spiritual leadership, character eclipses competence. Every time!

As the shadow of death slowly enveloped Paul's dungeon in Rome and the apostle prepared his younger friend to carry the torch of leadership after him, he continually highlighted the importance of character. He commended the single-minded focus of a soldier (2:3 – 4), the dedication of a winning athlete (2:5), the long-suffering diligence of a farmer (2:6), and the transparent goodness of a worker (2:15). Paul knew Timothy to be a man of sterling character, or he wouldn't have placed him in

The Missing Link

I was not born with a knowledge of the truth. Like everyone, I came into this world estranged from God, light-years from walking in the light. By His grace, I was born into a home where the name of Christ was spoken. By His grace, I grew up in a home that loved the Bible. And so by His grace, I learned about Jesus Christ from my mom and dad, who took me to church. Sunday school teachers loved me like Jesus loved children. Youth leaders, deacons, elders, and pastors modeled the life of Christ.

While serving in the Marine Corps, stationed far from home, a faithful mentor of mine with The Navigators taught me to see all circumstances through the eyes of a loving God. In seminary, under the discerning guidance of wise professors, I learned the deeper truths of Jesus Christ. And throughout my years in pastoral ministry, friends, fellow staff members, and several mentors have encouraged me and helped steer me through difficult waters.

I am the beneficiary of a priceless legacy. Other faithful men and women, who once received the torch of Christian leadership from the generation before, placed it in my hand and said, "Run. Hold this light high and guard it!" I am the last link in a chain that extends back to Timothy, Paul, and beyond. I am the last link, of course, if no one receives the torch from my hand.

Are you that man or woman? Take this light. Hold it high as you run and guard it well!

Ephesus to lead the most strategically important church in Asia. The apostle worried not so much about Timothy as the next generation of men he would equip and empower to lead.

— **2:20** —

As Warren Wiersbe has noted in his splendid book *Preaching and Teaching with Imagination*, "Parables [and other illustrations] start off like *pictures*, and then become *mirrors*, and then become *windows*. First there's *sight* as we see a slice of life in the picture; then there's *insight* as we see ourselves in the mirror; and then there's *vision* as we look through the window of revelation and see the Lord."[18] Paul's image of a foundation in verse 19 naturally calls to mind the image of a house. The Lord has laid a solid foundation of truth on which the structure of the church rests.

Like all households, the house of God contains various kinds of vessels, including good china for special guests and everyday dishes for regular meals. Before the advent of indoor plumbing, households also used a vessel called a "chamber pot." It was reserved for human waste. Rather than brave inclement weather in the middle of a cold night, one used a chamber pot, covered it with a lid, and then emptied it the following morning.

As we examine and apply Paul's illustration, we need to be clear about the context. His analogy bears a strong resemblance to the image used in his letter to the Romans to defend God's sovereign election in salvation (Rom. 9:20–24). In this case, the analogy has nothing to do with salvation and everything to do with service. In Romans, the vessels have no say in their use. Here, vessels may choose to become vessels for honor. In Romans, God cleanses and sanctifies. Here, vessels cleanse themselves.

— **2:21** —

Paul then introduced a condition, "if," followed by four "then" results. The only condition for becoming a vessel of honor is to cleanse oneself from all things dishonorable. This places the responsibility for cleansing with the individual. Again, the issue is not salvation, but service. Believers are positionally cleansed of sin, declared righteous in the court of heaven, and set apart for good works. *Functionally*, however, the Holy Spirit must guide us through a process of sanctification. While He will be faithful to complete the task, He nevertheless calls us to participate in His cleansing program.

The condition, "if anyone cleanses himself," uses the Greek verb from which we derive the English word "catharsis." One experiences catharsis when he or she is purged of something toxic. Furthermore, Paul chooses an intensified form of the verb, meaning the vessel must be thoroughly scrubbed and disinfected before it can be used for a noble purpose. Just imagine how long and hard you would scour a chamber pot before using it to serve stew!

Once the condition has been met, four results follow.

First, *the person becomes a "vessel for honor."* This not only refers to the vessel's inherent worth—any container is good enough to hold excrement, but we value vessels clean enough to serve food; the phrase also describes the container's intended purpose. The cleansed vessel will serve an honorable role.

Second, *the person is "sanctified"*; that is, set apart for a specific purpose. I don't use kitchen knives to repair something in the garage. Those utensils are reserved for food preparation. Similarly, cleansed vessels are stored in a special place and used only for their intended functions.

Third, the person is *"useful to the Master."* The adjective means "valuable" or "profitable." Before entering ministry, I trained to become a mechanical engineer while working in a machine shop. As an apprentice, I quickly discovered I could turn out high-quality parts only when I used high-quality tools. That's when I learned to prize fine tools.

Fourth, *the person is "prepared for every good work."* The verb translated "prepared" is a perfect passive participle, which can be literally rendered, "one who has been made ready and remains so."

— 2:22 —

Paul then explained just how one might cleanse himself or herself to be a vessel suitable for ministry. First, we must flee "youthful lusts," which most people associate with sexual sin. As youth gives way to adulthood, glands shift into overdrive and we have to learn restraint. But that's only part of the struggle. Timothy wasn't a teenager at the time of this writing, but a man in his late thirties or early forties.

The apostle used the "flee … pursue" formula in his first letter, which will help us interpret his meaning here.

> But godliness actually is a means of great gain when accompanied by contentment. For we have brought nothing into the world, so we cannot take anything out of it either. If we have food and covering, with these we shall be content. But those who want to get rich fall into temptation and a snare and many foolish and harmful desires which plunge men into ruin and destruction. For the love of money is

a root of all sorts of evil, and some by longing for it have wandered away from the faith and pierced themselves with many griefs.

But flee from these things, you man of God, and pursue righteousness, godliness, faith, love, perseverance and gentleness. (1 Tim. 6:6 – 11)

A comparison strongly suggests that "youthful lusts" are those things that rob a mature person of his or her contentment. Lust for money. Lust for power or control. Lust for admiration. Lust for achievement. People consumed by these lusts become impatient, dogmatic, competitive, argumentative, harsh, self-imposing, and stubborn — just the kind of personality that will shatter a congregation into a thousand factions.

But it's not enough to empty a vessel of unclean contents. Before it can be used, it needs a good scouring. Paul named four cleansing agents:

- "righteousness" that reaches outward to do what is right by others
- "faith" that reaches upward to place trust in God
- "love" that extends grace to others by seeking their highest, greatest good
- "peace" that is experienced within by resting in the friendship we share with God

Note the apostle encouraged those who wished to cleanse themselves to find others of like mind. We were never meant to walk the path of righteousness alone.

— **2:23** —

A person cleanses himself or herself by rejecting (lit., "begging off"; cf. Luke 14:18 – 19) what Paul calls "moronic" and "uninformed" speculations (1 Tim. 6:4; Titus 3:9). This includes pointless debate with other believers as well as those outside the body of Christ.

Debating the finer points of theology with another believer can be stimulating and fun. I have engaged in more than one rousing seminary row and enjoyed the mental sparring a great deal. But it's a lousy teaching tool. I don't remember changing my position on a significant point of doctrine, nor do I recall influencing someone else to shift his position through spirited, point-counterpoint debating. True to Paul's words, arguments do nothing but waste time and stir up animosity between people. The fact is, we have a big enough job living by the straightforward points of Christian doctrine without having to speculate about unclear issues.

We must also avoid pointless debates with nonbelievers. These would include arguments with people who either challenge Christian doctrine without having any knowledge of the Bible, or who want to debate philosophical or religious issues that have no relevance to Christian doctrine. I've never seen anyone decide to become a Christian as a result of losing an argument.

Paul's point is clear: arguing is futile. People who genuinely want truth don't dispute what you have to tell them. They ask questions. They seek clarification. But they rarely argue.

— **2:24** —

Having explained the futility of trying to correct or teach through debate, Paul offered a different approach. In just a few phrases, he described the ideal Christian leader. Leaders don't fight; they influence. Take note of how a spiritual leader influences those in opposition to divine truth.

First, *a spiritual leader is gentle.* We get a good idea of what Paul meant by this term in 1 Thessalonians 2:7. "We proved to be gentle among you, as a nursing mother tenderly cares for her own children." I've heard my sister, Luci, say she wishes Christians would "just be nice." That captures the spirit of Paul's counsel regarding an effective spiritual leader. We're to be thoughtful and courteous. The spiritual leader must abide by the basic rules of good manners.

Second, *a spiritual leader is ready, willing, and able to pass on biblical truth.* He or she has acquired biblical knowledge through diligent study and has learned how to communicate in a manner that helps others understand it as well.

Third, *a spiritual leader is long-suffering.* How valuable is patience! Some people walk around expecting to be offended and have a hair-trigger response when they feel wronged. The Greek word translated "patient when wronged" is a compound of "endure" and "evil." A spiritual leader allows personal insults to go unanswered in order to choose a different response. Paul describes that next.

— **2:25-26** —

If you've never been in Christian leadership, you may not know this, but the role includes having to say things that might be difficult to hear. You hope it's behind closed doors, in private. It should be done tactfully, with grace. Sometimes we must help a family confront a dad or mother. Sometimes we must confront a fellow minister or a fellow Christian leader. And we must correct those who actively oppose the orthodox teaching of Scripture.

Paul chose to use a different word for "gentleness" from verse 24 (there rendered "kind"). The term here means "mild and gentle friendliness." In Greek culture, respected leaders treated their subjects with gentleness, yet without sacrificing strength. Jesus used this term of Himself (Matt. 11:29), and Paul declared it to be a fruit of the Spirit (Gal. 5:23). Spiritual leaders are to exhibit this kindly strength when confronting those standing in opposition to divine truth.

Whether these people receive correction or continue to reject truth is not in the power of the spiritual leader. Paul introduced a condition with a Greek conjunction that leans in the negative direction. Therefore, "if perhaps" may be too neutral. A phrase that captures the negative spirit of the Greek conjunction might be, "in the rare event …"

Paul did not doubt the Lord's ability to bring a rebellious heart to repentance; he merely acknowledges how rarely it occurs. Most people opposed to the truth remain entrenched in their rebellion (Matt. 7:14). If someone opposing the truth "repents"—that is, changes mind and direction—it will not be the result of correction, but the power of God working from within. A person in the "snare of the devil" is a slave to sin (John 8:34; Rom. 6:17 – 18) and, therefore, cannot choose truth to restore his or her senses without direct divine intervention.

The effective spiritual leader understands this, having accepted that he or she is merely a means of communicating divine truth. Only God's power can cause a person to want to hear it.

Paul undoubtedly had hoped to send Timothy more letters sharing his wisdom and explaining insights gained from ministry in the western frontier. As it happened, time grew short. He had been in prison before. He had faced danger countless times throughout his ministry. And, in every circumstance, the apostle chose to see God's sovereign hand at work. In reading his earlier prison epistles, one gets the feeling Paul knew he would be released sooner or later. Not so with this second letter to Timothy. Still positive—even upbeat considering his circumstances—Paul nevertheless appears to have accepted that release from his dungeon will lead him to the presence of Christ.

So, having reflected on the past and having encouraged Timothy in the present, the faithful servant of God turns his protégé to face a future without him. God is sovereign and His foundation of truth is secure, but challenging days lie ahead.

NOTES:

1. Sam Johnson and Jan Winebrenner, *Captive Warriors: A Vietnam POW's Story* (College Station, TX: TAMU Press, 1992), 138–39.
2. William Ernest Henley, "Invictus," *Modern British Poetry*, ed. Louis Untermeyer (New York: Harcourt, Brace & Company, 1920), 10.

3. These are a few of the possible meanings where the object of the preposition *kata* is in the accusative case.

4. Gerhard Kittel and Gerhard Friedrich, eds., *Theological Dictionary of the New Testament: Abridged in One Volume*, trans. Geoffrey W. Bromiley (Grand Rapids: Eerdmans, 1985), 430.

5. Jonathan Edwards; see S. E. Dwight, *The Life of Jonathan Edwards* (New York: G. & C. & H. Carvill, 1830), 68–73.

6. Kittel and Friedrich, eds., *Theological Dictionary of the New Testament: Abridged in One Volume*, 1352.

7. F. B. Meyer, *Christ in Isaiah* (London: Morgan and Scott, 1917), 9.

8. Simone Weil, *Gravity and Grace*, transl. Emma Craufurd (Abingdon: Routledge, 1987), xxvi.

9. John R.W. Stott, *The Message of 2 Timothy* (Downers Grove, IL: InterVarsity Press, 1973), 52.

10. In a general sense, this applies to women as well as men, but in terms of the office of pastor, Paul used "men" in the restrictive sense.

11. William Shakespeare, *Henry V*, Act IV, Scene III.

12. Stephen Arterburn and Jack Felton, *Toxic Faith: Experiencing Healing from Painful Spiritual Abuse* (Colorado Springs: Waterbrook, 2001), 2–3.

13. Gerhard Kittel, ed., *Theological Dictionary of the New Testament*, trans. Geoffrey William Bromiley (Grand Rapids: Eerdmans, 1978), 4:143.

14. Ibid., 8:112.

15. To translate *yashar*, which has a broad semantic range, including "to make level, smooth, straight, just, pleasing, upright."

16. In fact, Walter Bauer and Frederick Danker, *A Greek-English Lexicon of the New Testament*, 3rd ed. (Chicago: Univ. of Chicago Press, 2000), 722, lists as the first definition, "cut a path in a straight direction."

17. "Exceedingly Great and Precious Promises," by unknown author, *A Selection of Hymns, from the Best Authors, Intended to Be an Appendix to Dr. Watts' Psalms and Hymns*, ed. John Rippon (Burlington, N.J.: Stephen C. Ustick, 1807), 127–28.

18. Warren Wiersbe, *Preaching and Teaching with Imagination* (Grand Rapids: Baker, 2007), 52.

THE FUTURE
(2 TIMOTHY 3:1–4:22)

I am a big fan of thinking positively. A can-do attitude gets things done in the face of adversity while pessimists cower in the shadows, complaining about today and whining for better times. Clearly, Paul was a positive thinker. He saw the potential for good to emerge from every circumstance. To him, the glass was always half full. He never doubted the power of God to turn any difficulty to the gospel's advantage. That's a major reason the apostle accomplished so much in such a short time—fifteen years, maybe twenty. But his thinking stayed realistic; he didn't maintain a positive attitude by ignoring evil.

Chapter 3 marks a subtle, yet significant, transition in Paul's letter. After reflecting on the past and commenting on present circumstances, the imprisoned apostle urged the younger minister to face the future. Without doubting the goodness or sovereignty of God, he declares in no uncertain terms, "difficult times will come." He says, in effect, "The gospel will prevail in the end, but the days between today and that glorious victory will be filled with ever-increasing evil. Anticipate victory, but prepare for battle."

Depravity on Parade (2 Timothy 3:1–9)

¹But realize this, that in the last days difficult times will come. ²For men will be lovers of self, lovers of money, boastful, arrogant, revilers, disobedient to parents, ungrateful, unholy, ³unloving, irreconcilable, malicious gossips, without self-control, brutal, haters of good, ⁴treacherous, reckless, conceited, lovers of pleasure rather than lovers of God, ⁵holding to a form of godliness, although they have denied its power; avoid such men as these. ⁶For among them are those who enter into households and captivate weak women weighed down with sins, led on by various impulses, ⁷always learning and never able to come to the knowledge of the truth. ⁸Just as Jannes and Jambres opposed Moses, so these *men* also oppose the truth, men of depraved mind, rejected in regard to the faith. ⁹But they will not make further progress; for their folly will be obvious to all, just as Jannes's and Jambres's folly was also.

Sometimes it helps to get straight to the point. No reason to play around with platitudes or pleasantries. Just state the truth as it is. While chapter breaks had no part in the original text, Paul's letter nevertheless takes a dramatic turn with the

KEY TERMS

ἀνθίστημι [*anthistēmi*] (436) "to oppose, stand against, resist"

Two Greek words, ἀντί [*anti*], "against," and ἵστημι [*histēmi*], "to stand, establish," combine to depict a person trying to prevent something from being established or remaining intact. When used of a person, it means to bring about his or her destruction, or to prevent him or her from accomplishing something.

κηρύσσω [*kēryssō*] (2784) "to preach, proclaim, be a herald"

Whereas an envoy (*apostolos*) was empowered to issue orders and make decisions on behalf of the sender, a herald (*kērux*) simply carried a message. Nevertheless, the act of proclamation carried such significance that the herald enjoyed special protection while on his mission. Anyone who harmed a herald risked facing the wrath of the sender.

φυλάσσω [*phylassō*] (5442) "to guard, watch, protect, care for"

This term is based on an older form of Greek that describes the activity of a watchman on a tower guarding a city. Paul used the verb in what is called the "middle voice," emphasizing the personal interest to Timothy. This term also denotes the duty of shepherds, who must protect their flocks from predators and thieves.

words of verse 1, "But realize this:" What follows is an autopsy of human depravity and a startling prediction of the atrocities people—especially religious people—are capable of perpetrating.

Paul's bleak picture of the future reminds me of a classic line from the pen of James Russell Lowell, who actively opposed slavery in America. Soon after the presidential election of Zachary Taylor, a southern slave-holder, Lowell lamented:

Truth forever on the scaffold,
Wrong forever on the throne.[1]

In ancient times, the bodies of dead criminals were hung on a scaffold just outside town as a vivid warning to all who would oppose the powers that be. As Paul writes from his dungeon and Nero tortures Christians, truth appears to have been hung on the gallows.

— **3:1** —

With the words "But realize this," Paul effectively poked Timothy's sternum with each syllable. The verb *ginōskō* ("to know") appears in the present tense, imperative mood, which is literally translated, "You keep on knowing this!" In other words, "Be ever mindful of this as you carry out your duties!"

What is "this?" Eight foreboding English words: "in the last days difficult times will come." Some have suggested Paul meant "the great tribulation" later described by John (Rev. 7:14; cf. Dan. 12:1; Matt. 24:21; Mark 13:19), but his use of the phrase more often refers to the time between the birth of the Messiah in Bethlehem and His return in Jerusalem to set up His kingdom. The last days are centuries long, and they will go from bad to worse.

The apostle didn't intend to frighten or discourage Timothy, only to give a correct orientation to his expectations. If, as some theologians have suggested, the time between the resurrection of Christ and his return in power is to be marked by the steady retreat of evil, Timothy was about to be disappointed. The Greek term translated "difficult" is used only one other time in the New Testament to describe the two demonized men living among the tombs near Gadara (Matt. 8:28). Empowered by evil, they broke the chains that bound them and terrorized the region with their "extreme violence."

"Difficult" is an understatement! The term means "harsh, hard to bear, vicious, dangerous, menacing." Classical Greek used the term to describe wild animals or a raging sea. One of my mentors preferred the word "savage." He used to warn, "In the last days, savage times will be upon us."

— 3:2–4 —

Paul then gave the reason for such "savage times." The tiny Greek conjunction *gar* ("for" or "because") introduces no less than nineteen adjectives and descriptive phrases characterizing human depravity. We cannot blame natural disasters, famine, pollution, poverty, or pestilence for the misery brought on the world; people are at fault. The term *anthropos* ("men") refers to all people everywhere … young and old, male and female.

These characteristics deserve our attention. We may be positive-thinking people, but we must be aware of the dangers and prepare to meet them.

"Lovers of self." All people are given to selfishness, but this describes a deeper level of self-love to which we would assign the term *narcissism*. Self-lovers see everything in the world only as it affects them. They skew their perception of every event to bolster their own sense of superiority, significance, or safety. Furthermore, they seek the comfort and promotion of self above all else.

"Lovers of money." *Materialism* is the modern term. Materialists seek wealth and possessions as a means of power, control, security, personal worth, and even love.

There's nothing wrong with being blessed with wealth. It's the love of wealth we must avoid (cf. 1 Tim. 6:10). Money-lovers are driven by greed.

"Boastful." The Greek term describes the ancient version of a con artist, a vagabond who moves from town to town, making big promises, raking in money, and then disappearing overnight. They seek glory for themselves without providing anything of worth to those around them.

"Arrogant." This compound Greek word combines *hyper,* "over," and *phainō,* "appear" or "seem," to express the idea of being exalted over others. In secular Greek the term may be either positive, in the sense of "distinguished," or negative. Hellenistic Jews, following the Old Testament, saw arrogance as Satan's quintessential quality.

"Revilers." The Greek word is *blasphēmos,* from which we get the English word "blasphemer." To blaspheme is to curse, slander, or treat someone with contempt. Blasphemy is any manner of speech that disregards or disrespects the value of another. While we now reserve the term for those who revile God, Paul uses the term in a more general sense. This person denigrates everything and everyone he or she deems inferior.

"Disobedient to parents." This is the first of five terms with the negative prefix *a-,* which we would render "dis-" or "un-". The root word is *peithō,* "to be convinced, be persuaded." The disobedient don't merely reject their parents' house rules; they are adults who reject the counsel of their parents. I never hire people who have unresolved parent issues; they also have issues with authority that extend to every aspect of their lives.

"Ungrateful." The prefix *a-* negates the word for "grace" or "gracious" to carry the idea of a generally unthankful attitude. These people walk around with a spirit of entitlement. When they don't get their way, they grouse as though robbed of something.

"Unholy." The prefix *a-* negates the positive quality denoted by *hosios,* which generally describes acts that are "sacred, lawful, dutiful." It also describes people who respect traditions and feel a sense of duty to eternal laws. The "unholy" person doesn't simply reject the laws of God; he or she refuses even to abide by rules of common decency. Pagan Greeks would condemn this person as a bad citizen and a lousy neighbor.

"Unloving." A person without natural affections toward others, or characterized by hardheartedness, offers nothing to others without expecting something in return.

"Irreconcilable." The Greek term used here literally means "without libation." When warring nations signed a truce or feuding individuals reconciled their

differences, they would pour out a drink offering (a libation) before a god and swear an oath. The expression "bring a libation" meant to bring an offer of peace. Someone "without libation" cannot admit wrongdoing, refuses to forgive offenses, and therefore remains at odds with everyone.

"Malicious gossips." The Greek word translated "malicious" is *diabolos,* "devil," the nickname given to Satan for his lying and his entrapment of people. The devil seduces people into sin and then bears the tale to God so as to create a rift in their relationship and widen it as much as possible. A human *diabolos* does the same within a community, a church, a faculty, a family.

"Without self-control." The term for "self-control" appears in 1 Corinthians twice. In 1 Corinthians 7:9, Paul suggests that people without sexual restraint should not try to remain single, but marry instead of "burn." In 1 Corinthians 9:25, the apostle illustrates the dedication of an athlete in training for competition, watching his diet, avoiding anything that might dull his competitive edge. Those without self-control cannot remain ethically upright, for morality requires a denial of self.

"Brutal." The Greek word means the opposite of "gentle" or "tame," often used of wild animals, especially lions.

"Haters of good." Overseers in the church were to be lovers of good (*philagathos*), which means they actively seek the restoration of God's original order to creation, even if they are unsuccessful. The Greek word means (lit.) "not a lover of good." This person finds greater affinity with a corrupt world.

"Treacherous." The verb form of this root word means (lit.) "to give, hand over." It is the same term used by Luke (Luke 6:16) to describe Judas. It is also a close cousin of the "giving over" of Jesus. Jesus was "given over" to the Sanhedrin by Judas (Mark 14:10), to Pilate by the Sanhedrin (Mark 15:1), and to the soldiers by Pilate (Mark 15:15). In most contexts, though not all, the term carries the idea of betraying the well-being of another for personal gain. This is someone who turns away from a friend when he most needs an advocate.

"Reckless." The literal meaning of the Greek word is "falling forward," presumably without the ability to stop. In English, we would say someone is "rushing headlong" into trouble. This person is rash and headstrong, easily provoked, and, therefore, susceptible to harming others without thinking.

"Conceited." The word means "wrapped in smoke" or "head-in-the-clouds," describing someone whose lofty view of himself towers above everything else.

"Lovers of pleasure rather than lovers of God." A "pleasure-lover" adopts a hedonistic lifestyle, elevating the desires of the moment above all else, even God. This is just another expression of self-love.

—3:5—

Paul concluded his list of "savage" behavior with perhaps the most despicable of all. Some dress themselves in the august robes of righteousness, yet pursue their lusts. They pretend to be godly in order to justify their own selfish desires. They reject the true power of godliness, which Paul associates with contentment (cf. 1 Tim. 6:5–6). This false godliness can range from depraved, demented fanatics flying planes into tall buildings, to corrupt media ministers fleecing the flock for personal gain, to businessmen seeking networking possibilities within the church, to sanctimonious Christians rationalizing their greed. John Stott adds this convicting thought:

> They evidently attended the worship services of the church. They sang the hymns. They said the "Amen" to the prayers, and they put their money in the offering plates. They looked and sounded egregiously pious. But it was form without power, outward show without inward reality, religion without morals, and faith without works.[2]

Paul urged Timothy to avoid people characterized by any of the nineteen earmarks of depravity.

This list provides us with a realistic portrait of our times. Savage indeed! Passages like this cause some people to avoid honest exposition of the Scriptures. As a young minister, I found this section of Paul's letter almost too bleak to accept at face value. Nevertheless, I believed if Timothy needed to remember these things, then so do all ministers of the gospel. Over the years, Paul's realism in this segment has kept me from becoming disillusioned.

The apostle didn't paint a rosy picture of ministry for Timothy. Satan has determined to stop the Lord from reclaiming His creation, so we shouldn't be surprised to see evil intensify. Moreover, people don't suddenly lose their depravity upon entering a church. Believers grow out of their evil gradually—some slower than others—and wisdom reminds us that not everyone in the congregation is what he or she appears.

—3:6–7—

Having instructed Timothy to avoid such people, Paul continued with the Greek conjunction *gar* ("for" or "because"). Among those kinds of people one finds a certain type of charlatan we still see active today.

Paul's description of "weak women weighed down with sins" doesn't characterize women in general, as some undiscerning expositors claim. This is a specific subset of women in Ephesus. False teachers targeted these particular households and wormed their way in, pretending to offer Christian teaching. (Such activity still occurs today. Pseudo-Christian sects offer literature that uses Bible verses and familiar terms from Sunday school, but with a subtle, sinister twist.)

Paul exposes the telltale characteristic of these teachers and their gullible students. They're always steeped in spiritual studies, much of it ostensibly Christian, yet they never believe in the simple gospel of salvation by grace, through faith in Jesus Christ. Coming to a "knowledge of the truth" means to receive salvation (1 Tim. 2:4; 2 Tim. 2:24).

— 3:8 —

An exhaustive search of a Bible encyclopedia and the Scriptures turns up no mention of either Jannes or Jambres. Jewish folklore attached these names to the sorcerers Pharaoh called upon to confront Moses (Ex. 7:11).[3] In the biblical account, God gave Moses and Aaron the ability to turn a shepherd's staff into a serpent. The magicians of the Egyptian court mimicked the miracle, either by illusion or the power of Satan, but the serpent produced by divine power quickly devoured the rival snakes. Still, Pharaoh hardened his heart against the Lord.

Paul condemns the false teachers that proliferated in Ephesus as incorrigibly depraved, and therefore "rejected" in regard to the faith. The term for "rejected" bears some explanation, otherwise one might interpret the verse to mean that God rejected the men for their false teaching. But that's true only up to a point.

The Greek word for "rejected" is *adokimos*, which is *dokimos* negated with the prefix *a-*. *Dokimos* derives its meaning from the verb "to watch" and pictures a metallurgist placing a sample of gold or silver under intense heat to observe how it responds. It came to be used of soldiers and athletes, whose mettle was proven by their endurance in combat or competition. One who is *dokimos* has been proven by testing. The *adokimos* are *dis*proven by testing, and therefore rejected by their own lack of merit.

— 3:9 —

As Paul's warning of a bleak future grew worse by the verse, Timothy undoubtedly felt overwhelmed. Fortunately, the apostle turned from the bad news toward a bit of good with a strong contrastive conjunction, "But ..." The peddlers of lies and the purveyors of evil would not get very far. Eventually, their false teaching would be swallowed up by the truth, and apostates would be shown for the fools they are.

As abolitionist poet James Russell Lowell mourned the election of a slave-owner to the presidency in the United States, he nevertheless believed in inevitable triumph of good over evil. He wrote:

Truth forever on the scaffold, Wrong forever on the throne. —
Yet that scaffold sways the future, and, behind the dim unknown,
Standeth God within the shadow, keeping watch above his own.[4]

A dozen years later, another American president signed and issued the Emancipation Proclamation, and in 1865, the United States outlawed slavery with the Thirteenth Amendment to the constitution.

Paul's point is simple: Evil has a limited shelf life. Deceivers will proliferate and their influence will expand. Falsehood may devastate some churches and persecute many genuine believers. Evil men may consume many lives with their hatred. But, ultimately, evil comes to nothing. Divine truth always prevails. In the end, God wins.

Joseph *did* live to see justice roll down. Pharaoh *did* finally let the Hebrews go and they *did* cross the Red Sea safely. Gideon's three hundred men *did* prevail against a vastly superior army. David *did* defeat his enormous, blaspheming foe. Daniel *did* survive the lions' den. Nehemiah *did* rebuild that wall around Jerusalem against incredible opposition. Jesus' resurrection *did* follow His crucifixion. And a handful of ordinary men called apostles *did* turn the world upside down.

Furthermore, Paul *did* escape his dungeon to enjoy the presence of his Lord for eternity, and we celebrate his God-endowed genius today, two millennia later. As for Nero? His name is a joke.

Application

How to Respond to Evil

If any single truth emerges from Paul's warning, it's that every believer will encounter evil. It's not a question of whether, but when. Therefore, Christians — especially ministers — must prepare themselves. After all, what good is a warning if we do not prepare? I find within Paul's realistic assessment of the future four principles, each suggesting a specific response to evil.

First, *difficult times will come as evil tries to destroy good. Accept this truth.* A positive attitude requires realistic expectations. The opponents of truth will fight hard to preserve their "right" to sin without conviction or consequence. We shouldn't be surprised when they reject appeals to reason and then respond unreasonably. Nor should we be shocked when they try to silence the truth through deception, resistance, and persecution.

The truth is: ministry to a depraved world will be difficult. Accept it.

Second, *deceivers will present themselves as genuine ministers of the gospel. Reject false teachers.* Not all opposition to the truth will come by force from the outside; some agents of evil will enter the church in disguise, bringing false teaching with them. Regardless of their outward appearance, their impressive Christian pedigree, or their stellar credentials, always compare their teaching to the Word of God.

If these people teach anything contrary to the Bible, presume to add new revelation, or claim to have exclusive ability to make the Bible understandable, *confront them.* If the confrontation doesn't bring a change, it may be necessary to discipline them. The church must be protected from error. If you fill a leadership role in your church, remove them from the premises. Otherwise, remove yourself from their presence.

The truth is: false teachers are toxic to the body of Christ. Reject them.

Third, *evil sometimes occupies positions of power that cannot be overthrown. Endure persecution.* As Paul writes this second letter to his protégé, Nero was using his immense power to torture and murder Christians. Meanwhile, Timothy served a church in a city overrun with false teachers. He undoubtedly suffered some measure of persecution as popular personalities tickled the ears of the congregation with teachings that appealed to their fallen natures. The power of evil appeared invincible ... for a time. When the smoke of its arrogance cleared, however, truth remained. And it still remains.

The truth is: the rule of evil is temporary. Reject evil when you can; endure evil when you must.

Fourth, *the primary weapon of evil is deception. Reveal truth.* While we must face evil head-on, we cannot take evil at face value. Evil people exaggerate their influence. They appear stronger or more influential than they really are. They create the illusion of righteousness, usually at the expense of godly people. Inasmuch as you are able, speak the truth openly, refuse to tolerate secrets, challenge the claims of false teachers by asking for evidence, and do not be afraid to call evil deeds what they are. Evil cannot stand the light of truth; it will either flee in shame or vainly struggle to cover it up. Shine the light!

The truth is that the power of evil cannot tolerate truth. Reveal it.

Making a Lasting Difference (2 Timothy 3:10–15)

[10]Now you followed my teaching, conduct, purpose, faith, patience, love, perseverance, [11]persecutions, *and* sufferings, such as happened to me at Antioch, at Iconium *and* at Lystra; what persecutions I endured, and out of them all the Lord rescued me! [12]Indeed, all who desire to live godly in

Christ Jesus will be persecuted. ¹³But evil men and impostors will proceed *from bad* to worse, deceiving and being deceived. ¹⁴You, however, continue in the things you have learned and become convinced of, knowing from whom you have learned *them*, ¹⁵and that from childhood you have known the sacred writings which are able to give you the wisdom that leads to salvation through faith which is in Christ Jesus.

Most people I know want to make a difference; in fact, they want to make a lasting difference in the lives of others. Most people I know do not want to drift along in mediocrity. They don't want to be swallowed up in anonymity or obscurity. They aren't driven by money. They aren't lured by fame. They fear neither hardship nor sacrifice. They don't fret about the risk involved. They don't work for an early retirement, because they weren't born with a "Best used by" date stamped on their foot. They want their lives to count for something.

A classic example of this yearning to make a positive difference occurred in 1914, when Ernest Henry Shackleton decided to accomplish a feat that had never been attempted. He determined to lead an expedition across Antarctica, from sea to sea via the pole. He knew he couldn't do it alone. He would have to recruit a team of strong-hearted adventurers like himself. As legend has it, he took out an ad in *The London Times*, although the original has yet to be located. According to the book *The 100 Greatest Advertisements, 1852–1958*, the ad appeared as follows:

MEN WANTED

For hazardous journey, small wages, bitter cold, long months of complete darkness, constant danger, safe return doubtful, honor and recognition in case of success.

Ernest Shackleton
4 Burlington st.

Later newspaper articles reported a deluge of candidates. More than five thousand men and a few women (!) submitted their names for consideration. Shackleton evaluated many of them, searching for talented, physically strong people with other intangible qualities, such as attitude, character, determination, creativity, and adaptability. He intended to transform a collection of the right individuals into a synergistic union of souls—a team.

The famed adventurer attracted the right kind of people by announcing his intentions clearly, calling for strong-hearted volunteers boldly, and stating the risks and rewards unambiguously. The aptly titled book *Endurance* records the story of Shackleton and his crew of men who wanted to make a difference.

Paul's adventure on earth was reaching its end. He would not leave his dungeon except to face the executioner's sword, and he undoubtedly knew it. In this segment of Paul's call to adventure, the apostle wanted to assure Timothy that he was, indeed, well equipped to make a significant difference for the kingdom of God. As we examine this passage, let me summarize Paul's message.

The past is like the present (vv. 10–11),
and the future will be like the past (vv. 12–13),
so, continue in the present as you have in the past to engage the future (vv. 14–15).

Paul says, in so many words, "I want you to make a difference, unlike all of the others around you."

— 3:10–11 —

After Paul's gruesome autopsy of depravity—which listed no less than nineteen fatal flaws—he grabbed Timothy's attention with the emphatic use of the pronoun "you." He said, in effect, "False teachers and other evil people behave that way; *you*, however, must be different because you are different."

All of the verbs in verses 10 and 11 appear in the aorist tense, which views action at a point of time in the past. We render aorist verbs as a simple past tense in English: "followed," "happened," "endured," "rescued." Paul turned Timothy's head to see where they had been together. Unlike the false teachers, who did not gain their knowledge from the apostles, unlike those who had not suffered for the sake of the gospel, unlike any who had not received more than a decade of training, Timothy had a long history in the trenches of Christian ministry. Paul then listed nine memories from the many years of Timothy's "following."

"Teaching." As Timothy unrolls the scroll and reads the letter for the first time, he remembers the years he has traveled with Paul. He recalls the times of teaching, where sitting under lamplight, Paul leaned over to say, "Now remember this . . ." or, "Let me show you what the Lord has revealed to me . . ." and he would instruct the younger man. Timothy also heard Paul's sermons and lessons from Old Testament Scriptures, given hundreds of times in dozens of cities and towns.

"Conduct." Paul's word means "manner of life." Not just how he behaved in front of people or even with close friends, but also how he conducted himself in private. The authenticity of a mentor means the world to an up-and-coming minister!

I remember traveling from my barracks to the office of my mentor one afternoon as a torrential downpour soaked the island of Okinawa. I arrived to see him through the window, bowed on his knees, pouring out his heart to God. He didn't know I was there, but I stood in the rain watching the conduct of this authentic Jesus-follower, and I felt encouraged to continue following as well.

"Purpose." Paul doesn't merely write out a mission statement. The Greek term *prosthesis*, "set before," held great significance to a Jew, who used it in close association with the Table of Consecrated Bread in the temple (Ex. 25:23 – 30; Lev. 24:5 – 9). The apostle's purpose — the goals of his life — have been "set before" God, just like the consecrated bread.

The next four words go together. *"Faith, patience, love, perseverance"* are cardinal virtues of the Christian life. Timothy observed Paul's daily trust in the Lord, his long-suffering through carping criticism and vicious attacks on his character from heretics, his tender love for the foolish, fickle believers in several dozen churches, and his strong-hearted endurance of many stonings, floggings, mock trials, and imprisonments.

Timothy personally witnessed his mentor experience the full range of emotions as Paul fulfilled the role of a spiritual father, and he personally bandaged the *"sufferings"* he experienced through *"persecutions,"* and he personally heard Paul's cries for relief from his "thorn." Those were vivid memories in Timothy's mind.

Paul's reference to Antioch, Iconium, Lystra, and Derbe took Timothy back to the region of his upbringing — where he first laid eyes on Paul. Even before the apostle invited the young man to become his apprentice, Timothy had witnessed the high personal cost of ministry (Acts 13:14 – 14:23). The apostle concluded his brief review of the past to acknowledge the hardships and to praise God for delivering him through them.

Paul briefly reviewed their storied history together to make a point. He said, in effect, "Timothy, we've come this far together and you've seen the best and worst of it. And we're still alive, still engaged in the work of the gospel."

— 3:12–13 —

The main verbs in verses 12 and 13 are future tense: "will be persecuted" and "will proceed." A look to the past brought the future into perspective. The persecutions Paul suffered will become the suffering of any believer who stakes his or her life on the gospel and dares to live it openly. Of course, Timothy recognizes that "all" included him. He undoubtedly heard his mentor warn him many times, especially after being run out of town by an angry mob, "If you want to live a godly life, if you want to make a lasting difference, you will be misunderstood, mistreated, maligned, and hated. Count on it."

Paul characterized the enemies of the gospel as "evil men" and "imposters." The latter term appears only once in the Bible and literally means "wailer," as in one who howls incantations as though possessed by a spirit. Classical Greek literature always uses the word in a derogatory sense, casting the "wailer" as traveling swindler of the weak-minded. One of Paul's earliest experiences with a swindler (Acts 13:3–12) was undoubtedly the first of many. He predicts here that many more "evil men" and "swindlers" will rise to places of prominence—perhaps even within congregations—and carry many into apostasy.

— 3:14–15 —

A look to the past, a glance toward the future. Now Paul wants Timothy to focus on the present. Like verse 10, he grabs the younger man's attention by repeating an emphatic "You," followed by a present tense imperative, "continue." The verb is *menō*, the same used by Jesus in His "abide in Me" speech in the upper room (John 15:1–11). It means "remain, live, stay." Furthermore, the present tense imperative has an ongoing force to it, such that the message is "keep on remaining."

In bringing Timothy to the present, Paul writes, in so many words, "Difficulty plagued our past, yet we continued on. Difficulty will only intensify as the gospel grows, but that doesn't mean we should do anything different. Continue doing what has been successful."

Paul summarizes his encouragement by reminding Timothy again of his strong Christian heritage and the extensiveness of his training. The younger minister evidently struggled with confidence such that he had to be prodded to remain at his post, to boldly confront evil and proclaim truth, and to put his knowledge into action. The words "learn" and "become convinced" don't express the same idea. We learn by gaining information, changing perspectives, and acquiring skills. To be "convinced," however, invades the will. Convictions motivate the person to transform knowledge into action.

Much like faith without works is dead, so theological training is pointless unless the minister, motivated by his or her convictions, decides to make a difference.

Ernest Shackleton and his team never completed the voyage they began. Their ship, *Endurance*, became lodged between two ice floes and eventually was crushed. As the ship sank, the crew scavenged wood and supplies in order to survive, and attempt to return home. Against all odds and overcoming astounding wilderness obstacles, the adventurer successfully returned all of his men to safety.

Shackleton returned home a hero and traveled the lecture circuit successfully, but he undoubtedly struggled to overcome the feeling of failure. Nevertheless, his "failed" expedition wasn't a wasted effort. Years later, another adventurer by the name of Edmund Hillary, who scaled Mount Everest, wrote,

> Of all the explorers I would like to have known, Shackleton was the most admirable ... It was as a leader of men and an overcomer of appalling obstacles

that Shackleton really excelled. Not for him an easy task and a quick success — he was at his best when the going was toughest. The enormous affection and respect he engendered in his expedition members (often mighty men themselves) shines through in their diaries and their writings.[5]

You may feel more like a failure than a success, or feel that your life is all in vain. But you can't be certain about all the lives you impact as you faithfully follow and obey Jesus Christ. Therefore, "continue in the things you have learned and become convinced of." Regardless of the outcome in your eyes, you are making a difference to someone. Press on!

Application

Two Steps to the Finish Line

Paul challenges Timothy to make a difference where he lives and serves. That is a tall order for one man with an entire city working against him. To make matters worse, the city is Ephesus and it appears as if Timothy doesn't have the support of his church. So, what can solitary, shy, struggling Timothy do to make a difference?

Paul gives his younger colleague two specific instructions that we would do well to apply where we live and serve.

First, *continue in the things you have learned.* Naturally, this presupposes the existence of learning, at least in regard to the Scriptures. You may not have been the beneficiary of biblical training. If not, that's where you begin.

For those who do have a strong Christian heritage, go back to your upbringing. Retrace your steps to the place where the foundation of truth was laid. Return in your mind to any positive influences — a parent, grandparent, teacher, pastor, mentor, or school — and recall the things you were taught. Review the lives of the people who model the truth, people who exemplified authentic godliness. What did they do? How did they live? In what ways did they teach and influence you? Return to the lessons from Scripture they passed on to you.

Now, continue in the things you have learned.

Second, *become convinced of the things you have learned.* From our earliest years, we begin forming impressions about ourselves, the world, the Lord, and the distinction between right and wrong, wisdom and foolishness. We absorb knowledge and even begin to exercise discernment. Then, at some point in our journey toward adulthood, we must become *convinced* of the things we have learned. That which we have heard and understood must become matters of belief. Knowledge must lead to conviction, because conviction prompts action. People usually make choices that result in the least amount of discomfort or inconvenience ... unless moved by conviction.

There is a powerful link between remembrance and continuance, between what we remember and how we continue. Those who finish well do so because they don't forget what they have been taught. Nor do they fail to form their own bone-deep convictions.

So the good question is: "Do you know what you believe? Can you defend it before several people who aren't believers? Are your convictions such that when you're outnumbered, you don't yield? Are they strong enough to hold you in check? For example, when you are out of town, all your normal accountability structures are gone, and you are free to behave as you choose without anyone back home knowing anything—do you have the kind of conviction that says, "I'm not going anywhere near that temptation"?

Go back to the things you have learned and become convinced of.

God-Breathed Truth (2 Timothy 3:16–17)

> [16]All Scripture is inspired by God and profitable for teaching, for reproof, for correction, for training in righteousness; [17]so that the man of God may be adequate, equipped for every good work.

I'll never forget the 1984 Summer Olympics in Los Angeles, mostly because of Gabriela Andersen-Schiess. By the time she entered the stadium to complete the final 400 meters of the very first women's Olympic marathon, her body had shut down. Fatigued, dehydrated, and nearly paralyzed from heat exhaustion, she twisted and gimped her way around the track, waving off doctors. A single touch from any one of them would have disqualified her. It took her nearly six minutes to complete that last turn, but she finished! When she staggered those final anguished steps across the finish line and collapsed into the arms of physicians, I stood to my feet and applauded the television, cheering like a madman.

Almost anyone can start strong. Few finish well. Of course, after running 26.2 miles, *any* finish is a good finish.

As any successful athlete will tell you, the decision to finish well begins with a commitment to arduous training, months or even years before race day. Timothy had benefitted from the very best training early in his life (1:5; 3:15), which continued for no less than fifteen years under Paul's tutelage (3:10–11). As the apostle himself now nears the finish line, he urges his apprentice to continue running as he had begun, for the toughest part of the race is yet to come (3:12–15).

Of course, Paul didn't write these words to Timothy only. Prompted and guided by the Holy Spirit, he wrote them for all who would run in his footsteps — not just full-time vocational ministers, but all believers. Moreover, the Lord personally has preserved and protected these words through two thousand years of persecution and turmoil so that we might read the words Paul wrote and heed his exhortation: "Train well; run well; and by every means, finish well!"

Ever the practical man of faith, Paul explains how in one compound sentence. It is *the* single most significant sentence in all the New Testament regarding the Scriptures because it touches on *the* watershed issue of faith in our times. What you believe about the Bible influences everything you believe and affects every decision you make.

— **3:16** —

The Greek term *graphē* means "writing" in the most general sense. It also took on various technical meanings, however, depending on the community. In legal circles, *graphē* described the product of a king or judge in the sense of "decree" or "prescription." The Hebrews referred to the Old Testament as the *graphai*, the plural form of *graphē*, which Matthew reflects in his gospel (e.g., Matt. 21:42; 22:29; 26:54).

Some expositors claim that Paul referred only to the Hebrew Scriptures when he made this declaration to Timothy. Careful examination of his phrasing, however, suggests otherwise. The phrase "sacred writings" (*hiera grammata*) in verse 15 clearly refers to the Hebrew Scriptures that Timothy has studied from his childhood. The phrase "every writing" in verse 16 parallels "sacred writings," placing these two phrases on the same plane. Furthermore, Paul uses the singular *graphē* in "every writing" instead of the plural form *graphai*, which would be the more familiar expression for the Old Testament. Paul clearly means for "every writing" to indicate each divine utterance written through a supernaturally inspired prophet. In other words, God did not close the canon of Scripture with the Old Testament;[6] the New Testament writings are equally inspired by God.

These writings — and no other — are "inspired by God." The phrase is rendered from a single word that combines *theos*, "God," and the verb *pneō*, "to breathe." The literal rendering of this adjective is "God-breathed." A noun based on the same root word is *pneuma*, from which we derive "pneumonia" and "pneumatic." This word picture involving air or breath lifts a deeply significant meaning from the creation account in the Hebrew Bible.

In the beginning, God created the first human, Adam, from the dust of the ground (Gen. 2:7), but he would have been nothing more than organized dirt had the Lord not done something miraculous—something He chose to do only for humanity. He breathed life into the man and he became a "living being"—that is, having both body and soul (cf. 1 Cor. 15:45).

We often call the words of poets and songwriters "inspired," but strictly speaking, this misuses the term. Only the words of prophets and apostles writing under the supernatural direction of the Holy Spirit are truly "in-Spirited." Only God-breathed words possess His life. Furthermore, because "God is light, and in Him there is no darkness at all" (1 John 1:5), He cannot lie. Therefore, any word given by Him through inspiration must be true. God superintended the transfer of His mind, His thoughts to human writers, so that they composed and recorded His Word without error.

The purpose of Scripture is fourfold: for teaching, for reproof, for correction, and for training in righteousness.

"Teaching" (*didaskalia*) is a crucial element in growth toward maturity. In the same way people who are never taught to read cannot reach their full potential, so people without teaching from the Scriptures fail to develop fully. God's Word gives you tools for life.

"Reproof" (*elegmos*) convinces us to behave differently by rebuking us, revealing areas that others may not see or that we prefer to ignore. The Spirit of God uses the Word of God to reveal the truth of sin or foolishness within.

"Correction" (*epanorthōsis*) builds on reproof. It means "restoration" or "reformation." Whereas reproof reveals our sinfulness or foolishness, correction shows us how to straighten out what we're doing wrong.

"Training (in righteousness)" (*paideia*) takes the soul transformation process even further. The Greek term from which we derive the English word "pedagogy" is based on the idea of guiding a child to adulthood. An instructor cannot teach merely by correction, pointing out where the student has gone wrong. That's like trying to drive by looking in the rearview mirror. Training shows the correct way to behave *before* mistakes are made.

Note also that Scripture does not give us righteousness. There's nothing magical about the book or the printing or even the words themselves. The Bible is not a good luck charm. You can't purify something by placing a Bible on it. The words can't be chanted like a spell to make things happen. The words in the Bible have meaning. God Himself purifies souls; Scripture then trains us to align our behavior so that it matches our new, righteous identity (2 Cor. 5:17; Eph. 2:10; 4:24; Col. 3:10).

God has revealed divine truth through the agency of prophets and apostles, who recorded it for all time "so that, in order that, for the purpose of"; the Greek conjunction *hina* in this context points to the specific end the Lord has in mind for each individual. Unfortunately, the adjective "adequate" (*artios*) no longer means what it once did. At one time, "adequate" meant "equal to the task," but now it smacks of mediocrity. No one who really wants a job would list "adequate" as a personal quality on a resume. Today, we would call the right person for the job "qualified" or "proficient." He or she has the right training and expertise to master the tasks we hope to see accomplished.

The Greek word for "equipped" is an expanded verb form of the adjective rendered "adequate," which is better translated "qualified." It's the passive participle, "an equipped one," strongly suggesting that the equipping is by divine activity (i.e., a "divine passive"). Furthermore, God intends for us to be supernaturally equipped to accomplish every kind of good work (cf. 2:21).

To run well and to finish well, one cannot cultivate a casual relationship with Scripture. Listening to expository preaching is a great start. Purchasing a study Bible is a wonderful next step. Devoting time to a commentary, as you are doing now, takes you deeper. Don't stop! When you have devoured this volume, get yourself another one expositing the same books of the Bible. Listen to more than one voice. Take it even a step further. Consider formal classes, either through a nearby seminary or online.

Does this sound extreme? Let me follow up with another question. How important is finishing well? What priority do you give the call of God to be "equipped for every good work"? I want to join Paul in urging you to set aside time-wasting activities to devote yourself to training in the Scriptures. Hear it. Read it. Study it. Memorize it. Meditate on it. Live it. Do all this, and you will finish well.

Gabriela Andersen-Schiess trained long and hard for the 26.2 mile (42.192 km) race to the Los Angeles Coliseum and barely had enough left to finish in thirty-seventh place. Not impressed? She finished ahead of seven other runners. Six never even finished.

Application

The First Step in Making a Difference

As a pastor, I don't want to lead a church that merely claims to believe scriptural truth. With every cell in my body, I *long* for the body of Christ to *live* scriptural truth.

I want that so badly, it sometimes hurts. That's why I firmly believe my primary duty in the pulpit is expository preaching that always includes practical, specific application. Sermons based on the inerrant Word of God must drive toward a practical application of the passages they explore. And each practical application must describe not only what godly behavior looks like — legalism already does a fine job of that — but *how* believers might "be equipped for every good work" (3:14). Paul chose those words carefully. We want believers who are trained and qualified to live obediently, since it takes that to transform their parts of the world with good deeds.

If I am to fulfill my role in equipping the men and women of God through expository preaching, my work begins in my study with in-depth analysis of the passage. I then follow a pattern I learned from my mentor, Dr. Howard Hendricks, in doing so. I answer four questions.

First, *what does the passage say? (Observation)*. Not "what does the passage mean?" We'll determine that soon enough. Initially, we must observe what the Scriptures *say*. What words did the human author put on the page, and in what order? What conjunctions did he use? What verb tenses did he employ? Who or what is the subject of each verb? What objects do the verbs take? I carefully check out the definitions of key words, using lexicons and dictionaries to understand their usage within the culture and time frame of the original work. Some people even go so far as to diagram each sentence. Not until we have a fairly good grasp of what the passage says are we able to move into what it means. This takes time, concentration, patience, and prayer.

Second, *what does the passage mean? (Interpretation)*. Once I have examined the terms and observed how they are arranged, I discern what thought the human author intended to express. I avoid the implications of his meaning at this stage, and I save applications for later. Right now, I am focusing only on what he meant by his words. I may have to rely on the context of his statements, consider his purpose for writing, account for colloquial expressions, and respect the influence of his culture. I must also recognize the impact of genre. Is the passage poetry, narrative, parable, or prophecy?

Third, how does the passage fit? (Correlation). Once I have determined the author's meaning, I must recognize that the passage is but a part of a whole body of work produced by a single, supernatural Author, God Himself. I must consider parallel passages or other portions of Scripture that speak to the same issue. This helps me recognize the purpose of the passage in the Lord's overall plan for His people. It also keeps me in check so that any principles I derive from my study are supported by other portions of divine revelation. Using a concordance is essential, since it helps me find other biblical references where the same words appear.

Finally, *how does the passage affect the way we live? (Application)*. As the last step—not the first or second—after taking time to examine the passage carefully, I begin to derive timeless principles from the passage. "Timeless principles" are those precepts that affect all people, regardless of when, where, or with whom they live. The exact expression of the principle may take different forms depending on a person's environment, but the underlying principle remains the same. For example, the principle "be kind" is universal; the expression of kindness takes infinite forms.

Expository preaching then follows a similar pattern in the pulpit, unfolding the passage for the congregation so its members, too, understand what it says, what it means, how it fits, and what timeless principles it teaches. The introduction, illustrations, and conclusion all enhance this overarching goal of explaining the Word of God in interesting and creative ways. Then, like seeds flung by a sower, we pray it finds fertile hearts, and we trust the Holy Spirit to nourish its growth.

Every Pastor's Job Profile (2 Timothy 4:1–5)

[1]I solemnly charge *you* in the presence of God and of Christ Jesus, who is to judge the living and the dead, and by His appearing and His kingdom: [2]preach the word; be ready in season *and* out of season; reprove, rebuke, exhort, with great patience and instruction. [3]For the time will come when they will not endure sound doctrine; but *wanting* to have their ears tickled, they will accumulate for themselves teachers in accordance to their own desires, [4]and will turn away their ears from the truth and will turn aside to myths. [5]But you, be sober in all things, endure hardship, do the work of an evangelist, fulfill your ministry.

"Do not enter the ministry if you can help it."

You might be surprised to know who wrote that piece of advice. Perhaps an intellectual cynic? An atheistic antagonist? A burnt-out pastor unloading his frustration? Actually, they are the words of Charles Haddon Spurgeon, quoting the British Puritan pastor Joseph Alleine, as recorded in his now-classic *Lectures to My Students*.[7] Hardly a man who had grown bitter against his calling.

At age seventeen, Spurgeon accepted a call to preach at his first church. Then, at the age of twenty, he accepted the call to pastor the New Park Street Chapel, following in the footsteps of Benjamin Keach, John Gill, and John Rippon. He served that congregation thirty-eight years until just before his untimely death at the age of fifty-eight. Soon after he began preaching, the chapel was enlarged to contain the growing crowds. Then services were moved to concert halls until completion of the Metropolitan Tabernacle, which could accommodate 6,000 in a single service (with no public address system!) And he preached several sermons each week. Before his death, membership had grown to more than 14,500.

Spurgeon extended the ministry to include an educational institute, The Pastor's College, funding the effort from his own pocket for more than twenty years. He established a publishing house, which continued to publish his sermons twenty-five years after his death. They actually ran out of money before they ran out of sermons to print. And he founded an orphanage, which still operates as a charity today.

Every person in ministry should own a copy of *Lectures to My Students* and read it often. I have worn out my first copy and continue to read my second. Spurgeon's insights on the realities of ministry have encouraged me and upbraided me throughout the years. And in "Lecture II: The Call to Ministry," Spurgeon quotes the sage advice given by Joseph Alleine to a young man considering ministry, advice given to Spurgeon, who in turn offered it to his students: "Do not enter the ministry if you can help it."

Why would Spurgeon find this advice so helpful that he would express it to a room full of students preparing for ministry? If he loved the Lord and enjoyed his vocation as much as he did, why would he discourage anyone so bluntly? Because no one should pursue ministry hurriedly or unadvisedly or without the assurance of a divine call.

This heaven-sent command to serve is not a voice, audible or inaudible. The call of God begins with a nagging dissatisfaction with any vocation or life work that does not serve God specifically and directly. As Spurgeon so wisely stated, "If any student in this room could be content to be a newspaper editor, or a grocer, or a farmer, or a doctor, or a lawyer, or a senator, or even a king, in the name of heaven and earth, let him go his way. For a man so filled with God, would utterly weary of any pursuit, but that for which his inmost soul pants."[8]

The call of God includes a sense of destiny combined with an all-absorbing passion to work for the Lord. When complete and confirmed, the call of God manifests itself as an undeniable, unavoidable assurance that one should do nothing else. Unlike other "callings" in life, which might be described as an internal imperative to do something specific, a divine call to ministry is God's leading an individual *away* from other worthy pursuits to devote himself or herself to vocational ministry. This call also blends giftedness with diligence and responsibility, resulting in the benefit of others. If the gift is teaching, others are taught. If the gift is preaching, congregations are challenged. If the gift is counseling, others overcome emotional and spiritual difficulties to become healthy, Christlike believers.

As the apostle nears the end of his letter—and the end of his life—he intensifies his focus on Timothy and the younger man's ministry. He gives Timothy, and all pastors by extension, a solemn charge consisting of four parts:

- a subpoena (v. 1)
- specific commands (v. 2)
- realistic predictions (vv. 3–4)
- personal reminders (v. 5)

— **4:1** —

Anyone who has been called before a judge in a courtroom and required to solemnly vow "to tell the truth, the whole truth, and nothing but the truth" knows how daunting that moment can be. Paul's language appears reminiscent of an ancient subpoena, an official command issued by the court to appear or face punishment. In effect, he calls Timothy to enter the supreme court of heaven and to stand before the Almighty Judge to receive a solemn charge. The Judge is none other than God. And, as God, Jesus Christ will be the person before whom all humanity will stand to receive judgment (John 5:22–23).

Paul could not have more forcefully called Timothy to attention, saying as it were, "Timothy, you will eventually stand before this One to give account for your work. He will judge your motives. He will assess your public ministry, evaluate your private life, and sift through the secrets of your soul. Therefore, heed the counsel I am about to give."

— **4:2** —

The apostle names five specific commands associated with Timothy's call to ministry: preach, be ready, reprove, rebuke, and exhort. At some level, every minister of the gospel is responsible to fulfill these duties, but Paul directs them to the role of pastor. Therefore, every pastor's calling requires faithful obedience to these divine mandates. And, just like Timothy, they answer to the Supreme Judge.

"Preach the Word." The term *kēryssō* means "to herald, proclaim." The official representative of the king (called a *kēryx*) bore the king's message—not his own—to the realm or to a specific person. And he enjoyed the protection of the king as he carried out his duty. To harm a herald was to invite the wrath of the court. Paul has called himself a *kēryx*, a proclaimer (1:10), and now passes the title to Timothy.

The message a pastor carries is "the Word," a reference to the "sacred writings" (3:15) and "all Scripture" (3:16), the special revelation of God to humanity. Others may sit, others may passively listen, others may watch, but the pastor must stand and deliver. His calling is to the Word of God, and the Word of God is his only basis of authority. To depart from the faithful proclamation of Scripture is to lose all credibility.

"Be ready in season and out of season." The literal translation of the imperative verb is "stand over." A guard stands over the city, a treasure, or a person to protect his charge against attack. Often translated "appear" or "confront," the verb carries the ideas of urgency and vigilance.

No one knows the precise cultural meaning of the phrase "in season and out of season," but it's plain enough. A pastor must stand ready at all times and in every circumstance—when it's convenient or when it's not. When it's early or when it's late. When the crowds are large or when there are only a few. When he is being affirmed and loved, or when he is being criticized. He is to be on the job, no matter what.

"Reprove." This term means to "prove, convince, refute, persuade."[9] It carries the idea of replacing incorrect ideas with correct ideas—much like a teacher might show a student of science a new theory to explain a particular phenomenon. As it relates to sin, this is a command to help others understand the truth regarding their sinfulness. The pastor cannot hedge or hold back. Sin needs to be exposed. Otherwise, the people have no hope but remain trapped in a cycle of ignorant wrongdoing.

"Rebuke." To rebuke is to call attention to wrongdoing and to assign responsibility. The term is a close cousin to "reprove," except that the desired response is humility instead of conviction. Rebuking also implies the possibility of a consequence, so that the pastor must declare the truth and its consequences if ignored.

"Exhort." One name for the Holy Spirit, "Paraclete," derives from the verb *parakaleō*, which pictured the relationship of a coach to his or her athlete-in-training; that is the term used here. The pastor must become a diligent, long-suffering teacher of grace in a training regimen for the church. This provides necessary balance. A steady diet of reproof and rebuke alone will demoralize people, leading them to despair. A coach challenges and corrects, but a coach must also comfort and encourage.

The phrase "with great patience and instruction" applies to all five commands as a group, not just to "exhort." The term rendered "great patience" combines the words *makro* and *thymos*, to mean (lit.) "long-tempered." The pastor must have a long fuse, meaning he's slow in seeking redress for wrongs committed against him. That's not to say he should become a doormat; he still must reprove and rebuke when he encounters wrong, even against himself. But he keeps himself above the fray, so that emotions don't create a knee-jerk reaction or pull him into poor behavior.

It's difficult to remain patient. A pastor encounters members of the congregation who have never outgrown their pre-Christian mentality. Truth be told, some prefer to stay undeveloped, untransformed. They choose to resist the ministry of the Holy Spirit and remain carnal. Such individuals tend to give the pastor and everyone else the greatest amount of headaches. Nevertheless, the pastor must patiently carry out all five divine mandates with patience.

— 4:3–4 —

So, why must the pastor remain so uncompromising in his duties? Paul transitions from the five divine mandates with the connecting conjunction *gar* ("for, because") to reveal every pastor's future. Verses 3 and 4 contain five future tense verbs concerning the future of Timothy's congregation, and those of future ministers. While Paul wrote to Timothy, his warning encompasses a wider scope.

"They" in this prediction refers to people in general—unbelievers in the surrounding community and people in Christian circles within the church. The time will come—future for Timothy, but already here for those living after him—when people will not "endure" sound teaching. Paul chooses an intriguing Greek word, translated "endure," which means "to be patient with, in the sense of enduring possible difficulty."[10] The idea is that they find the truth of God to be so torturous to their sinful desire that they must "endure" in the same manner Christians must "endure" hardship. The next few phrases explain their two-step plan to overcome their affliction of divine truth.

First, *they will surround themselves with people who tell them what they want to hear.* These people reject preachers who exposit the Bible as it was written and who interpret its words at face value. At all costs they will choose preachers who avoid the word "sin," preferring pep-rally sermons that "give people a boost for the week" and "focus on the goodness of God."

Second, *they'll close their hearing to truth in favor of myths.* Myths are stories that tell of supposedly ancient events in order to justify the universe as it exists and to rationalize certain behavior (see comments on 1 Tim. 1:3–4; see also the historical note "Jewish Mythology: 'The Demon-Men of Canaan'" in Titus 1). Basically, myths serve the desires of people by using contrived history to substantiate and affirm their choices. The Bible, of course, doesn't justify or rationalize sin; the Bible challenges us to rise to its standard of right and wrong.

—4:5—

Paul again grabbed Timothy's attention with the emphatic use of the pronoun "you" (cf. 3:10, 14) and then gave him four personal instructions, using four imperative verbs.

"Be sober." The Greek term has both a literal and figurative meaning, just like the English term. To be sober is to have one's mind clear of anything that might impair thinking. Instead, the pastor must acknowledge, teach, and obey divine revelation with single-minded focus.

Paul says in effect, "Stability must characterize the faithful pastor in an upside down world. Remain steady as she goes. Stay balanced. Remain a model of self-control. Don't attempt to compete with the ear ticklers. An insane world needs a steady voice."

"Endure hardship." Paul chose a term used in only three places in the New Testament, two of them in this letter (see 2:9; James 5:10). In calling pastors to endure hardship, his use of *kakopatheō* immediately draws the Greek reader's mind back to 2:8–9: "Remember Jesus Christ, risen from the dead, descendant of David, according to my gospel, for which I *suffer hardship* even to imprisonment as a criminal; but the word of God is not imprisoned" (emphasis mine).

Like Paul, who followed in the suffering of Christ for the sake of the gospel, every pastor can expect to walk this same way of suffering. He will receive unfair criticism. He will be misunderstood. People will shut their ears to truth and chase after myths, and the faithful pastor will be characterized as foolish, dated, irrelevant. But just as Christ rose from the grave vindicated, so truth eventually will crush apostasy and myth.

"Do the work of an evangelist." The term "evangelist" occurs only two other times in the New Testament (Acts 4:11; Eph. 4:11) and denotes a bringer of good news. In the secular sense, this person distributed news of a royal birth or brought reports of victory from the battlefront.

In this case, of course, the good news is none other than the gospel. Take note, however, of Paul's phrasing: "Do the work of an evangelist." This involves more than merely presenting God's plan of salvation. The "work" includes feeding the hungry, clothing the poor, sheltering the homeless, caring for widows and orphans, fighting for justice, and rescuing the helpless.

The work of an evangelist puts the words of the gospel into action.

From My Journal

Called of God

In the summer of 1959, as I interviewed to become a student at Dallas Theological Seminary, Dr. Donald Campbell, the registrar, looked at me, then at my wife, and then back to me. After a pause, he asked a question I will never forget. "Mr. Swindoll, would you be happy and fulfilled doing anything else?"

I had a good job waiting for me back in Houston; at full seniority, no less. I could have made a fine living. We had no children. We could have settled into a nice little house near family and all that was familiar to us. We could have created a comfortable future for ourselves.

I thought for a moment, although my heart already resonated with the answer. "No, Dr. Campbell, I would not be satisfied doing anything else." He told me years later that if I had given any other answer, they never would have accepted me as a student. As it happened, they accepted me on probation, because a guy like me came with more than a few risks for the school.

Fortunately, I am the recipient of a legacy established by a long line of flawed, imperfect vessels. People like Paul. People like Timothy. People deemed unsuitable from a worldly perspective, yet bearing the only qualification that matters. A minister is called of God.

"Fulfill your ministry." The Greek term translated "fulfill" means "to bring to complete fullness or satisfaction." This reminds me of a large sailing vessel with its sails unfurled, filled with wind, pushing the ship toward its destination, allowing the crew to fulfill their purpose.

The word for "ministry" is *diakonia*, the same term for the service of deacons (Acts 6:1), which Paul described earlier in 1 Timothy 3. He didn't, however, limit *diakonia* to the office of deacon. Paul saw the work of "waiting tables" — in both the literal and figurative meanings — as the duty of all ministers: elders, pastors, and himself (1 Tim. 1:12).

Application

The Four Duties of a Pastor

Most jobs come with a profile, a document that, along with other details, outlines the employee's primary objective. It identifies the specific duties he or she is expected to complete. Paul had earlier established the primary objective for all ministers:

> He gave some as apostles, and some as prophets, and some as evangelists, and some as pastors and teachers, for the equipping of the saints for the work of service, to the building up of the body of Christ. (Eph. 4:11–12)

After echoing this objective in 2 Timothy 3:16–17, Paul outlined the four primary duties of a pastor.

First, *the pastor must faithfully and consistently preach the Word of God.* There is a subtle, yet profound, difference between teaching and preaching Scripture. Both explain the meanings of the words and phrases. Both draw timeless principles from the text and then apply them. But teaching and proclamation differ in their intent. The goal of teaching is Scripture knowledge, with suggestions for application. Preaching, however, seeks to compel hearers to act on what they have learned from Scripture. Teaching feeds the mind; preaching challenges the will.

Effective preaching doesn't have to be emotionally rousing; sometimes emotional appeals help, sometimes they become a distraction. Effective preaching doesn't draw attention to itself; if people leave the church commenting on a preacher's style — whether good or poor — then the point of proclamation has been lost. The mark of effective preaching is lasting change that builds momentum over time and can be seen as progress in the right direction. The church as a whole begins to behave differently as members begin to make better choices as they encourage one another to do the same. With effective preaching, the Lord's sheep begin to move in the right direction without prodding.

Second, *the pastor must confront wrongdoing and correct error.* The pastor must maintain an uncompromising standard of purity with respect to doctrine and teaching. He carefully screens teachers to be certain they understand Scripture and then remain faithful when instructing others. And when teaching strays from the Bible, he confronts, corrects, encourages, and instructs with gentleness and patience. Unfortunately, at times he also must be firm. Guarding the flock from error may require the spiritual leader to remove teachers from their posts when their teaching proves either incompetent or willfully contrary to Scripture.

The pastor also must be aware of the cultural and academic trends that influence people during the six days they aren't in church. He must prepare himself with sufficient knowledge so that he is able to confront false teaching with answers from the Bible. Faithful shepherds protect the flock of God.

Third, *the pastor must lead the effort to evangelize the community.* One of the primary reasons Jesus established the church is to carry the good news to the world and to make disciples. The Holy Spirit empowers local churches to reach out and to bring their communities to faith in Christ. A visionary church is the lengthening shadow of its visionary pastor.

Note, however, that the pastor is not the only evangelist. Nor is he necessarily the primary evangelist. Many churches think of their pastor as a hireling, expecting him to fulfill their responsibilities on their behalf. The pastor is a shepherd. He leads the flock's evangelistic efforts, but he is not a one-man substitute for what the entire church has been commanded by the Lord to do.

Fourth, *the pastor must serve the congregation.* As noted in the explanation above, the term for "ministry" in the command "fulfill your ministry" (v. 5) is the word used for the office of deacon. *Diakonia* is the act of waiting on tables, the New Testament metaphor for service to others. This is the most basic function of the pastor.

The pastor serves the needs of his congregation in several ways. He coordinates the emotional and spiritual care of individuals in the congregation. He also helps see to their physical needs during times of loss or distress. He offers counsel and other resources to keep families together and healthy. He is engaged in activities that touch their lives on those special occasions. In other words, he marries, baptizes, and buries members of his congregation. He anticipates the needs of individuals and families in order to guide the church appropriately.

The job profile of a pastor is not for everyone. In the absence of a calling, such duties would soon become toilsome, leading to resentment and burnout. But when God calls a man to serve as pastor, nothing other than these duties will satisfy him. He *must* preach, reprove, evangelize, and serve. In doing so, he "fulfills" his ministry.

Looking Back—No Regrets (2 Timothy 4:6–8)

---

⁶For I am already being poured out as a drink offering, and the time of my departure has come. ⁷I have fought the good fight, I have finished the course, I have kept the faith; ⁸in the future there is laid up for me the crown of righteousness, which the Lord, the righteous Judge, will award to me on that day; and not only to me, but also to all who have loved His appearing.

When people know the end of their earthly journey is at hand, they tend to glance backward just before passing into that eternal future. The late Henri Nouwen, for example, reflected on his life during a particularly difficult period. His journal entries were published after his death in the book, *The Inner Voice of Love*.

> The years that lie behind you, with all their struggles and pains, will in time be remembered only as the way that led to your new life. But as long as the new life is not fully yours, your memories will continue to cause you pain. When you keep reliving painful events of the past, you can feel victimized by them.[11]

As people look back, some feel satisfied by what they see; others cringe with regret. Disappointment over unwise decisions or sinful actions can keep the turmoil of regret perpetually agitated. The toxic effects of regret can destroy one's later years, not unlike the man who wrote these sad words:

Across the fields of yesterday
He sometimes comes to me,
A little lad just back from play—
The boy I used to be.
And yet he smiles so wistfully
Once he has crept within,
I wonder if he hopes to see
The man I might have been.[12]

The miserable main character of the French novel *Vipers' Tangle* reached the end of his life and found within his heart a twisted, writhing knot of hatred and regrets. He confessed in his diary:

> But the horror of growing old consists in this, that one's age is the sum total of one's life, and not one figure of it can we change. It has taken me sixty years—I thought—to "create" this old man now dying of hatred. I am what I am. I should have to become somebody else ... Oh God! ... Oh God ... if only you existed![13]

So it is for all who come to the end of their days serving only self and loving no one else. Having forsaken God, they sulk and groan to their graves feeling God-forsaken.

That could have been Paul. He had every reason to feel resentful. He had been the target of abuse for years. He had endured dozens of betrayals, undoubtedly mourning the sorrow of each one. He had borne the brunt of false accusations from every stripe of charlatan and heretic in the first century. He had endured danger, imprisonment, flogging, and even stoning for the sake of the gospel. So, by the time of this letter, he looked much older than he should have, stooped and scarred, probably aching in every formerly broken bone.

It would not have been unreasonable for Paul to expect a comfortable retirement as a reward for such dedicated service to the Lord and His church. Instead, he is writing from his deathbed—such as it was. It couldn't have been more than a place on the floor of a dungeon, cleared of debris. He had no money, few provisions, inadequate clothing, and dwindling morale. The only thing in abundant supply was solitude. Other than Dr. Luke, he had no familiar face to encourage him. And yet, his last words betray no hint of bitterness or resentment or regret. In place of all that his indomitable spirit emerges.

His letter reveals a man concerned about others far more than himself. Throughout the letter, Paul has focused on Timothy and, by extension, on those who follow in his footsteps. Imperative verbs have conveyed urgent instructions. His repeated use of the second person pronoun, "you," guided his instructions to the younger minister's heart.

- "I constantly remember *you* in my prayers night and day" (1:3).
- "*You* therefore, my son, be strong in the grace that is in Christ Jesus" (2:1).
- "*You*, however, continue in the things you have learned" (3:14).
- "But *you*, be sober in all things, endure hardship, do the work of an evangelist, fulfill your ministry" (4:5).

Then suddenly, "you" gives way to "I," "me," and "my." Paul shifts his focus away from Timothy to reveal something of himself. As the veil between this life and his eternal future draws closer, the apostle glances over his shoulder. Consider the self-reflective words of a man prepared to die without regrets.

—**4:6**—

Paul uses two interesting figures of speech to describe his last days. The first involves a ritual unfamiliar in twenty-first-century Western culture, but common in Paul's world. A "libation" was a familiar Jewish custom in which a worshiper poured red wine across the base of an altar. The wine represented the blood of a lamb given as a sacrifice. The apostle's word picture also drew upon the Hebrew poetic expression "poured out" (Ps. 22:14; Job 30:16), in which a person is emptied of strength to the point of death. To be "poured out" is to be drained of one's life energy.

During an earlier imprisonment, Paul wrote to the Christians in Philippi, "Even if I am being poured out as a drink offering upon the sacrifice and service of your faith, I rejoice and share my joy with you all" (Phil. 2:17). He felt his life draining away during his long wait for trial, and he was prepared to give his life for the Lord. Even so, he considered the sacrifice of his life worthwhile for the sake of their salvation and continued growth in grace (Phil. 1:21).

His second figure of speech depicts a journey, speaking of his death as "my departure." But this colorful Greek term *analysis* (lit., "untying again") paints no less than four word pictures.

First is the idea of examination. Transliterated into English, *analysis* carries the idea of unbraiding a rope, dividing the complex unit into its individual strands. Paul anticipates that his death will result in his life and accomplishments being unraveled, laid bare for all to see.

Second is the idea of release from bondage. The term *analysis* was used of unyoking a beast from its burden. Paul regards death as unyoking his life from the toils of responsibility. When used of humans, it pictures the breaking of shackles and leg irons. Death means freedom.

Third is the idea of moving one's residence. Greeks used the term *analysis* to describe striking a tent in order to relocate. We have a similar expression in English: "We're pullin' up stakes." Paul sees death as a relocation to a much better land.

Fourth, and the most poignant, is the idea of a voyage. Sailors used the word *analysis* in the sense of departure. They untied their ship from its moorings in order to launch the vessel. Paul's death will release him from his earthly moorings to make the voyage to the realm of his Heavenly Father.

— **4:7** —

A longing look to his eternal future prompted Paul to glance over his shoulder. He remembered the challenges and victories of the past, just as every person facing death would. Teachers see the faces of former students. Nurses remember patients that impacted them most. Politicians consider their legacies. Parents want to see the faces of their children and grandchildren. Pastors think of their time in the pulpit, hoping they remained faithful to the Word. Missionaries hope to leave a region transformed into an outpost of God's kingdom. All ministers of every discipline want to have created a legacy of faithfulness. Accomplishments? Of course. But faithfulness first and foremost.

Paul glanced backward to see a fight, a course, and the faith. Interestingly, he shifted the normal word order in Greek to emphasize the subject of each verb. He wrote literally, "The good fight I have fought, the course I have finished, the faith I have kept." The effect for the reader is to focus on the calling to which Paul responded and to stress the faithful fulfillment of his duty.

The term for "fight" is *agōn*, meaning "a striving for victory." We get our word "agony" from the Greek concept of giving all of oneself to win a contest or to reach a goal (cf. 1 Tim. 4:10). Paul recalled the day the Lord stopped him in his tracks with a blinding revelation of Himself, challenged and convicted the earnest-yet-arrogant man of religion, cleansed him of his sin and healed his blindness, and then called, equipped, sent, supported, and strengthened him for ministry. He reviewed the arduous course he had run—a thirty-year super-marathon—and affirmed that he had given it his all. He had held nothing back.

Earlier, when apostate teachers presumed to challenge Paul's credentials and question his commitment, he reviewed his race to that point:

> Are they servants of Christ?—I speak as if insane—I more so; in far more labors, in far more imprisonments, beaten times without number, often in danger of death. Five times I received from the Jews thirty-nine lashes. Three times I was beaten with rods, once I was stoned, three times I was shipwrecked, a night and a day I have spent in the deep. I have been on frequent journeys, in dangers from rivers, dangers from robbers, dangers from my countrymen, dangers from the Gentiles, dangers in the city, dangers in the wilderness, dangers on the sea, dangers among false brethren; I have been in labor and hardship, through many sleepless nights, in hunger and thirst, often without food, in cold and exposure. Apart from such external things, there is the daily pressure on me of concern for all the churches. (2 Cor. 11:23–28)

Without a shred of pride, the knowledge that he has "agonized" well gave Paul satisfaction, the issue of results or success notwithstanding. Yet, he had not only run well, he has finished well. His declaration "the course I have finished" uses a word that combines the ideas of purpose and completion. Furthermore, the perfect form of the verb appears reminiscent of *tetelestai*, the Greek translation of Jesus' declaration from the cross, "It is finished!"

No one, even Paul, chooses his or her course. The course is prepared for us. We can choose, however, whether to run it. No two courses are the same, yet we are called to run our respective courses with equal faithfulness and determination. Moreover, you might be surprised by the difficulty of the course laid before you, but the Lord is not. He knew beforehand the challenges you would face, and He has promised to equip you to overcome them. Not necessarily all at once, but daily, on an as-needed basis.

Paul's course had led him through some horrific turns and more than a few treacherous sinkholes. Eventually, it led him to a dungeon beneath the streets of Rome. But that's not the end of his journey. It is only the waypoint for another leg. The end of his journey on earth would put him on a course toward glory. Cultivating that eternal perspective and maintaining it for the duration of one's life journey requires trust.

Paul's third declaration has a double meaning. First, he continues to trust in the Lord and the soundness of the gospel he has been commissioned to preach. Second, he has guarded the treasure entrusted to him (cf. 1:12, 14; 1 Tim. 6:20); he preserves divine truth with the purity in which he has received it and he wields that truth to confront and eradicate apostasy in the church.

— **4:8** —

Having acknowledged his present circumstances and having glanced over his shoulder with satisfaction at the sum total of his life, Paul gave a longing look toward his future. And he saw vindication.

I have chosen that word carefully, but it might lead to some misunderstanding; so let me first explain what vindication is *not*. Vindication is not an opportunity to gloat over those who sinned against us. Vindication is not the ability to say, "I was right while all my critics were wrong." Vindication is not the right to judge others after being misjudged. All of those are worldly concerns that lie in the past. Vindication looks forward. Vindication, in the oldest sense of the word, is the state of being delivered from peril. Vindication is to be free from allegations or blame, to be justified, to be declared righteous, to receive what has been promised. Vindication is the ultimate reward of faithful running. It says, "Your dedication, despite criticism, has proven to be worthwhile. Your hope is now seen" (cf. Rom. 8:24).

Of all the blessings of vindication, the idea of justification reigns supreme. Paul describes his reward as a "crown." This recalls the custom of a victorious athlete receiving a laurel wreath, symbolizing all that he is to receive. Particularly successful or noteworthy competitors received royal treatment upon returning home. Officials would break a large opening in the city wall and then cover it with a brass plate engraved with his name. All his debts were cancelled as the victor was granted tax-free status for the rest of his life. Merchants often guaranteed the victor and his family a lifetime supply of food. A victorious athlete could literally rest on his laurels.

The "crown" Paul would receive is that of righteousness. Neither Paul nor anyone else can earn righteousness. Paul's faithful running and strong finish didn't earn him any merit against his sin. Righteousness is a gift of God, given by grace to those who trust in His Son. During life on earth, righteousness is promised; in eternity, righteousness is received. Paul finished the race and received what had been promised: a verdict of "not-guilty" from the Supreme Judge in the court of heaven.

Paul's self-analysis and his ability to face death with no regrets are especially poignant considering the circumstances in which he is writing. The irony highlights the vastly different ways that heaven and earth judge the content of a person's life. Paul is writing his letter from prison, awaiting the day he will stand before Nero or one of his delegates to be judged. In a worldly sense, a person who has failed will stand before the very definition of earthly success. That is, in terms of wealth, no one could rival the emperor of Rome; but Paul owned nothing more than the filthy clothes on his back. In terms of power, Nero ruled the entire Mediterranean world; Paul probably couldn't even stand erect in his cell. In terms of human laws, Nero *was* the law; Paul fully expected to be declared "guilty" and then beheaded as a criminal.

But the realm of eternity judges differently. Where are the two men now?

Application

Three Soul-Searching Questions

Now is always a good time to consider three searching questions lifted from Paul's self-evaluation. Pause long enough to ask and answer them honestly. I guarantee this: they will change the way you think about tomorrow.

Question 1: *Have I acknowledged the reality of my present situation?*

Paul considered his circumstances and accepted them at face value. That means he didn't try to imagine them better than they were; that's self-delusion. And he didn't try to convince himself he would be miraculously released (Acts 5:18–20; 16:25–27); that's wishful thinking at best, presumption of the Lord's will at worst. Without discounting any potential future, he accepted the truth of his place in life, saying, "I'm pouring out my life as an offering to the Lord." Paul maintained this same attitude in every circumstance throughout his life—whether free or imprisoned, healthy or ill, surrounded or sequestered.

Right now, reflect on your present circumstances. Things could be better; things could be worse. Regardless, this is your place in life to be experienced by you and no other. If you can change anything for the better, by all means do so! If you currently enjoy great blessing, savor these days with gratitude and share them with those you love. Let your life count for eternity. Acknowledge your circumstances realistically and then submit them to His sovereign care.

Question 2: *When I remember the events of my past, are there regrets I need to address?*

Now is the time to ask that question, while you have the time and the ability to do something about regrets, before they haunt your deathbed. Have I offended or harmed someone without having made it right? Is that person alive? Have I apologized and attempted to restore that relationship? Or, if that person is gone, have I taken my offenses to the foot of the cross and sought the Lord's forgiveness and allowed Him to relieve me of that burden? Am I truly free of lingering guilt?

Have I accepted the consequences of foolish or sinful behavior as an expression of God's mercy? Or do I kick against the rails of Providence ... or just as senselessly, continue to kick myself? Have I repented fully, received the Lord's grace, turned to walk in a new direction, and allowed the residue of my actions to keep me sensitive to His leading?

Is there a person I need to thank? Someone who deserves to hear my sincere appreciation for his or her positive impact? Don't save that for the person's eulogy. Take time *now* to express your gratitude.

Address regrets now, before they poison your spirit or steal joy from the days you have yet to live.

Question 3: *Can I claim the assurance of some future reward, some future crown?*

Paul knew what awaited him, regardless of how or when he died. In addition to eternal life—which he did not earn, but received by grace through faith in Christ—he fully expected to receive a number of honors he did labor to earn. Do you have that assurance? The Bible mentions five crowns:

- *the crown of rejoicing* (Phil. 4:1) ... for leading others to faith in Christ
- *the crown of righteousness* (2 Tim. 4:8) ... for eagerly awaiting Christ's return
- *the crown of life* (James 1:12) ... for suffering for the glory of God
- *the crown of glory* (1 Peter 5:4) ... reserved for elders and ministers who serve congregations willingly, faithfully, and consistently
- *the crown of mastery* (1 Cor. 9:25) ... for keeping the flesh in subjection

Revelation 4:10–11 projects a beautiful image of believers—the twenty-four elders—in heaven casting their crowns before the One who awarded them. As we all join this magnificent act of worship, we will be face down on a brilliantly transparent, shining, mirror-like street, where we'll see ourselves for the first time as God see us.

Stop and imagine yourself there. What will you bring to that wondrous ceremony?

I urge you in the years you have left—who knows how many or how few?— turn your attention to things eternal. Turn your eyes away from the person who makes your life miserable. Resolve to clear away the trash of regret. Determine to stop dragging around the anchors of resentment and blame. Begin living today in light of that eternal tomorrow. When you do that, you will discover an inner joy you've never known.

A Circle of Honor and Dishonor (2 Timothy 4:9–15)

> [9]Make every effort to come to me soon; [10]for Demas, having loved this present world, has deserted me and gone to Thessalonica; Crescens *has gone* to Galatia, Titus to Dalmatia. [11]Only Luke is with me. Pick up Mark and bring him with you, for he is useful to me for service. [12]But Tychicus I have sent to Ephesus. [13]When you come bring the cloak which I left at Troas with Carpus, and the books, especially the parchments. [14]Alexander the coppersmith did me much harm; the Lord will repay him according to his deeds. [15]Be on guard against him yourself, for he vigorously opposed our teaching.

In 1975, the newly appointed librarian of Congress, Daniel J. Boorstin, discovered a shoebox tucked away in a vault. It held the contents of Abraham Lincoln's pockets the night he was murdered. Among the contents were newspaper clippings praising the president's deeds. One slip of newsprint seemed especially worn to Boorstin, who noted that it contained a speech by John Bright in the British House of Commons, praising Lincoln as "one of the greatest men of all times."

Today, many people would heartily agree with Bright; but in 1865, millions considered Lincoln either incurably evil or a complete buffoon. The president's critics were unrelenting and numerous. His was a lonely agony of a man, desperately working to hold his nation together and guide it down a moral path.

I find Lincoln's carrying those little sepia slips of affirmation touchingly pathetic. I imagine this now-celebrated leader all alone, unfolding the clippings under the flickering lamp on the desk of the oval office, seeking comfort and support to face another day of unappreciated leadership.

Leadership and loneliness go hand in hand. That's a surprise to people who have not been called to fill leadership positions. Most would think that leaders spend so much time with other people that a rich social life becomes almost automatic. But nothing could be further from the truth. The fact is, loneliness stalks where the buck stops.

- How often Moses must have felt the cold shoulder of loneliness when leading for forty years the mutinous, murmuring people of Israel.
- How Joshua must have longed for a partner with whom to share the responsibilities of leading the conquest of Canaan.
- How loneliness must have stalked the halls of David's palace during Absalom's rebellion and in the days of grief after the young man was killed.
- How utterly alone the great prophets felt—so strong-hearted and fiercely loyal to God, yet repeatedly misunderstood, maligned, and often martyred.

It should, therefore, come as no surprise that Paul suffered loneliness in the dark of his cell. He had always kept the company of students and colleagues on his journeys. Now, either duty or dereliction took every familiar voice, every kind face, far from Rome. Only Luke dared to risk imprisonment and persecution to supply Paul's needs and, perhaps, tend to his medical difficulties. The lonely leader closes his letter with a touching plea that reminds us that the heroic apostle was, after all, just a man: "Come before winter" (4:21).

Soon, autumn's chill will begin to aggravate Paul's old wounds. In the meantime, down in the dark solitude of a foul-smelling dungeon shared with other doomed men, memories crowded the weary minister's mind—some painful, some pleasant. As Paul neared the end of his letter, he recalled two painful memories and five faithful friends.

— **4:9** —

Paul pleaded twice in this segment for Timothy to come soon. The Greek command translated "make haste" doubles as a plea for speed and zeal. He obviously didn't know how much longer he had to live. His trial could come at any time, after which he would have only a couple of days before execution. He would likely spend those in the maximum security facility, an abandoned underground cistern accessible only by a three-foot-diameter hole in the floor of a heavily guarded antechamber. Try to imagine that.

— **4:10** —

Paul eloquently lamented the first of two painful memories. The name Demas appears only two other places in the New Testament, and then only in passing. Demas sent greetings along with Luke at the end of Paul's letter to the Colossians (Col. 4:14) and to Philemon (24). Paul considered the man a "fellow-worker," a high compliment from the apostle. But something happened inside Demas. He once followed Christ earnestly, or Paul never would have invited him to join his entourage. He once demonstrated courage and determination, for traveling with Paul would have demanded nothing less (Acts 15:37–38).

No more. Demas had abandoned Paul for what the apostle termed a "love [for] this present world," which is no insignificant condemnation. Paul used the distinctly Christian verb *agapaō*, normally reserved for people, to say that Demas "loved this present world." "This present world" refers not only to the worldly pursuits of money, power, status, pleasure, or possessions. Jesus identified the enemy of God's kingdom as "the world" (John 15:18–19).

"The world" does not mean the earth per se. The planet does not have a mind, so it cannot be evil. Nature has been twisted and corrupted by evil, but it is not evil in itself. In fact, Paul personified nature as an innocent bystander, suffering the ill effects of evil, groaning for redemption by its rightful Owner (Rom. 8:20–22). Instead, "the world" represents the fallen world system, which operates according

During his second imprisonment in Rome, Paul found himself virtually alone. He had sent Titus to Dalmatia, Crescens to Galatia (in which Iconium was a major city), and Tychicus to Ephesus. Demas deserted him for home in Thessalonica, leaving only Luke to care for his needs.

to Satan's values and is subject to the curse of sin (Gen. 3:14–19). "The world" also represents the people who live by its values and willingly serve its ends. Jesus originally came to redeem the world (John 3:17; 12:47), but the world rejected Him (John 3:18; 12:48); therefore, He began to separate "His own" from the world (John 10:14, 26–27; 13:1; 15:19).

To say that someone loves "this present world" is to say he or she is an enemy of God's kingdom (cf. 1 John 2:15–17).

Thankfully, Paul's memory didn't linger on Demas more than a few moments. He quickly recalled the names of five faithful men whom we might place in the apostle's circle of honor. The first is Crescens, about whom we know almost nothing. His name appears nowhere else in Scripture. That he is mentioned with four other notable men suggests Paul thought highly of him. Paul likely deployed him to Galatia sometime between his first and second imprisonments.

Paul originally asked Titus to join him in Nicopolis (Titus 3:12), where he planned to winter before setting sail for Rome. We have no reason to believe Paul didn't follow through on this part of his plan. Regardless, sometime during his stay in Rome, he sent Titus to Dalmatia, also known as Illyricum. The assignment could not have been easy. The people were notoriously stiff-necked, stubbornly resisting Roman subjugation and reportedly harboring brigands and pirates. Strabo, a contemporary of Titus, called the region of Illyricum despicable "because of the wildness of the inhabitants and their piratical habits."[14]

Crescens was too far away in Galatia to make the trip in reasonable time, and Titus couldn't very well leave Dalmatia without leadership — not yet, at least.

— **4:11** —

Paul named Luke as the only man to have remained faithfully by his side. Because prisons provided only the very least provisions, prisoners depended on family and friends to bring food, water, clothing, and medical supplies — usually by bribing the guards. By this time, Luke had written his gospel. Acts, his chronicle of the earliest days of the church, concluded with Paul's first Roman imprisonment. Therefore, the "beloved physician" (Col. 4:14) knew of Paul's many injuries (2 Cor. 11:23–28) and had, no doubt, witnessed many of them personally. He was invaluable to the apostle.

Mark refers to John Mark, the cousin of Paul's oldest Christian friend, Barnabas. This short affirmation of Mark's "usefulness" testifies to the forgiveness and redemption available between brothers in Christ.

Years earlier, Paul conducted his first missionary journey under the leadership of Barnabas, whose cousin, John Mark (Col. 4:10), abandoned the mission partway through (Acts 13:13). So, when the time came to assemble a team for a second journey,

> Barnabas wanted to take John, called Mark, along with them also. But Paul kept insisting that they should not take him along who had deserted them in Pamphylia and had not gone with them to the work. And there occurred such a sharp disagreement that they separated from one another, and Barnabas took Mark with him and sailed away to Cyprus. But Paul chose Silas and left, being committed by the brethren to the grace of the Lord. (Acts 15:37–40)

Time passed. Mark matured. Paul forgave. What an incredible compliment to be called to his aid. Paul obviously knew the request to come to Rome carried significant danger, but he also knew that now he could depend on Mark. Great-hearted Paul had come full circle, and he wasn't reluctant to reveal it.

— **4:12** —

The fifth faithful man in Paul's circle of honor was Tychicus, whom Paul probably met in Ephesus (Acts 20:4). He had traveled with the apostle and served as courier, bearing his letters to his hometown of Ephesus (Eph. 6:21), to Colossae (Col. 4:7), and probably to Philemon (Col. 4:9). He may have relieved Titus on Crete (Titus 3:12), allowing Titus to join Paul in Nicopolis. Then, sometime before his second imprisonment, he sent Tychicus to Ephesus.

Some have wondered why Paul would tell Timothy this. If Timothy had been serving in Ephesus, wouldn't he know? I think this argues against the view that Tychicus carried this second letter. He more likely served in some other city and had received instructions to relieve Timothy in Ephesus, allowing the latter to leave for Rome immediately.

— **4:13** —

Paul asked Timothy to attend to him in Rome, even asking him to hurry (v. 9) and to come before the onset of winter (4:21). His faith allowed him to add two practical requests to "when you come." He asked for his cloak, presumably to keep him warm as the chill of winter will soon envelop Rome. And he asked for his books, which undoubtedly included a copy of the Scriptures.

— **4:14-15** —

Paul's circle of dishonor includes Demas, who slipped away from Paul and the faith as the influence of the world eventually revealed his true spiritual condition. Alexander, however, never pretended to be Paul's colleague. He had "vigorously opposed" the apostle, his ministry, and his gospel almost from the beginning.

The name Alexander appears in the New Testament in three contexts: a Jew who tried to address the rioting crowd in Ephesus (Acts 19:33); an apostate teacher in Ephesus whom Paul disciplined with Hymenaeus (1 Tim. 1:18–20); and "Alexander the coppersmith." Because the name was so common, we cannot know for certain if these three were the same man. I tend to think, however, one man in Ephesus caused Paul no end of problems and continued to plague Timothy.

The verb translated "did" means "to show, inform, prove." It has reference to being an informant. A literal rendering from the Greek reads, "He accused many evils to me." Apparently, he caused Paul great harm through false accusations. To whom, we do not know. City officials, perhaps. Or, more likely, to the church body, trying to sway their allegiance away from the gospel to embrace Alexander's false teaching.

Paul didn't expose Alexander in order to embarrass him for two thousand years. He called attention to the danger of Alexander as a warning to Timothy. Paul would soon die. Alexander would remain. As one teacher of truth passed from the scene, the apostate would simply train his sights on the next.

Leadership and loneliness go hand in hand. The spiritual leader cannot expect to receive much in the way of human affirmation. He holds confidential information that often prevents him from explaining his decisions. Therefore, misunderstanding clouds what might otherwise be close relationships. He must make difficult choices that benefit the community but bring discomfort to a few individuals. The backlash from a loud minority usually goes unanswered as a supportive majority remains silent.

The spiritual leader usually deals with opposition alone; no one wants to be around for an unpleasant confrontation. Affirmation, if any, usually comes much later, and often anonymously. The spiritual leader must live with his eyes on the horizon; he lives two or more years in the future, while everyone else lives in the moment, doing what must be done to maintain progress. So the leader must savor his plans in solitude until the day he can cast the vision and inspire those around him.

While loneliness stalks where the buck stops, the spiritual leader eventually learns to enjoy his or her solitude. Others may misunderstand, but the Lord knows all. The community may not appreciate difficult choices, but the Lord affirms obedience.

The leader must stand against error, but the Lord is the Author of truth. The leader must learn to thrive on his or her visions, but they usually find agreement in the Lord's heart. Therefore, the loneliness of leadership becomes the leader's opportunity to cultivate a deeper intimacy with the Almighty. Spiritual leadership has its burdens, but sharing camaraderie with God is more reward than any leader deserves. So, in the end, leadership in the Father's kingdom is a privilege like no other.

Application

The Needs of the Needy

It's easy to forget that heroes have human needs like everyone else. We place them on a superhuman pedestal, but even ancient heroes of the faith struggled as we do today. Paul's closing lines reveal a man strong in his faith and sure of his convictions, yet very much in need. His pleas for help offer four timeless reminders for difficult times:

First, *when you're lonely, you need caring, close friends.* That's about as obvious as saying, "When you're hungry, you need food." Unfortunately, modernism and our Western culture have conditioned us to feel shamed by our need for companionship. God made us for relationships—with Himself and with one another. Paul never counted "rugged individualism" among his chief attributes. He surrounded himself with people without becoming a people-pleaser; he drew strength and comfort from his colleagues without compromising his dependence on the Lord.

Develop a rich social life that gives you the opportunity to cultivate several close, caring relationships. Make this a priority now; caring friends won't suddenly emerge when you're lonely.

Second, *when you're hurt, you need loyal advocates.* An advocate is more than a friend; an advocate is someone who supports or defends you in a cause, someone who acts in your best interest on your behalf, especially when you are unable to defend yourself.

Every person who goes through any kind of legal proceeding needs an attorney. Attorneys used to be known as "advocates." When you go before a judge, your lawyer becomes your go-between. Similarly, when we're hurt, we need a go-between, someone to act in our best interest, to serve on our behalf, and to represent us before those who have the power to help or harm us. They encourage, they help us see things objectively, they relieve the burden of survival, and they help find solutions we would be powerless to discover on our own.

Third, *when you are loved, you need to be grateful.* If you are loved by a circle of people, you are rich indeed. Share the wealth. Why keep all that love to yourself?

When was the last time you looked at another individual and said, "I love you"? Others need to know you love them, and they need to hear the first person singular, "I." Not a casual, "Luv ya!" but the complete, "I love you."

You may not be the casually expressive kind, someone who doesn't frequently or easily express emotion. Well, *get over yourself!* This isn't about you; it's about the people in your life who would cherish your words. If you believe it, express it. If they love you, show your gratitude by telling them often.

Fourth, *when you're needy, admit it.* When was the last time you picked up a phone, called someone, and said, "Hi, today's a really tough day for me. I need you right now"? If you're like most people, two things keep you from expressing that kind of raw vulnerability: pride and fear.

Pride lies at the root of so many sins and fear holds us hostage to our misery. The simple admissions "I need help" or "I need you" have the power to shatter both of those deadly constraints. They establish quick bonds with friends, they welcome advocates, they multiply the potential solutions to problems, they free others to step into our lives and share the burdens of suffering or loneliness.

Paul, perhaps the most stalwart, resilient, long-suffering, faithful follower of Christ in the entire Bible, didn't suffer without asking for help. As a man of grace, who extended grace to so many, he believed in grace enough to ask for it and to receive it gratefully when offered. Let's follow his model.

Grace to the Very End (2 Timothy 4:16–22)

---

[16]At my first defense no one supported me, but all deserted me; may it not be counted against them. [17]But the Lord stood with me and strengthened me, so that through me the proclamation might be fully accomplished, and that all the Gentiles might hear; and I was rescued out of the lion's mouth. [18]The Lord will rescue me from every evil deed, and will bring me safely to His heavenly kingdom; to Him *be* the glory forever and ever. Amen.

[19]Greet Prisca and Aquila, and the household of Onesiphorus. [20]Erastus remained at Corinth, but Trophimus I left sick at Miletus. [21]Make every effort to come before winter. Eubulus greets you, also Pudens and Linus and Claudia and all the brethren.

[22]The Lord be with your spirit. Grace be with you.

Staring death in the face can bring out the best in people. The real prospect of death carrying us away from this world forces us to push aside pettiness as we focus on what is most significant. Perhaps the most vivid recent example of this would be the events of September 11, 2001. Before that day ended, four planes had crashed. The twin symbols of American commerce that once stood tall and erect over Manhattan had fallen. The Pentagon had a smoldering, 200-foot hole in its west side. The wreckage of another airliner littered a remote patch of Pennsylvania countryside, leaving no survivors to tell their heroic story. Our nation watched televisions helplessly in stunned silence and grief as the death toll continued to mount—to hundreds and then to thousands.

We will never know all of the events that transpired that awful morning, but we do know that the immediate reality of death brought out the best in most people. Firemen and policemen became our heroes, charging into buildings to help people hoping to escape smoke, fire, and ultimately the complete collapse. Hundreds within the Pentagon helped their colleagues exit the destroyed portion of the building, even as their own clothing and skin burned. And who can ever forget that courageous group of thirty-eight passengers on United 93, charging the cockpit to regain control of the airplane? Who knows what might have happened if all of these people failed to recognize what is significant and then do what must be done?

Sometimes, death, or even the prospect of death, can bring out the very best in people.

As you read these words, wherever you happen to be, pause for a moment and consider your answer to this question: "If you knew you had no more than a few hours to live, what would emerge from within you?"

Now is the time to begin to answer that question. Will you be full of grace, or will lingering grudges push bitterness to the surface? Will grace flow from your lips, or will lingering regrets cause you to curse? Will grace fall over you like a blanket, or will you feel naked and ashamed? Will grace put a rod of iron in your spine, or will you quiver with fear and dread? Today is the day you must decide how you will face death. Choose grace today, practice grace each day thereafter, and perhaps you will resemble Paul in the last days of your own life.

By now you are familiar with his circumstances. He is sitting in a dungeon awaiting trial, although the verdict is a foregone conclusion; he will face the executioner's sword. Except for Dr. Luke, he has no one to comfort him. Cold, hungry, lonely, aching, and probably sick, he endures injustice without bitterness. He had been deserted at his trial by everyone, but he held no grudges. He might possibly die alone like a common criminal, yet we find no self-pity in his final words. In a real sense, Paul faces a kind of personal Gethsemane. The result of his crushing could have been bitter bile or sweet grace.

By now you also know Paul well enough to know which he produces.

Nero's campaign to scapegoat Christians not only turned killing them into a spectacle, it made their persecution fashionable. According to Tacitus, Pliny, and other contemporary historians, all kinds of allegations put believers before judges for condemnation. They were accused of hatred against humanity and convicted of atheism, because they worshiped a God who cannot be seen and they refused to acknowledge the gods of Roman fantasy. Rumors twisted the Eucharist ceremony into a cannibalistic rite. Christians refused to join their Roman neighbors in sinful rites that ascribed deity to Caesar, so they were accused of sedition.

Paul could have been arraigned on any of these charges, but their merit was beside the point. He was living under a regime in which truth had become irrelevant and logic conscripted to serve the emperor's whims. John Pollock writes, "Of Paul's final trial, nothing is known beyond a tradition that he was condemned by resolution of the Senate on the charge of treason against the divine emperor."[15] (If ever there were a more obvious oxymoron! Divine emperor, indeed. As John Ortberg has noted, today we call our children Paul and "we call our dogs Caesar and Nero."[16])

After all Paul had done for his colleagues and friends, you would think at least they would come and stand in his defense, but to support a Christian at his trial would have been a death wish. As it happened, Paul's friends in Rome either had been captured and tried, or they fled like rats from a sinking ship. In spite of that, however, take note of Paul's grace: "May it not be counted against them."

In the oppressive last days of his life on earth, Paul instead saw God's divine hand moving to give him mercy and to propagate the gospel among his persecutors. His vertical orientation in service to the Lord left him no energy for horizontal bitterness. In fact, we find no evidence of resentment, but only of gratitude.

He declares that the Lord stood by him to accomplish two objectives. First, that the "proclamation" might be "fully accomplished." The first term is *kērygma*, the content of "preaching." Earlier, Paul had called himself a *kēryx*, a herald, an envoy, a proclaimer (1:10). The second term is a compound word consisting of "full" and "to carry." Paul doesn't delude himself with the thought that proclamation of the gospel will end with him. His citizenship granted him the right to be tried in Roman courts, so he views his trial as yet another divine means by which the good news can reach the elite of Rome. His status also will spare him a painful and humiliating death in the Colosseum.

Regardless of the final outcome of his next trial, Paul knew he would emerge from his dungeon a free man. He fully expected the Lord to rescue him "from every evil deed," not by helping him avoid suffering or pain, but by triumphing over it. The Lord does this by trumping the evil deeds of humanity to give them divine purpose. He also triumphs over evil by giving eternal glory to the one who bears suffering with patience, endurance, faithfulness, and *grace*.

Paul didn't come by his eternal perspective overnight. It had been a part of his worldview for many years. During his first imprisonment in Rome, he wrote to the Philippians:

> Now I want you to know, brethren, that my circumstances have turned out for the greater progress of the gospel, so that my imprisonment in the cause of Christ has become well known throughout the whole praetorian guard and to everyone else, and that most of the brethren, trusting in the Lord because of my imprisonment, have far more courage to speak the word of God without fear. . .
>
> What then? Only that in every way, whether in pretense or in truth, Christ is proclaimed; and in this I rejoice.
>
> Yes, and I will rejoice, for I know that this will turn out for my deliverance through your prayers and the provision of the Spirit of Jesus Christ, according to my earnest expectation and hope, that I will not be put to shame in anything, but *that* with all boldness, Christ will even now, as always, be exalted in my body, whether by life or by death. For to me, to live is Christ and to die is gain. (Phil. 1:12–14, 18–21)

While the Lord would rescue Paul through his execution and allow him to enter glory for eternity afterward, Paul gave God glory in the midst of his anguish. He used the term *doxa* in 2 Timothy 4:18, from which we derive the word *doxology*, by which we sing our praise of God. *Doxa* derives from the verb *dokeō*, which means "to believe, think." To be glorified is to be revealed in such a way as to be thought good. To be glorified is to be vindicated in the eyes of all witnesses. Paul championed the righteousness of God while suffering in prison and plans to proclaim His goodness by dying well.

— 4:19 —

Per his usual style, Paul closed his letter with several greetings. He mentioned Prisca and Aquila. He first met the couple in Corinth soon after Emperor Claudius had expelled Jews from Rome (Acts 18:1–3). They became close friends immediately, sharing the craft of tent making and the conviction of the gospel. When Paul left Corinth for Ephesus, the couple followed (Acts 18:18) and eventually settled there.

We don't know the specific circumstances, but they had proven to be his advocates even when it placed them in jeopardy (Rom. 16:3).

He also addresses the household of Onesiphorus. By now, the man himself probably had died or was lost somewhere in the Roman persecution.

— 4:20 —

Paul added a few postscripts as matters of business. He mentioned two men of personal interest to Timothy. Erastus of Corinth, probably the city manager mentioned in Romans 16:23, had been a ministry partner with Timothy. Paul had sent the two ahead of him to prepare Macedonia for his visit after leaving Ephesus (Acts 19:22). Trophimus, originally from Ephesus (Acts 21:29), had been a part of Paul's ministry team (Acts 20:4) and apparently traveled with the apostle after his release from prison. He told Timothy he was forced to leave him in the care of friends in Miletus, a city just forty miles south of Ephesus. By now, however, the man had certainly recovered.

I find Paul's grace evident even in this short aside from a postscript. He could have bitterly sneered, "Why is it that they're safe from danger while I'm here? Why are they allowed to live in relative comfort while I'm condemned to die?" Instead, we find Paul extending greeting and encouragement. He delights in their safety and prosperity. What a man, this Paul! Grace heaped upon grace.

— 4:21 —

After another request for Timothy to visit, Paul sent greetings from four Christians in Rome, mentioned nowhere else in Scripture. While we have no information on them, I see in their mention another example of Paul's grace.

Earlier Paul complained that all had deserted him (4:9–11) and that he stood alone before the Roman court in his first trial. Where were Eubulus, Pudens, Linus, Claudia, and "all the brethren"? They lived in Rome, yet only Luke was attending to Paul. The apostle could have judged them for their silence, but instead he sent greetings to Ephesus on their behalf.

— 4:22 —

Paul directed his closing benediction first to Timothy individually. The pronoun "your" is singular. He again expressed his desire for the Lord to embolden and empower the younger man's timid spirit.

He then expressed his desire for grace to fall on all who would hear or read his final words. The "you" is plural. To the end, Paul wanted grace to be the legacy of his ministry. And without a doubt, his wish was granted. Many expositors and ministers of the gospel refer to this faithful servant of God as "the apostle of grace." With all of them, I say, "Amen!"

NOTES:

1. James Russel Lowell, "The Present Crisis," in *Poems by James Russell Lowell* (Boston: Ticknor, Reed, and Fields, 1849), 2:57.

2. John R.W. Stott, *2 Timothy: Standing Firm in Truth* (Downers Grove, IL: InterVarsity Press, 1998), 88.

3. Not unlike the traditional names given the wise men in the Christmas story, Gaspar, Melchior, and Balthasar. Scripture doesn't name the magi, and for all we know, there could have been thirty of them, or three hundred!

4. Lowell, "The Present Crisis," 2:57.

5. Sir Edmund Hillary, as quoted in *Shackleton's Boat Journey*, by F. A. Worsley (New York: Norton and Co., 1977), 12.

6. The Lord did, however, cease special revelation after John, the last of the apostles, died. He closed the canon with Revelation.

7. Charles Haddon Spurgeon, quoting Joseph Alleine in *Lectures to My Students: A Selection from Addresses Delivered to the Students of Pastor's College, Metropolitan Tabernacle* (New York: Sheldon & Company, 1875), 42.

8. Ibid., 42.

9. Kittel and Friedrich, eds., *Theological Dictionary of the New Testament: Abridged in One Volume*, 222.

10. Johannes P. Louw and Eugene Albert Nida, *Greek-English Lexicon of the New Testament: Based on Semantic Domains*, electronic ed. of the 2nd edition (New York: United Bible Societies, 1989), 1:307.

11. Henri Nouwen, *The Inner Voice of Love* (New York: Image Books, 1999), 34.

12. Thomas S. Jones Jr., "Sometimes," in *The Little Book of Modern Verse: A Selection from the Work of Contemporaneous American Poets*, ed. Jessie B. Rittenhouse (Boston: Houghton Mifflin, 1913), 89.

13. François Mauriac, *Vipers' Tangle*, trans. Gerard Hopkins (Chicago: Loyola Press, 2005), 213.

14. Strabo, *Geography*, 7.5.10 (Loeb Classical Library; *The Geography of Strabo* [Cambridge, MA: Harvard Univ. Press, 1924], 3:271).

15. John Pollock, *The Apostle: A Life of Paul* (Colorado Springs: Victor, 1985), 307.

16. John Ortberg, "Talking Religion and Politics without Getting Co-Opted," *LeadershipJournal.net* (May 5, 2008).

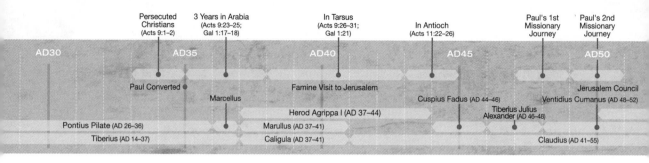

AD30   AD35   AD40   AD45   AD50

Paul Converted

Marcellus

Famine Visit to Jerusalem

Herod Agrippa I (AD 37–44)

Cuspius Fadus (AD 44–46)

Jerusalem Council

Ventidius Cumanus (AD 48–52)

Tiberius Julius Alexander (AD 46–48)

Pontius Pilate (AD 26–36)

Marullus (AD 37–41)

Tiberius (AD 14–37)

Caligula (AD 37–41)

Claudius (AD 41–55)

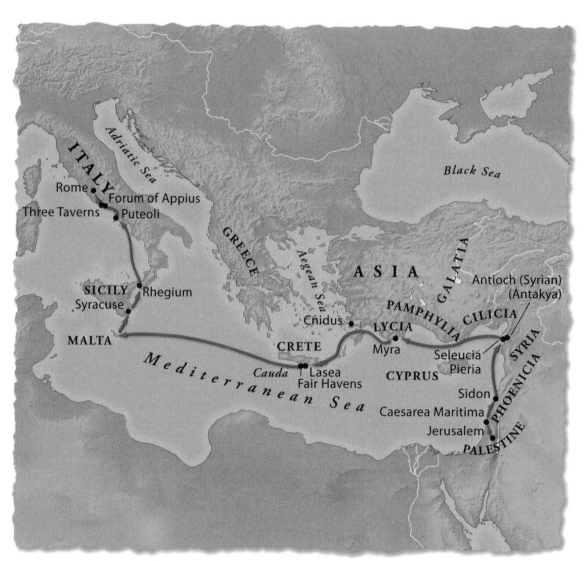

Paul first encountered the island of Crete while on his way to Rome to have his case heard before Caesar. While there, he discovered an isolated church, leaderless and lost.

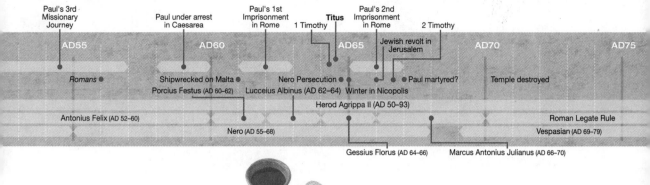

Paul's 3rd
Missionary
Journey

Paul under arrest
in Caesarea

Paul's 1st
Imprisonment
in Rome

Titus

Paul's 2nd
Imprisonment
in Rome

1 Timothy

2 Timothy

AD55

AD60

AD65

Jewish revolt in
Jerusalem

AD70

AD75

Romans ●

Shipwrecked on Malta ●

Nero Persecution ●

● Paul martyred?

Temple destroyed

Porcius Festus (AD 60–62)

Lucceius Albinus (AD 62–64)

Winter in Nicopolis

Herod Agrippa II (AD 50–93)

Antonius Felix (AD 52–60)

Roman Legate Rule

Nero (AD 55–68)

Vespasian (AD 69–79)

Gessius Florus (AD 64–66)

Marcus Antonius Julianus (AD 66–70)

TITUS

Introduction

By the time Paul the apostle wrote his younger colleague Titus, he had experienced the full range of sorrows and joys in Christian service—everything from exaltation as a mythical god, which Paul despised, to the kind of abuse reserved for criminals, in which he gloried. He had become a seasoned soldier in the great war against evil, and his body bore the scars of many victories. After twenty-five years in the field, the dogged apostle could point to each mark on his body and begin a tale of how the Lord had proved Himself faithful and then recall the insight he had gained as a result. And because Titus had been a disciple of Paul much of that time, he could finish most of his mentor's war stories.

No one understood better than Paul how costly ministry can be and how deeply one can be wounded when serving others. It's not a vocation in which someone can maintain a cool, professional detachment. Service to Christ demands the whole heart of the minister and promises to crush it every time. Yet in that crushing, God has pledged not merely survival but an even greater share of "abundant life" (John 10:10). He promised to make His people more like Himself—purer, wiser, stronger, gentler—starting with His appointed leaders.

Paul's heart had been crushed many times, enough to make any sane man quit the ministry and return to the safe, predictable trade of tent making. He had experienced the heartbreak of a heated rift with Barnabas, the man Paul considered his own father in the faith (Acts 15:36–41). He had submitted himself to the

253

Practicing What You Preach

Section	Salutation		Leadership of the Church	
Passages	1:1-4	1:5-9	1:10-16	2:1-10
Summary	Paul's authority as an apostle.	Authority of Titus. Qualifications of elders based on visible evidence.	Counterfiet authority of rebellious people and false teachers.	Visible qualities that authenticate teaching from God.
Key Terms	• Knowledge of the truth • Preaching	• Self-controlled • Exhortation • Faithful • Word • Teaching • Blameless	• Deeds • Good deeds	• Self-controlled • Word of God • Doctrine • Sound Doctrine • Sound Speech • Doctrine of God • Speak • Encourage • Train • Good deeds

Ministry of the Church			Conclusion
2:11-15	3:1-8	3:9-11	3:12-15
Grace that leads to godliness.	Grace demonstrated as submission to authority and good deeds.	Rebellious people to be identified and removed.	Closing instruction.
• Self-controlled	• Self-controlled		
• Grace of God	• These truths		
• Instructing • Speak • Reprove • Rebuke	• Remind • Insist		
	• Deeds of righteousness		
• Good deeds	• Good deeds		• Good deeds

KEY TERMS

διδασκαλία [*didaskalia*] (1319) "teaching, doctrine"

Paul uses this term no less than eleven times in his instruction to Timothy and four times in this letter to Titus. It appears alongside several synonymous terms, such as "faithful word" (1:9), "sound speech" (2:8), and "truths" (3:8). This teaching, which is so essential to Christian maturity and especially needed on the isle of Crete, is based on "the knowledge of the truth that is in keeping with godliness" (1:1 NET).

ἔργον [*ergon*] (2041) "deed, work" *fruits*

The Greek language uses this word to describe anything a person does to affect the world around him or her, "an act, deed, thing done," as opposed to something merely thought or believed. As one commentator notes, "everywhere in the Greek world we find a certain tension of word and act. Philosophy assumes their logical and ethical harmony."[1] The correlation between belief and behavior was a problem for everyone, Christians and pagans alike.

σώφρων [*sōphrōn*] (4998) "self-control, moderation"   *v schizo ati*

The root term, which is loosely based on a combination of *sōzō* (safe) and *phrēn* (mind), rarely appears in the Bible but was ranked high among secular Greeks as a civic virtue. A society was said to be "of sound constitution" when the competing classes all agreed on direction or leadership. The Gospels use the adjective to describe the young man who lived among the tombs after Jesus freed him from the maddening control of demons. Of eleven occurrences in Scripture, it appears six times in Titus. ✻

ὑγιαίνω [*hygiainō*] (5198) "sound, whole, wholesome"   *clear*

English derives the word "hygiene" from this Greek verb, which means "to be healthy." Greek literature uses the word in both the literal and figurative senses. Something was said to be "hygienic" when it was clear of contamination.

ὑπομονή [*hypomonē*] (5281) "courageous enduring, steadfast progressing"

In the secular Greek world, *hypomonē* is a heroic, unswerving dedication that might include "the bearing of pain by the wounded, the calm acceptance of strokes of destiny, heroism in face of bodily chastisement, or the firm refusal of bribes."[2] Along with faith, proven character, and hope, this quality carries the elect toward their eternal destiny in heaven.

φανερόω [*phaneroō*] (5319) "to manifest, make visible, reveal, shine"

Classical Greek made little use of this term, which means "to make visible what was invisible." It is causative, meaning that it causes something to take place, and it gives particular emphasis to the prior state of being unseen. Therefore, it finds wide use in the New Testament, which records a remarkable time of divine revelation. Grace had always been active in God's plan for the world, but it reached its ultimate expression in the appearing of Jesus Christ on earth.

authority of the apostles in Jerusalem, only to face the unenviable task of opposing the chief apostle, Peter, because of his doctrinal compromise (Gal. 2:11–21). He had invested in the lives of protégés like Titus, Timothy, Luke, Priscilla and Aquila, Silas, and John Mark, yet—for various reasons—eventually found himself alone as he awaited trial in Rome (2 Tim. 4:9–11). Throughout his ministry, self-serving dissenters and obstinate men of influence challenged Paul's authority and undermined his teaching in every church he had founded and/or nurtured. And for every faithful Timothy and Titus, Paul could point to a Demas and Hymenaeus, who had not only deserted him but also abandoned genuine belief in Christ (2 Tim. 1:15).

Misunderstanding, controversy, slander, and outright betrayal dogged every step of the apostle's journeys. Disciples thrilled him and failed him. Friends came and went. Thriving churches flirted with apostasy. Congregations continually looked to him for guidance and then thanked him by rejecting his authority or questioning his integrity. In success, he was accused of boasting; in prison, dismissed as a failure. No one knew better than Paul how rewarding, yet how frustrating ministry can be. He suffered repeated disappointment with people, but no earthly sorrow could diminish the reward uniquely enjoyed by vocational ministers: sweet intimacy with the Almighty.

The scars he had received over the years would be his gift to Titus, who needed these reminders as he struggled to stabilize churches on the unruly island of Crete.

THE HONORABLE MINISTER

Titus most likely became Paul's student during the apostle's first missionary journey in AD 48, although he is rarely mentioned in other books of the New Testament. His name means "honorable," and he apparently served as prime example of how a Gentile can become a genuine follower of the Messiah without first becoming a Jew. This experience would serve Titus well during his appointment to the island of Crete.

The earliest converts to Christianity came to Jesus Christ through the door of Judaism and the Old Testament. The Son of God was, after all, the Jewish Messiah.

> **TITUS IN THE NEW TESTAMENT**
>
> Galatians 2:1–5
> Acts 15:1–35 (per Galatians 2:1–5)
> 2 Corinthians 2:12–13
> 2 Corinthians 7:4–9, 13–14
> 2 Corinthians 8:1–6, 16–24
> 2 Corinthians 12:14–18
> 2 Timothy 4:9–15

And if Jesus was the "true vine" and His Father the vinedresser, then His roots ran deep into Israel's soil. Therefore, how could the fruit of this vine be any less Jewish? How could one partake of the new covenant without first partaking of the former, the old covenant? The men who came to be known as "Judaizers" argued, in effect, *Certainly, Gentiles should be circumcised and learn the law of Moses. They should enter a relationship with Christ by the door God had prepared: Judaism.*

The issue of Christian circumcision became the first doctrinal error to threaten the gospel as churches began to sprout from Gentile soil across the Roman Empire. To settle the issue once and for all—or so everyone thought—Barnabas and Paul agreed to join a contingent of Judaizers on a trip to Jerusalem to lay the matter before the men who had been personally trained by Jesus. Paul would argue that salvation comes by grace alone through faith alone in Christ alone, and in order to demonstrate the power of the gospel apart from the old covenant, he introduced the testimony of Titus, a Gentile and a Christian whose stature put many Jews to shame.

Several years later, around AD 56, Paul began receiving disturbing reports while establishing and strengthening the church in Ephesus. The church in Corinth had taken the gospel as a license to sin and openly condoned a man's affair with his stepmother! Further investigation revealed that sin had permeated the church and threatened to erode it from the inside out. After sending a stern letter (1 Corinthians) and making a painfully confrontational visit in person, Paul sent Titus with an even stronger letter in hand (now lost) and a directive: help the leaders reform the church in Corinth (2 Cor. 2:1–4; 7:6–13).

While the difficulties required Titus to remain much longer than planned, he faithfully completed his task and then brought good news to Paul: mission accomplished. The Corinthian believers had decisively confronted the sin in their midst and they again held Paul in tender regard. Moreover, they had given generously toward a famine relief fund that Paul was collecting (Rom. 15:26). Unfortunately, a new threat had emerged before Titus departed. The pendulum had swung from license to legalism, which made the environment ripe for Judaizers, false teachers "of the circumcision." After reporting this latest challenge to Paul, Titus likely returned to Corinth.

Titus had proven himself so faithful on difficult assignments that troubled churches apparently became his specialty. Near the end of Paul's life, Titus had been sent to the Roman province of Dalmatia (2 Tim. 4:10), also known as Illyricum, where Paul had once preached the gospel with some success. A church struggled to survive in a region that stubbornly resisted the rule of Roman law and remained a notorious haven for pirates. According to the Roman historian Polybius, "the Illyrians were not the enemies of this people or that, but were the common enemies of all."[3] Strabo, a geographer and contemporary of Titus, claimed the people of Illyricum failed to see the usefulness of their resources "mostly because of the wildness of the inhabitants and their piratical habits."[4] Such had been the last recorded assignment of the rough-and-ready leader, Titus.

Paul describes his protégé as enthusiastic for service (2 Cor. 8:17), motivated by love (2 Cor. 7:13), and sensitive to wounded sensibilities (2 Cor. 12:18). He calls Titus a "true son in a common faith" (Titus 1:3), "a brother" (2 Cor. 2:13), his "partner and fellow-worker" (2 Cor. 8:23). All of these qualities, along with the confidence of his mentor, made Titus the ideal man to bring order to the rugged, undisciplined assemblies of Christians on the island of Crete.

PERPETUAL LIARS, EVIL BEASTS, AND LAZY GLUTTONS

Paul first encountered the people of Crete while being transported to Rome for his audience with Caesar's tribunal (Acts 27:1–13). A strong northerly wind forced his ship to travel along the island's southern coast and to take refuge in Fair Havens for a period of time. Though technically under arrest, Paul's guard gave him unprecedented freedom to visit churches and conduct ministry (cf. Acts 27:3), which undoubtedly occupied the apostle's time on Crete.

The island first heard about Christ from Jewish pilgrims returning from Jerusalem with amazing stories of Pentecost (Acts 2:11). Their belief, while genuine, did not receive the same kind of apostolic nurturing that churches on the mainland enjoyed. Long after the Council of Jerusalem had decided important issues regarding the role of Old Testament law in the life of the Christian (Acts 15:19–20), Cretan believers struggled without the benefit of competent teaching. This isolation also made them particularly susceptible to the influence of local traditions, itinerant philosophers, and Roman temptations. Unfortunately, Paul's work of stabilizing and strengthening the island churches barely started before the captain of his ship insisted they leave Fair Havens for the more comfortable harbor of Phoenix. Against Paul's warning of probable shipwreck, the men tried to reach the western tip of the island, only to be blown out to sea by a violent wind. Turning back proved to be impossible.

The apostle probably returned to Crete sometime after his release from house arrest in Rome, resumed his organizing and stabilizing work, and then left Titus in charge with much to accomplish. This makes the most sense of Paul's words, "For this reason, I left you in Crete" (1:5) — not "sent" but "left," implying that Paul had been present on the island with Titus. It is unlikely this occurred during Paul's journey to Rome. Luke accompanied Paul and described the events in vivid detail, yet mentioned nothing about leaving one of their number behind. Most likely, after leaving Rome, Paul traveled to Crete to carry out the plan he formulated earlier, left Titus in charge, set sail for Ephesus, where he appointed Timothy, and then visited the believers in Macedonia for several months.

As Paul's ship disappeared over the horizon, Titus assumed the immense responsibility of proclaiming Christian truth and finding stable, disciplined men to give that truth a strong foundation and a permanent home on Crete. Paul's delegated authority gave him a good start, but he would need the encouragement of a seasoned laborer.

The work of Titus among the Cretans was not going to be easy. The island population had earned a reputation for low culture, brutish behavior, and an enthusiasm for everything but work. Judaizers inspired those with a work ethic to embrace legalism while pagan philosophers tugged eager appetites toward license. The cosmopolitan mixture of traders and tramps constantly challenged the faithfulness of genuine believers, many of whom failed to practice what they believed. Put simply and directly, the church on Crete was an unholy, disorganized mess.

"SET IN ORDER WHAT REMAINS"

Paul wrote his letter to Titus for two reasons. First, the younger pastor needed something to set him apart from any other man who would presume to exercise authority over Cretan churches. This letter, quite likely read at Christian gatherings, delegated apostolic authority to Titus and charged him with the task of organizing and strengthening the communities of believers on that island. His receiving this commission in the hearing of the people he was to lead certainly would have settled any disputes before they arose.

Paul also wrote his letter to describe the nature of a genuine church and to define its mission and message. While the letter is brief—consisting of only forty-six verses in three chapters—it forms a concise, yet remarkably complete guide for pastors today, especially those establishing new churches. Notably, Paul does not diagram a specific organization of the church from which we can draw a chart. Nor does he suggest that each should be linked into any kind of hierarchy. It would seem that any means of organization and governing is acceptable, so long as the church accomplishes its primary purpose: *to be the means by which the elect come to belief in Christ, to nurture their understanding of the truth so that it results in godly behavior, and to help them overcome challenges until they enter God's presence for eternity* (1:1–2).

Like the strands of a rope, Paul's miniature church manual braids together three primary themes.

The first theme is *God as Savior*. Whereas other Scriptures often distinguish the roles of the Father, the Son, or the Holy Spirit in the plan of salvation, the Pastoral Epistles (1 and 2 Timothy and Titus) take great care to emphasize tri-unity of God. In Titus, we find references to "God promised" (1:2), "God our Savior" (1:3; 2:10; 3:4), "God the Father and Christ Jesus the Savior" (1:4), "the grace of God appeared" (2:11), "our great God and Savior, Jesus Christ" (2:13), "the washing and renewing of the Holy Spirit" (3:5), and "Jesus Christ our Savior" (3:6). Each person of the Trinity partakes in every aspect of redemption, which is accomplished by grace through the faith of an individual, apart from any good he or she might accomplish.

The second theme is *sound doctrine*, which Paul articulates in 2:11–14 and 3:4–7. It is the core truth around which everything in the church must wind. He repeatedly stresses the importance of right thinking throughout the letter, variously calling it "knowledge of the truth" (1:1), "the faithful word" (1:9), "sound doctrine" (1:9; 2:1; 2:7), "sound speech" (2:8), "the doctrine of God" (2:10), and "trustworthy statement" (3:8). He also charges everyone with the responsibility to communicate this truth to each other and to the outside world through "preaching," "exhortation," "rebuking," "teaching," "training," "reminding," and—most important of all, "good deeds."

Paul's third theme is *godly behavior*, which he often calls "good deeds" (1:6; 2:7, 14; 3:1, 8, 14) and describes with specific detail in both positive and negative terms throughout the letter. Church leaders must be "above reproach" or "blameless," while rebellious people make themselves known by their evil deeds. Church members should show evidence of genuine faith by being "sensible" (1:8; 2:2, 5, 6, 12) in addition to possessing other admirable qualities. Godly behavior not only validates and reinforces genuine belief; it benefits everyone and authenticates church doctrine before a watching world.

These three interdependent themes—God's redeeming grace, knowledge of truth, and righteous behavior—define Christian maturity and should characterize every believer in every church. Furthermore, this is the goal of Christian ministry and should be the primary reason for churches to exist. The challenges may change with the times and the structure of the organization may adjust to engage culture, but the mission and message of the church will always remain the same. Moreover, as I noted in reference to 1 Timothy 3:1–7, "As go the leaders, so goes the church."[5] While Paul clearly intended to describe the quintessential characteristics of a healthy congregation, his first and primary audience was none other than Titus, whom he expected to faithfully model what he was charged to cultivate in Cretan churches: grace, truth, and godly behavior.

NOTES:

1. Gerhard Kittel and Gerhard Friedrich, eds., *Theological Dictionary of the New Testament: Abridged in One Volume*, trans. Geoffrey W. Bromiley (Grand Rapids: Eerdmans, 1985), 254.
2. Ibid., 582.
3. Polybius, *Histories* 12.6 (*The Histories of Polybius*, Loeb Classical Library [Cambridge, MA: Harvard Univ. Press, 1922–27], 1:269).
4. Strabo, *Geography* 7.5.10 (*The Geography of Strabo*, Loeb Classical Library [Cambridge, MA: Harvard Univ. Press, 1924], 3:271).
5. Cf. Peter Scazzero, *The Emotionally Healthy Church: A Strategy for Discipleship that Actually Changes Lives* (Grand Rapids: Zondervan, 2003), 36.

A LEADER WORTH FOLLOWING
(TITUS 1:1–4)

---

[1]Paul, a bond-servant of God and an apostle of Jesus Christ, for the faith of those chosen of God and the knowledge of the truth which is according to godliness, [2]in the hope of eternal life, which God, who cannot lie, promised long ages ago, [3]but at the proper time manifested, *even* His word, in the proclamation with which I was entrusted according to the commandment of God our Savior, [4]To Titus, my true child in a common faith: Grace and peace from God the Father and Christ Jesus our Savior.

Every once in awhile, I receive a letter that keeps me up at night. The following letter reminded me of the overwhelming responsibility pastors bear when they stand before a congregation.

Dear Chuck:

I was deeply moved by your talk on Martin Luther. In fact, I tried to sing with you at the end, but I cried instead. I feel so small. Our heroes look so big. So deep. So much better than me. I'm so comfortable. And I'm so mediocre.

I want to know something. When you were 27, were you like you are now? Had you already read all the right books? Did you know all the hymns? Were you as deep? Was Christ so real in your life that your words pierced people's hearts? I ask that because I want to know if there is any hope for me. I am not broad, nor very deep. I wasn't raised in the church. I don't know the hymns. I still have to read all the words. I wasn't raised to be a big reader, either. I want to read the right books, but I get very frustrated when I go to Christian bookstores. Who needs books like *Pray Your Way to Big Bucks*, or, *If You're Sick, You're a Lousy Christian*, or, *Positive Thinking: Never Say "Sin,"* or a book full of goofy rhymes to replace talking with God?

I've also heard you say that one becomes like those with whom he spends his time. I'm surrounded by mediocre people. The more I mature in the Lord, the less people I find worth imitating. I'm not so mature, though, that God is the only model. You're one of my models. I want to know, are you like my other "models"? Do you rip your wife apart in front of other people? Do you talk big but turn wimpy when it's time for action? Are you worth imitating?

How can I be excellent? I don't care about impressing anyone. I just don't want to be mediocre.

This man is the real deal. He desperately wants to know if his spiritual leaders are, in fact, worth following. The issue at stake for this man is authority. To whom does the pastor answer and how can I know his message is genuine? He has naturally looked for evidence of spiritual authority in the deeds of his spiritual mentors. Very wise.

As Paul left Titus on the island of Crete to organize and stabilize the churches, the apostle understood the need to establish a clear line of authority from God, through an apostle, and finally to the man assigned to lead. He would do this in a letter, beginning with a carefully crafted salutation.

—1:1–2—

Paul began his letter to Titus as he did nearly every New Testament letter. He identified himself, validated his apostolic authority, greeted his recipient, and then pronounced a blessing. But if we look a little closer, we will discover that the first four verses form one long, compound sentence, each phrase of which anticipates an important theme in the message to follow. Paul's opening line foreshadows the themes of authority, grace, doctrine, and preaching.

Paul identified himself using the term *doulos theou*, "bond-servant of God." Gentile cultures in the Roman Empire considered bond-slaves less deserving of respect than animals. Romans prized their freedom and took great delight in subjecting "lesser peoples" to servitude. But Paul sees no honor in the world greater than bearing the title "bond-servant of God," and he finds no greater freedom than slavery to the Almighty. He couples this idea with the term "apostle," a designated envoy. In secular Greek culture and in the Septuagint, an "apostle" referred to someone sent to accomplish a task on behalf of the sender. Paul claimed authority, not on the basis of his impressive résumé, but on the command of the One who sent him — that is, Jesus Christ Himself.

Let's face it; no man or woman deserves to stand before God's people on his or her own merit. No amount of education, success, longevity, popularity, charisma, or personal power qualifies an individual to be God's mouthpiece to others. Pastors who presume to stand in the pulpit to deliver any message not derived from Scripture stand on unsure ground. Paul claims the authority of a sent servant, an envoy who wields the power of the Sender.

Titus, of course, already knew this by personal experience. He never questioned Paul's calling or authority. Paul asserted his apostolic authority for the benefit of those who would hear the letter read in public, including any false teachers who surely lurked within congregations of genuine believers. The apostle would soon delegate this authority to Titus, along with a clarification of his mission on Crete (1:5).

Having declared his role as God's envoy, Paul then described his threefold purpose.

First, *Paul is the means by which God's "chosen" come to belief in Jesus Christ (1:1).* The NASB and NIV faithfully render the phrase "*for* the faith of those chosen of God" (emphasis mine), because the Greek preposition *kata* has a broad range of uses and can be variously translated "down," "against," "according to," "along with," or a number of other ways. Consequently, translators struggle to make definite sense of it. However, when *kata* is combined with certain types of words, the possible range of meaning narrows significantly. Given the immediate context, the most reasonable translation is "*for the sake of* the faith of God's chosen ones." I understand this to indicate Paul's desire to be the means by which the elect (predestined believers) come to trust in Christ, thus beginning their spiritual journey.[1]

Second, *Paul is to nurture believers' knowledge of the truth so that their outward behavior will reflect their inward belief (1:1).* According to some expert teachers, learning is said to take place when an individual's behavior changes as a result of gaining new information. Once truth has been understood and assimilated, it's only natural to begin making different choices. For instance, a person who genuinely understands the law of gravity should behave accordingly when standing on the ledge of a skyscraper.

Moreover, practice makes perfect. The Greek word for knowledge is *epignōsis*, which refers to experiential knowledge or practical wisdom. Someone without *epignōsis* can genuinely believe a truth, yet lack the practical skills to apply it effectively. I understand perfectly well how a piano works and I sincerely believe that each key will strike a corresponding note. But that's the extent of my expertise! I lack the practical skill to make beautiful music come from the piano.

Paul saw his role as more than bringing people to belief in Jesus Christ. He longed to have them understand the complexities of grace and to help them skillfully apply it to every aspect of their lives. This is "knowledge of the truth which is according to godliness," a key component of spiritual maturity.

Third, *Paul is to continually help believers overcome challenges until they enter their eternal destiny after this life has ended (1:2).* Note the beginning-middle-end progression of his mission.[2] Paul wanted to bring people to belief in Christ, nurture their growth in grace, and encourage them to anticipate the day they inevitably meet Him face-to-face. And he anchored the absolute certainty of this eternal destiny to the solid rock of God's promise, which is secured by His immutable character and was made long before time began. Paul's reminder that God cannot lie foreshadows a future discussion about false teachers (1:10–16), who pin their hope of eternal life to one's ability to obey the law.

The promise of certain victory over the present struggle and the assurance of eternal life is a central feature of Paul's theology, which he fully develops in his letter to the Romans (Rom. 8:18–31). For him, clinging to the assurance of victory becomes the means of living by the Spirit. He can boldly live like a victor over sin and evil because he already knows the eventual outcome.

— **1:3** —

Paul then concluded the "from" portion of his salutation by describing the means by which he exercised his apostolic authority and accomplished his ordained purpose: expository preaching. That is, preaching that explains the meaning of Scripture and applies it to daily life. Three terms linked together define this primary activity of a pastor:

Manifest + God's Word + Proclamation = Expository Preaching

The Greek word translated "manifested" means "to make visible, make clear." In the Gospels, the term describes the process of explaining the meaning of a parable (Mark 4:22). This is not to suggest that one must have special training or mystical knowledge to understand the Scriptures. In fact, the New Testament was originally written in Koine Greek—the language most commonly spoken across the Roman Empire—so that anyone capable of reading could have direct access to the mind of God. Specialized education can help bridge the gap between today's culture and the ancient world, but there's nothing mystical or magical about it.

Instead of revealing hidden meanings, the preaching pastor translates the principles of God's Word into daily life, first through his own spiritual growth and then by explanation of them from the pulpit. Paul's deliberate connection between genuine belief and godly behavior, which defines Christian maturity, begins with the spiritual leader. While his authority comes from God's Word, faithful obedience gives him credibility.

— **1:4** —

Paul's extended salutation concluded with the name of his recipient, Titus, whom he called "my true child in a common faith." Again, on the surface, Paul's letter was a personal message from a mentor to his protégé, but he intended for the conversation to be overheard by those whom Titus had been commissioned to lead. Consequently, he carefully calculated the manner in which he addressed Titus.

The Greek phrase literally means, "my true-begotten child with respect to a common belief." A true-begotten child is one born into a family through natural means as opposed to becoming a family member through adoption. A true-begotten child, therefore, bears his or her father's traits. Furthermore, a "common belief" links Paul and Titus within the same bloodline, as it were. Paul's allusion to family and legacy suggests that Titus was much like himself and was thus qualified to stand in his place. This ancestral link also made Titus heir to all of Paul's authority and rank, much like the son of a noble.

Paul obviously expected that Titus would need the authority and rank delegated to him in order to accomplish the difficult task that lay before him on Crete. After all, a major component of his mission included identifying authentic spiritual leaders and then establishing them in positions of authority. If the churches were to flourish, they had to know their leaders were worth following and that the truth they taught was indeed divine truth.

Application

Who Are You and What Is Your Purpose?

I find Paul's short salutation challenging. I sometimes lose perspective when the details and stresses of life begin to crowd my calendar and nibble away at my sanity. I forget who I am and what I'm supposed to be doing. And I admit the challenges of ministry have taken me to the brink of resignation more than once. During those difficult times, I have to be reminded of my identity and my purpose.

Paul understood the importance of this for a minister, who often serves alone, with no one nearby to offer encouragement and support. The apostle knew how suffering and opposition can wither a man's courage. He knew firsthand that when all else fades away, one's calling has to be enough, for that may be all a bond-servant of God has to keep him or her going.

Paul's letter commissioning Titus for service on Crete opens with a clear statement of his identity and purpose, which gives us an opportunity to ask and answer four questions.

First, Paul identifies himself as "a bond-servant of God and an apostle of Jesus Christ" (1:1). What is your identity? God has equipped you with a unique set of abilities, and He has seasoned them with experiences. If you haven't already, perhaps it's time to take an inventory. If you have trouble identifying them yourself, ask the people who know you best. You might compose a short email to give these people an opportunity to prepare a thoughtful response.

Here's how you might start your letter:

Dear _____:

After _____ years of life, I thought it was high time I stop and ask myself what unique abilities and experiences the Lord has invested in me that I might use for His glory. To be honest, I don't spend a lot of hours sitting around thinking about me, so I need your help. I'm not fishing for compliments or affirmation, so please don't feel the need to praise me. What I need from you is more difficult. Take a few moments to consider the following question and answer as honestly as you can.

What unique abilities or experiences might (your name here) use to serve the Lord and bring Him glory?

Thank you for helping me,

—————————————————

Second, Paul declares his primary purpose for living, which includes three specific points: to be the means of believing sinners coming to faith, to strengthen their knowledge of the truth, and to establish them in their certain expectation of eternal life (1:1–2). What's your primary purpose? To what are you committed? Think about this carefully. What do you most want to see fulfilled as a result of your being here on earth? Avoid any answer that has a "should" feeling connected to it. Try to be specific, and by all means, be honest. If you don't like your answer, you have an opportunity to change it later.

Third, Paul identifies his calling: to proclaim God's Word (1:3). What's your calling? What are you doing to fulfill your purpose? What are you doing that keeps you from fulfilling your purpose and when can you change your focus? If you are actively engaged in fulfilling your purpose, do you still delight in it?

Fourth, Paul affirms his relationship with Titus (1:4). His commitment to the younger man is resolute and intimate. To whom are you committed? Are you cultivating a deep and intimate relationship with these treasured people? Do you have a true son or daughter in the faith? Do you have someone with whom you spend an extra amount of time investing your life? Or will your abilities and experiences disappear when you depart this world for the next?

V. Raymond Edman offered a sobering challenge while still president of Wheaton College:

> Is there delight deeper or more delectable than that of duty diligently done? To know one's responsibility, to face its circumstances, both favorable and unfavorable, to follow the line of duty without deviation caused by difficulties or distraction, and to fulfill the task as assigned—all this brings great joy. Between finding out our task and fulfilling the same, there lies the discipline of duty, often arduous and difficult, even to the point of impossibility. Battle against: "the wrath of men / the waste of years, the waves of despair / and the wickedness of the adversary." … The

discipline of duty is not easy nor light, its performance is painful and perilous, but its culmination is delight.[3]

We're all somewhere along the way in our journey. You may have come to an arduous or perilous part; the river is wide and the current is strong and the water is deep. Maybe there's some personal pain you're enduring. Perhaps you had to make some unpopular decisions that have caused others to doubt, misunderstand, and even malign you. If you have established your identity, purpose, and calling, and if you have cultivated meaningful relationships, you are well-equipped to emerge victorious.

If you haven't taken the time to prepare this crucial foundation, may I suggest you start now? The crisis you face may be the Lord's opportunity to confirm your current path or to set you on a new one. As Hudson Taylor once observed, "It doesn't matter how great the pressure is, what really matters is where the pressure lies — whether it comes between you and God, or whether it presses you nearer His heart."

NOTES:

1. To learn more about predestination, see my exposition of Romans 9:1–33 in my *Insights on Romans* (Grand Rapids: Zondervan, 2010), 186–202.
2. I contend that the three prepositional phrases (*kata pistin … [kata] epignōsin … ep' elpidi*) all modify "bond-servant and apostle," yet follow a logical order, one building on the other.
3. V. Raymond Edman, *The Disciplines of Life* (Wheaton, IL: Scripture Press, 1948), 247–53.

SECTION 1: THE LEADERSHIP OF THE CHURCH (TITUS 1:5 – 2:10)

For Paul, church leadership and the gospel message were one and the same. No division. Just as divine truth took on human flesh and the gospel lived among us in the person of Jesus Christ, so the message of the church resides in its leaders. Yes, the Word of God was faithfully received and recorded by prophets and apostles and then preserved to be our sole, 100 percent reliable source of divine truth. Nevertheless, the Lord established the church so that that body of Christ might *live* the Word before the world, to be light in the darkness — just like Jesus. Therefore, Paul can barely imagine any division between the leaders and divine truth. To communicate this essential truth, Paul uses almost circular reasoning, writing in effect, "Church leaders can be identified by their conformity to divine truth (1:5 – 2:10); conformity to divine truth produces church leaders (2:11 – 3:11)."

For the sake of clarity, I have divided the body of the apostle's letter into two sections:

- the leadership of the church (1:5 – 2:10)
- the mission of the church (2:11 – 3:11)

Not surprisingly, Paul begins with a description of church leadership, giving all of his attention to matters of character, virtually ignoring organizational structure. After all, no model of church rule, no system of checks and balances can contain the evil intentions of humanity. By contrast, if men possess godly character, they will lead the church well regardless of the model they adopt.

Looking for a Few Good Men (Titus 1:5 – 9)

⁵For this reason I left you in Crete, that you would set in order what remains and appoint elders in every city as I directed you, ⁶*namely,* if any man is above reproach, the husband of one wife, having children who believe, not accused of dissipation or rebellion. ⁷For the overseer must be above reproach as God's steward, not self-willed, not quick-tempered, not addicted to wine, not pugnacious, not fond of sordid gain, ⁸but hospitable, loving what is good, sensible, just, devout, self-controlled, ⁹holding fast the faithful word which is in accordance with the teaching, so that he will be able both to exhort in sound doctrine and to refute those who contradict.

Shortly after I arrived in San Diego for Marine Corps basic training, our Drill Instructor placed a red armband on one recruit in our squad, designating him the leader. Then, several weeks later, while on the rifle range, the Drill Instructor unceremoniously tore it from his arm and shouted my name. As I stood at ramrod attention, he pinned it on my arm, saying, "You're the leader now. You've got what it takes. Do *exactly* as I say or I'll give it to someone else." That was my first indication that I might have the qualities of a leader. He obviously saw something I didn't.

If there's any segment of our society that understands the need for qualified leaders, it's the military. From the moment a new batch of undisciplined, wide-eyed recruits steps off the bus at the training center, the hard-nosed instructors begin identifying leaders, and they make their choices with uncompromising efficiency. They don't worry about feelings, seniority, politics, or popularity because, when bullets fly and missiles explode, others' lives depend on capable leadership. Unqualified leaders get warriors killed; qualified leaders accomplish their mission. Simple as that!

Considering the eternal stakes involved in Christian ministry, I'm amazed to see some churches take the issue of leadership so lightly. A healthy church must have qualified leaders in order to accomplish its primary purpose, which Paul outlined in three points. I paraphrase them like this:

The purpose of the church is (1) to become the means by which the elect come to belief in Christ, (2) to nurture their understanding of the truth so that it results in godly behavior, and (3) to help them overcome every challenge until they claim their eternal destiny (cf. 1:1–2).

The Christians of Crete needed capable spiritual leadership above all else. While Christianity flourished on the mainland under the apostles' teaching and Paul's expert guidance, the isolated Christians on that island struggled to develop stable, productive fellowships. Unfortunately, the heavily populated island — known to ancient writers as "the island of a hundred cities" — required more time than Paul had to give. He initiated the work and then handed the assignment over to Titus, charging him with two separate, yet interrelated tasks: "set in order what remains," and "appoint elders in every city."

— 1:5 —

The phrase rendered "set in order what remains" begins with a double compound word that means literally, "thoroughly set straight further." It suggests that Titus should continue the pattern Paul had established. The apostle found the churches broken or twisted by apostasy and was determined to realign them. "Set straight" is derived from the Greek word *orthoō*, which medical writers used to describe the process of setting and splinting broken bones. We get our words "orthodontics" and "orthopedics" from this term.

Paul's precise meaning of "set straight" becomes clearer as we encounter the primary topics addressed in the letter: *unqualified leaders, false teaching*, and *unbecoming behavior.*

Furthermore, he instructed Titus to straighten out "what remains," which could refer to the remaining disorder in each church or to the unruly churches Paul had not visited. Given the size and complexity of the mission, he most likely meant both. The phrase "as I directed you" lets us know that Paul didn't leave Titus to muddle his way through on his own. The word translated "directed" is yet another compound word, consisting of a verb meaning "to order, set in place, establish" with a prefix meaning "thoroughly." After years of dedicated service to Paul, Titus had been thoroughly trained. He knew exactly what his mentor expected. Titus was to train another generation of leaders in the same manner Paul prepared him (2 Tim. 2:2).

Paul used two Greek terms, *presbyteros* and *episkopos*, interchangeably when referring to "elders." Many expositors agree that both refer to the same position, but a slight difference in emphasis is worth noting. Whereas *presbyteros* highlights the person, *episkopos* stresses his function. The former means simply "older man," while the latter means "overseer." Nevertheless, each term takes the other for granted. In other words, older men were venerated for their wisdom and were expected to guide the community. Conversely, those recognized as superintendents of the community were assumed to be older men. Age alone, however, did not qualify a man to lead the congregation. This office of the church fit well with the image of a shepherd, which Peter employed in his letter, referring to Christ as both Shepherd and Guardian (1 Peter 2:25). Therefore, this role implied certain qualities, which Paul decides to make explicit in his open letter to believers on Crete.

— 1:6 —

Too often, churches seek the wrong qualities when choosing their leaders. The world wants an impressive résumé that demonstrates a track record of proven success in business. While corporations want shrewd businessmen, full of charisma and wielding powerful influence, the church needs men who conform to a different standard. A church needs *servant-leaders*, who bear the same qualities our Lord demonstrated when He came "to serve, and to give his life" (Mark 10:45). Godly leadership models grace, extends mercy, demonstrates compassion, exudes joy, cultivates an atmosphere of peace, and encourages others to participate by using their gifts and abilities. He pursues the opinions of others, applies keen discernment, and then heeds their wise counsel. Perhaps most of all, the godly leader will seek the highest good of others, refusing to seek his own way or maneuver himself into a position of power.

Men like these are incredibly rare, yet invaluable to the church. Paul described the kind of man suitable for this high and holy office using no less than seventeen terms, each one defining an indispensable quality of spiritual leadership. Paul's choice of terms deserves close examination.

"Above reproach" means (lit.) "blameless" or "without accusation." This is not a requirement for sinless perfection or a pristine past; it's a general assessment of a man's maturity and reputation. John Calvin paraphrased this idea as "not marred by disgrace." This general quality of character frames all the rest, which can be divided into three broad categories: home life, public life, and church life.

Regarding "the husband of one wife," the Greek reads (lit.) "a one-woman man." At the most basic level, this describes a man who is married to one woman and continues to live in fidelity and harmony with this same woman. (See the excursus " 'A Husband of One Wife' and the Issue of Divorce" for an extended explanation of this qualification.)

"Having children who believe" describes a man who has effectively accomplished in his home what we hope he will facilitate in the church. The Greek term *teknon*, generally translated "child," doesn't imply any particular age range, but usually has in mind any offspring still living under the roof and authority of his parents. As it is used in this phrase, the term is plural, suggesting that we consider his children in general, not any particular one. Let's face it; many of the very best families have a child who goes astray, at least for a time. The patriarch of an otherwise believing household is not disqualified for having a prodigal child. As Kent Hughes wisely suggests, "Good leadership is not determined in the absence of difficulty, but in the prudent discipline of handling problems when difficulties come."[1]

"Not accused of dissipation" calls for a man whose life is not known to be chaotic, disorderly, wasteful, or otherwise filled with drama. Some lives seem to move from crisis to crisis with occasional calm in between, which tends to leave a man little emotional and intellectual capacity to guide others. While no one is immune to the travail of living in a fallen world, the elder should have learned by experience how to manage his affairs.

"[Not accused of] rebellion" is probably better rendered, "insubordinate, undisciplined," or "unwilling to take direction." Everyone is subject to someone. The elder, as a leader, must be free of authority issues. Not attempting to dominate others, he must allow himself to be an example of submission for those he leads.

—1:7—

"Not self-willed" is a negative way to describe a submissive spirit. A self-willed person despises authority—that is, the proper authority of others in his life. He wants his own way, to do as he pleases. He is stubborn and reluctant to submit to the decisions of others. A self-willed man is arrogant, self-interested, driven by strong independence, and has a general spirit of entitlement. He is as much strong-willed as self-willed and self-serving.

"Not quick-tempered" means that a man chooses what will move him to appropriate anger, such as blasphemy, abuse, molestation, or brutality. He doesn't, however, possess an underlying spirit of anger that manifests itself in his "flying off the handle." A man who is "not quick-tempered" avoids outbursts of anger or angry words, especially when confronted or contradicted.

"Not addicted to wine" should not be restricted to alcoholism. This idea includes those who frequently fail to recognize their limits regarding alcohol. Moreover, an elder carefully avoids surrendering control of his body to the effects of any substance.

"Not pugnacious" describes a man who is neither contentious nor quarrelsome. Intense emotions do not fuel his interactions with others, even in the midst of disagreement. Elders are not to have a combative spirit about them.

"Not fond of sordid gain" refers to a disposition that is not "sordidly greedy of gain" or "insatiable of wealth and ready to procure it by disgraceful means," as translated from the classical Greek writers Herodotus and Aristophanes. Savvy and successful businessmen can make wonderful elders when they come by their wealth honorably and have a generous spirit. But beware of misers! They tend to want even less for the church than their own homes.

—1:8—

"Hospitable" (lit., "loving of strangers") denotes loving someone who is foreign or different. A hospitable man welcomes those who are different and easily overcomes the natural tension that exists between them because of their differences.

"Loving what is good" describes a deep-seated love for and submission to the Lord—His Word and His will—as it is carried out in His way and in His time. Such a person is quick to examine his actions and his motives in a constant effort to do what is right.

"Sensible" suggests being reasonable, having sound judgment. This term, translated several times as "self-controlled," describes a quality Paul wants to see in "older men" (2:2), "younger women" as taught by the older women (2:5), "younger men" (2:6), and the church at-large (2:12). In other words, sensibility should be the defining quality of the congregation, starting with the leaders. Gene Getz begins his analysis of this trait with the observation, "a prudent man is a humble man."[2] Humility and prudence keep a man focused on what is best for the congregation he serves and what honors Christ, who is the Head of the body.

"Just" means "conforming to custom, fulfilling obligations, and observing legal norms."[3] The classical Greeks called it "virtue"; however, the New Testament writ-

EXCURSUS

"A Husband of One Wife" and the Issue of Divorce

According to Titus 1:6, a pastor or elder must be "the husband of one wife." The Greek reads (lit.) "one-woman man." I have in my library no less than fourteen volumes on Paul's letter to Titus. That's a good thing. What's not good is this: they convey no less than eleven opinions on the precise interpretation of "one-woman man" and its practical application. Small wonder there is so much confusion!

At the most basic level, this refers to a man who is married to one woman and living in harmony with her. It implies sexual purity and a reputation for devotion to his mate.

It's helpful to note that all the qualifications listed for Titus and Timothy (see also 1 Tim. 3:1–7) point to matters of character. Because this qualification appears second in both lists, just after "above reproach," we gain a sense of its importance in Paul's mind. Marriage carries with it such exacting responsibilities and reveals so much about a person's inner, true character; it serves as an excellent barometer of a man's character. How a man conducts himself in his marriage says a lot about how he will bear the responsibilities of spiritual leadership among his congregation. John Phillips writes with helpful wisdom:

> Marriages bring disciplines as well as delights. It is an arena where love and loyalty can be practiced, where lessons in personal relationships can be learned, where theories are tested in the crucible of experience, where limits have to be observed. A good husband is faithful to his wife, a good provider, a spiritual leader, loving his wife as Christ loved the church.[4]

Another commentator adds:

> Many a wise pastor has advised potential leaders whose marriages need attention not to seek church office, despite the fact they are technically married. God requires the church to determine whether a potential elder's marriage is whole, healthy, and solid. As a corollary, men with damaged or deficient marriages should not pursue church leadership positions thinking that others will not care or notice. They will care and they *will* notice.[5]

In an ideal world, all overseers are to be blameless and flawless, faithful husbands and fathers. Unfortunately, sin mars the ideal. Depravity is ever among us, taking its toll on husbands as well as wives. As a result, inconsistencies and failures plague us all. Therefore, it would be hypocritical to be too rigid concerning the issue of divorce. It seems nonsensical to me that a man who lived with several women before conversion and then marries a woman after his conversion can be received as a pastor or elder, yet a man

ers take it further, recognizing Jesus as the ultimate example of justice. To be "just" is to be innocent like Christ, even as a sufferer of injustice. A just man seeks fairness for others but rarely for himself.

"Devout" speaks of someone who authentically and completely devotes himself to the Lord. He doesn't seek perfection, but he does walk a consistent walk with Christ in which he remains open to change, ready to sacrifice his own way, and sensitive to the Spirit's conviction and encouragement.

"Self-controlled" in this instance comes from the Greek word meaning (lit.)

whose marriage ended in divorce (often against his desire) would be denied an opportunity to lead, regardless of the reason for his divorce. Obviously, the issue is complicated.

Taking everything into consideration, let me offer these contrasting lists to clarify my position. When Paul writes that the overseer is to be "a one-woman man" in Titus 1:6 and 1 Timothy 3:2:

I *do not* believe	I *do* believe
• Paul means to exclude those who have never married.	• Paul means to underscore specifically the importance of steadfast morality and consistent fidelity to one's spouse and marital vows.
• Paul means to exclude those who are widowed, whether remarried or not.	• Paul means to keep the standard high, as close to ideal as possible.
• Paul means to suggest that one must be married to serve as an overseer.	

Therefore, I have determined it is both safe and wise when selecting overseers to *give preference* to those who have faithfully remained married to the same spouse, and therefore embody the literal interpretation of "one-woman man" (the ideal). I recognize, however, that there are legitimate exceptions to this ideal standard, such as the case of a faithful husband whose unfaithful spouse refused to continue their marriage. Against his desire and despite his best efforts to reconcile, he becomes divorced from that first spouse and, perhaps, marries another, to whom he remains utterly faithful. I would call such a man "a one-woman man."

Obviously, determining who is at fault in a divorce can become a dubious and tedious exercise. All marriages involve a combination of two lives — both sinful — with each contributing to the cause for divorce. We can call neither partner completely innocent or "above reproach." Only God can see the secrets of their hearts, sort the details, and sift motives to determine who caused the marriage to break down. So, I return to my general policy. When selecting overseers, it is both safe and wise to *give preference* to those who have faithfully remained married to the same spouse, and therefore embody the literal interpretation of "one-woman man."

From My Journal

Be Generous Before You Change Your Mind

When I was a student at Dallas Seminary, Cynthia and I lived in a little campus apartment. Apartment #9. A tiny egg-crate nook surrounded on all sides by other student apartments. I'm not saying the walls were thin, but when I told her a joke, our neighbors laughed. And, of course, money was just as thin.

Fortunately, we had friends back home in Houston, Texas, who cared for us. One of the men in our church home, Mr. Kane, really believed in turning the grace he had received into tangible expressions of his faith by paying our seminary tuition all four years. He did the same for sixteen other students from the Houston area.

But that's not all. He realized on one occasion that we were getting a little threadbare. He didn't like the way our clothes looked when we came home for a visit, so he drove to Dallas, took us all to a wonderful men's shop after a great lunch, and then bought all of us brand new sport coats. You know, Mr. Kane never talked himself out of doing that. He could have said, "Well, I don't want the boys to feel like they can't make it on their own." The fact was, we couldn't. And we were far from humiliated by his generosity. Hardly! I can still remember … we tore into that men's shop like kids in a candy store. Our hearts raced with gratitude.

Giving thought to being generous? Go there! Sure, it might be a sacrifice, but you will not regret it in the long run. I urge you to act quickly before you talk yourself out of it!

"having dominion or possession over oneself." Because our goal in Christian ministry is to cultivate maturity, we will naturally encounter a great deal of immaturity along the way, which requires immense self-control at times. The spiritual leader must not allow his emotions to dictate his responses.

— 1:9 —

"Holding fast the faithful word" refers to men who base their lives on sound doctrine as it has been taught by a trustworthy authority. During New Testament times, it was the teaching of the apostles; today it is Scripture. Protestants do not hold the traditional teaching of the church to be inerrant or infallible, recognizing the Bible alone as God's Word. Deviation from two thousand years of consensus on a matter, however, should be viewed with a healthy skepticism. If an elder cannot in good conscience teach what he has been taught, he should remove himself from service until he can be certain of what he believes.

The first and last qualities — "above reproach" and "holding fast the faithful word" — are synonymous, so far as Paul is concerned, and they form bookends around the qualities in between. Faith and deeds are inseparable. For the apostle, the only worthwhile teaching is "truth that is in keeping with godly behavior" (1:1). The characteristics of the spiritual leader qualify him for two crucial activities in the church that Paul introduces with the words, "so that" (1:9).

The elder must be able to "exhort in sound doctrine." The verb "exhort" comes from *parakaleō*, from which we get "Paraclete," a term referring to the Holy Spirit. A modern equivalent to this New Testament term is "to coach." A good coach knows his trainee intimately. He affirms strengths and encourages success. He recognizes weaknesses and formulates a plan to help the trainee overcome them. He knows when to push and when to comfort. Most important of all, he is a good example himself. His own belief can be seen in his good deeds, and he wants the same for those he leads.

The elder must be able to "refute those who contradict." Throughout the New Testament, the Greek word for "refute" has the specific sense "to show people their sins and summon them to repentance"[6] (Matt. 18:15; Luke 3:19; John 16:8; 2 Tim. 3:16; Heb. 12:5; 2 Peter 2:16; Jude 15; Rev. 3:19). Paul had no interest in winning philosophical debates or splitting theological hairs. For him, the danger of "those who speak against" lies not only in their false teaching, but their ability to spread their corrupt behavior.

As John Calvin stated, "A pastor needs two voices, one for gathering the sheep and the other for driving away wolves and thieves. The Scripture supplies him with the means for doing both so that the person who has been correctly instructed in the Scriptures will be able to guide those who want to learn and refute those who are enemies of the truth."[7] If the congregation is to grow in maturity and serve its purpose, its leaders must be worthy examples for the individual members to emulate. They must know the truth, live the truth, teach the truth, and defend the truth against a clever, ruthless enemy.

Application

Government of the Church

Sometimes I wish the Lord had instructed Paul to outline a specific pattern for establishing and organizing a church. A nice, thick manual with floor plans, organizational charts, rules of order, and a set liturgy would make things so much easier for a pastor. Then we could simply defer to God and His "Divine Constitution and Bylaws" rather than try to balance the infinite opinions and perspectives that inevitably compete in any church. As a result, perhaps, we could focus fully and only on worship, instruction, fellowship, and evangelism.

Of course, the Lord did precisely that for Israel. Moses faithfully recorded God's exact design specifications for His house of worship, including floor plans, organization, rules of order, and liturgy ... yet the people still failed to worship Him and obey His Word. That's because unfaithful men held positions of authority in the temple and then led the people astray.

Clearly, the secret to establishing and maintaining a faithful church cannot be found in any specific form of church governance. I think a church should be superintended by qualified elders and led by gifted and godly pastors, but that's my preference. Other forms include:

Hierarchical — typical of mainline denominations, where a central body directs the churches via a command structure not unlike civil governments.

Presbyterian — rule from within by a council of elders who may, or may not, report to another governing body.

Congregational — majority rule by members of the congregation, who meet regularly to decide on every matter of the church.

As we examine the structure and quality of the leadership Paul demands for the churches on Crete, we must be careful not to see more than what he wrote. Whole denominations have justified their particular method or structure based on this passage and similar instructions in 1 Timothy 3. The fact is, neither Christ nor Paul prescribes a specific model of leadership for the church. Within certain guidelines, we are free to implement any method that addresses the needs of the congregation, which can be different in each culture and may change with time. During the apostolic period, churches remained autonomous, but that doesn't mean that cooperation or hierarchy is necessarily wrong. The church in Ephesus had both deacons and elders (1 Tim. 3), but Paul described only elders for Titus. And few churches, if any, hired fulltime staff to guide them, but today that is clearly a good idea.

Instead, we find in Scripture—clues within Christ's teaching, descriptions in Acts, and specific instructions in Paul's letters—certain principles that must govern whatever model we choose to follow.

Note that Paul called for *"elders in every city"* (1:5), not *"an elder in every city."* *Leadership of the church is always plural, never concentrated on one man.* As a church grows and impacts a larger segment of the surrounding community, the body of leadership must grow with it. As the responsibility grows heavier, more shoulders are needed to bear it or, by and by, the man who tries to do it all will crack under the strain. He will eventually experience an emotional or physical breakdown, or he will begin to believe his own press and become a dictator, or he will ignore his blind spots and permit moral decay to erode his character. Church leadership was never meant to be a one-man show.

Furthermore, Paul instructed Titus to hand-select elders for each congregation. *Leaders of the church should be appointed, not elected (1:5).* The practice of selecting elders came from centuries of tradition, especially as observed by the Hebrews in the synagogue. Nowhere in Scripture are leaders elected to their posts by congregations; they are always selected by other mature leaders who are themselves qualified to recognize the necessary traits for leadership.

Most important of all, Paul demanded leaders to be men of character, regardless of their age, wealth, experience, power, or position. *Leaders of the church must demonstrate proven Christian maturity (1:6–9).* Many churches seek successful businessmen to serve on their board of elders, which is not necessarily wrong by itself, but there must be more to prove such men are qualified. If business savvy is the chief qualification, no one should be surprised when the church begins to resemble a corporation with a cross stuck on top.

An "elder" holds a *spiritual* office and must demonstrate that his is a life lived under the control of the Holy Spirit. His qualities must include continual submission to the Spirit's control; being an example of loving leadership in his own home; a humble and contrite heart that remains keenly sensitive to the presence of sin or any act of pride, stubbornness, or selfishness; a quick willingness to confess his own wrongdoing; a strong commitment to conform his behavior to the instruction of

Scripture; and a humble vulnerability before the Lord as a result of in-depth self-analysis as described by David in Psalm 139:23 – 24.

A person who lacks these spiritual qualities should never hold a position of authority in the church, no matter how successful he is in business or how much influence he wields in the community. The role of an "elder" requires traits that conform to a different standard, that of *godly leadership*, servant-leadership as our Lord modeled when He came "to serve and to give his life" (Mark 10:45). Godly leadership models grace, extends mercy, demonstrates compassion, shows forth joy, cultivates an atmosphere of peace, and encourages others to participate by using their gifts and abilities. He pursues the voice and opinions of others and then heeds their wise counsel. Perhaps most of all, the godly leader will seek the highest good in the lives of others, refusing to seek his own way or to maneuver himself into any position of power.

Dealing with the Difficult and Dangerous (Titus 1:10 – 16)

---

¹⁰For there are many rebellious men, empty talkers and deceivers, especially those of the circumcision, ¹¹who must be silenced because they are upsetting whole families, teaching things they should not *teach* for the sake of sordid gain. ¹²One of themselves, a prophet of their own, said, "Cretans are always liars, evil beasts, lazy gluttons." ¹³This testimony is true. For this reason reprove them severely so that they may be sound in the faith, ¹⁴not paying attention to Jewish myths and commandments of men who turn away from the truth. ¹⁵To the pure, all things are pure; but to those who are defiled and unbelieving, nothing is pure, but both their mind and their conscience are defiled. ¹⁶They profess to know God, but by *their* deeds they deny *Him*, being detestable and disobedient and worthless for any good deed.

Standing for the truth is not a popular pastime. Defending the truth is for neither the fainthearted nor those who want to be liked above all else. No, only people of courage should take on such a difficult, thankless task. Talent and intelligence are fine qualities in a leader, but the essential quality must be courage. That's because the realm of truth is not a playground; it's a battleground.

Spiritual leaders must soon come to terms with a difficult reality: every community of believers will encounter opposition — sometimes from the outside, more often from within. This difficulty can be demoralizing to the congregation unless its leaders recognize that evil always has been, and always will be, a threat to the

From My Journal

When Will I Learn?

After almost five decades in pastoral ministry, you'd think I would have outgrown my youthful idealism. Certainly by now I should have left behind the silly notion that if I worked hard enough, preached strong enough, prayed long enough, and invested enough of myself in the lives of people, then my church would eventually struggle free of depravity's clutches and create something close to paradise on earth. Certainly by now I should have realized that the success I long for doesn't lie just behind whatever crisis I happen to be facing at the time. When will I accept that the health, and healing, and happiness I long to see God's people enjoy will not be theirs until we enter His new creation together? I suspect in another fifty years!

Long ago, I finally acknowledged that no church will ever be perfect. As long as Satan is alive and free to roam about, ignorance, selfishness, sin, and depravity will undermine any attempt of ours to bring even the slightest bit of heaven to earth. Furthermore, "the deeds of the flesh" are ever with us. My theology is sound enough to recognize that the fall of humankind will not be erased until Christ returns and casts the "ruler of this world" (Eph. 2:2; 1 John 5:19) into the abyss at the end of time. Yet, admittedly, each encounter with evil still takes away my breath.

Why should I be so stunned? Why should discouragement nearly always take me to the brink of quitting after all these years of seeing God's people through repeated carnal escapades? When will I lose this often-painful idealism? Never, I hope. If I ever do, *then* it will be time to call it quits.

A call to ministry is a call to a perpetual tension between the life that is and the victory that is available. It is a bitter-sweet, painfully joyful life of service to sin-sick people, for whose triumph the Father continually yearns. It is the decision of men and women who know of a better place, yet choose to live among those struggling to arrive. Therefore, may I never grow calloused to the hideous, disfiguring capacity of sin. May I never lose hope in the power of the Holy Spirit to overcome it here and now, even before Christ's ultimate victory. As long as I continue to mourn over each casualty of evil as if it were the first, as long as I continue to expect delight beyond each crisis and find repentance and restoration beyond each fall, I am where I belong. I am called to this life of unrealistic expectations, this foolishly optimistic vocation called "pastor."

If God is pulling His people toward their destiny, I suppose that makes the spiritual leader His rope. Though the tension gets almost unbearable and, sometimes, I fear my rope is coming unraveled, no one should pity me. While one end drags the church through each difficulty, the other feels the firm, reassuring grip of an ever-faithful God. And, for reasons not even I can explain, there's no place I'd rather be.

Maybe that's why it's not a job; it's a calling.

church. It was true in Paul's day, and it continues to be our challenge today. Moreover, we have an aggressive adversary who attacks those committed to the truth of God. As the apostle reminded the believers in Ephesus, "our struggle is not against flesh and blood, but against the rulers, against the powers, against the world forces of this darkness, against the spiritual forces of wickedness in the heavenly places" (Eph. 6:12).

— **1:10** —

In addition to many other schemes, Satan is the master of deception. To afflict the church, he artfully drapes his lies in the regal robes of truth. He seduces charming, intelligent men and women, promising the world in exchange for their help in deceiving others. And how convincing they are! Keeping their true nature carefully concealed—even from themselves—they deftly move among the elect, up through the ranks of authority, and into positions of power. Lacking truth, they win friends and influence people by means of a contrived charisma that's difficult to resist, even for those who despise falsehood. Nevertheless, a trained eye can spot them. Paul's letter to Titus explains how. He instructs his younger colleague to watch for three clues.

First, *their teaching is nonscriptural.* Paul used three terms—"rebellious men," "empty talkers," and "deceivers"—to characterize the relationship between false teachers and the source of all Christian truth.

The word translated "rebellious men" is better rendered "unaccountable men." These individuals on Crete not only rejected their former authority, they refused to submit themselves to any oversight or give accountability to anyone (1 Tim. 3:1 – 11; Jude 8). This particular brand of false teacher establishes *himself* as the religious authority, typically through personal power fueled by the adoration of undiscerning followers. Moreover, such men look to themselves as the source of spiritual "truth," passing off their speculations as revelation, clearly in direct contradiction with Scripture (1 Tim. 1:4).

Beware of spiritual leaders who publicly call themselves "bishop," "prophet," "apostle," or "God's anointed," yet have no one empowered to strip them of their title should they fail to honor it with godly behavior. Even Paul subjected himself to the elders in Jerusalem (Gal. 2:2), which Titus witnessed. Paul, in turn, held the elders accountable when they deviated from the teaching of Christ (Gal. 2:11 – 17). No one outgrows the need for accountability.

"Empty talkers" comes from a compound word, the first part of which means "empty, vain, futile" and "denotes the world of appearance as distinct from that of being."[8] One can scarcely find a more derogatory term in the Old Testament. It harkens back to the words of Solomon, who called worldly philosophies "vanity," "futility," and a "striving after wind" (Eccl. 2:15–17). Old Testament prophets used the concept of "empty" to describe the worship of false gods (Jonah 2:8–9) or the worship of the one, true God in the absence of good deeds (Isa. 1:13–17). In Ephesus, the teachers of vanities diverted attention from the Scriptures and the apostles' teaching to focus on "strange doctrines, myths and endless genealogies, which give rise to mere speculation" (1 Tim. 3:3–4). To make matters worse, "their talk will spread like gangrene" (2 Tim. 2:17), poisoning those who hang on their every word.

One of my mentors used to say, "You can always spot those who don't teach the truth by the way they say absolutely nothing beautifully." "Vain talkers" speak with smooth, captivating, even persuasive assuredness, but they have little or nothing on which to base their teaching. They cleverly present their personal opinions as spiritual truth.

The term used for Paul's third category, "deceivers," is curious. Whereas the commonly used term *apatai* ("deceivers") would have sufficed, Paul combined it with *phrēn* ("heart, mind") to form a new compound: "mind-deceivers." I suspect Paul coined the term to describe the false teachers who deliberately engaged in mind-bending control, not unlike the cloistered cults that proliferated in the United States during the 1970s. A classic signal that one has become the target of mind control is the fear that holding dissenting opinions will bring negative consequences.

The particular threat to the churches on Crete came from those whom Paul called "the circumcision," a name typically assigned to Jews, whether Christian or not (Rom. 3:30; 4:9; Gal. 2:7–9; Eph. 2:11; Col. 3:11). Most likely, however, Paul intended a more specialized meaning, referring to Christian Jews who insisted that the path to Christ necessarily passed through the gate of Judaism (Acts 15:1; Gal. 5:11; 6:12–13). This particular heresy, though struck down by the elders in Jerusalem, stubbornly refused to die on the mainland and apparently continued to thrive on Crete. In the absence of strong Christian communities, where believers studied together and benefited from mutual accountability and encouragement, households on the same island became easy targets for false teachers.

This same tactic is commonly used today. Pseudo-Christian religions, such as Mormonism and the Watchtower Society, seek out poorly informed believers who have little or no involvement in a local church. They organize at-home Bible studies where Scripture is gradually displaced by other teaching material, and to avoid alarming their prey, these false teachers cleverly couch their lessons in terms that many would recognize from Sunday school. Their doctrine, however, is anything but orthodox Christian truth.

— 1:11 —

Paul goes on to describe a second mark of false teachers: *Their motives are evil.*

"Sordid gain" bears the same connotation we give the phrase "drug money." The mere possession of wealth obtained through false teaching brings shame on the person holding it. Make no mistake, most false teachers do what they do for the money. They may try to hide their real motives, but they can't for long. Eventually, as they become more isolated from reality and deluded by the same spell they cast over their followers, they adopt a brash, shameless spirit of entitlement when demanding financial support. Many justify their exorbitant, opulent, and luxurious lifestyles by claiming, "I teach prosperity and I live prosperity." As their financial base grows broader and deeper, false teachers naturally become more flamboyant, even eccentric, mostly because they lack the moral compass and checkpoints that Scripture provides. This leads to the third and, for Paul, the primary characteristic of false teachers in the next verse.

THE LIES OF LIARS ABOUT A LIAR!

When Paul quotes "a prophet of their own," he undoubtedly does so with tongue in cheek. The line, "Cretans are always liars, evil beasts, lazy gluttons" (1:12) reportedly comes from the pen of Epimenides, an almost mythical, sixth-century BC poet-prophet. According to Cretan legend, Epimenides sought shelter in a cave while searching for a lost sheep and fell asleep for fifty-seven years. When he emerged, not only had the ancient Rip Van Winkle gained astounding knowledge of medicine and natural history, he could travel great distances outside his body, commune with the gods, and prophesy with great accuracy.

When his fellow Cretans insisted that Zeus was born on Crete and claimed to possess his grave, Epimenides (supposedly) wrote in his poem "Cretica,"

They fashioned a tomb for thee, O holy and high one —
The Cretans, always liars, evil beasts, idle bellies!
But thou art not dead; thou livest and abidest for ever,
For in thee we live and move and have our being.

For centuries, mathematicians and logicians have mused over the paradox created when Epimenides, a Cretan, declared all Cretans to be liars. Was he telling the truth or was he lying? Moreover, the supposed source is a man whose history has been exaggerated to the point of disbelief by Cretans! Like the legendary King Arthur, we can't even be certain Epimenides ever existed.

The many layers of deception — the lies of liars about a liar who lied — perfectly illustrate the difficulty Titus faced. Paul's deadpan remark, "This testimony is true," probably gave the younger pastor a good laugh. Sometimes you simply have to laugh at absurdity just to keep from crying.

—1:12—

This third mark of false teachers is this: *Their behavior is disgraceful.*

In a twist of irony (and perhaps with tongue in cheek), Paul draws on the testimony of a pagan prophet who stated that "Cretans are always liars, evil beasts, and lazy gluttons" (1:12). Please note that this prophet himself was a Cretan! Then, in a double twist of irony, Paul declared the false prophet's oracle to be true.

We must remember that Paul intended his letter to be read in the presence of the Cretan believers, using a cultural inside joke, as it were, to make a sober point about the conduct of false teachers on Crete. It also served as a reminder to the Cretan believers that they had inherited a new identity as Christians (cf. 3:3–7). In highlighting this difference between false teachers and genuine believers, Paul returned to a primary theme of his letter: one's conduct exposes one's belief.

In his letter to Timothy, who served under equally difficult circumstances in Ephesus, Paul summed up the character and methods of false teachers in 1 Timothy 6:3–5.[9] Paul now advised flatly in Titus 1:11: They "must be silenced." This sounds harsh, especially in our era of wholesale religious tolerance. At first, I thought a clearer understanding of the original word might make Paul's command easier to take, but it literally means "to muzzle," usually by stuffing something in a person's mouth! His mandate to Titus, made in the presence of the congregations, could not have been more plain: *Shut them up.* He says, in effect, "Confront false teachers without delay or they will tear the churches apart."

—1:13—

For the sake of the flocks, Paul instructed Titus to "reprove them severely." The word "reprove" is the same term rendered "refute" in 1:9 to describe the role and responsibility of an elder. While this reproof must be prompt and forthright, which undoubtedly *feels* harsh to the false teacher, it is not intended to insult or humiliate him. Paul did not call for Titus to crush the enemies of truth with a withering verbal assault, but to redeem them. Note his purpose: "so that they may be sound in the faith." The Christian message always has restoration at its motivation. The discipling work of a healthy church is to restore the fallen and to strengthen the weak.

—1:14—

Paul's comments suggest that two kinds of false teaching challenged the churches on Crete: Jewish mythology (v. 14) and rigorous abstinence (asceticism, v. 15).

By the time of Jesus, Jewish literature overflowed with fables about angels and demons, how they procreated and interacted with people, and how their activities affected history. False teachings based on a blend of Greek philosophy with Jewish mythology thrived on these writings and reproduced like weeds during the

JEWISH MYTHOLOGY: "THE DEMON-MEN OF CANAAN"

Most of us are fairly familiar with Greek mythology, perhaps from school or even movies. We know such names as Zeus, Apollo, Aphrodite, and Hercules. But Jews had their ancient myths too. Loosely based on history and Scripture, each generation passed along a bizarre folklore that often became more influential than divine truth. As an aside and strictly for your enjoyment, here is a sample of Jewish mythology, in my own words.

Long ago, when the veil between the realms of earth and spirit was still thin, heaven dispatched powerful creatures known as Grigori to watch over people. Many called them *Irin*, or "watchers." The greatest among them, Semjaza, appointed nineteen vice-regents — Samiazaz, Arakiba, Rameel, Kokabiel, Tamiel, Ramiel, Danel, Ezeqeel, Baraqijal, Asael, Armaros, Batarel, Ananel, Zaqiel, Samsapeel, Satarel, Turel, Jomjael, and Sariel (Enoch 6:7–8 (*1 Enoch* 6:7–8) — to command his army of two hundred guardian angels. But during the days of Jared, the angels looked on the daughters of Canaan and found them irresistible. So, they swore an oath to band together, forsake their mission, and to take wives from among the race of men.

The rebellious angels began having sexual relations with the women, to whom they revealed the power of charms and spells, astrology and earth signs, and how to make potions from certain kinds of berries, leaves, and roots. Azazel, one of the Grigori, taught men how to fashion weapons out of metal and how to make pottery. By and by, the women bore a race of giants called the *Nephilim*, who became immensely powerful, having the form and shape of enormous men with the superhuman qualities of angels. Moreover, they ate everything in sight and took what they wanted from others, simply because they could. And when the food ran out, they devoured men and "began to sin against birds, and beasts, and reptiles, and fish, and to devour one another's flesh, and drink the blood" (*1 Enoch* 7:5–6).

Finally, the archangels — Michael, Uriel, Raphael, and Gabriel — could remain idle no more. They petitioned the Lord, saying "Thou seest what Azazel hath done, who hath taught all unrighteousness on earth and revealed the eternal secrets which were (preserved) in heaven, which men were striving to learn … And the women have borne giants, and the whole earth has thereby been filled with blood and unrighteousness" (*1 Enoch* 9:6–7, 9–10).

So the Lord sent Uriel to instruct Noah, the son of Lamech. He instructed Raphael to dig a pit in the desert of Dudael, to bind Azazel hand and foot, to cast the rebel angel into it, and to cover him with jagged rocks and darkness until the day of judgment. The Lord ordered Gabriel to strike down the Nephilim by turning them against one another in battle, and He sent Michael to seize the other Grigori and "bind them fast for seventy generations in the valleys of the earth," after which they would be judged and cast into the eternal fire.

All of these things were recorded by Enoch. During the time he was hidden in the heavens, the Lord commissioned him to prophecy against the tormented Grigori, which he faithfully did.

first three centuries after Christ. Unfortunately, these sensational stories diverted attention away from the truth as revealed by Jesus Christ and taught by the people who were trained by Him. Crete's preoccupation with legend didn't stop with Epimenides. The congregations needed to get back to basics.

— 1:15 —

Some teachers promoted a life of strict abstinence from anything pleasurable—a lifestyle called "ascetism." Greek philosophy taught that the universe consisted of two vastly different realms: the realm of pure idea or thought, which was the realm of God; and the material realm, which is where we live. For the Greeks, the realm of the idea—the spiritual realm—could be experienced by humans only as they distanced themselves from the distractions of the physical world. To this, Jesus said in effect, "Nonsense!" (Mark 7:15; Luke 11:39–41). In the beginning, God created all things, both material and immaterial, and called all of it good. Paul affirmed that everything should be received and enjoyed with gratitude as it comes by His grace (1 Cor. 8:8; Col. 2:20–23; 1 Tim. 4:1–5).

Unlike the Greek philosopher's view of the universe, the Jewish (and therefore, Christian) concept sees material things as neither good nor evil by themselves. Material things can be *used* for good or evil, however, depending upon the intent of the person. Therefore, Paul said, "To the pure, all things are pure." When believing people conduct themselves according to God's will, even the most detestable things can become a means of good in their hands. But a person who is still a slave to evil (Rom. 3:9–18) can do no good on his own. Even the Bible—God's holy, written Word—can be twisted to serve the depraved and deceptive agendas of false teachers.

— 1:16 —

To conclude his discourse on the most difficult challenge of the church in Crete, Paul returned to a central theme of the letter. Genuine belief in the truth of God produces a lifestyle of godly behavior. And the absence of good deeds is good cause for suspicion. False teachers merely profess to understand spiritual truths but are, in fact, incapable of godly behavior, because they do not possess the truth they claim. Paul's deliberate use of circular reasoning illustrates the futility of false teaching.

John Stott, based on his study of Paul's letters to Timothy and Titus, astutely boiled the issue of false teachers and false teaching down to three questions: "First, is its *origin* divine or human, revelation or tradition? Secondly, is its *essence* inward or outward, spiritual or ritual? Thirdly, is its *result* a transformed life or merely a formal creed?"[10] Teaching that does not lead to mature Christian conduct is false teaching. Beware!

Application

The Unglamorous Work of Spiritual Leadership

As we read Paul words to Titus, clearly a large group of "rebellious men" were wreaking havoc among the churches on Crete by their "empty talk" and outright deception. Unfortunately, this kind of rebellion didn't stop after the first century. Every generation has its "boars in God's vineyard," who sow discord among His people and use the church for personal gain. Moreover, every church has its troublemakers. Unfortunately, they never correct themselves. "Rebellious men" and women almost always thrive and multiply unless confronted.

Seminaries usually equip spiritual leaders with the skills necessary to teach the Bible and to care for the spiritual needs of people. They even help them gain organizational skills. But far too little is said about the less attractive side of leadership: confronting deceivers and opposing rebels. Consequently, many young and inexperienced men put on the mantle of leadership in churches rife with power struggles and quickly become overwhelmed. Praying and "hoping for the best" just won't suffice.

So, what counsel does a leader need in times like these? When preparing to confront a deceiver or a rebel, consider these five suggestions:

1. *Begin by committing everything ahead of you to prayer.* Make certain that your elders are standing with you and support your plan to confront the wrongdoer.
2. *Instead of walking into the conflict alone, choose two or three mature and wise people you trust to go with you.* Make sure they have been well prepared for what they will encounter.
3. *Wherever you find biblical foundation for your words and actions, stand on it.* Let God's Word provide you with the direction you plan to take. Some that come to mind, along with Titus 1:10 – 16, are Proverbs 27:6; Romans 16:17 – 18; Galatians 6:1 – 2; Ephesians 6:10 – 12; and 1 Peter 5:2 – 4. This will give you courage to press on.
4. *Speak the truth in love.* Address the specific areas that need to be dealt with. Stay calm. Do not get sidetracked by your own anger or by allowing the out-

break of an argument or threatening words to surface. Remain focused on what is best for the church. This is not an issue between the two of you, but between the offender and the church of God. (That is extremely important for you to keep in mind.) Conflict resolution is hard work—stay patient, stay strong.

5. *Pursue a resolution.* Avoid "making deals" with the offender, or quoting secondary sources (gossip), or allowing the subject to change. Remain firm, fair, and resolute. If the offender shows no sign of repentance, or if after initial promises to comply with your requests, you see no evidence of change, arrange a time for him or her to meet with your governing board. Explain that the purpose of that meeting is to "officially remove the offender from the church." Do not attempt to carry that out in your initial meeting. Have your entire body of elders present for a decision of that magnitude. Assure the offender that his or her genuine repentance is essential.

The Character of the Church (Titus 2:1–10)

---

[1]But as for you, speak the things which are fitting for sound doctrine. [2]Older men are to be temperate, dignified, sensible, sound in faith, in love, in perseverance.

[3]Older women likewise are to be reverent in their behavior, not malicious gossips nor enslaved to much wine, teaching what is good, [4]so that they may encourage the young women to love their husbands, to love their children, [5]*to be* sensible, pure, workers at home, kind, being subject to their own husbands, so that the word of God will not be dishonored.

[6]Likewise urge the young men to be sensible; [7]in all things show yourself to be an example of good deeds, *with* purity in doctrine, dignified, [8]sound *in* speech which is beyond reproach, so that the opponent will be put to shame, having nothing bad to say about us.

[9]*Urge* bondslaves to be subject to their own masters in everything, to be well-pleasing, not argumentative, [10]not pilfering, but showing all good faith so that they will adorn the doctrine of God our Savior in every respect.

We are all being watched. Not only by angels, who move among us unseen, and by Satan's evil host, who lurk in the shadows waiting to multiply evil. We are being watched by children and teenagers, who want to know how the world really works and whether we actually believe everything we say about good and bad, right and wrong. We are being watched by older believers, who hope the coming generation will faithfully carry on what they have built. We are being watched by younger believers, who need reassurance that the path they follow is a good one. And, of course, we are being watched by those who have not chosen to believe. Our behavior either confirms their suspicion that Christianity is a hoax, or it invites them to draw near for a closer look. There may be a few who even read God's Word and then observe our behavior to see if they match.

We are all being watched. Paul says so. Note the progression of his letter thus far. He has insisted on belief that can be observed (1:1). He sent Titus, who had observed Paul's belief in action during their years together and most recently on Crete ("as I directed you" [1:5]). He directed Titus to appoint spiritual leaders whose behavior had been observed and then was judged to be "above reproach" or "blameless" (1:6). He commanded the Cretan leaders to silence false teachers, whose behavior reflected faulty doctrine (1:16). Then, Titus and the appointed elders were to cultivate godly behavior within the congregations, primarily by setting a worthy example.

Now Paul expressed his desire for each congregation to pursue godly behavior "so that they may encourage" (2:4), "so that the word of God will not be dishonored" (2:5), "to be an example of good deeds" (2:7), "so that the opponent will be put to shame" (2:8), and "so that they will adorn the doctrine of God our Savior" (2:10).

The character of the church is being watched, both from the outside and from within.

— 2:1 —

Paul separated this section of his letter from the previous with a strong contrast: "But as for *you*." He has described the false teachers as "detestable and disobedient and worthless for any good deed" (1:16). By contrast, he now commanded Titus to teach "pure doctrine," or more literally, "healthful" instruction. The Greek word rendered "pure" is a term from which we get our word "hygiene." It refers to that which is healthy and wholesome. Paul wrote, in effect, "Let your teaching be uncontaminated, wholesome, and health-giving. May the good hygiene of your teaching disinfect what has been contaminated and then stimulate healthy growth."

The apostle then outlined how Titus should organize the rejuvenation of each congregation's character, first by dividing them into distinct categories. In addition to the visible leaders of the church like Titus and himself (2:1), Paul named five groups, all of whom were being watched:

- older men (2:2)
- older women (2:3)
- younger women (2:4–5)
- younger men (2:6)
- bondslaves (2:9)

—2:2 (Older Men)—

While we typically think of older men as wiser, more mature, and stronger in faith, those who are up in years do not always justify our expectations. The passage of time and the experience of life invite each person to gain wisdom, but many refuse the offer and, instead, become critical, cynical, cranky, negative, even lazy. But age can frequently benefit others. Moses begins his most productive forty years at age eighty. As the Israelites prepared to conquer the Promised Land, Caleb chose the most rugged, best-defended territory at the ripe old age of eight-five, saying, "Give me this hill country!" (Josh. 14:12). Most of the Old Testament patriarchs and heroes accomplished the most good during their latter years. Paul expected older men to cultivate in themselves six qualities that he hopes will define the church at large.

First, they are to be "temperate," which means to avoid extravagance and over-indulgence in any area. A temperate person keeps things in balance and within limits. In the literal sense, the term refers to freedom from intoxication, but Paul intends the broader sense of being free from the excess of good things, such as work, medications, food, or sex, and being free from addiction to destructive things, like illegal drugs or pornography.

"Dignified" comes from a term that usually refers to people or things that are majestic. On the negative side, it means to avoid becoming frivolous, trivial, tedious, or superficial. On the positive, a dignified person is worthy of respect.

"Sensible" is the defining quality that Paul seeks for all Cretans, perhaps because they have consistently and universally lacked this mark of maturity. Sensible means "moderate, prudent, modest, restrained, disciplined."[11] It's the only term the apostle applies to both genders and every age.

"Sound in faith" is (lit.) "hygienic in faith." This concept, along with the next two, is merely an extension of the "hygienic teaching" commanded in 2:1. This wholesome belief in Christ is a lifestyle that begins with trusting Him as Savior and then extends, progressively, to every aspect of life.

"[Sound] in love" refers to *agapē*, the other-focused, exercise-of-the-will kind of love best exemplified by the Lord.

From My Journal

Uncommon Sense

The longer I live, the more I value a virtue that Paul mentions several times in these verses: *sensibility*.

He urges older men to be "sensible" (2:2). Shortly thereafter, he encourages younger women to be "sensible" (v.5). On the heels of that, he underscores the same trait in young men (v.6). And then, yet again, he writes that all of us who have been born again should "live sensibly, righteously, and godly in the present age" (v.12). By mentioning it no less than four times in this brief space, it's obvious that *sensibility* should play a huge role in everybody's life.

Throughout my many years in ministry, including every church I've served as pastor, I've had to deal with folks who have gone off the deep end. They got fanatical, or they pushed grace too far, or they lacked self-awareness, or they refused to be realistic and reasonable when a relationship broke down. Truth be told, I have to admit to periodic lapses of sensibility in my own life. How easy it is to "grind an axe" on some pet subject while I'm preaching or to go too far defending myself when criticized, rather than remaining calm and quietly confident—in a word, sensible.

I recall marrying an older bride and groom a number of years ago. She had become rather independent and set in her ways and he was the dominant type—super-intense, and on top of that, jealous. It quickly became obvious a mixture so volatile would soon lead to an explosion unless both could somehow remain "sensible." I spent three or four sessions with them before the wedding, emphasizing the importance of maintaining balance and urging both of them to guard against extremes. I even gave them a couple of premarital, practical projects to work on in the hope of helping them cultivate sensible ways to adjust to each other. Only a few months after their wedding they were back in my study, glaring at each other (I think their honeymoon may have lasted a couple of days, if that). She was furious at him for his refusal to "give her more space."

I suspected her living alone so many years might require a lengthy adjustment period and might make her more sensitive to sharing her living space, so I calmly asked what she meant by her need for breathing room. Are you ready? He had taken all the interior doors in their house off their hinges and stacked them in the garage because he "didn't want either of them to have any secrets." He also began the habit of checking the odometer in her car when he left for work each morning and rechecking it upon returning. He followed up with a verbal interrogation at supper. "Where did you go today? What took you eighteen miles from home?"

That did it! Out of spite, she deliberately spent untold hours in her car driving wherever and then relishing his doubt about her fidelity. Both took their behavior to ridiculous extremes. Both needed the essential virtue: sensibility. Its absence proved devastating.

As I recall, their marriage lasted less than two years.

"[Sound] in perseverance" uses a profoundly significant Greek term that embodies the essence of spiritual maturity. In Paul's other letters, this quality produces godly behavior (Rom. 2:7), endures tribulation, and leads to proven character (Rom. 5:3–4; 2 Cor. 1:6; 2 Thess. 1:4), delivers believers to their eternal destiny (Rom. 8:35), produces hope (Rom. 15:4), results from intimacy with God (Col. 1:10–11), and remains singularly focused on Christ (2 Thess. 3:5). Perseverance is the best indicator of genuine faith during life and the crowning proof of authentic belief after death.

— 2:3 (Older Women) —

Having described the desired character of older men, whom the congregation should find worthy examples, Paul turned his attention to "older women." In 1 Timothy 5:9, the apostle referred to "older" widows as those who were at least sixty years old. Nevertheless, we can safely interpret "older women" in the relative sense, saying that women of any age should teach women who are younger than themselves.

While the terms he uses of older women differ from those describing older men, his use of the word "likewise" suggests that their qualities parallel those of older men. In the same way as older men are to be dignified and worthy of respect, older women should be "reverent," which comes from a Greek compound word meaning (lit.) "temple-fitting." The implements and furniture in the temple were specifically created for service to God and were consecrated for that purpose. The idea of reverence suggests that a person, by her conduct, demonstrates that she belongs to God and that her life has been reserved for His worship. The command could be rendered, "Older women, just like older men, are to behave like someone specially reserved for service to the Lord."

These older women were to become the opposite of "malicious gossips," which is translated from *diabolos*, the same term used in the Septuagint to describe Satan as "the accuser" or "the adversary" (1 Chron. 21:1; Job 1; Zech. 3:1). The "tale-bearer" always has a story to share about someone and, not coincidentally, her information never elevates the subject's reputation in the minds of others. Furthermore, older women were not to be "enslaved" to alcohol. On the contrary, older women were to be "good-teachers" — another compound word coined by Paul — for the sake of the younger women.

Although younger women may seldom approach older women for advice, they watch. They learn by example, even when they aren't completely aware of the fact they are being taught. Young girls often grow up rebelling and resisting the way their mothers do things. Then, years later, they instinctively nurture their families and care for their homes exactly as they observed their mothers function.

— 2:4–5 (Younger Women) —

In this way, older women would "encourage" younger women. The verb Paul chose is based on the same term translated "sensible" earlier. By their example, by their "good-teaching" behavior, they would "bring to sensibility" younger women, resulting in no less than seven observable qualities, many of which are self-explanatory. Three terms deserve special attention.

"Pure" comes from the Greek word usually translated "holy." Younger women are to become like their older examples: reserved for God's holy purposes. Their behavior should demonstrate that they, like the sacred implements of worship in the temple, belong to the Lord.

"Workers at home" should not be understood and applied as many did during the 1970s. Family advocates saw women working outside the home—in offices and factories—as a threat to the integrity of the household. But Paul did not write this to prohibit women from working outside the home. In fact, the issue never became controversial until after the Second World War. Before then, families cared most about the basics of survival—food, water, shelter, clothing, and protection—and they worked *interdependently* to get what they needed. The term here is the noun "homemakers," in the same sense as the crown jewel of women described in Proverbs 31:10–31. She's no mousey, subservient waif existing beneath her husband's shadow. She's a powerful, industrious, resourceful partner, fully engaged in cultivating her family's well-being and in the building of a family legacy!

"Subject to their own husbands" calls for young women to demonstrate self-willed deference to the desires of their husbands, a deference motivated by earned respect. While Paul calls for young women to subject their wills to the leadership of their husbands, the conditions of Ephesians 5:22–30 apply. There Paul describes a symbiotic relationship in which the husband's loving leadership is devoted to serving his wife, which inspires the kind of respect that makes it a delight for her to show deference in return.

Like older men and older women, younger women are objects of scrutiny by a watching world. Paul reminded them that the credibility of God's Word is at stake. Nonbelievers may not obey the commands of God, but they nevertheless understand the inherent link between belief and behavior among believers ... and they expect the two to match.

— 2:6–8 (Younger Men) —

In turning his attention to younger men, Paul again used the words "likewise" and "self-controlled" (the same word rendered "sensible"). Because young men tend toward being impetuous and rash, unrestrained in their conduct, impulsive, and volatile, Paul said, in effect, "Titus, help younger men learn how to apply the brakes to life. Help them understand how to bridle their tongues and control their tempers. Help them know how to curb their ambition and to purge themselves of greed. Show them how to master their sexual urges and impulses, how to follow their minds instead of their glands. Teach them to be responsible stewards of money rather than squanderers. Show them the rewards of unselfish leadership and the folly of self-centered pursuits." And how was Titus to do this? By example. Paul called for good deeds, doctrine that is free of corruption, dignity (the same term used of older men in 2:2), and "hygienic" speech that is above reproach.

According to Paul, the skeptic and the false teacher will find no opportunity to attack the gospel when godly behavior, wholesome speech, and uncorrupted doctrine bear witness to it. This is not the duty of the spiritual leader alone; this unassailable integrity should characterize the entire congregation, man and woman alike, from elder to tot.

— 2:9–10 (Bondslaves) —

The final segment of the congregation whose conduct either authenticates or invalidates the genuine teaching of Christ consists of "bondslaves." As in his other letters, Paul bypassed any attempt to overturn this centuries-old custom, perhaps for one of three reasons. First, he may have given the matter special attention in another document, now lost. Second, the practice in the Roman Empire had become dominated by indentured servanthood, whereby the relationship between bondslave and master became the ancient equivalent of employee and boss. Third, and most likely, Paul foresaw that genuine belief in Christ would eventually transform the culture and make slavery go the way of the Dodo. Eventually, that is what happened.

Regardless, if Paul intended to overturn the institution of slavery, he knew that it would not occur overnight. He therefore wrote Titus to pursue the cause of Christ on the island of Crete by establishing and fortifying churches, whose conduct might win converts without a word. Bondslaves were to steward faithfully and conscientiously the interests of their masters with the same eagerness they would their own. Again, as with the other groups within the church, Paul desired that their godly behavior would "adorn the doctrine of God."

An old story of Saint Francis of Assisi tells of the day he said to one of his students, "Come with me, let's go down to the village and preach to the people who need our Savior." Off they went.

Once at the gate they stopped, bent down to speak kind words to a crippled old man, and gave him a cool drink of water and a few coins. Then they saw some children playing with a ball out in the field, so they joined their game and had fun with the children. While they played, a lonely widow watching at her doorstep drew their attention. When they finished the game, they visited with her, bringing a few words of cheer and encouragement to the old lady living alone. A fearful young man lurked in the shadows, ashamed of what he had done the night before. They prayed with him, spoke with him openly and freely about forgiveness, grace, and mercy, and they encouraged him to pursue a more productive future. On the way out of town they stopped at a small store and greeted the merchant, asked about his family, and thanked him for his faithful work through the years.

Finally Saint Francis said, "Let's go back." The novice stopped and said, "But wait, when do we preach?" The older friar answered, "Every step we took, every word we spoke, every action we did has been a sermon."

The most effective presentation of the gospel begins with a Christlike life. Therefore, the defining character of the church should be everyday, authentic godliness.

NOTES:

1. R. Kent Hughes and Bryan Chapell, *1 & 2 Timothy and Titus: To Guard the Deposit* (Wheaton, IL: Crossway, 2000), 297.

2. Gene Getz, *The Measure of a Man* (Ventura, CA: Regal, 2004), 56.

3. Kittel and Friedrich, eds., *Theological Dictionary of the New Testament: Abridged in One Volume*, 169.

4. John Phillips, *Exploring the Pastoral Epistles: An Expository Commentary* (Grand Rapids: Kregel, 2004), 233.

5. Hughes and Chapell, *1 & 2 Timothy and Titus*, 296.

6. Ibid., 222.

7. John Calvin, *1 & 2 Timothy & Titus* (Wheaton: Crossway, 1998), 184.

8. Gerhard Kittel, ed., *Theological Dictionary of the New Testament*, ed. and trans. Geoffrey William Bromiley (Grand Rapids: Eerdmans, 1978), 4:519.

9. See the comments in this commentary, above, on 1 Timothy 6:3–5.

10. John R. W. Stott, *The Message of 1 Timothy & Titus: Guard the Truth* (Downers Grove, IL: InterVarsity Press, 1996), 183.

11. Kittel and Friedrich, eds., *Theological Dictionary of the New Testament: Abridged in One Volume*, 1150.

SECTION 2: THE MISSION OF THE CHURCH (TITUS 2:11–3:15)

According to Paul's theology, being always precedes doing. In other words, what we do is a direct result of who we are, and who we are determines what we choose to do. Therefore, people who have been transformed by God's grace should behave like Christ. Moreover, groups of these transformed people should naturally become hands and feet, faithfully obeying the instructions of their Head.

In this section of Paul's pastoral field manual, divine truth becomes the apostle's focus. If the church's leaders are faithful men and women whose hearts have been transformed by God's grace, the message and ministry of the congregation should reflect that same grace in the world. Unfortunately, the task will be no easier for the people of God who comprise the church than it was for the Son of God during His time on earth.

Tough Grace (Titus 2:11–15)

[11]For the grace of God has appeared, bringing salvation to all men, [12]instructing us to deny ungodliness and worldly desires and to live sensibly, righteously and godly in the present age, [13]looking for the blessed hope and the appearing of the glory of our great God and Savior, Christ Jesus, [14]who gave Himself for us to redeem us from every lawless deed, and to purify for Himself a people for His own possession, zealous for good deeds.
[15]These things speak and exhort and reprove with all authority. Let no one disregard you.

Wherever grace exists, there will always be those who abuse it. Take, for example, grace in the form of freedom. The United States grants to all residents the right to speak openly, even critically, without fear of persecution or punishment. Tragically, some turn that freedom into license to exploit women for the sake of profit. The courts have been reluctant to crack down on this obvious abuse of free speech for fear of unduly curbing liberty.

Freedom has limits. But those limits cannot come from an outside authority, or freedom ceases to be freedom. Complete liberty can remain unlimited only if free people choose to limit themselves through godly character. As Benjamin Franklin insightfully noted to a friend, "Only a virtuous people are capable of freedom. As nations become corrupt and vicious, they have more need of masters."[1]

The same can be said of another kind of grace: love. Paul called love the greatest of all Christian attributes (1 Cor. 13:13), yet how often have we seen one married partner abuse the love he or she receives? A devoted wife faithfully cares for her husband and nurtures their children, only to have her love returned empty, left behind for the sake of career or selfish pursuits. An attentive husband provides safety and sustenance for a woman who can find only fault, eventually abandoned for the arms of another man.

Sometimes "love must be tough."[2] Sometimes, love has to take a strong stand in order to keep the relationship from disintegrating.

What's true of freedom and what's true of love is also true of grace. People have abused grace from the day God decided against destroying Adam for his sin. In his letter to the church in Rome, Paul described the response of darkened minds to God's saving grace: "Are we to continue in sin so that grace may increase? ... Shall we sin because we are not under law but under grace?" (Rom. 6:1, 15).

Grace has limits, and, therefore, there are times when grace must be tough.

Paul examines this foundational doctrine of the church as it impacts a believer, from rebirth to resurrection:

- grace by salvation (v. 11)
- grace through sanctification (v. 12)
- grace in glorification (v. 13)
- grace as redemption (v. 14)

— 2:11 (Grace by Salvation) —

Paul's shift in focus to the message of the church begins with a bedrock truth, literally rendered, "*Appeared* the grace of God, salvation to all humanity." The term "appeared" best translates the Greek term *epiphainō*, from which we derive our word "epiphany." We might view it as a "eureka!" kind of word, adding an element of delight and surprise to the idea of discovery. Humanity didn't receive grace and salvation after a diligent search, or by pleading for help, or by approaching God. "*Appeared* the grace of God" by His own initiative, motivated solely by His goodness, despite our unworthiness. The Creator spontaneously and voluntarily reached down to rescue humanity from our own self-imposed, sinful condition.

Paul isn't teaching universalism by this verse. The offer of saving grace has been extended "to all men," yet most of the human race will decline the salvation He offers—as inconceivable as that is!

— 2:12 (Grace through Sanctification) —

In the spiritual life of the believer, salvation refers to the past, that moment of rebirth "from above" (John 3:3–8). The theological term *sanctification* refers to the believer's present condition: *set apart for God's purpose.* This present condition, like salvation, is God's doing on our behalf, not something we do for ourselves (Rom. 8:28–39). While we are commanded to conform our behavior to match our identity as God's specially reserved instruments, the Lord did not leave us to carry out this supernatural task on our own. This grace we have received not only saves us from eternal condemnation for sin; it also "instructs."

The term used here is *paideuō,* based on the common Greek noun for "little child." Paul could have chosen *didaskō,* which refers to formal, classroom instruction. This nuance is important. *Didaskō* would suggest we voluntarily show up for class; *paideuō* places us in the role of the ignorant, like helpless tots receiving instruction from a loving parent. From Him we learn how to live, long before we're ready for book-learning.

Note that we receive both negative and positive instruction. In other words, we are taught what *not* to do and what we *should* do instead.

Negatively, we learn to reject "ungodliness," which translates the Greek word *asebeia.* The root term is *sebomai,* which originally meant "to fall back before" or "to shrink from," as one would do in the presence of a deity. By the time of Paul, the word described a general attitude of reverence or worship. The Greek prefix *a-* negates whatever it's attached to, so the term refers to attitudes and actions of "not-reverence." *Asebeia* refers to a lifestyle of irreverence, which inevitably breeds contempt for God. Such behavior that despises God we learn to reject.

In addition, grace teaches us to reject "worldly desires." Paul does not use this phrase to condemn pleasure derived from wealth, food, entertainment, technology, or other physical delights. Elsewhere, Paul cautioned believers to reject the false teaching that earthly pleasures are necessarily bad (Col. 2:20–23). Moreover, he instructed his other disciple, Timothy, to enjoy everything as created by God and to receive it with thanksgiving (1 Tim. 4:1–5). In other words, in the spirit of wisdom and gratitude to the Giver of all good things, savor a good meal, take pleasure in wholesome entertainment, delight in the wonders of modern technology, and praise God for all of your provisions.

For Paul, "world" represents everything that is not "in Christ" or of Christ (1 Cor. 6:2; 2 Cor. 4:3–4; 5:18–20; Gal. 6:14; Eph. 2:1–7, 12–13; Col. 2:8). Therefore, "worldly desires" refers to those things the Enemy covets — sinful by definition — or to the desperate, idolatrous kind of longing that leads to sin. Grace trains us to avoid desiring the things that the world desires and to avoid craving anything with worldlike motives. Grace instructs the believer to enjoy wealth as a gift from God, while the world craves wealth as a means of power, self-gratification, or validation.

In a positive sense, grace teaches believers how to turn away from futile, destructive behavior to pursue that which is "sensible" (of sound mind), "righteous" (that which is deemed good in the court of heaven), and "godly" (characterized by respect or reverence of God). The final phrase of verse 12, "in this present age," highlights the tension believers experience as their standard of conduct runs counter-current to that of the world.

— 2:13 (Grace in Glorification) —

Salvation reflects on the past. Sanctification considers the present. Glorification anticipates the future.

The English word "hope" suggests wishful thinking. A child might say, "I hope someone gives me a remote-control car for my birthday." He might get his wish, or he might not. The Bible, however, uses a Greek term meaning "an assured expectation." When someone purchases an airline ticket, she holds in her hand the hope—the assured expectation—of an assigned seat on that flight. Paul uses this term in a specific way to describe the future day when Jesus returns to rule the world and to renovate it to His liking.

"Glory" refers to the state of things as God desires them. Jesus spoke of His own glorification as the time when God's righteous character was revealed through His Son's resurrection. Eventually, believers will share the glory of Christ (Rom. 8:17; Col. 1:27; 3:4) when they receive a resurrected body like His (Phil. 3:21). At that time, the bodies of believers will be "glorified." Our bodies will reflect the full image of God, which had been distorted by the fall. Furthermore, the struggles and battles and disappointments and failures and wrongs and heartaches and grief and death of "the present age" will be displaced by the next, in which we will experience no pain, no strife, no tears, no sorrow, and no death.

— 2:14 (Grace as Redemption) —

Paul concluded his mini-discourse on grace with the doctrines of substitution and redemption. Jesus took our place and paid the penalty of our sin so that we might be freed from slavery to sin. We were indentured to evil, compelled to do its bidding. But Jesus bought us out of bondage so that we would no longer serve that old master.

While we have been purchased out of slavery to "lawless deeds" and now are owned by a new master, note how Paul describes our new activity. We were compelled to do evil under the old master; under the new master, good deeds arise from within, driven by "zeal," which the Greeks understood as "passionate commitment" or "enthusiasm." The Puritans refer to this dramatic internal change of motivations as "the power of the new affections."

In Texas, we have a species of oak tree known as "live oak." Unlike its cousins, the live oak doesn't drop its leaves in the autumn or go dormant during winter. It stays green all year long. As with all trees, however, the live oak must discard old leaves and grow new ones. This occurs when new growth displaces old growth; new leaves push the old ones off the branch.

Similarly, new affections displace the old, and the Christian gradually grows in his or her respect and reverence for the Lord. Transformed from within, we act on our desires to please the Father with good deeds, just like His Son. In a real sense, we outgrow our desire for sin because the grace of God has saved us, continually sanctifies us, and has predestined us for glory (Rom. 8:28–39).

— 2:15 —

Paul charged Titus with the responsibility to proclaim the truth of grace to the churches, and through the churches, using three strong imperatives:

Laleō, "to speak." This verb frequently implied casual speaking. In other words, Paul wanted Titus to infuse every conversation with this teaching on grace.

Parakaleō, "to exhort." Our title for the Holy Spirit, "Paraclete," derives from this verb, which pictures the relationship of a coach to his or her athlete-in-training. Paul expects Titus to make this teaching on grace the training regimen for church leaders and members.

Elenchō, "to correct." This term carries the idea of replacing incorrect ideas with correct ideas, much like a math teacher might show a student the right method of solving a problem. Paul challenged Titus to "prove," "convince," "refute," and "persuade"[3] the churches to abandon false teaching for the doctrine of grace.

Paul encouraged Titus to stand on the apostolic authority delegated to him in the letter he held in his hands and undoubtedly read before the congregations on Crete. We must remember that this took place before the New Testament had been written and compiled. Christian teaching took place by word of mouth, so an authentic teacher needed apostolic authority to set him apart from anyone claiming to present divine truth.

Today, a spiritual leader stands on the authority of Scripture, the sixty-six books of divinely inspired, inerrant truth of the Bible.

Preaching grace is dangerous business. Some will try to abuse grace, finding in spiritual freedom a license to commit more sin without fear of divine discipline (Rom. 6:1, 15). Theologians call such people "antinomians" or "those without law." To counter this abuse, others try to place external limits on grace. Theologians call these people "legalists." But grace cannot be restricted by laws, or it ceases to be grace (Gal. 2:21). Therefore, any limits on behavior must come from within. God must give His people a nature like His own if they are to live in complete freedom, yet without serving sin. To paraphrase Ben Franklin, "Only a *transformed* people are capable of freedom."

Unfortunately, no believer is completely transformed, and the great majority of church members have barely begun the process. That means that grace and freedom have been granted to people who possess little or no internal restraint, a prospect that can be terrifying to a spiritual leader. Believe me! After nearly five decades in pastoral ministry, the temptation to corral grace with a few well-placed and appropriate restrictions can be overwhelming. That's when grace must be tough.

During those times, I have to remind myself the Lord didn't call pastors and elders to become surrogate parents or policemen to the congregation. We're unable to "fix" anybody! He calls for godly, qualified men to proclaim grace, the foundational doctrine of the church. Our job is proclamation; He's in charge of transformation.

Application

Preach Grace

The mission of the church is to become a visible example of God's grace to humanity. We are to bring that otherworldly substance we call "grace" to earth so that it can be seen, heard, and experienced by all people. God calls certain men out of ordinary life so they might become shepherds, men charged with the awesome privilege of "equipping the saints for the work of service, to the building up of the body of Christ" (Eph. 4:12). To that end, Paul summarizes the work of a pastor, explaining *what* he should teach (2:12 – 13) as well as *how* he should teach (2:15).

At the risk of oversimplifying the pastor's role, the content of his instruction should follow that of grace itself.

- Grace teaches us how to deny ungodliness and worldly desires (1:12a).
- Grace teaches us how to live sensibly, righteously, and godly (1:12b).
- Grace offers us hope of victory over all evil in glory (1:13).

As I reflect on my preaching over more than forty-five years, I can honestly say that nearly every sermon I have preached and virtually every lesson I have taught falls into one of those three categories.

Now, let me do a little mentoring as I direct the next few paragraphs specifically to pastors. Paul explains *how* the pastor should convey these divine truths using three words: *speak, exhort,* and *reprove.*

Speak. Let the lessons of grace flow through casual, authentic conversation with individuals as you build relationships with them. These interactions shouldn't become ad hoc sermons or occasions for formal instruction. Simply be yourself—transparent and natural. I cannot count how many times members of my congregation have recalled what I considered a lighthearted conversation, telling me how my words became the catalyst of major life change for them. Invariably, I've found myself surprised ... and always gratified.

Exhort. Dedicate yourself to expository preaching. Why any pastor would choose to preach any other way is beyond my comprehension. While expository preaching requires many hours of diligent study, I find it far less stressful than trying to come up with a clever message each week, loosely tied to Scripture but built on my own wisdom. I can sustain that for a few months, maybe, before I run out of personal life lessons to share.

When I preach through books of the Bible, I never have to wonder what I'm going to preach from Sunday to Sunday and I never have to proof-text my own witticisms. When I preach on a topic, such as marriage or child rearing, each sermon is derived from a specific passage related to the subject. The messages are God's, as are the timeless principles that emerge during study, because everything comes directly from His Word. And if I have studied well and remained open to the Holy Spirit's leading during my preparation, the applications almost write themselves.

Reprove. Commit yourself to gentle, yet firm confrontation of error wherever it appears. Trust me, no one hates having to do this more than I do. Relationships are difficult enough without having to correct someone's faulty teaching or directly asking a strong personality to be mindful of his or her influence. But the stakes are unimaginably high, as we are preparing for eternity. Reproof doesn't imply being contentious, tactless, or heavy-handed. If you're careful to preserve the dignity of a man or woman in error, your correction will bypass his or her defenses. If you are gentle and humble, the reproof can be effective. Then, follow up soon afterward with a sincere and encouraging affirmation; who knows, you may win a friend for life.

Revealing the Unseen (Titus 3:1–8)

---

[1]Remind them to be subject to rulers, to authorities, to be obedient, to be ready for every good deed, [2]to malign no one, to be peaceable, gentle, showing every consideration for all men. [3]For we also once were foolish ourselves, disobedient, deceived, enslaved to various lusts and pleasures, spending our life in malice and envy, hateful, hating one another. [4]But when the kindness of God our Savior and *His* love for mankind appeared, [5]He saved us, not on the basis of deeds which we have done in righteousness, but according to His mercy, by the washing of regeneration and renewing by the Holy Spirit, [6]whom He poured out upon us richly through Jesus Christ our Savior, [7]so that being justified by His grace we would be made heirs according to *the* hope of eternal life. [8]This is a trustworthy statement; and concerning these things I want you to speak confidently, so that those who have believed God will be careful to engage in good deeds. These things are good and profitable for men.

Planet Earth is home to two very real worlds. We inhabit a tangible world, which we experience through the senses and measure in units of space and time. We also inhabit an intangible, eternal world — invisible, yet just as real. Most people acknowledge only the tangible world, because they either cannot see the other world, or simply *will* not. William Irwin Thompson likened such people to flies crawling across the ceiling of the Sistine Chapel, blissfully unaware of the magnificent shapes and forms and colors that lie above them (or beneath them, as it were). Not only do they fail to appreciate the magnificence of the world they inhabit, they haven't the capacity to recognize their own blindness.

In the Lord's inexplicable, yet undoubtedly wise judgment, believers have been given the task of revealing the invisible universe to our unsighted family, friends, coworkers, neighbors, and even enemies. He commissioned His church — leaders and followers alike — to instruct the world at large on the existence and benefits of grace. In addition to speaking, exhorting, and correcting (2:15), we are to demonstrate grace through our behavior.

While I find speaking, exhorting, and correcting to be challenging work, *living* the truth through my actions is far more difficult … yet far more effective. Let's face it; the world has no lack of convincing talk and noteworthy spokesmen. People need to see results. Apparently, nothing much has changed in two millennia. Note the repetition of "deed" throughout Paul's letter to Titus, particularly in this section (1:16 [2x]; 2:7, 14; 3:1, 5, 8, 14).

—3:1—

Paul expected Christians to obey "rulers" and "authorities," which represent both the offices of government and those who occupy them. His commands left no room for anything short of complete, submissive obedience. Not merely respect, but compliance with their laws and directives.

I admit this can be difficult. Some American presidents quickly earn my respect, but others—to be completely honest—make obedience a major struggle. Just when I think I can't imagine a less deserving leader in the Oval Office, I remind myself that when Paul wrote this letter, Nero what in charge of the Western world. Thoroughly pagan. Morally bankrupt. Despotic, cruel, oppressive, murderous, unjust, homosexual, and sadistic. *Corrupt to the core.* No one embodied the very spirit of antichrist more than Nero—not for several centuries at least. Yet Paul called for obedience and urged believers to be prepared to do good works.

This attitude contrasts sharply with traditional Jewish society, which urged strict separation from local culture. The Israelites struggled to maintain appropriate separation from their idolatrous neighbors in the Promised Land, so the Lord chastised them by allowing Babylon to carry them far from home. While in captivity, the Hebrews learned how to maintain their identity as God's covenant people, even as they shared living space with other captured cultures. But by the time of their return to their land, this crucial ethic of separateness had become an obsession.

In the first century, Jews living outside Israel formed tight-knit communities, reluctantly submitting to local laws and authorities and treating local culture with thinly veiled disdain. Rather than elevate God in the minds of pagan cultures, and instead of winning respect and admiration as His covenant people, Jews provoked hatred. Christianity, then considered a sect of Judaism, risked perpetuating the same counterproductive tension. Paul worried for good reason. According to the Roman historian Tacitus, Nero persecuted Christians a few years later "not so much for the imputed crime of burning Rome, as for their hate and enmity to human kind."[4] The apostle naturally wanted to protect believers from persecution, but he also recognized that a church cannot effectively evangelize a community while treating its citizens with contempt.

—3:2—

In addition to respectful submission to authorities and even support for their efforts, Paul urged kindness to neighbors in four specific ways.

"Malign" is rendered from the Greek word *blasphēmeō*, from which we get the English term "blaspheme." It means to curse, slander, or treat someone with contempt. Blasphemy is any manner of speech that disregards or disrespects the status of another. Even the very least of humanity deserves respect for no other reason than they, deep within, bear the image of God, who values them so much He sent His Son to redeem them.

In many households, parents strictly forbid the use of the word "stupid." I think that's a wise policy. I can think of few occasions when the term "stupid" doesn't malign someone.

The Greek term behind "peaceable" literally means "nonfighter." This person walks away from quarrels; he or she simply decides not to fight, even if fighting could gain an advantage.

Moreover, we are to be "gentle." That's not to suggest we must become the doormats of the world. The term used here combines the ideas of "dignity" and "reasonableness." Aristotle used the word to denote indulgent consideration of human infirmities. Gentleness honors the spirit of the law rather than rigidly holding to the letter of it. A king was said to be gentle when he used his power in appropriate measures to preserve the common good of his subjects.

Some fellow citizens of the tangible world don't want to be at peace. Every neighborhood (like every school) has at least one bully, a person who cannot live without making someone nearby miserable. To be peaceable and gentle does not mean we have to lie down when pushed. One can stand up to a bully without a fistfight or responding unreasonably.

Paul's next phrase, "showing consideration for all men," wonderfully describes the spirit of grace. Greek culture prized "consideration" as a quality of refined leadership, a mark of strength. Paul draws on this secular idea, adding to it the necessary ingredient of love (1 Cor. 4:21). Our general demeanor toward others should be humble courtesy, demonstrated by kind responses. Furthermore, Christians must offer this dignity to "all men," the Greek idiom for "all people everywhere." Regardless of race. Regardless of skin color. Regardless of religion, or lack of such. Regardless of political leanings. Regardless of economic status or salary or occupation or education or marital status. *All.*

— **3:3–4** —

Paul slips the little connecting conjunction *gar* ("for" or "because") into the text to set his readers straight on the reason for extending grace to non-Christian authorities and neighbors. First-century pagans would have affirmed the grace-oriented behavior he described, but not for reasons Paul would affirm. Greeks, and Romans especially, saw kind and gentle behavior as a means to selfish ends: social advancement and self-righteousness. Quite the opposite, Christians extend grace because nothing separates them from their pagan overlords and lost neighbors except the grace of God.

We were "foolish" instead of "sensible." We were "disobedient" instead of "subject to rulers"; "deceived" and "enslaved" rather than prepared for good deeds; "hateful" and "hating" rather than peaceable, gentle, or kind. "But" someone changed all of that. Someone changed us. "The grace of God appeared ..." (cf. 2:11–12). Christ's "kindness" and "love" appeared. God came looking for us, even as we continued our rebellious, selfish pursuits.

— **3:5–7** —

A detailed description of God's kindness and love nullifies any suggestion that believers deserve any credit for their place "in Christ" or for their improved character. Motivated only by "kindness" and "love" (v.4), God saved us, not because we are good, but because He is good. His mercy saved us, not our righteousness. He saved us first by "washing of regeneration" and further by "renewing."

"Regeneration" in the Gospels refers to the resurrected, perfected life believers can expect in the age to come (Matt. 19:28; Mark 10:30; Luke 22:30). When Christ returns to reclaim Planet Earth from the clutches of evil, He will purge all creation of sin and transform what remains. In this new creation (Rev. 21), all who are "in Christ" will be recreated. Paul draws on this imagery to declare that the process of re-creation has begun in the life of Christians. Regeneration is rebirth (cf. John 3:3–8). Regeneration in this life, before the "age to come," begins with God's granting believers a new nature.

If "regeneration" is the gift of a new nature, then "renewing by the Holy Spirit" helps us grow into it. Regeneration occurs once at the moment of belief; renewing occurs progressively over time. Paul doesn't focus on our participation in that process, choosing instead to highlight God's grace in the person of the Holy Spirit. People cannot renew themselves any more than they can regenerate themselves. It is all a work of God.

"Whom" (v. 6) refers to the Holy Spirit. We receive the Holy Spirit through Jesus Christ. (Note Paul calls Jesus "Savior," deliberately paralleling "God our Savior" in v. 4.) Jesus saves those who trust Him by "justifying" them. Justification is the sovereign act of God whereby He declares righteous the believing sinner while we are still in a sinning state, still engaged in periodic acts of sinfulness. Moved by kindness, love, and mercy, the Lord declares us righteous in the court of heaven because of what His Son has done on our behalf, not because of what we can do for ourselves.

God saves, regenerates, renews, and justifies believers in order to guarantee their status as heirs of His kingdom—not merely citizens in the "city of God," but part owners with Christ (Rom. 8:17). How's *that* for grace?

— 3:8 —

Experts in the Greek language point out that verses 4 through 7 form one, long sentence, arranged in stanzas like poetry. Like 1:1 – 4 and 2:11 – 15, it is tightly packed theological truth, the gospel in a nutshell. Paul calls it a "trustworthy statement," probably because it was not original to him. Ancient societies frequently used rhyme and meter to help them remember important truths. This may have been a longstanding mnemonic device passed from church to church for many years. The apostle calls other such statements "trustworthy" in his letters to Timothy (1 Tim. 1:15; 3:1; 4:9; 2 Tim. 2:11).

Paul uses an emphatic form of the verb "to confirm" when urging Titus to "speak confidently" the gospel. The voice of a sole spokesman for truth would have to be both confident and repetitive against so many voices of error on the island of Crete. The same is true anywhere, for this is, after all, the primary purpose of a pastor. He is responsible to proclaim grace clearly and emphatically. He cannot allow reluctance to delay him, he must not allow hesitation to interrupt him, and he should not be apologetic. If a pastor stands on the authority of God's Word, he can afford to be bold.

Take note of the ultimate purpose for Titus's ministry: that right belief may produce "good deeds." Evangelical churches tend to emphasize sound doctrine—and should continue to do so. But right belief does not automatically lead to godly behavior. I fear we have been overly influenced by modernism, which places faith in education to reverse the evils of the world. "Fill their heads with knowledge," says the humanist, "and, sooner or later, they will have no choice but to behave properly."

Biblical and theological knowledge are critical ingredients in the believer's transformation, but right belief is only a part. The believer must become part of a fellowship of other believers and actively engage the world in accomplishing good. These, too, become critical ingredients. And somehow, mysteriously and supernaturally, the Holy Spirit uses biblical truth, Christian fellowship, and good deeds to transform the individual. According to Romans 8:28, He promises to use "all things"—good circumstances and evil—to produce good in us. But here, Paul urges Titus and all pastors to supply God's people with only the best ingredients.

Paul's concluding statement, "These things are good and profitable for men," hints of a concern larger than the well-being of the Christians on Crete. Non-Christians do not see, or choose not to acknowledge, the invisible world they inhabit. They remain blind to their accountability in the realm of the unseen, but tragically, their blindness will provide no defense before the court of heaven. Paul wants Titus to strengthen the congregations, not only to protect and preserve believers, but also to become a means of curing non-Christian myopia.

A Christian makes the unseen world visible when sound doctrine and good deeds work together, when faith prompts action, when grace received becomes grace given away.

Application

Authentic Evangelism

In his book *Evangelism Explosion*, D. James Kennedy tells a true story:

> I once heard a man walk up to a woman and say, "How are your kidneys today?" That's the truth! I actually heard the man ask that question. Her response? Did she hit him with her purse? No, she said the following: "Oh, they're much better today, thank you, Doctor." I overheard those words in a hospital room. The doctor had earned the right to ask that personal question. If you doubt that, stop the next lady you meet on the street and ask it yourself, and see what happens.
>
> All of which is to say, we need to earn the right to ask personal questions.[5]

Christians tend to flock together and rarely associate with any but their own kind. Therefore, those outside the church have little reason to think they won't be judged and condemned. They know only the caricature of God as a snarling bully with a grudge against fun, so they naturally assume we are like him. (Unfortunately, some Christians do little to dispel that myth.) It's no wonder we have such a difficult time explaining the gospel! We haven't earned the right to talk about something so personal.

Let me offer a couple of principles to consider as you attempt to reveal the unseen realm to the people in your life.

First, *only authenticity and integrity can win a hearing*. Be real. Don't buy into the myth that always being in the right will make people want to hear what you have to say. Own your mistakes. If you've said too much and offended, apologize. If you're angry, either confront your offender tactfully or let it go. If you form a wrong opinion, admit it. No one likes a know-it-all, and no one trusts a holier-than-thou attitude.

Furthermore, lead your life with integrity. That means you speak the truth and you follow through on your promises. That's the kind of practical holiness everyone respects, Christian and non-Christian alike.

Second, *you cannot convince anyone of a truth you're not living.* If you want to talk about the forgiveness of God, you'll have to model forgiving others. If you want to discuss the love of God, then faithfully love your wife or husband as Christ loved the church. People notice inconsistencies quickly, but they're just as quick to see godly character. They're also smart enough to know that if you really believe something, you'll have no trouble living it.

The Tough Side of Ministry (Titus 3:9–11)

[9]But avoid foolish controversies and genealogies and strife and disputes about the Law, for they are unprofitable and worthless. [10]Reject a factious man after a first and second warning, [11]knowing that such a man is perverted and is sinning, being self-condemned.

I have long maintained that a pastor must possess two common qualities that are rarely found in one man: a tender heart and a tough hide.

Every calling has its occupational hazards, and pastoral ministry is no exception. J. Oswald Sanders, in his outstanding book *Spiritual Leadership*, writes, "To aspire to leadership in God's kingdom requires us to be willing to pay a price higher than others are willing to pay. The toll of true leadership is heavy, and the more effective the leadership, the higher it goes."[6] Pastoral leadership requires a man to share the personal burdens of the flock while enduring their criticism. If he doesn't cultivate a tender heart, a shepherd's compassion can quickly callous over, transforming him into a jaded, cynical, ecclesiastical bureaucrat. Unfortunately, cultivating a tender heart requires a man to make himself continually vulnerable, knowing full well the pain he is bound to suffer.

Despite the need to remain tender, a pastor cannot ignore the second quality: a hide like a rhino. If he doesn't cultivate a thick, tough hide, the arrows of evil find an easy target. Cruel criticism, heretical dissension, and unholy power struggles — to name just a few. A tough-skinned shepherd recognizes that we live in a fallen world where truth will not stand on its own; it must be backed by strength and dogged, unflinching tough love. Enemies of truth wage a relentless, ruthless war to crush the gospel, so shepherds must learn to be tougher and more determined than their attackers.

Paul understood that while all leaders battle criticism, dissension, and power struggles, those engaged in ministry—at all levels and in every respect—become targets of some of life's most vicious, personally offensive attacks. The battle-hardened apostle wanted to prepare his younger protégé, Titus, for the conflicts awaiting him on Crete. The apostle's years in spiritual leadership had taught him that pleasing people instead of standing on principle feels easier, but only in the short term. The long-term suffering for both the minister and the church can be devastating.

Effective spiritual leadership does all things with compassion, but never at the expense of conviction. Effective spiritual leadership never fails to confront when necessary. Invariably, Christians who have strayed from the truth and refuse to repent find their way into churches only to spread the disease of division and strife. Just as a surgeon must cut out diseased tissue, so leaders in churches must confront those who would infect the body of Christ with discord and divide congregations into factions.

—3:9—

Paul charged Titus with the task of proclaiming the gospel with bold assurance of its truth and encouraged him to carry out his mission with divinely appointed authority ("speak confidently", v. 8). "But," the apostle warns, "avoid" three deadly theological distractions: "foolish controversies," "genealogies," and "strife and disputes about the Law." While the doctrine of God's saving grace (vv. 4–7) is "good and profitable" (v. 8), the other topics mentioned are "unprofitable and worthless."

Paul calls some theological debates "foolish," using the Greek word *mōros*, from which we derive our word "moron" or "moronic." In Greek literature, something that is *mōros* is futile, empty, or pointless. When Jesus used the illustration of salt that has lost its saltiness, the term *mōros* was used by the one who recorded the lesson.

Christian community must include healthy theological debate. God gave us one another to challenge our interpretations of Scripture and to put our theological conclusions to the test. The best theological journals won't publish papers that haven't been peer-reviewed (i.e., scrutinized by fellow experts). Some debates are pointless, however, in that their conclusions either have no bearing on our behavior or prompt unbiblical behavior.

No one knows for certain what specific problem Paul had in mind when he warned against "genealogies." His letter to Timothy places this problem in the same category as "myths" (1 Tim. 1:4), which he warned against in Titus 1:14. Some have suggested that early Christians saw spiritual superiority in having Jewish heritage. After all, the new covenant did spring from the old.

"Strife" means "quarrel" or "contention," but "disputes" might be too subtle a translation of the Greek term. *Machas* has a decidedly more violent nuance, used most often of physical combat and even war. I am aware of two seminary students who were disciplined after their quarrel over the doctrine of sanctification escalated into a fistfight! "Strife and disputes about the Law" had become a national pastime in Israel, which led to widespread hypocrisy among the religious elite.

Paul undoubtedly had been a heavyweight champion among his fellow Pharisees, so he knew better than most the futility of quibbling over the minutiae of the Mosaic law. He understood that where there is light, there are bugs. Warren Wiersbe, a man seasoned by many decades in ministry, wisely wrote, "I have learned that professed Christians who like to argue about the Bible are usually covering up some sin in their lives, are very insecure, and are usually unhappy at work or at home."[7] Spiritual leaders must learn to avoid, or "stand aside" from, such people. They will consume our time, drain our energy, and weaken our testimony.

— 3:10 —

While a pastor must avoid pointless arguments and allow room for some unproductive discussion — totalitarian control is not the objective — there comes a time for intervention, and sometimes confrontation. After one or two "warnings" (lit., "admonitions" or "corrective teachings"), after two attempts to set someone's crooked doctrine straight, such a person proves to be a "factious man" if he persists. The Greek term is *hairetikos*, which we transliterate to form the English word "heretic." According to Kenneth Wuest, "The noun means, 'fitted or able to take or choose, schismatic, factious.' A heretic is one therefore who refuses to accept true doctrine as it is revealed in the Bible, and prefers to choose for himself what he is to believe."[8]

"Reject" is a strong command. In the same manner as a pastor must reject myths (1 Tim. 4:7) and reject controversies (2 Tim. 2:23), so he must discipline someone who creates factions in the congregation.

— 3:11 —

Paul calls such a person "perverted." Today, the term has developed a nuance of "sexual deviance" that isn't intended here. The word means "twisted, distorted,

From My Journal

One of My Darkest Days

The desk calendar in my church study remained open at Wednesday, April 26, 2006. Four days had passed, but my calendar stayed frozen in the moment that my ears heard words I found almost impossible to believe. On that day my world screeched to a halt. Without wishing to sound dramatic, that became my personal day of infamy. It will go down as one of the darkest days of my life. This is what I wrote in my journal as I reflected on that terrible, tragic date.

My own much loved friend and partner in ministry had fallen. His secret, dark world of sin had been exposed in all its ugliness. The adversary had struck two vital ministries with a severe blow. My wife and I suddenly lost trusted companions who were so gifted, yet so weak and so flawed. I grieve the loss personally and the heartache it brings to many I love. My heart goes out especially to two bewildered and broken spouses and family members.

It will take time for me to heal, for all of us to recover. We'll not rush. There will be moments when our eyes will fill with tears as we remember and reflect and regret. Grief revisits until it is resolved.

Finally we will emerge from all of this. We will recover from our heartbreaking sadness and our inner scars will heal. But their marks will remain as mute reminders of great days, but by then only memories. And innocent days, but by then only dreams. We will be older but much wiser. We will remind ourselves as we stand that we "must take heed, lest we fall." Like these two friends, we have loved and lost, but long to see recovered and restored.

And so as I return to my desk this next week to press on in God's sacred work, I will turn the page on my calendar to a new date, but I will never forget this day of infamy. I will be more aware than ever that if someone as gifted and lovely as my two friends can be overtaken in a fault, so can I. And were it not for the matchless grace of God and His empowering Spirit, it would already have happened to me and to all those I hold dear to my heart.

My dear Father, help me to walk closer to You than ever before in my life. When I am tempted again may I be stronger because of the memory of this sad, dark day. When I am alone, may I be surrounded by the reminders that I live my life before You, my God, You who are holy, holy, holy. And should I or any of my friends ever fail You, may we remember that Your great arms are still open to prodigals who find their way back, needing to hear Your voice saying softly and tenderly, "I love you, I forgive you. Welcome back home." Through Christ I pray, amen.

turned inside out." This is Paul's first-century way of saying, "You can't reason with an unreasonable person." Furthermore, this inside-out thinking is likely the result of sin, which causes the person to work tirelessly to justify his or her actions in order to silence his or her own conscience. But the more one tries to silence that person's conscience, the more bizarre the justification becomes.

Paul uses the present tense of the verb "to sin," declaring the person to be in a continual pattern of wrongdoing. The factious person *is sinning* and he or she knows it. After one or two attempts to straighten out a mind that sin has distorted, the pastor must consider the good of the community and compel the factious person to leave.

How a spiritual leader, especially a pastor, protects the flock from factious people reveals a lot about his heart and hide. On the one hand, rhino-hide pastors without a tender heart become totalitarian taskmasters and frequently have control issues that will eventually hinder the church. Paul does not intend his instructions to transform the church into a police state in which no dissenting opinions are tolerated. He writes these instructions to protect the church from internal corruption. No pastor or body of elders should delight in the disciplinary removal of a brother or sister. The removal must be conducted in love, and always with a view toward restoration, not condemnation (Gal. 6:1 – 2).

On the other hand, a bleeding-heart, permissive, people-pleasing pastor will soon find the church eroded and fractured from the inside, despite outward appearances of unity. Rather than risk offending anyone or face potential criticism, he allows theological error to undermine biblical authority. Eventually, the dissenters gain enough power to run the pastor off, or they leave, taking half the church with them.

If a pastor wants to maintain the integrity of biblical truth in a church, he must love his congregation by loving divine truth enough to risk misunderstanding and negative criticism. Otherwise, he should step aside and choose another, less hazardous vocation.

Application

Rejecting a Factious Man

"Factious men" have plagued more than one church I've served. These are people who seemed to delight in making my life miserable ... and others as well. It has helped me down through the years to remember that Paul was troubled over Alexander the coppersmith, who did him much harm (2 Tim. 4:14); John had to deal with strong-willed Diotrephes, who refused to accept what John said (3 John 9–10); and Nehemiah was forever plagued with Sanballat, Tobiah, and Geshem, whom he openly called his "enemies" (Neh. 6:1).

The Bible names other troublemakers, but I'll stop there. After more than forty-five years in pastoral ministry, let me assure you who engage in some form of spiritual leadership, we're not alone when it comes to people who conduct their lives in ruthless ways. Such critics stop at nothing in resisting our leadership, questioning our motives, and disrespecting our role. They can be downright vicious! One of my mentors—now dead—didn't hesitate to call them "savages."

In a small church I served many years ago, for reasons I never could figure out, a man in leadership made me the target of his attacks—sometimes in subtle ways, other times in an offensively verbal manner. It didn't help that he carried a Smith and Wesson .38, which he kept loaded (one time he emptied the bullets on the desk in my study, reminding me that he was armed). That has a way of intimidating a young pastor. I wasn't the only one the man bullied. Unfortunately, my fellow elders also knew him to be a "factious man," but we failed to follow the instruction Paul writes to Titus. It wasn't long before the bully became "the church boss." Instead of warning him twice, clearly and firmly, then removing him from the fellowship of the church ("rejecting the factious man"), I'm disappointed to admit we tolerated his sinful attitude, frequent outbursts of anger, and outrageous actions.

I sigh as I look back and recall our passive, disobedient response to this kind of sin. He became a major reason that little church struggled to grow. Yet none of us had the courage to confront him and take bold action against his wrongdoing.

That difficult place of ministry taught me well. I learned my lesson! I made it a policy *never again* to allow myself or others to be bullied and *never* to sit back and permit a "factious man" to undermine the leadership of any church I serve. Being a servant of God does not require the shepherd of the flock to become a doormat for others. Reject those who are "factious." *Stand up to them!* What are you afraid of? Why are you letting it go on?

Standing up for what is right almost certainly involves risk, takes guts, and may require sacrifice. When the dust settles after a bold confrontation, don't expect everyone to immediately recognize who was right and who was wrong. And don't expect your supporters to stand up and cheer. The ranks tend to thin when the hard work of discipline runs its course.

"Rejecting a factious man" almost always wins loud protests from some and silent affirmation from most. Get used to it. If this seems too difficult or too strong, or if your motivation becomes unclear, read Galatians 1:10 … and don't fail to answer Paul's question: "Am I now trying to win the approval of men, or of God?" (NIV).

Closing Instructions (Titus 3:12–15)

¹²When I send Artemas or Tychicus to you, make every effort to come to me at Nicopolis, for I have decided to spend the winter there. ¹³Diligently help Zenas the lawyer and Apollos on their way so that nothing is lacking for them. ¹⁴Our people must also learn to engage in good deeds to meet pressing needs, so that they will not be unfruitful.

¹⁵All who are with me greet you. Greet those who love us in *the* faith. Grace be with you all.

We could easily get the wrong impression of Paul if we listened to those who see him only as a great intellect, a mind with deep theological understanding, a disciplined soldier of the cross, or a firm and passionate veteran of spiritual warfare. His letters reveal a confident theologian, a ruggedly independent spirit, a man unafraid of challenges, willing to wade into uncharted territory for the sake of the gospel.

That certainly describes Paul, but it's only one side of this complex man. If everything you knew about Paul came from the first part of his letters — the opening segments of Romans, the Ephesian letter, the early part of Timothy's letter, and much of his letter to Titus — he could appear formal, aloof, maybe even cold. The concluding lines of his letters, however, reveal a tender man who loves deeply and readily acknowledges his need for companionship. Take the time to read Romans 16, 1 Corinthians 16:17–24, and Colossians 4:7–18 and you will discover a remarkably large circle of close friends — ministry partners in whom Paul invested time, energy, and affection.

As a pastor, I am especially drawn to the closing lines of Paul's letter to Titus. This passage forms a tiny crack in time that offers us a glimpse into his inner circle of ministry trainees. We see his personal and professional interaction with men who served alongside this great man of God and benefitted from his personal tutelage. Imagine! An internship with Paul the apostle.

From these last four verses of Paul's letter, I find three priorities of ministry that every minister of the gospel must keep in perspective:

- being together: God made us to need others.
- helping others: life is enriched by giving aid to others.
- doing good: God redeemed us to do good.

— **3:12** —

At the time of Paul's writing, he appears uncertain as to which man he will send to Crete to replace Titus. He names two candidates: Artemas and Tychicus.

The name Artemas could be the masculine form of the feminine name Artemis, the goddess of fertility worshiped in Ephesus (a.k.a. Diana). Or, more likely, his name is a contraction of a compound Greek word meaning "gift of Artemis." Either way, his parents obviously venerated the pagan goddess, suggesting he came to faith in Christ from a typical Greek upbringing.

We know a little more about Tychicus, whose name means "fortunate." After the uproar in Ephesus, Tychicus and other members of Paul's entourage evangelized Macedonia (Acts 20:1–4). Early in Paul's first imprisonment in Rome, he sent Tychicus with letter in hand to the church of Ephesus, commending him as "beloved brother and faithful minister in the Lord" (Eph. 6:21), and then on to Colossae as "our beloved brother and faithful servant and fellow bond-servant in the Lord" (Col. 4:7). During his second imprisonment in Rome, as the apostle summoned Timothy to be with him during his last days, he explained that all of his younger colleagues were gone, including Tychicus, whom he had sent to Ephesus.

We don't know for certain which man Paul sent to replace Titus; we know only he trusted both to complete the work on Crete. Like Titus, both were Greek converts and likely uncircumcised, which Paul undoubtedly saw as an advantage in the battle against Judaizers (1:10–11, 14; 3:9; cf. Acts 15:1; Gal. 2:11–13; 6:12–15; Phil 3:2–3).

Paul directed Titus to meet him in Nicopolis, where he planned to spend the winter. This name means "city of victory," which several cities in the Roman Empire shared in common. Most likely, Paul refers to Nicopolis of Achaia, a Roman colony on the western shore of Greece, across the Ionian Sea from the southern tip of Italy. This would have been an ideal place to rest and the perfect launching point for his visit to Rome in the spring. Paul wrote of his plans to visit Rome as part of his intended missionary journey to Spain (Rom. 15:24–25), but he arrived there in chains instead (Acts 28:16, 30–31). After his release and a visit to Crete and other trouble spots, he apparently hoped to resume his mission to the western frontier.

Evidently, his plans were interrupted as he was arrested and sent to Rome again, only this time for execution.

— 3:13–14 —

Paul encouraged Titus to provide for Zenas and Apollos, who may have carried the letter to Titus on their way to Crete.

Paul describes Zenas as a *nomikos*, the Greek term for a lawyer. Scholars debate whether he was an expert in Jewish law or represented clients in Roman courts.

Because "Zenas" means "Zeus-given," I doubt he had been trained among the Pharisees; therefore, I believe him to be a converted Greek.

Apollos could have been none other than the gifted orator and evangelist, whom Priscilla and Aquila mentored in Ephesus (Acts 18:24 – 18). This Jew had been educated in the great libraries of Alexandria and cultivated a unique ministry in which he "powerfully refuted the Jews in public, demonstrating by the Scriptures that Jesus was the Christ" (Acts 18:28). I cannot help but wonder if Paul didn't ask him to visit Crete as part of his ministry, not only to evangelize Jews but also to add his expert voice to that of Titus in refuting Judaizers.

Paul had requested "diligent" care for the two evangelists, meaning "with earnest" and "without delay." Those who traveled in ancient days depended on the hospitality of trusted friends. Paul evidently saw an opportunity to teach the believers on Crete the value of helping trusted ministry workers. He said, in effect, "Use this opportunity as a means of teaching the believers on Crete how to engage in good deeds."

— 3:15 —

Paul concluded his letter to Titus as he began, with an affirmation of the faith and grace that bound the two men as brothers and united all of the believers on Crete. The "you" in his benediction is plural — "y'all," as we say in the South. Because the letter was intended to be read in public, all of Paul's brothers and sisters on the island received his personal greeting.

As I reflect on Paul's ministry and his reliance on others to complete it, I am amazed the Lord chooses to involve people in His sacred work. God doesn't *have* to involve people. He could call in His host of angels to get the job done far more efficiently. He could bat an eyelash, and everything He desires would become reality. Instead, He calls people to become instruments of His grace and He equips the church to be the mouthpiece of the gospel.

God invites the contributions of men and women who submit to His sovereignty and remain faithful to His calling. If He wants a message declared, He employs human lips. If He wants a truth written, He inspires a human mind and empowers human hands. If He wants grace to be modeled, He calls, saves, justifies, sanctifies, and transforms people to become His examples of loving mercy. The Lord allows us to become an integral part of His victory over evil so we may share in the spoils at the end of days. Then, because He gave us the gift of this opportunity, we will shout in unison, "*We* won!"

NOTES:

1. Benjamin Franklin, *The Writings of Benjamin Franklin*, ed. Albert Henry Smyth (New York: MacMillan, 1907), 9:569.
2. James Dobson, *Love Must Be Tough: New Hope for Families in Crisis* (Dallas: Word, 1996).
3. Kittel and Gerhard, eds., *Theological Dictionary of the New Testament: Abridged in One Volume*, 222.
4. Tacitus, *Annals* 15:44; see *The Works of Tacitus* (London: Woodward and Peele, 1737), 2:698.
5. D. James Kennedy, *Evangelism Explosion*, 4th ed. (Wheaton, IL: Tyndale, 1996), 56.
6. J. Oswald Sanders, *Spiritual Leadership* (Chicago: Moody Press, 1994), 115.
7. Warren W. Wiersbe, *The Bible Exposition Commentary* (Wheaton: Victor Books, 1989), 2:268.
8. Kenneth S. Wuest, *Wuest's Word Studies from the Greek New Testament: For the English Reader* (Grand Rapids: Eerdmans, 1984), Tit 3:10.